The rise of suburbia

Themes in Urban History

General editor: Derek Fraser

The rise of suburbia

edited by F.M.L. THOMPSON

Leicester University Press   St. Martin's Press   1982

First published in 1982 by Leicester University Press

Copyright © Leicester University Press 1982

Designed by Arthur Lockwood
Text set in 10/11 pt Linotron 202 Times,
printed and bound in Great Britain at
The Pitman Press, Bath

British Library Cataloguing in Publication Data
The Rise of Suburbia. – (Themes in urban history)
  1. Suburbs – England – History
  I. Thompson, F.M.L. II. Series
  307.7′4′0942   HT133
  ISBN 0–7185–1177–8

Library of Congress Cataloging in Publication Data
Main entry under title:
The Rise of Suburbia.
  (Themes in urban history)
  1. Suburbs – Great Britain – History – Addresses,
  essays, lectures. I. Thompson, F. M. L. (Francis
  Michael Longstreth) II. Series.
  HT133.R57   307.7′4   81–21304
  ISBN 0–312–68433–9   AACR2

FOREWORD

Urban history is an expanding field of study, sustained by a considerable volume of research. The purpose of this series, originally conceived by the late Jim Dyos, is to open a new channel for the dissemination of the findings of a careful selection from that research, providing a conspectus of new knowledge on specific themes.

For each volume in the series, each of the contributors is invited to present the core of his work: the essays, originating in theses but now specially written for this volume, are combined under the control of the editor, who writes an introduction setting out the significance of the material being presented in the light of developments in that or a cognate field.

It is hoped that in this way the fruits of recent work may be made widely available both to assist further exploration and to contribute to the teaching of urban history.

In this, the third volume of the series, Professor Thompson has brought together studies of suburbs which allow a comparison both within metropolitan suburban development, and between greater London suburbs and that classic of middle-class 'villadom' – Headingley in Leeds. The book thereby provides valuable insights into the growing differentiation of the Victorian urban experience.

Derek Fraser
University of Bradford

CONTENTS

LIST OF ILLUSTRATIONS

LIST OF TABLES

ABBREVIATIONS

Note Places of publication are given only for those works published outside the United Kingdom.

AG   *Acton Gazette* (from 1880, *Acton, Chiswick and Turnham Green Gazette*; from 1892, *Acton and Chiswick Gazette*)
BEP   Brown Estate Papers
Bexley R.   *Bexley Record*
BPL   Bromley Public Library (Local History Department)
Bromley R. *Bromley Record*
BUDC   Bexley Urban District Council
CRO   County Record Office
EC   Ecclesiastical Commissioners
GC   Goldsmiths' Company
GLRO   Greater London Record Office
HCSC   House of Commons Select Committee
HLRO   House of Lords Record Office
LCC   London County Council
LCD   Leeds Corporation Deeds
LM   *Leeds Mercury*
MCT   *Middlesex County Times*
MLR   Middlesex Land Registry (at the GLRO)
PP   Parliamentary Papers
PRO   Public Record Office (minutes of evidence at parliamentary committees are also available at the HLRO; PRO references – given only once for each bill – are to printed versions transferred from British Transport Commission historical records)
VCH   *The Victoria History of the Counties of England*

NOTES ON THE CONTRIBUTORS

J.M. RAWCLIFFE obtained his M.A. degree at the University of Kent. He was a Principal Lecturer in History at Stockwell College of Education, Bromley, and a Visiting Professor at the University of Monkato, Minnesota, and is now Head of History at St Olav's Grammar School, Orpington.

MICHAEL JAHN read Geography at University College London and also obtained his M.Phil. degree there. He has been Assistant Librarian at University College London since 1969 and is in charge of the History Library.

COLIN TREEN read Geography at the North West London Polytechnic, and obtained his Ph.D. at the Department of Economic History at the University of Leeds. He has taught at the Leeds Polytechnic since 1972 and is now Senior Lecturer in the School of Architecture and Landscape there.

MICHAEL CARR read Geography at the University of Cambridge, and obtained a B.Sc. (Econ.) degree and his Ph.D. at the University of London; he has also obtained an M.Ed. degree from the University of Nottingham. He has been Head of Geography and Principal Lecturer in Geography at Homerton College, Cambridge, since 1966.

Introduction:
The rise of suburbia

F.M.L. THOMPSON

Introduction:
The rise of suburbia

F.M.L. THOMPSON

Suburbia rose between 1815 and 1939, an unlovely, sprawling artefact of which few are particularly fond. To be sure, there were suburbs long before the nineteenth century in the sense of places beyond city limits, the outskirts of towns hanging on to the central area physically and economically, for the most part composed of the ramshackle and squalid abodes of the poorest and most wretched of the town's hangers-on and its most noxious trades. Already, from the middle of the eighteenth century, the great suburban sea-change had started in London, the decisive social upgrading which made places distanced from the city centre desirable residential areas for those who could afford it rather than mere dumping grounds for the unfortunates unable to live in town houses. Nevertheless, while the idea of the residential suburb as an attractive emblem of material and social success and not as evidence of failure and rejection was in circulation before 1815, and its realization on the ground was already sprouting particularly in South London, it was not until the years after Waterloo that modern suburban development got properly under way on a significant scale. It is equally true that suburban expansion did not stop in 1939, never to be resumed. The Second World War certainly brought an abrupt and general halt, but much new building since 1945, particularly round provincial towns, has replicated the established suburban mode of attaching new building estates and complete fresh suburbs to the existing built-up area. By and large, however, what has persisted into the second half of the twentieth century is the commuting arrangement, the separation of residence and workplace despite the planners' efforts to reunite them in new towns. It has been expressed on the ground more in the shape of physically distinct dormitory towns, urbanized villages, and infilling and redevelopment in older suburbs, than in any massive suburbanization of the outer fringes of existing settlement. The great divide of the Second World War may be more visible as a distinction between the types of environment created than as a difference between the social complexions of the communities that live in them or the dependent relationship of those communities to mother cities, but it is a sufficiently clear distinction to make it sensible to view the sprawling phase of

2

suburban growth as a completed process with as definite a beginning and end as any complex historical process ever has.

While it was going on, the process gratified landowners, developers, builders and the occupants of the new suburbs, or at least continued to lure them with prospects of profits, status, and happiness, but pleased practically no one else. Contemporary social and architectural critics were fascinated and appalled by the mindless, creeping nature of the sprawl with its apparently insatiable capacity for devouring land, destroying the countryside, and obliterating scenery for the supposed purpose of enabling more people to live in semi-rural surroundings. The ceaseless activity of the builders, the alarming rapidity with which they turned pleasant fields into muddy, rutted building sites, the confusion of hundreds of building operations going on simultaneously without any discernible design, the impression that little schemes were starting up everywhere at once and were never being finished, were in themselves frightening portents of disorder and chaos as if a machine had escaped from its makers and was careering wildly out of control. If the business of development was more than a little disturbing, its end product was generally viewed with distaste, ridicule, or contempt. The suburbs appeared monotonous, featureless, without character, indistinguishable from one another, infinitely boring to behold, wastelands of housing as settings for dreary, petty, lives without social, cultural, or intellectual interests, settings which fostered a pretentious preoccupation with outward appearances, a fussy attention to the trifling details of genteel living, and absurd attempts to conjure rusticity out of minute garden plots. 'A modern suburb,' wrote a contributor to the *Architect* in 1876, 'is a place which is neither one thing nor the other; it has neither the advantage of the town nor the open freedom of the country, but manages to combine in nice equality of proportion the disadvantages of both.' And in 1909 Sir Walter Besant deplored 'the life of the suburb without any society; no social gatherings or institutions; as dull a life as mankind ever tolerated.'[1] It was this kind of perception of suburbia as little short of a social disaster, the blind creation of an aesthetic and cultural desert, which not only gave it a despised image in the minds of architects and town planners but also convinced them that it was the result of lack of system and control. The coincidence, since 1945, of a change in the direction of development with the imposition of reasonably effective planning regulations has further convinced them of the correctness of this diagnosis.

Urban historians and geographers arrived later on the suburban scene, after the frontier had been closed. They were led by Jim Dyos, who was born in one inner suburb, Kentish Town, and made his reputation with the history of another, Camberwell; it would have pleased him to see this early volume in the series which he conceived being devoted to his own first love, suburban history. In his pioneering *Victorian Suburb*, Dyos was chiefly concerned to rescue the suburb from historical oblivion and to show that its reputation for insignificant and uninteresting anonymity was unwarranted.[2] Putting Camberwell under the historical miscrocope he demonstrated that the apparently random jumble of streets, house patterns, and neighbourhoods which made up the completed inner suburb of 1900 was in fact an intricate mosaic of building estates and developments, each piece with an identifiable and intelligible form created in an explicable and hence an orderly and rational, although not necessarily lovely or admirable, way. Each piece of the jigsaw had an identity and character shaped by the way in which a particular developer at a particular time visualized in terms of buildings the resolution of an equation involving the potentialities of the site and its location, building costs and current tastes in house types, and the nature of the likely demand for housing in the district. The solutions varied between districts at any one time, because individual decisions and the circumstances influencing them differed; but above all they varied over time, reflecting not merely changing tastes and expectations but also the changing general position of Camberwell itself, at one moment on the outer fringe and 50 years later well behind the suburban frontier. Chronological layers of development were therefore unravelled, of initial occupation and re-occupation and subdivision of houses, of social aspiration and social decay, within existing neighbourhoods and influencing the character of districts yet to be developed, plotting and explaining the progress, or decline, of Camberwell from sought-after suburb on the edge of the country to integral part of the fully urbanized central metropolis. The book is a triumphant demonstration that the suburb and the sub-districts of which it is composed, far from being featureless wastelands possess individuality and character in the distinctive layouts and buildings of their physical structure. Even more it is a demonstration of how property deeds, building leases, maps, estate papers, business records, and a great array of printed sources can be made to yield an understanding of the diverse influences which determined the timing of the making of the suburban environment and its physical and social shape, an understanding which shows that in the process of creating suburbs seemingly blind and mindless market forces were only translated into shapes on the ground through perfectly rational and orderly decisions by people.

At the same time as Dyos was publishing, urban geographers, many of them with historical interests, began in the early 1960s to turn their attention from urban morphology in general to suburban forms and suburban growth in particular. Much of this work adopts the same approach and essentially empirical method, uses the same sources, and tackles the same questions, as those favoured by urban historians, seeking to explain the detailed timing and configuration of specific suburban developments in terms of the pre-development structure of landownership, the pattern of tracks, paths, and field boundaries, the actions of individual owners and developers, the influence of the means of transport, and the operation of the drives and pressures of social class.[3] Other geographers, much influenced by the work of urban sociologists in America, adopted a more consciously theoretical and abstract approach in extending to suburban and fringe areas the analysis of land use patterns in terms of physical and social distance from the city centre, and in measuring the degree to which their study areas conform to the Chicago model of social segregation, itself no more than a generalized description of the spatial distribution of the industrial, commercial, and residential sectors of a particular city.[4]

The stiffening of historical research by the incorporation of a conceptual framework is all to the good, and while the labours of the 'factorial ecologists' among the geographers have done little to illuminate the suburban scene, if only because the census materials with which they work are both crude in relation to social classifications and in relation to recognizable suburban districts, in general the parallel and often converging streams of urban history and urban geography have set the course for the post-Camberwell study of suburban history. Studies have been published of the suburbs of metropolitan Essex,[5] Paddington and Hammersmith,[6] Hampstead,[7] Victoria Park, Manchester,[8] Kelvinside,[9] and

4

Edgbaston,[10] as well as a general account of the interwar explosion of London's outer suburbia.[11] Since suburban history, appropriately enough, retains a semi-detached relationship to urban history and there is no clear line between town and suburb, the latter frequently becoming part of the central area as a result of later expansion, the histories of particular towns often discuss suburban development.[12] Even so, the tally of modern scholarly studies of suburbs is not a long one, and much more remains in unpublished theses: this volume, in publishing the authors' distillations of theses on Bromley, Ealing and Acton, Bexley, and Headingley, Potternewton, and Chapel Allerton in north Leeds, very nearly doubles the number of available studies of particular suburbs, preserves the balance between the metropolis and provincial towns which has already been established, and adds to our understanding of how and why the suburban environment came into existence.

Almost without exception these studies start with an outline of population growth since 1801, a statement of the relative and absolute increase in the size of the population living in towns, and a more detailed account of the size of the total population and its decennial rates of growth in the mother city or conurbation of the study area. There is an underlying assumption, sometimes made explicit, that the vast increase in the numbers of town-dwellers, or at any rate a high proportion of that increase in any town of considerable size, could in the nature of things – given that more people must occupy more space, and that the space within existing town limits whether defined administratively or geographically was already full – only be housed in suburbs established on the outskirts. Having provided some explanation of the growth in overall urban population, whether in demographic terms or in terms of the economy of the particular town and the sources of expansion in its employment and incomes, the questions for the suburban historian become those of which sections of the net increase in total population moved to the suburbs and why, and which parts of the surrounding space were turned into suburban residential areas, when, by what stages, by whom, and why in some particular shape rather than any other.

Indeed, it makes very good sense in the British context to consider population growth as fundamental, and to look for some threshold in town size beyond which a traditional urban structure of a unified and physically, socially, and economically integrated townscape gave way to a modern arrangement of central town and dependent suburbs. For the nineteenth century it is valid to see suburbanization as a facet of urbanization, a necessary part of and condition for the wider process. It would be hazardous to make any firm pronouncement without local knowledge of the history and topography of every large town, but by mid-century it is likely that every place with more than 50,000 inhabitants thought of itself as possessing some suburbs; Brighton had its Kemp Town and Hove, Newcastle its Jesmond and Gosforth, Hull its Cottingham when they reached about that size. Nevertheless, before accepting that suburban development was a necessary consequence of the scale of urbanization it is worth asking whether the connexion is as strong as the nineteenth-century experience suggests.

There were certainly theoretical alternatives to the suburban mode for accommodating expansion in urban populations, and other countries provide working examples of them in practice. The development of residential suburbs of distinctive

Other alts to suburbs e.g. American cities or build upwards. Land prices!?

appearance and distinctive class was one form of lateral expansion. Another form of lateral expansion was by simple accretion at the town edges of buildings and street patterns that reproduced and continued the character of the established town, in new quarters with mixed residential, commercial, and industrial functions, and with intermixed residents from different social classes. This, apparently, is what happened in most American cities until the 1870s; they remained compact 'walking' cities, despite considerable growth in size, with no pronounced social – as distinct from ethnic – segregation. It was only with the appearance of the new technology of mass transit by tramways that socially segregated districts began to develop, the vehicle of segregation being the suburb.[13] Towns could also expand upwards rather than sideways, throwing up vertical streets in tenement and apartment blocks. This was the way with most continental, and the large Scottish towns; by this means Paris and Vienna remained classically compact cities, in contrast to London, the scattered city, and one stepped outside Rome, for example, in the later nineteenth century literally into an empty surrounding desert.[14] That English towns did not follow these models was an act of choice, not of necessity.

The largest English towns – Liverpool, Manchester, Birmingham, Leeds, and Sheffield, as well as London – were suburbanized, and socially segregated, half a century or so before the arrival of cheap mass transit, which was not developed effectively in the English setting before the 1890s. It can be argued that horse omnibuses and railways, if they chose to offer suburban train services, provided transport that was neither for the masses nor cheap but was nonetheless sufficient to carry the better-off minority out to suburbs. There is a great deal in this argument, but since the Americans possessed the same pre-tramway transport technology without using it to support the same style of living, omnibus and suburban train should be regarded as permitting, rather than creating, the suburb. In any case it was entirely possible for a place like Camberwell, 1½ to two miles from the City, to remain quite substantially a 'walking suburb' at least until the 1870s, and yet to be unmistakably suburban in character and function regardless of the degree of reliance on walking to work.[15] The high density, high rise development of continental and Scottish cities, on the other hand, has been explained by high building land values and, in some cases, stringent building regulations designed to prevent building outside municipal limits for reasons of internal security and social control. The building regulations were important, and were not paralleled in Britain; Scottish municipal regulations were generally tougher than English ones, which outside London tended not to exist at all until mid-century, but they acted to increase building costs through control of materials and structures and did not regulate the availability of sites. Where building was allowed building land values were markedly higher in continental towns than in England, and the ready availability of supplies of relatively cheap building land with a gradient of values generally descending from city centres was a prerequisite for suburban development. On the other hand, recent experience suggests that it requires a very sharp rise indeed in plot value in relation to building cost, raising the site element from a traditional 5 to 10 per cent of overall cost to one-third or even one-half, before high density tall buildings become the only economic use of building land. In Scotland, moreover, the generally higher building land values did not inhibit the development of Kelvinside with its suburban densities, suburban profiles, and suburban qualities, once a demand for that kind of thing appeared among the wealthier Glaswegian middle class.[16] High land prices encourage high buildings, and low land prices are favourable to suburban development, but neither can be regarded as decisive influences.

England's own pre-suburban experience, moreover, has to be taken into account. There was marked urban growth in the course of the eighteenth century, particularly after 1750, the proportion of the population living in towns increased from about one-fifth to around one-third, and the actual numbers of town dwellers roughly from one million to three million.[17] Some of this increase in urbanization was accounted for by an increase in the number of places which could be called towns, each of them still quite small in 1801. But much of it was the result of the growth of large towns: leaving London aside, by 1801 Liverpool, Manchester, Birmingham, and Bristol were well over the 50,000 mark, Leeds, Sheffield, and Newcastle upon Tyne were not far behind in the 30–40,000 range, and Norwich, despite having fallen back in the city league table, was of similar size. All these towns had grown up to this point without generating any true suburbs, although they had small settlements of town housing outside the central areas for the wealthy and a spattering of country houses for the wealthiest. What is more, attempts to build suburbs as places of defined appeal and status were generally unsuccessful before the 1820s. In Liverpool the plan to build a residential suburb for the well-to-do on the earl of Sefton's estate in Toxteth Park, to be called Harrington, was a flop in the 1770s and 1780s, and it was not until the 1820s, and then in a different direction at Everton, that the suburban idea began to take hold with Liverpool's wealthy merchants. In Manchester Ardwick was beginning to grow as a suburb for the wealthy perhaps just a few years earlier, while in Birmingham a grandiose scheme to create a new hamlet of some pretensions in Ashted hung fire in the 1790s, and development in Edgbaston was sporadic and unimpressive until the 1820s.[18]

Even eighteenth-century London, while obviously exceptional in sheer size and complexity, already at the beginning of the century a concentration of over half a million people and at its close a conurbation of nearly one million, was not unequivocally a special case of suburban precocity. Such an expansion in numbers clearly involved an expansion in the built-up area to house them, and successive stages in the growth of the town were plainly marked by new communications carried round the contemporary edges of settlement, for example the New Road, now Marylebone and Euston Roads, in the 1760s and the Regent's Canal in the 1800s; while new bridges across the Thames from mid-century signalled the spread of south London from Southwark into Newington, Walworth, and Lambeth. The great bulk of this expansion was urban in form, an extension of established patterns of streets of terraced housing, of squares in the more fashionable parts, of close-packed courts and alleys and jumbles of tenements in the less favoured areas intermixed with industrial and commercial activities, a general growth in size of the environment for town life in the varied and evolving forms in which it already existed in the older inner areas of dense settlement. Beyond these districts of the expanding town a ring of satellite villages flourished and grew in the eighteenth century, linked to the metropolis by thin ribbons of substantial villa development and short strings of roadside terraces. In the backlands behind these ribbons several schemes of estate development were successfully launched in the later eighteenth century, conceived as new towns and accorded appropriate names to advertise their individuality: Hans Town, Somers Town, Pentonville, Camden Town, and so on. At the time these were geographically suburbs, in their distance and semi-

WHAT IS SUBURB?

detachment from the centre, and to a degree were socially suburban in being, for their élites, places of residence divorced from their places of work. Physically and architecturally, however, they were extensions of the town, laid out in streets and squares and built in repetitive three and four storey terraces whose plain regularity Victorians found so monotonous and unimaginative, and whose accommodation was often found too large and expensive for single family occupation.[19] The impression, derived from the shape and appearance of the built environment rather than any knowledge of how the inhabitants lived, which remains unresearched, is that the atmosphere of these new towns was more urban and akin to other socially and economically similar parts of older London than it was new and distinctively suburban. The overgrown villages which lay beyond, Hackney, Highgate, Hampstead, Clapham, or Camberwell, were a clear step closer to being prototype suburbs with the charms of their surrounding country and their local cream of successful merchants and professional men going up to town daily in their carriages. Even so, their mixed development of large individual houses in park-like grounds for the wealthiest, and small squares and short runs of terraced town housing for others, and their mixed use for family summer stations removed from the heat and stench of the city, and for holiday resorts, as well as for some permanent residence, gave them a pleasantly varied appearance and a diversified social life rather than an unmistakably suburban stamp.

There is, of course, a tautological trap in implying that the full stamp of suburban approval can only be given to that species of low density development of residential districts arranged in roads, avenues, ways, and walks rather than streets and squares, studded with detached and semi-detached low rise houses set in individual garden plots, and peopled with middle-class commuters, which only appeared in the nineteenth century. It then becomes a matter of spatial definition, not of argument, that pre-nineteenth century methods of dealing with the expansion of towns and treating their outskirts were not truly suburban. Nevertheless architectural historians are in no doubt that detached and semi-detached houses built for single family occupation are of the suburban essence, and that such houses did not exist before the nineteenth century; heralded in the revolutionary plans for the Eyre estate in St John's Wood in the 1790s, they were first realized on the ground in the successful development of that estate from 1815 onwards, and became the origin, through much mutation and debasement, of virtually all suburban houses.[20] It is arguable, also, that it was only in the setting of this kind of house, where the family could distance itself from the outside world in its own private fortress behind its own garden fence and privet hedge and yet could make a show of outward appearances that was sure to be noticed by the neighbours, that the suburban life style of individual domesticity and group-monitored respectability could take hold. It has often been remarked that the key feature in the attractions of suburban living is that it offers a retreat from the noise and bustle of the metropolis to the privacy and seclusion of the family home. The daily retreat has to be made possible by some means of getting to work, and its security has to be insured against challenges and interruptions from different life styles by a high degree of social homogeneity and exclusiveness in the residential neighbourhood, but its core is the single family house where a private domestic life can be lived. 'The flight to the suburbs,' writes Donald Olsen, 'involved the temporary rejection of the rest of society, of that part that extended beyond the immediate family of the householder: the most satisfactory suburb was that which gave him the maximum of privacy and the minimum of outside distraction.'[21] In a male-dominated society this was an essentially male view of the attractions of suburbia since it was the man who went out to work and then sought daily relief from the strains of business and the demands of relations with colleagues and strangers by escaping to the supposedly undemanding comforts of the family home, while his wife was left to make what she could out of day-long isolation in the cherished privacy and seclusion. The creation of an environment in which this division of middle-class male lives between a public world of work contacts and a private world of family life was what the rise of suburbia was all about. The question then is, why did the pursuit of privacy, or its realization in building forms, happen at this particular time?

At one level the answer is that someone in a position to influence the shape of building operations – urban estate owner, developer, architect-surveyor, or builder – invented the semi-detached house, and that once invented it caught on. The someone, moreover, can be precisely identified as John Shaw, the architect-surveyor to the Eyre estate, and his designs for the detached and semi-detached villas of St John's Wood were a stylistic event of far-reaching importance. Domestic architecture has its own traditions, its own processes of change, and its own internal logic, and it is possible to place this particular departure in a sequence of efforts to produce scaled down and watered down versions of aristocratic housing arrangements suited to smaller incomes: town terraces were imitations in gradations of compression and austerity of upper-class town houses, and the semi-detached was the ultimate reduction of the country house through intermediate layers of villas. Unless it is assumed, however, that designers and builders dictate to the housing market and that occupiers are obliged to live in whatever kind of house it pleases the builders to provide, a design-based explanation remains superficial. In a competitive world a new product is successful only if there turns out to be a demand for it.

It is unlikely that a potential demand for this type of housing had been around for many years without a supply to satisfy it appearing. It is not easy to see any decisive shifts in the factors controlling the supply of building land or of houses in the years before the suburban take-off which could support an explanation from the supply side. Admittedly, the trend over the eighteenth century was for the owners of sizeable building estates to make increasingly systematic and carefully organized efforts to regulate and supervise the layout and design of developments on their properties, and insofar as they and their advisers were cautiously conservative in their ideas they tended to legislate in their building agreements for tried and tested types of town housing and to try and prevent aberrations or experiments. It would be a mistake to suppose, however, either that competently and effectively controlled building estates exercised a stranglehold over supplies of building land, or that their owners had the power to frustrate market forces by autocratic decree. All the evidence suggests that there were plentiful supplies of building land much of which was available without any restrictions on what was to be built; that many urban landowners who did attempt to use building agreements and leases to impose their concepts of permissible development drew the terms carelessly and imprecisely, with many loopholes for builders to do undesirable things; and that even the most regulatory landowners were unable to enforce a character of development which the location and housing demand for the site would not sustain.[22] There were, therefore, no effective legal or political constraints on the availability of building land which could have prevented the erection of single family houses if there had been an effective demand for them, and while there has been little systematic work on the intractable subject of building land values there is nothing to indicate that land costs were so high in the eighteenth century as to inhibit low density development, or that there was any decisive drop as a precursor of suburban growth. What evidence there is suggests a rising trend for building land values through the nineteenth century, with cyclical variations, and contains no sign that the starting point of this trend marked any discontinuity from the eighteenth century; that, indeed, would have been inconsistent with the well-observed tendency of land values on the urban fringe to move smoothly from high agricultural values for accommodation land, prime hay or grazing land, or market gardening, to the bottom rungs of building values.[23]

If land would always have been available somewhere on the outskirts of the city for builders to build what they liked, it is equally unlikely that any changes in building costs or in the organization of the building industry made semi-detacheds possible where they had not been possible before. Building costs certainly rose during the French Wars as a result of rising prices for building materials, and then fell, but this was a cyclical rather than a secular movement. A short-term fall in costs, and plentiful supplies of cheap finance for builders, may have given an initial impulse to suburban building in the 1820s, but in broad perspective nineteenth-century suburban growth should be viewed as taking place in a context of slowly rising costs, if only because of the improving quality and equipment of the suburban house, rather than being pictured as a response to increasing cheapness.[24] The building industry itself did undergo major changes, with the emergence of a few large-scale contractors in the early nineteenth century and the transformation of the small building unit from a joint enterprise of building tradesmen headed by a senior craftsman as undertaker to the small capitalist building firm with a builder employing members of the different building trades as wage workers. The emergence of the building contractor, however, was not a precondition of suburban development, since the great bulk of this work was for long done by multitudes of small-scale and ephemeral speculative builders; and although it is possible that the small capitalist was better able to engage in speculative house building than the craft enterprises he replaced, it is apparent that these eighteenth-century predecessors, headed perhaps by a carpenter or a mason, were perfectly capable of taking risks and building on speculation for the market as they saw it.[25]

Plentiful supplies of comparatively cheap building land and a building industry capable of producing speculatively for a range of incomes permitted the growth of suburbs, but there do not seem to have been any changes in these factors sufficiently sharp or pronounced to have caused that growth to get under way. It is possible, however, that the effective supply of building land was increased by transport improvements opening up fresh and more remote areas for settlement, without any change in the inclinations or policies of landowners being required. In a general sense modern suburbia could not have happened without the omnibus, commuter train, and tram, powerfully reinforced in the twentieth century by the motor; without such means the geographical spread and the growing distances between home and work could not have been supported. While transport improvements and extensions clearly sustained the general process of suburban expansion and intensification, this does not necessarily imply a causal connexion or indicate which way it operated. New transport ventures are rather more likely to be designed to cater for an established traffic than to create an entirely new one, even *did transport bring or just allow suburb?*

though once operating they have great potential for stimulating large increases. In any event when new railways did produce a clear suburban response, as they did in Bromley in the 1850s and in west London in the 1860s and 1870s, this happened long after the attractions of the suburban way of living had been successfully demonstrated, and the new transport promoted the development of an already tested product in a fresh locality. It is less easy to imagine new forms of transport poking their fingers out into the country in the hope of initiating a way of life that had not yet been tried and shown to be socially and commercially successful. On the other hand, flexible and adaptable forms of transport were at hand in the crucial period at the beginning of the nineteenth century that were capable of playing their part in enlarging the residential area through extension of their services, so soon as a demand for them arose.

By the early years of the century there was already a well-developed network of short-stage coach services in the London area, running between such peripheral villages as Paddington, Camberwell, Clapham, Islington, or Edmonton and the City and West End. Fares were high, coaches small, and journeys slow with long stops at the public houses which were the picking up points, so that this kind of passenger transport was not suited to the regular commuter who would have needed to use a private carriage or his own feet for a truly suburban daily journey to work. Nevertheless the short-stage provided the essential link with the centre for the more occasional traveller, for shopping, visiting, or entertainment, which permitted Paddington or Clapham families to evolve a suburban pattern of life. The horse-drawn omnibus, introduced in 1829 on the Paddington–City route, was a development of the short-stage concept, adding a larger capacity vehicle with rear entry for easy access, boarding and alighting at the passenger's wish, faster journeys, and lower fares.[26] Bus services expanded rapidly in the 1830s, freed from the previous prohibition of picking up or setting down in central London, and quickly became established as one of the most important determinants of the character of early suburban development. Buses made possible daily journeys to work at times of day, journey speeds, and fares which were convenient to the affluent to middling middle class of professional men, civil servants, merchants, bankers, larger shopkeepers, and perhaps some senior clerks. Buses, therefore, allowed families in such groups to live at a distance from work and dispense with private carriages, and permitted those who could never have aspired to own private carriages to do likewise. They permitted middle-class neighbourhoods to function without coach-houses or mews, households to be run with only female servants, and houses to be smaller and less expensive because quarters for male horse servants were not needed. These all became standard features of early Victorian suburbs, and they were all dependent on the horse bus. *buses*

The horse may rightly be credited with much influence over the form which the suburban environment took, and with permitting its colonization of growing territories in the 30 years or so before the 1850s, when suburban train services first began to have any significant effect in allowing or stimulating further suburban growth. It would be going too far, however, to suggest that the availability of horse-drawn public passenger transport was decisive in triggering the birth of the suburb. The sequence of events was that the suburb came first and the short-stage coach or omnibus followed once the potential passengers were established. It is true that this came to be such an automatic development that people came to live in districts with very poor, or no transport services in the confident expectation that a

11

new bus route would be opened as soon as there was a sufficient concentration of residents to furnish profitable customers, so that settlement in advance of transport was simply a matter of timing and the mechanics of business and no proof that settlement went ahead without regard to transport services.[27] This reasoning could, however, be applied with little modification to the pre-suburban world, in which the organization and equipment of the horse and coach trades were fully capable by the later eighteenth century of responding to the emergence of new bodies of customers by providing new services. While suburban development needed some form of transport services in order to take root and flourish, it is thus likely that in the initial phases at least it was the development which called forth appropriate kinds of transport, and unlikely that there had been any powerful but latent suburbanizing force held in check by any absence of enterprise or innovation in transport.

If, therefore, the building and occupation of districts of single family homes, and hence the origins of suburbia, cannot be satisfactorily explained by independent changes in the supply conditions, it is natural to suggest that the initiating impulse came from the side of changes in housing demand. The two possibilities are that the desire for a domestic life of privacy and seclusion was a new experience for any sizeable section of the middle class, only gathering force for the first time around the beginning of the nineteenth century; or that the desire had long been present and that what happened was some change in the means of satisfying it, a shift in effective demand. From the vantage point of the major provincial towns the origins of successful suburbs can be explained quite simply in terms of effective demand at the group rather than the individual family level. Before the 1820s or 1830s there simply were not enough comfortably off middle-class families in Birmingham or Manchester, Liverpool or Leeds, to populate an exclusive residential district as distinct from the occasional square or crescent, or individual mansions scattered in the surrounding country. The failure of earlier attempts to develop respectable or prestigious suburbs can be laid at the door of lack of demand because of the small size of the local bourgeoisie. Once this passed some critical level, which happened at different points between the 1820s and the 1850s according to the overall size, social structure, and prosperity of different towns, middle-class residential suburbs took hold, although the great provincial cities were still hard put to it to sustain more than one smart suburb at a time and, as the case of Leeds shows, the limited size of the market made mixed character suburban development not uncommon.[28]

Middle-class numbers look like a sufficient explanation for the provincial case, without drawing on any analysis of middle-class ideology or taste. An argument from smallness of numbers, however, is unlikely to convince if applied to eighteenth-century London. Much work remains to be done before its social structure can be understood or depicted with precision, but it is tolerably clear that by the end of the century something like one fifth of its population belonged to the middling ranks of society. In round numbers this means that there were 30,000 to 40,000 middle-class families, and although the group comprised a broad and varied range of occupations, social positions, and incomes, stretching from £80 to £100 a year at the lower end of the shopkeeper and small employer scale up to £500 to £800 a year of the wealthy merchants and prosperous professional men, at which level it shaded off into the upper classes where super-rich bankers, brewers, and large-scale traders were on terms with the aristocracy and gentry, it must nevertheless have contained several thousand families able to afford houses worth

£40 to £50 a year or even more.[29] Single family homes with ample servant accommodation could well be provided at that sort of rent, and a total demand numbered in thousands could well have supported several suburban districts. The simple answer is to say that it did indeed do just that, and the Claphams, Newingtons, Camberwells, Islingtons, or Hackneys of the eighteenth century were precisely the type of suburbs that this upper middle class wanted.

Such a conclusion, however, merely prompts a rephrasing of the issue: if eighteenth-century upper middle-class Londoners wanted their suburban settlements to be reiterations of town housing in town formations, why did their early nineteenth-century descendants want something entirely different? The clue, it has been suggested, lies in the kind of life for which the detached or semi-detached house set in its own garden was the necessary physical setting. The clear separation of work and home, the insistence on social distancing, the treatment of the home as a feminine domain, the importance attached to domestic privacy and the exclusion of the vulgar prying multitude, can all be seen as parts of a code of individual responsibility, male economic dominance and female domestic subordination, and family-nurtured morality which served to give the bourgeoisie a social identity and mark them off from the upper class and the lower orders. The separation of work from domestic life was occurring in the later eighteenth century as a result of changes in production technology and business organization which made the home an unsuitable or impossible place for many kinds of trade and manufacture; the emphasis on personal religious and moral responsibility and behaviour from the Clapham Sect and the Evangelicals, whose message was powerfully reinforced by the French Revolution and fears of disorderly, irreligious mobs, gave a central role to the family as the main instrument of moral education; and the socially segregated suburb of separate family houses shortly emerged to supply the ideal environment for practising the newly reformed life style incorporating these religious, moral, and social aspirations.[30]

There is great intellectual attraction in this ideological explanation of the launching of modern suburbia, since it grounds a new form of middle-class housing demand firmly in a set of ideas and ideals whose own origins have roots in changes in the economy and developments in religion, bypasses any enquiry into changes in real incomes and effective demand, and yet makes it possible to regard a shift in the character of demand as the decisive suburbanizing force. Some doubts need to be resolved, however, before this interpretation can be wholly accepted. Was the cult of privacy and regulated domesticity a class phenomenon, did its practice require a particular kind of housing, and does the chronology fit, so that the development of the ideals and conventions can be shown to have preceded suburban growth? The upper class, or some of it, cultivated the virtues of family life, propriety, and rectitude, and translated these values into elaborate arrangements to provide privacy, sexual segregation, delimitation of specialized spheres of activity, and separation from the servants, in the planning of their houses, at much the same time as the middle classes were developing their domestic rituals.[31] Within the working classes some sections of the skilled artisans and regularly employed developed ideas of respectability which included pride in the home and the cultivation of family life. It may well be that the conventional view is correct, which ascribes a conversion of aristocratic and upper working-class minds and attitudes to the triumph of the bourgeois ideal, but such a conquest has not been conclusively demonstrated and it remains possible that groups in all classes were responding simultaneously to a common set of influences on morals and manners.[32] This may not have much practical significance for the initiation of suburban growth: the aristocracy had town houses and country houses and did not need any more; skilled workers could not afford to live far from their work and were obliged to take what houses were available and adapt them as best they could to the needs of family life; only the more affluent members of the middle classes both required and could afford the new suburban houses as settings ideally suited to the practice of domesticity. It does, however, bear on the question of whether a specific type of house was essential, or much better suited than alternative types, to the realization of privacy and seclusion.

Long town streets of terrace houses without gardens were prone to stimulate a lively, public, gregarious street life, which bustled with noise, strangers, and external distractions, and perhaps most damagingly of all for internalized family discipline and self-sufficiency, encouraged the random and promiscuous mixing of children out of reach of parental control. Terrace housing was not, however, inherently inimical to a more inward-turning life of seemliness and propriety. While many terrace houses were, or became, multi-tenanted, this descent into multi-occupation by several households was largely the result of later nineteenth-century social deterioration of streets and neighbourhoods which had started life with reasonably high status, and the normal terrace house was not only perfectly capable of acting as a single family home but was in fact usually designed and initially occupied as such. It was, moreover, well adapted for a domestic régime of clearly separated spheres of activity, as a French visitor to London noted in 1817:

> These narrow houses, three or four storeys high – one for eating, one for sleeping, a third for company, a fourth underground for the kitchen, a fifth perhaps at the top for the servants – and the agility, the ease, the quickness with which the individuals of the family run up and down, and perch on the different storeys, give the idea of a cage with its sticks and birds.[33]

In addition there is no suggestion that the terrace house in any way encouraged the presence of workplace and residence in the same building, indeed it seems probable that most terrace houses were always exclusively residential. Suitably placed in quiet locations terraces were serviceable vehicles for sheltered middle-class living, and although they were falling out of favour from the 1820s because of the superior merits and convenience of detached and semi-detached houses for privacy, this was a slow process and terraces were still being built in new middle-class suburbs well into the 1860s.[34]

Above all the crystallization of the ideas of privacy and domesticity and their general acceptance among the middle classes, and others, was also a long-drawn out process, stretching from the 1780s to its culmination in the 1850s and 1860s. It is by no means clear that the development of the new domestic ethos preceded the new suburban growth, and if the two processes went on alongside each other it is at least as likely that the environment influenced the behaviour pattern as that the desired behaviour pattern helped to shape the environment. The spatial dispersion and separation of the suburban environment was, after all, highly likely to foster the further development and refinement of attitudes which emphasized the attractions and virtues of privacy, withdrawal of the family on to its own social resources, avoidance of embarrassing chance encounters with strangers, and peaceful recuperation from the worries of business. The suburban environment in itself had no moral qualities apart from those attributed to it by its inhabitants, and when these decided that suburbs were morally good because of their immunity from the wickedness and immorality of the city a fresh source of support was tapped to sustain the continuing suburban expansion. Certainly physical expansion and cultural development fed upon one another, but it would be hazardous to award causal primacy to either.

Work on the earliest nineteenth-century suburbs has concentrated on analysing the process of constructing the built environment and on explaining in detail why developments followed particular layout patterns and builders put up particular kinds and values of houses in specific places. If it were possible to match this level of research on the development and construction side with equally intensive study of the previous backgrounds, attitudes, and aspirations of the new inhabitants who constituted the demand for the kind of housing without which these ventures could not have succeeded, it might be possible to resolve the problem. Since the new suburban dwellers left no body of records of their life styles, their cultural outlook, or their motives in moving, this may never happen. Meanwhile it would be sensible to look to the suburban garden for the roots of the demand for suburban living, something which brought the possibilities of privacy and seclusion with it but which was desired in a straightforward way for its own sake because it was a piece of tangible evidence, however minute, that the dream of being a townsman living in the country was something more than just an illusion. The essential quality of the new suburbs was that they were on the edge of the country with open views beyond, even if subsequent development leapfrogged past them and hemmed them in as inner suburbs. An essential attribute of the single family house was the garden, preferably one in front to impress the outside world with a display of neatly-tended possession of some land, and one at the back for the family to enjoy. It can be suggested that a desire for individual gardens was surfacing among the potential suburbanites at just about the time when building suppliers chose to put the article on the market. It was in the 1790s that the countryside was ceasing to be feared or despised as boorish, backward, or hostile and was coming to be admired by cultivated opinion as the home of all that was natural and virtuous. In 1810 John Nash outlined his scheme for the development of Regent's Park, using the well-tried and conventional building forms of Georgian London, terraces and crescents, but placing them in a new rural setting instead of in a gridiron of streets and squares, so that each resident should have the illusion of looking out on his own country park. Even more important, in 1824 Nash tacked Park Villages East and West on to the imposing formality of the elegant Park terraces, villages which were indeed an aristocratic garden suburb in miniature, rusticated cottages, each one different, each one in its garden, planted in an urban context.[35] Even here *rus in urbe* was realized on the ground for the fashionable aristocracy and very wealthy, a model not only for developers and builders to imitate but also a pattern for the ambitious middle classes to seek to emulate. An aristocratic fashionplate – and in its early, contemporary, stage St John's Wood villadom was almost equally wealthy – it can be argued, transmuted middle-class yearnings for a whiff of the country, which had hitherto seemed unacceptable and inappropriate in town dwellers, into a positive and respectable demand. There were, after all, vast numbers of towndwellers who had come from rural backgrounds; some of them, presumably, hankered after the country they had left, and some of these had the means to indulge such nostalgia In late eighteenth-century London from one half to two-thirds of the adults had been born in the country; and it is probable that the mid-nineteenth-century pattern of internal migration which shows that at least two-thirds of the residents of south London and Liverpool suburbs, and presumably other suburbs likewise, had moved to the suburbs from neighbouring and largely rural areas and had not moved out from the central zone, also applied earlier.[36]

Some portion of the new suburbanites undoubtedly did desert the old town centres, escaping from increasing dirt, noise, stench, and disease, dissatisfied with the social confusion of mixed residential areas and with the inconvenience of traditional town houses for the style of life they wanted to pursue. But if they were heavily outnumbered by those coming direct to the suburbs from rural and small town surroundings, it is to these that we should look for the mainspring of suburban housing demand, and there is little difficulty in supposing that they were more interested in clutching at some small reminder of country life than in seeking an environment suited to the practice of an ideology of which they were most likely not yet aware. All that was needed to release this pent-up demand, it seems, was a demonstration that moving to a town did not necessarily have to mean moving to a town house and accepting a fully urbanized way of life. Since terrace housing of the traditional town form continued to be built in middle-class suburbs into the second half of the nineteenth century, it is conceivable that this had mainly in view the demand from established towndwellers who wanted to move to something familiar but in more pleasant surroundings, while the market for detached and semi-detached houses lay among the new arrivals. In any event, if demand for the new kind of suburban housing was stirred by fashionable and aristocratic example it is likely that it showed itself mainly in those sections of the middle class which felt closest to the aristocracy, least antipathy to them, or most anxiety to model themselves on what they took to be gentlemanly habits, the groups least likely to be concerned to develop a distinctively and assertively bourgeois culture. It is arguable that suburban growth and the suburban life was set in successful motion by the more imitative and self-effacing sections of the middle class in pursuit of the illusion of bringing the country and gentrification into the urban setting, more intent on appearing to merge themselves unobtrusively into a superior class than on seeking means to express their own class identity.[37]

Much of this reasoning remains to be tested by further research. The results of recent research which are published in this volume all rest on the implicit assumption that once the commercial viability of the suburban process had been established and an effective demand for its product had been shown to exist, thereafter the creation of further suburbs became almost a self-sustaining activity, a consequence of urban population growth and the growth and changing distribution of real incomes, which continued indefinitely, subject to cyclical fluctuations, until at least partially arrested by political regulation. This point had been reached by the 1830s, and it is reasonable to argue that from that time those who controlled the necessary resources, landowners, developers, builders and their financers, would channel those resources into the construction of suburban estates confident – frequently over-confident – that a continuing demand existed for his general type of housing. Suburbia had caught on, it was developing its culture, its social rituals, its conventions; the lawnmower had arrived, for those with large enough lawns; it was becoming the ambition of all those who could afford it to live as close to the edge of the country as possible, preferably no doubt employing a gardener. The questions had become, on the supply side, to judge whether and when a particular town and a particular locality could sustain a piece of suburban development, and to decide how to trim and adjust the suburban type in layout and house size to suit the location and the local market, and on the demand side to judge between the reputations, attractions, and costs of the different suburban districts on offer. Demand, of course, changed over time, not merely as fashions in house styles changed or as the special character of older suburbs altered and declined as the frontier moved outward, but also in terms of the social and income groups which composed it; the chapter on Bexley gives an insight into the social deepening of the suburban market particularly in the 1930s in response to falling costs and rising real incomes, but this can be seen happening earlier, on less impressive scales, in both Acton and north Leeds, and was a feature of the 1880s and 1890s which brought the lower middle class into suburbia in a considerable way.[38] Variations in the level of demand over time, as well as changes in its social make up, were as important as changes in the conditions affecting new building, in determining the cycles of vigorous expansion and slackness which characterized suburban development; and at the level of the particular suburb or individual building estate within it they were of supreme importance in settling its success or failure. At the general level, however, the motives of suburbanites in wanting to be, or at least passively consenting to be, suburbanites had ceased to be a problem requiring investigation; the suburban way of life in a suburban environment ranging from costly and leafy to inexpensive and gimcrack, was plainly what was preferred by the majority of those who could possibly afford it – it even came to be assumed by planners and policy-makers, with dubious justification, that it was what most of the working classes would want too if the means could be found to provide it for them.

The four case studies which follow, however, do a great deal more than show how, when, and why shapes on the ground took the particular form they did in four suburban localities in response to general impulses, although they do this in a way to satisfy curiosity about the influences which have moulded the local environment. Four general points stand out, which can only be made through studying the suburbanizing process in action in specific places: the importance of rural, pre-development features in influencing the shape, form, character, and timing of suburbanization, coupled with the limitations which market forces placed on the power of landowners and developers to decide what should be built; the varying role of transport services in different situations; the mixed social character of suburban districts, coupled with strong self-zoning tendencies; and the long drawn-out and much interrupted nature of the process of growth in any particular neighbourhood.

It has frequently been observed that the fully built-up environment exhibits the marks and scars of its rural antecedents, and that field paths and boundaries, ancient tracks, and property boundaries show through in the pattern of roads, the territories of housing estates, and the social and chronological frontiers between distinct housing types of the urbanized scene. These studies confirm the observation with many local illustrations, but go much further in revealing the complex character of the shadows which pre-development features cast before them. The structure of property rights involved in taking the development process through from the open land of farming, market gardening, or country house park to the suburban street is most expressly and schematically formulated in Treen's approach, but is implicit in all the other cases.[39] At the level of the individual building estate or building plot the availability of the land for development depended on the readiness, and legal capacity of the landowner to release it; the identity of the pre-development landowner, and the mixture of financial and social influences on him, therefore played a critical part in determining the timing and type of building operations. What emerges, however, is that there was no one type of pre-development owner or pre-development situation which was specially prone to stimulate development. In Bromley, land transfers which brought in new, speculative owners were of great importance as preconditions of development, while in north Leeds long-established, absentee aristocratic landowners attempted, without great success, to act as direct developers of their estates well in advance of any strong demand for villas in the area.[40] Ownership changes on the urban fringes might, indeed, indicate either the arrival of land speculators who would proceed to exploit the building potential they perceived, as happened with the north Leeds aristocratic estates from the 1870s onwards, or the settling of the wealthy on small residential country estates where they could hold development at bay for many years, until finally forced into retreat by the overwhelming pressure of suburban encirclement, as happened in parts of Bexley.

Readiness to speculate on rising land values and to release land for building was less a product of recent acquisition, or of the business connexions of a landowner, although these were important in some instances, than of non-residence and of the kind of advice on estate management a landowner was receiving. The social standing of the landowner and the strength of his links with the area could have a strong influence on the class of development favoured, the gentry, pseudo-gentry, and dignified corporate owners such as the Goldsmiths' Company with their estate in Ealing, aiming for the prestige of the upper end of the wealthy middle-class market, while owners and developers of lower status were likely to pursue the line of greatest profit through the most intensive type of available development regardless of its social class. The power of the landowner to translate his wishes into actual buildings, however, was tightly circumscribed by the commercial realities of each particular situation, its existing reputation, its immediate surroundings, and the strength of local demand. Many ambitious schemes failed through over-optimistic estimates of site potential, and on the whole the apparatus of landowner control through supervision of layout and design, and through stipulation of minimum values for houses to be erected, is best seen as providing effective reinforcement for general influences of place and status already working in the desired direction, but as being ineffective in turning back contrary tides.[41] The direction of these tides was frequently set by the first few pieces of new development in a neighbourhood, and the style of housing added casually to an existing village or settlement in an early phase of minimal growth could well determine the character of a much later phase of full-scale development. Thus the Stevens Town district of Ealing developed as an area of working-class housing in the 1870s and 1880s on the basis of a few workmens' cottages which had been built there without much thought in the 1840s; a few lower middle-class houses built in Acton in the 1850s set the tone for the whole district in the 1880s; some industrial development in Lower Burley, north Leeds, in the 1840s set the scene for covering most of the district with working-class back-to-backs in the 1860s; the handful of superior villa residences built near Bexley village in the 1880s and 1890s were still exerting their influence towards making this a high status area in the 1930s, while the initial lower class development further north in Welling was perpetuated in its later rapid growth.[42] In this way the first tentative, small-scale and often unplanned steps in development can be seen as themselves becoming pre-development features in relation to subsequent phases of comprehensive development, exerting strong influences on the social character of the final suburban product.

It has long been recognized that transport services played an important part among the general influences on suburban growth, but the exact nature of that part, and whether improved transport was an essential, causal, or permissive element in suburbanization, have been matters of dispute. Improved transport in the nineteenth century meant, above all, railways, and the prevailing view is that only in a few exceptional cases can railways be regarded as an important cause of suburban growth, and that generally 'the development of suburbs . . . preceded the provision of railway services, by periods of at least a decade or two for each of the larger cities'.[43] In part this view relates to the suburbs of the large provincial cities which at least until 1900 were little more than two to three miles from city centres, too short a distance for suburban trains to be practicable; the unimportance of railways in provincial suburban growth is confirmed in the study of north Leeds, where the intrusion of the Leeds–Thirsk railway was an impediment rather than an assistance to development. In part, however, the view concerns London's suburbs, and rests on the stringent assumption that railways only caused suburban growth when railway policy on fares and services took an actively promotional line, an assumption that virtually reduces the railway suburbs to Edmonton and Waltham-stow, where the Great Eastern's workmen's fares and workmen's trains reluctantly but decisively promoted the rapid development of working-class suburbs after 1864. The outer suburbs at more than five or six miles from the centre could not have developed as dormitories without commuter rail services, however skeletal, and even if railway companies did little or nothing to encourage such growth through special fares or convenient services the presence of a railway should be regarded as a necessary, although not a sufficient, condition for outer suburban growth. The building of railways preceded the development of suburbs in Bromley, Acton and Ealing, and Bexley, but the interval between opening a station and substantial suburban expansion varied between a few years and many decades, and the absence of any immediate railway-triggered expansion in Bexley confirms the proposition that railways made the outer suburban dormitories possible but did not create them.

Where other conditions were favourable – an attractive location, an established nucleus of village or small market town, landowners keen to act as developers, a handful of existing residents with city connexions, and a propitious moment in the trade cycle – the promotion of a railway could be the catalyst of expansion, producing a genuine railway suburb. This happened in Bromley, where local landowners were the chief promoters of the railway which was opened in 1858, ushering in a decade of rapid growth spearheaded by a small number of affluent middle-class households able to afford the high cost of commuting. Very soon, however, it became apparent that residential expansion was proceeding in spite of the inconvenience, inefficiency, and inadequacy of train services, and Bromley passed into the same situation as Ealing until the 1860s, where the Great Western completely neglected its suburban services, or Bexley in the 1930s, where headlong housing expansion ran well in advance of train services or access to stations, a situation in which transport services followed after development was under way.[44] A much more complicated statement about the relationship between transport and development emerges from the close analysis of railway promotions and train services in outer west London, and here it is possible to see the interdependence of the two, with the promotion of new lines in advance of suburban housing both by speculative landowners and by a railway company reliant on suburban traffic, the District, and the improvement of services by main line companies at hours and frequencies to suit the commuters' needs, acting as stimuli to revive building activity from a preceding depression. Here railway services acted as a chief instrument for communicating upswings in the building cycle to the district in the middle phases of its development, even if they had been of little importance in starting the initial development.[45]

In the inner suburbs where distances were too short for railway operation, and in the provinces, horse buses were of great importance to middle-class commuters and these were invariably introduced only after suburban development had taken hold.[46] From 1870 onwards horse trams were being rapidly introduced, and as a means of cheap mass transit they had a much more widespread effect than workmen's trains and fares in enabling the lower middle class and the artisans to push out into suburbia and to threaten the exclusiveness of middle-class suburbs. The encroachment of trams was resisted in Ealing, as in Edgbaston, Hampstead, Kemp Town, Kelvinside, and Victoria Park, because it threatened to bring in a lower class of people and bring on social deterioration, and as in other places the resistance was in the end unsuccessful. By the early 1900s electric tramways were being projected into virgin territory, well ahead of suburban settlement.[47] While it is salutary to be reminded that in Leeds the horse trams did not run early enough in the morning for working-class commuters, and were largely used by the middle classes, in general they were a working-class form of transport and a reminder that suburbs did not remain exclusively middle-class.[48] Further research may well show that tramway suburbs were more significant than railway suburbs, not perhaps as entirely new settlements called forth out of green fields, for no transport service seems to have been capable of doing that save in exceptional circumstances, but as places which experienced a dramatic transformation in social character and physical scale as a direct result of tramway penetration.

The Bexley evidence shows clearly that the development of dormitory suburbs for the working and lower middle classes in Bexleyheath, West Wickham, and Welling was strongly boosted by the trams linking them to industrial employment on Thameside. Where workplaces remained within walking distance, as they did in the inner parts of north Leeds, workers could afford to live within the suburb and work outside it, and they were catered for in the fingers of back-to-back housing which intruded on the social homogeneity of the district. Elsewhere, in outer London, commuting to a job in the centre was out of the question for the working classes before the coming of cheap public transport, and yet pockets or even substantial neighbourhoods of working-class housing appeared in these outer suburbs long before the trams or workmens' trains. The nineteenth-century suburban dream was a middle-class dream; the nineteenth-century suburban reality was a social patchwork. Of course, whole building estates and entire sub-districts were successfully developed with solidly middle-class housing, finely attuned to the different grades of income and status within that class; but the creation of a complete single class suburb was an illusion. In part this conclusion is an effect of the boundaries which are chosen to define the area of an individual suburb. It would be perfectly possible to take a district of single class housing and call it a suburb in itself, and indeed many sub-districts of unitary social standing did establish their own place-names which became essential elements in their identities, such as Bedford Park or Grove Park. There is perhaps no reason to suppose that administrative areas, entire parishes or townships such as Ealing, Bexley, Bromley, or Headingley, should be treated as potentially single suburbs. In the main, however, this conclusion does not rest on definitional ambiguities. It is not so much that each parish or township contained a multiplicity of separate, but related suburbs each of its own class, as that the very process of establishing a suburban community and the imperatives of building development produced some degree of social mixture.

Even in the purest middle-class suburban case, where the incomes to support the community were entirely generated by the minority of affluent commuters at the top of the social pyramid, these households required the support not only of indoor domestic servants but also of a considerable array of service activities to keep houses, gardens, clothes, linen, transport, roads and streets, and persons in good running order, and the workers in such industries, trades, and services needed to live locally. The pure case, uncluttered by other businesses and occupations inherited from a pre-suburban economy, probably did not exist in practice, but the small working-class districts of Bromley in the 1860s and 1870s appear to have come close to satisfying the requirements of this model. In the thoroughly mixed case lower grade housing was built far in excess of the size of a working and lower middle-class population in this directly and locally dependent and supporting role, and the extra labour force thus settled tended to attract employment to the area in a mutually supporting process which generated small-scale manufacturing, public utilities, and service industries in the suburb serving wider markets; this seems to have happened in Acton, with its laundries, dye works, and manure factory, in Hanwell with its light industry, and to a lesser extent in parts of Ealing. In the intermediate case a similar excess of working and lower middle-class housing was built, but industrial development within the boundaries of the suburb remained restricted and many of the residents were employed outside the district, in jobs which they could reach on foot; this seems to be broadly true of Lower Burley and parts of Headingley.

The three studies which examine the building of districts of working-class housing before the coming of cheap public transport are all concerned to explain how this happened and why it happened in particular places. In general, workmen's cottages and lower class terraced housing tended to go up on sites which developers and builders did not think sufficiently attractive to be eligible for anything of a better and more expensive grade, and these sites tended to be those nestling against some undesirable existing feature – a factory or workshop, a railway line, or a previous piece of lower class development.[49] Frequently these were also small parcels of building land, and the restricted possibilities of sites of only a few acres may have attracted the smaller, less ambitious, and more precariously financed builders who could only build the cheapest kind of houses. In this way fragmented ownership producing individual sites of small size may have encouraged lower class development, a process reinforced by piecemeal development where one small island of working-class housing could set the tone for the whole adjoining area. Site size alone, however, was not a determining factor, since in Acton the British Land

Company acquired a very large building estate of 70 acres and promptly set about creating a new working-class community on it.[50] There is indeed a suggestion that the freehold land societies and successor companies of the third quarter of the century may have directly contributed to the building of lower-middle-class and artisan housing in the suburbs, since they were primarily in business to create smallish building plots within the reach of potential owner-occupiers, who tended to be found more in those groups than higher up the middle class. This was not necessarily the case, however, for although the inconveniently shaped and placed part of the British Land Company's estate in Bromley was developed in this way, its prime part was successfully covered with prime villas which were occupied by representatives of the wealthy middle class.[51]

The most likely explanation, perhaps, hinges on the endemic over-optimism of developers and builders about the likely level of affluent middle-class demand for houses. They were forever setting out with high hopes for the demand for large and comparatively expensive houses, and forever finding that there were too few of the middle classes to go round. In this situation a developer or builder with strong financial resources and some personal commitment to a vision of the ultimate social complexion of his building estate might halt operations and wait to resume them at the same social level when the appropriate class of demand revived. An entrepreneur with no personal ties to the reputation of the neighbourhood, and perhaps a pressing need to turn over his capital rapidly and obtain some immediate returns, was however likely to take the obvious course of shifting his target down market by going in for a lower and cheaper grade of housing. Small builders operating on tight margins, and land societies anxious to keep their sites moving so as not to have their assets locked up in undeveloped land, fitted this description, and maybe for these reasons were more frequently than others responsible for introducing the working classes and lower middle classes into districts that had initially seemed destined for superior middle-class settlement.

The recurrent optimism, or greed, of landowners, developers, and builders, lured on by the often illusory prospect of large gains to be made from speculation on development into providing an over-supply of building land and of houses, is strongly represented in these studies. The result was that the development of individual estates was frequently a highly protracted and much interrupted affair, perhaps stretching over nearly half a century, and this in itself meant that the completed fabric might be a patchwork not only of successive architectural styles but also of social classes, as different layers of fashion and effective demand passed over and beyond a district.[52] It was this slowness of development which was likely to leave any particular estate raw and incomplete for years on end, that gave H.G. Wells the impression, fictionalized in *The New Machiavelli*, that Bromley in the mid-nineteenth century was the victim of 'an invading and growing disorder' that was replacing the social order and harmony of a neat little market town by a mindless, wasteful, anarchy which was suburbia:

> The outskirts of Bromstead were a maze of exploitation roads that led nowhere, that ended in tarred fences studded with nails . . . and in trespass boards that used vehement language . . . It was a multitude of uncoordinated fresh starts, each more sweeping and destructive than the last, and none of them ever really worked out to a ripe and satisfactory completion. Each left a legacy of products – houses, humanity, or what not – in its wake. It was a sort of progress

that had bolted; it was change out of hand, and going at an unprecedented pace nowhere in particular.[53]

After many years the ragged incompleteness disappeared, suburban neatness and tidiness colonized the builders' rubble and waste and turned it into gardens, and the underlying order and rationality of suburban development was finally embodied in a fully built environment. In Bexley in the 1930s, in a very different market situation and with the appearance of large-scale building firms exploiting economies of scale and capable of building a complete semi-detached in three days, the process which had formerly taken decades was completed in a year or two.[54] Whether H.G. Wells would have been better pleased with the result because it was achieved rapidly without intervening years of chaos may be doubted. The suburban result, however attained, represented what a great many people wanted to live in; it is not necessary to admire it in order to wish to understand how it happened.

NOTES

1 *Architect*, XVI (1876), 33; Sir Walter Besant, *London in the Nineteenth Century* (1909), 262; both quoted in D.J. Olsen, *The Growth of Victorian London* (1976, 1979 edn), 200, 210, whose chapter 'The villa and the new suburb' contains an excellent account of attitudes towards suburbia.
2 H.J. Dyos, *Victorian Suburb: A Study of the Growth of Camberwell* (1961).
3 For example, J.T. Coppock and H.C. Prince, *Greater London* (1964), especially the chapters by Prince, 'North-west London, 1814–63', and J.H. Johnson, 'The suburban expansion of housing in London, 1918–39'.
4 The main American influences have been R. Park, E.W. Burgess, and R.D. Mackenzie (eds.), *The City* (Chicago, 1925); H. Hoyt, *The Structure and Growth of Residential Neighbourhoods in American Cities* (Washington, 1939); G. Sjoberg, *The Pre-Industrial City* (Glencoe, Ill., 1960); H.M. Mayer and C.F. Kohn (eds.), *Readings in Urban Geography* (Chicago, 1964); P.M. Hauser and L.F. Schnore (eds.), *The Study of Urbanization* (New York, 1965). Among British applications see J.W.R. Whitehand, 'Fringe-belts – a neglected aspect in urban geography', *Trans. Inst. Brit. Geographers*, XLI (1967); and most recently, C. Roy Lewis, 'A stage in the development of the industrial town: a case study of Cardiff, 1845–75', *Trans. Inst. Brit. Geographers*, NS, IV (1979), and M. Shaw, 'Reconciling social and physical space: Wolverhampton, 1871', *Trans. Inst. Brit. Geographers*, NS, IV (1979).
5 W. Ashworth, 'Types of social and economic development in suburban Essex', in Centre for Urban Studies Report no. 3, *London, Aspects of Change* (1964).
6 D.A. Reeder, 'A theatre of suburbs: some patterns of development in West London, 1801–1911', in *The Study of Urban History*, ed. H.J. Dyos (1968).
7 D.J. Olsen, 'House upon house', in *The Victorian City*, I, eds. H.J. Dyos and M. Wolff (1973); F.M.L Thompson, *Hampstead: Building a Borough, 1650–1964* (1974); and *idem*, 'Hampstead, 1830–1914', in *Middle-Class Housing in Britain*, eds. M.A. Simpson and T.H. Lloyd (1977).
8 M. Spiers, *Victoria Park, Manchester* (1976).
9 M.A. Simpson, 'The West End of Glasgow, 1830–1914', in Simpson and Lloyd, *op. cit.*
10 D. Cannadine, *Lords and Landlords: The Aristocracy and the Towns, 1774–1967* (1980), part 2.
11 A.A. Jackson, *Semi-Detached London* (1973).
12 Most recently in M.J. Daunton, *Coal Metropolis: Cardiff, 1870–1914* (1977).

13 The evidence and arguments are marshalled in D. Ward, 'Victorian cities: how modern?' *J. Hist. Geog.*, I (1975), and D. Cannadine, 'Victorian cities: how different?' *Social Hist.*, IV (1977). And see S. Bass Warner, jnr. *Streetcar Suburbs: The Process of Growth in Boston, 1870–1900* (Cambridge, Mass., 1962).

14 S.E. Rasmussen, *London: The Unique City* (1937; Pelican edn, 1960), 13–14.

15 Dyos, *Victorian Suburb*, 69.

16 Simpson, *loc. cit.*

17 Figures for eighteenth-century urban population depend on the definition of 'town' which is adopted; those in the text are taken from C.W. Chalklin, *The Provincial Towns of Georgian England* (1974).

18 *Ibid.*, 90, 110–11, 88; Cannadine, *Lords and Landlords*, 91–3.

19 J. Summerson, *Georgian London* (1945), chapter 20, has no hesitation in classifying the outlying parts of 'Greater Georgian London' as suburban.

20 *Ibid.*, 158–9; Olsen, *Growth of Victorian London*, 213.

21 *Ibid.*, 211; the section on 'Privacy', 210–16, is the best summary of contemporary, and twentieth-century views of the role of the pursuit of privacy in the creation of suburbia.

22 These issues have been much discussed, for example in Thompson, *Hampstead*, 85–90, 365, and Cannadine, *Lords and Landlords*, 395–401.

23 See, for example, Thompson, *Hampstead*, 224–31. There is much detailed evidence on building land values in the contributions to this volume.

24 K. Maywald, 'An index of building costs in the United Kingdom, 1845–1938', *Econ. Hist. Rev.*, 2nd ser., VII (1954).

25 H. Hobhouse, *Thomas Cubitt: Master Builder* (1971); F.M.L. Thompson, *Chartered Surveyors: The Growth of a Profession* (1968), 79–93.

26 T.C. Barker and M. Robbins, *A History of London Transport*, I (1963), 4–22.

27 Thompson, *Hampstead*, 239, 251–2; and see below, 243, for interwar examples.

28 See below, 'The process of suburban development in North Leeds, 1870–1914.'

29 L.D. Schwarz, 'Income distribution and social structure in London in the late eighteenth century', *Econ. Hist. Rev.*, 2nd ser., XXXII (1979); and G. Rudé, *Hanoverian London* (1971), 48–51.

30 This is a highly simplified version of the thesis emerging from the research on the separation of spheres and the rise of domesticity which Leonore Davidoff and Catherine Hall of the University of Essex have in progress. There are hints of a similar theme in John Burnett, *A Social History of Housing, 1815–1970* (1978), 95–6, 102–3.

31 M. Girouard, *The Victorian Country House* (1979 edn), 15–31.

32 H. Perkin, *The Origins of Modern English Society, 1780–1880* (1969), chapters 8 and 9; a classic statement of the argument that the bourgeoisie imposed their ideology on the rest of society.

33 L. Simond, *Journal of a Tour and Residence in Great Britain*, I (1817), 64, quited in Burnett, *op. cit.*, 104.

34 Thompson, *Hampstead*, 276–80. Smart terraces were still being widely built in the 1870s, for example in Gosforth, Newcastle upon Tyne. On the other hand, a prime reason for the failure of the town-style development of Pimlico to find its intended middling middle-class market in the 1850s and 1860s, and hence for its comparatively tarnished image, was the competition of the more modern villa suburbs being built at the same time.

35 A. Saunders, *Regent's Park* (1969), 86–7, 133.

36 J.R. Kellett, *The Impact of Railways on Victorian Cities* (1969), 408–9.

37 This is consistent with what is known about the political conservatism of suburbia somewhat later in the nineteenth century: J. Cornford, 'The transformation of conservatism in the late nineteenth century', *Victorian Studies*, VII (1963–4).

38 S.M. Gaskell, 'Housing and the lower middle classes, 1870–1914', in *The Lower Middle Classes in Britain, 1870–1914*, ed. G. Crossick (1977).

39 See below, 160, table 14.

40 See below, 41, and 163.
41 See below, 50, 111, 170, and 224.
42 See below, 122, 171, and 227.
43 Kellett, *op. cit.*, 354–76.
44 See below, 38, and 243.
45 See below, 114.
46 G.C. Dickinson, 'Suburban road transport in Leeds, 1840–95', *J. Transport Hist.*, IV (1960).
47 Cannadine, 'Victorian cities: how different?', 467; and see below, 135.
48 See below, 176, and 226
49 See below, 62, 98, and 171.
50 See below, 64, 107, and 172.
51 See below, 59, and 103.
52 See below, 141.
53 H.G. Wells, *The New Machiavelli* (1911; Penguin edn, 1946), 33ff esp. 39.
54 See below, 265.

Bromley:
Kentish market town
to London suburb,
1841–81

J.M. RAWCLIFFE

Bromley: Kentish market town to London suburb, 1841–81[1]

J.M. RAWCLIFFE

This chapter is a study of the formative phase in which a small market and coaching town became an outer London suburb. It also seeks to examine the processes by which the broad movements of metropolitan expansion, drawing migrants to London and dispersing people into the outer suburbs, were translated into houses and communities. The activities of developers, speculators, resident gentry, and small traders all contributed to this development within the context of both physical and tenurial aspects of local topography. The period chosen for detailed study is the 40 years between 1841 and 1881, during which the great estates in Bromley parish underwent radical change. The process of expansion did not end in 1881, but it will be argued that during these 40 years the future characteristics of Bromley as a middle-class suburb were broadly determined. The factors which today make the London borough of Bromley an attractive suburban place of residence are essentially those which led to its rapid development in the nineteenth century, during which Bromley changed from being a small market town into one of the leading Kentish suburbs of London. The method used to give this process specific substance is essentially that of sampling, apart from a section on transport developments. A few key estates have been studied in detail in order to show the means by which change took place, whilst selected individuals have been investigated in order to illustrate the role of personalities alongside the general and impersonal economic and social forces.

In 1840 Bromley was still a market town, quite distinct from London, but nevertheless of considerable importance because of its key position on the main road out of London to Tonbridge and Tunbridge Wells, and also to the coastal towns of Hastings and Dover. Only ten miles from London Bridge, Bromley was an important staging post for travellers to and from the capital, and the first well-established market town out of London, with a reputation for good inns and hotels.

This large and 'extensive parish'[2] had an acreage of 4,646 acres and a population

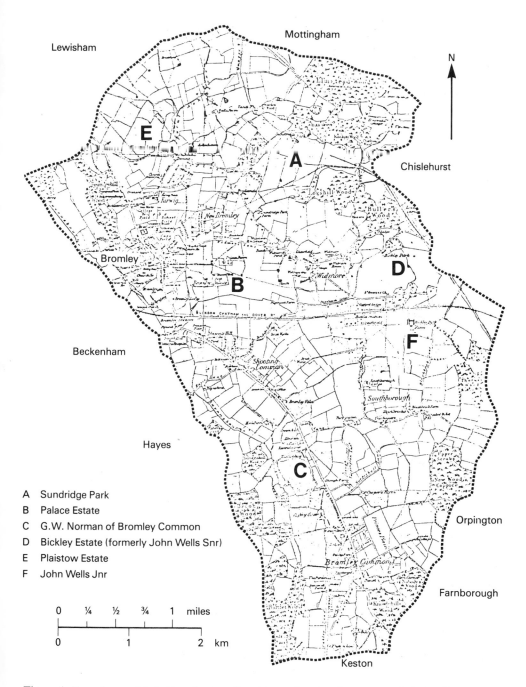

Bromley: Kentish market town to London suburb, 1841–81
J.M. RAWCLIFFE

Lewisham

Mottingham

N

Chislehurst

E

A

Bromley

D

B

Beckenham

F

Hayes

C

A   Sundridge Park
B   Palace Estate
C   G.W. Norman of Bromley Common
D   Bickley Estate (formerly John Wells Snr)
E   Plaistow Estate
F   John Wells Jnr

Orpington

Farnborough

Keston

0   ¼   ½   ¾   1   miles

0   1   2   km

Figure 1. Bromley parish in the nineteenth century, showing the estates of the leading landowners. The letters indicate the location of the main estates mentioned in the text. Boundaries have been omitted because of the separated nature of the holdings. The map is based on the 6″ O.S. map of 1862.

29

of 4,325 people in 1841.[3] The bulk of the population lived around the Market Square and along the long High Street which extended for three-quarters of a mile on the dry higher ground above the Ravensbourne Valley. To the west, across the valley, lay Beckenham Parish, another future suburb which in 1841 had a population of 1,608.[4] To the south of Bromley the main road passed through the hamlet of Mason's Hill, a half-mile from the town, before it crossed Bromley Common. This had been enclosed in 1821 and had since seen the building of some 'neat houses and villa residences'.[5]

Within this large parish were several scattered hamlets and the general appearance of the parish was rural, with a large number of the male population employed as agricultural labourers on the numerous farms, the majority of which were either estate farms or worked by tenant farmers. The tithe award of 1841 showed that approximately half of the parish was arable with hops, grain, and root crops being grown.[6] In addition the eastern and southern parts of the parish were still extensively wooded, and the census of 1851 shows that several individuals derived their livelihood from trades connected with forestry, ranging from sawyer to charcoal burner. G.W. Smith, a builder of Bromley Common, described the rural crafts of his youth around 1870:

> Our district being well-wooded, during winter, most of the old people worked in connection with the woods. As a youngster, I can remember the Charcoal burners at work in Crofton Woods, stacking the wood and covering it with earth, all [sic] the wattle and hurdle makers. Then the hop pole shavers and hop makers, pale cleavers and sawyers, all worked in the woods.[7]

Bromley's relative proximity to London and its interesting and well-drained higher lands made it attractive as a place of residence. By the 1840s the parish contained several well-established family seats. To the south were the Warde-Normans; to the north, at Sundridge, the Scotts; the Wells at Bickley bordering Chislehurst, and adjoining the town to the east, the lands of the Bishop of Rochester. Land had been granted to the Bishops of Rochester in the ninth century and at least three palaces had been subsequently built in Bromley, the last by Bishop Thomas in 1775. The important Bishop's estate provided the town with both prestige and employment. It also helped to limit the development of the parish by the complex nature of the leases, and though the estate by 1840 was in need of improvement, the proximity of this important estate adjoining the town, added to its status.

In addition, many people with business interests in London were taking up residence in Bromley and its surrounding area, because of the proximity of, and ease of access to London. Charles Freeman, writing in 1832, said that

> No parish perhaps, considering its short distance from the Metropolis and that coaches pass through it almost every hour in the day, could afford a more desirable retreat from the hurry and bustle of the Town; besides which it is rendered peculiarly so, on account of its pleasant and healthy situation.[8]

Estimates of the number of coaches passing through Bromley at this time vary,[9] but all indicate the importance of the town in the long-distance coach trade on the south-eastern fringe of London. As late as the early 1830s Bromley's coach trade and prosperity were increasing. This is evidenced by two facts. Firstly, a substantial road improvement was carried out in 1831 in Bromley town by which the High Road was straightened by widening the passage on the western side of the Market Square. This enabled traffic to avoid the congestion of the Market House and Square. Secondly, around 1830, the White Hart, one of Bromley's leading coaching inns was remodelled.

> It has undergone so extensive an alteration, that it now forms one of the neatest buildings of this kind on the road from London to Hastings the whole of the old front having been taken down, and the present stands back from the road about twenty-eight feet . . . a good carriage drive is formed and the inconvenience that was experience before the improvement is now entirely removed.[10]

The booming coach trade was to be relatively short-lived for between 1836 and 1838 the London and Greenwich Railway was built with its station five miles from Bromley at Greenwich. The final blow came in 1844 when the South-Eastern Railway Company opened the circuitous route to Dover via Redhill and Tonbridge. The proximity of the stations at Greenwich and Sydenham, allied with the fact that the remainder of north-west Kent was without a railway, had almost immediate effects.

The rapid decline of the coaching trade passing through Bromley in the 1840s can be seen in the evidence given by certain witnesses speaking against the extension of the North Kent line to Gravesend. In evidence before the House of Commons Select Committee on Railway Bills (Group A) in 1845 the landlord of the White Hart, William Pawley, lamented that the inn no longer kept him. He argued that this had not always been so 'before the S.E.R.'[11] Then he had kept 50 pairs of horses for coaching and posting 'now only 12'. In his evidence it becomes clear that his prosperity had come from the long distance traffic when 'thirty coaches a day passed through Bromley to Sevenoaks. Now four'.[12]

Pawley's grievances were threefold. Firstly he had lost the long distance coach trade which had brought him a considerable income as the White Hart was an important staging post. This decline was indicated by another witness who said that he had received £800 to £1,000 per year from one innkeeper for corn, 'now £1'.[13] Secondly the opening of the Tonbridge line had meant that those who formerly had travelled by coach to London from places north of the railway line, such as Westerham and Sevenoaks, now took short-run transport to Edenbridge or Tonbridge Railway Station. Pawley hoped that a railway would attract people who travelled from the Sevenoaks and Westerham area to a Bromley station, rather than southwards to the South Eastern Railway. Pawley said that by doing this the traveller would 'save half a crown in money and his time'.[14] Finally he argued that the end of the regular long distance coach trade deprived him of substantial lodgers in the hotel. One resident had recently left after only three months because he could not satisfactorily travel to London.[15] This view was echoed by Mr J. Thorpe of Hayesford, one mile to the south of Bromley town, who in complaining about the poor communications with London, said that in the neighbourhood of Bromley were 70 to 100 gentlemen's seats and villa residences 'occupied by persons engaged generally in business in London, and persons of independent property'.[16]

Thus the absence of a railway became Bromley's most pressing problem in the years up to 1858, and, as rail communications improved in the region as a whole, other towns became more attractive for those seeking a suburban home. For those living in Bromley, 'Conveyance to London became more difficult as the coaches, one after another, were taken off the road; and the large schools which had long flourished in and near the town, found more convenient localities.'[17]

Bromley's favourable location had led in earlier times to a flourishing market, but Freeman noted in 1832 that 'within the last fifteen years it had not been so well supplied and attended as before'.[18] With improved communications elsewhere in the region Bagshaw in 1847 wrote of Bromley as 'a small but decayed market town'.[19] Bromley's economic plight had worsened when the Bishop of Rochester left the town and the situation was not helped by the long drawn out sale negotiations which were not completed until 1846. The sale of the Palace was made difficult by an abortive railway bill which would have brought a station and thus increased land values. The failure to obtain the bill put the would-be purchasers in a much stronger position and this was one of the reasons for the protracted sale.

Bromley in the 1840s has been referred to as a 'deserted village', and the loss of

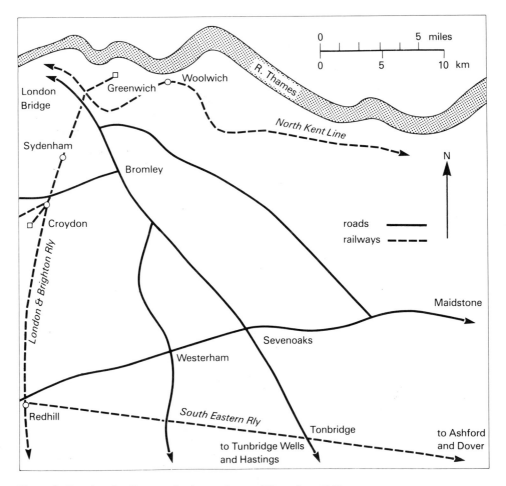

Figure 2. Road and rail routes in the environs of Bromley, 1852.

the Bishop was keenly felt for he had been a liberal supporter of schools and charities and his household and many visitors enhanced local trade. 'Tradesmen looked hopelessly on the future; many left the town, and some retired to the outskirts, on their little savings, rather than risk business longer in a place that appeared to be doomed.'[20]

Nevertheless, Bromley had inherent advantages. Her favourable situation remained, and Coles Child, the new Lord of the Manor, was not only an equally generous benefactor, but improvement-minded. In the short term the town suffered, but while the parish's population growth between 1831 and 1851 was only 3.1 per cent, the population of the Registration District as a whole grew by 22.4 per cent.

As we have seen, Bromley and its immediate neighbourhood contained several large houses and the prestige and healthy situation had attracted many city

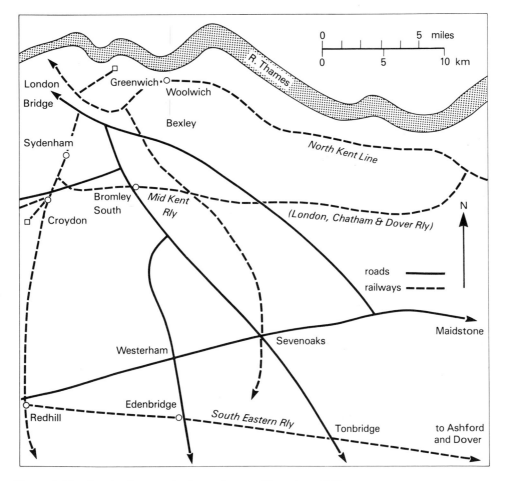

Figure 3. Road and rail routes in the environs of Bromley, 1868.

Table 1   Growth of the population of Bromley, 1841–81

	population (Bromley parish)	% increase	population (Bromley registration district)	% increase	England and Wales population ('000's)	% increase
1841	4,325		16,077		15,929	
1851	4,127	−4.6	17,637	9.7	17,983	12.9
1861	5,505	33.4	20,368	15.5	20,119	11.9
1871	10,674	93.9	32,184	58.0	22,789	13.3
1881	15,154	42.0	48,972	52.2	26,046	14.3

Source: Census enumeration abstracts, 1841; Population tables 1851–81. National figures from B.R. Mitchell and P. Deane (ed.), *Abstract of British Historical Statistics* (1962), 8–9.

merchants who, in spite of the declining coach services, continued to maintain their London connections. It was to be such as these who actively promoted the railway, not only to assist their own travel, but also to benefit from the increase in land values which a railway would bring. As John Nokes, a landowner of 1,700 acres, said in 1845, but for deficient communications and the lack of a station 'I should lay out a great many thousand pounds in building, and I could have let to different builders something like a hundred acres.'[21]

1   The coming of the railway

However, it took another 12 years before the railway came to Bromley, and when it did two leading landowners, Coles Child of Bromley Palace and William Dent of Bickley were the leading proponents. Both men were on the committee of the Mid Kent (Bromley to St Mary Cray) Railway Company which first met on the 11 April 1856, and William Dent was elected Chairman. There was considerable difficulty raising the necessary capital and during 1858 the Mid Kent realized that the extension of their line eastwards beyond Southborough Road would be beyond the means of the Company acting alone. By this time the Shortlands, Bromley, Southborough Road sections were all but ready and the Mid Kent exchanged running rights on their line for similar rights between Beckenham and Shortlands, with the West End and Crystal Palace Railway. Similar agreements were made with the South Eastern,[22] and the East Kent Railway Companies,[23] whereby the former agreed to finance a second track in return for running power, whilst the East Kent received running power over the vital Mid-Kent line on their route westwards to London.

On 22 November 1858 Bromley's new station at Mason's Hill was opened. Aspirations were high. As the author of an anonymous history of Bromley said in 1858 the town

> may be termed old-fashioned; a fair specimen of a small town in the old coaching days, but wanting the coaches and every fourth man you meet to be an ostler . . . Coaches passed through every hour . . . but the Railway having absorbed nearly

all the traffic, has rendered the Town of late years, one of the worst to get to or from, of any at the same distance from London: this state of things will shortly be altered . . . with excellent Railway accommodation.[24]

The fares charged and the length of the journey precluded all but the affluent from travelling daily to work in London. The average weekly wage in London at this time was £1 5s., whereas the daily third-class fare was 1s. 3d. a day or 7s. 6d. per week from Bromley to London Bridge, whilst the first train from Bromley was at 7.54 a.m., which with a journey time of 40 minutes, was not designed for the majority, whose daily work had usually begun before the first train departed. Similarly the first train from Shortlands did not depart until 8.35 a.m. on its 37-minute journey. The railway service was designed for the richer of the middle classes and they welcomed the opportunities provided by the railway to travel to the City and the West End.

However, the working agreements of 1858 only papered over the basic disagreements between the larger companies, the South Eastern and the East Kent, and the smaller ones, the West End and Crystal Palace, and the Mid Kent. Rather than the service to London becoming more efficient, the rivalries and friction between them led to a deterioration in the service at the expense of the passenger. Those who boarded the Mid Kent trains at the Mid Kent stations suffered particularly as they were subjected not only to changing at Beckenham Junction, but also to the vagaries in the Company's running rights, in allowing their rivals' trains to operate. Besides, this was a time when trains were run by timetables rather than by signals, which added to the risk of collision. As early as May 1859 a writer in the *Bromley Record* was complaining of the use of old rolling-stock which was constantly breaking down. In this case the writer laid the blame on the South Eastern. The effect was that the published journey time was frequently exceeded due to cancellations, delays or breakdowns. The frustrations of a Bromley traveller are well illustrated by a letter in *The Times* on 15 January 1864:

Sir – I live with thousands of others, down the Mid Kent Railway below Beckenham, ten miles from London Bridge, all of us requiring to be in town more or less punctually every morning. The recent 'facilities of new lines', as the phrase goes, have only woefully obstructed our business journeyings, and made our homes practically now twenty miles off London. I arrived at the London Bridge Station this evening to go home by the train appointed in the railway bills to start at 6.15; and found our train had taken a trip to Charing Cross, leaving 200 or 300 of us waiting about 15 or 20 minutes on a very unsafe, cold, exposed, narrow platform, kicking our heels about while engines and trains passed to and fro, like Cheapside omnibuses, in dangerous proximity; and after undergoing this ordeal, we arrived at Bromley precisely at 7.20, just one hour and five minutes from the time our train should have started, in making a journey of ten miles. And this is no solitary instance, and far from being one of our worst Mid Kent grievances.

In the course of our ten miles of railway journey leading to our homes, we ill-used travellers undergo another purgatory at Beckenham (about two miles only from Bromley). There that 'enterprising concern', the London Chatham and Dover Company, pushing itself about here, there, and almost everywhere, stops our Mid Kent way, and will not allow its neighbours' engines to move us one bit further, and here often we city folk sit shivering in our carriages or pace the cold station till it please the West End magnate to arrive from Victoria, and to drag us on our two or three miles to Beckenham or Bromley, while many of us would have better walked, were it not for cold and wet weather, over dark roads.

The morning up-journey to town brings little, if any comfort with it. Our West End magnate usurps again her obstructive dominance and we are 'taken on behind' as far as Beckenham, and left there till some mysteries of shunting of trains and half trains from main lines and 'sidings' take place; and also to wait often till one and sometimes two of the trains of our Chatham and Dover masters release us from our sidings, and allow our poor snubbed Mid Kent to sneak up to the City with us, . . . and often afraid, too, one would think from its snail-like motion as it nears its quarter, to show its humbled face in its own station.

. . . that Parliament will step in and free the national highway, as the railway now is, from the selfish obstructions thrown in our way by the quarrels of rival companies and other causes. Our Mid Kent arrangements are getting worse and worse. A few years ago we had trains running almost every hour from London Bridge to Beckenham and Bromley. Now should we be prevented getting home by the renowned 6.15 train . . . we have not another train till 8.10 . . . the next one is 10.50. The trains are so very slow, too, we might get the fifty miles to Brighton . . . Again, no fewer than seven of our Mid Kent daily trains which used to run through, are not allowed to go further on their journey than Beckenham . . .[25]

A combination of the increased demand for a service which was in fact deteriorating had led to the beginning in 1863 of what was to be a 15-year campaign to get a branch line for Bromley. On 10 November 1863 a meeting was held at the White Hart Hotel which agreed unanimously that 'this meeting considers the present railway accommodation to the City very inefficient'. The meeting agreed, 'That the proximity of the direct Tonbridge line of the South Eastern Company affording the means of constructing a short line into the very heart of the town . . . terminating close to the Market-place of Bromley, affords a favourable opportunity of remedying the evil.'[26] A committee was established and a deputation sent to meet the directors of the South Eastern Railway Company. The petition from 'the residents of Bromley (many of whom being engaged in London), are daily travellers by railway between Bromley and the City',[27] was met by a firm refusal. A possible reason as to why the deputation met with a cool reception from the South Eastern Railway Company may be that in June the Company had considered a bill for the Amalgamation of the Mid Kent. At this meeting Coles Child, who was a director of both companies, had spoken against the proposal, arguing that the Mid Kent was of little worth paying only $3\frac{1}{2}$ per cent as opposed to the larger company's $6\frac{1}{2}$ per cent.[28]

Pressure for a branch line had come from commuters who were primarily concerned with the quality of the service, and they were able to draw on influential and articulate support, as the letter to *The Times* indicated. These early demands for a second railway are in contrast with the reasons which led to the first. In the former case a small group of landowners had been the major proponents. Now it was the very commuters, many of whom had been attracted to live in Bromley since the first service was introduced, who were agitating for improved facilities. It is from amongst this same group that we find similar protest being made to the Vestry and later the Local Board, for improved public health and the better use of public money.

A second attempt at bringing a branch line to Bromley failed again in 1865 and it was to be another seven years before a branch line was again considered. On 22 November 1872 a public meeting was held with William Starling, a local property developer, in the chair. In his opening address,[29] he argued that Bromley was worse off than any other suburban town and he asserted that Bromley had been trifled with and made fools of by the South Eastern and the London Chatham and Dover Railway Companies. He thought the former the better of the two, but believed that both companies felt that travellers ought to be satisfied if the journey to London took no more than 45–60 minutes. He felt that the London Chatham and Dover Company would oppose the line, but that the branch line which would run

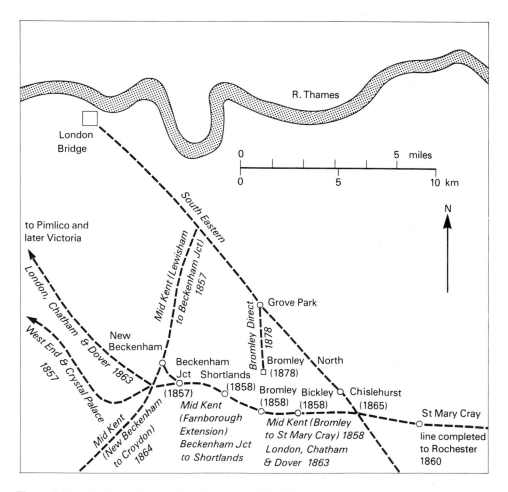

Figure 4. Local railways in the Bromley area, 1857–78.

from Hollow Bottom (Grove Park) over $1\frac{3}{4}$ miles to Bromley would be in the interests of the South Eastern Company as the branch line would run from their main line.

Chislehurst Station which had opened in 1865 was cited as an example of a profitable suburban station. In its first year its receipts had been £69 per week, but by 1872 had reached between £700 and £800, due to the subsequent villa development which the railway had attracted. 'If the railways are not alive to their own interests the managers are unfit to hold the position they occupy', Starling said. The meeting was well supported and the venture was given the backing of the town and the Local Board because a second railway 'was in the interests of the town and health of those who travelled daily to the City'. Once again the grievance was the poor rail service, but the demand for a branch line must also be seen against the increase in population between 1861 and 1871 and the substantial villa development since the first railway in 1858. Not only had the existing services deteriorated but the town had developed in many ways, new residents had been attracted by the prospect of good rail access to the City, whilst the rapid rise in population had also strained the resouces of the Local Board. New areas of population had developed and there was a need for a new station at the northern end of the town, which by linking with the South Eastern Railway Company at Grove Park would reduce the distance to London by two miles.

It was estimated that the total cost of the line would be £18,600 consisting of £10,000 for the building of the line, £6,000 for the land and £2,600 for the engineer. The point was made that land was still cheap, as the route of the line did not run through any house property. On the other hand development was going on apace. Advertisements in the *Bromley Record* offered land 'opening up very eligible plots for building purposes'. However, the line was no nearer fruition, although in October 1873 the *Bromley Record* reported that the project 'had not been abandoned',[30] and there was a letter in the same issue from William Gurley-Smith advocating the branch line and urging landowners and both companies to unite 'to lay down a line which would receive their countenance and prevent a costly opposition'.[31] The reasons for the branch line remained the same for 'it would get rid of the horrible nuisance of changing carriages at Beckenham that ruffles the tempers of the mildest, terrifies aged and infirmed people, and drives the business man away from Bromley.'[32] The twin fears of the lack of adequate rail facilities and the subsequent curb to future development remained.

On 14 January 1874 a Bill was deposited in the joint names of 'your worthy townsman, W.D. Starling, Esq.' and his co-directors,[33] and on the 27 February another public meeting was held, which was attended by 250 townspeople.[34] This time, a builder and Local Board member, Charles Muffett, was in the chair. The meeting again voiced disquiet at the inadequate rail facilities which were 'no accommodation at all'. The lack of direct access to Cannon Street and Charing Cross, the change at Beckenham Junction and the length of the journey were all discussed. One speaker said that they were 'treated more like cattle than Christians', and that they spent at least 100 minutes a day in travel, whilst those travelling from Beckenham and Chislehurst took only 40 minutes.[35]

It was suggested that if one railway had led to a doubling of the population between 1861 and 1871, Bromley 'would become still more patronized, and a greater number of people would come to reside in the locality, if the proposed line were made.'[36] The builders and property developers thus saw further opportunities through a branch line, but also were aware that if it did not come then other more favourably placed areas would forge ahead.[37]

The meeting finally accepted a proposal by William Starling, that was carried unanimously, 'that the present railway accommodation for the inhabitants of the town is insufficient; there being no direct communications with the Cannon Street and Charing Cross stations, and a very serious loss of time occasioned by the change of carriages at Beckenham Station.'[38] A second motion was also carried that the proposed branch line 'was calculated greatly to benefit the residents and traders of Bromley and largely increase the value of property in the immediate neighbourhood of the town'.[39] The meeting concluded by hoping that Sir Samuel Scott would be reasonable. 'While the line could afford to the town a great boon, it would do no damage to Mr Scott's estate and injure neither ornamental or residential property.'[40]

There could be no firmer indications of the motives for a branch line than these, for at the meeting the interests of the commuter, the trader and the property developer coalesced to support a line which they hoped would bring increased trade, higher property values and further building opportunities to the town. William Starling, the chairman of the venture, was a local surveyor and land speculator, despairing of getting the South Eastern Railway Company to build the line, had formed the Bromley Direct Railway Company. Anticipation of the railway itself generated property speculation to the north of the town near where it was assumed the terminus would be. The result was that there were several applications to the Local Board for the stopping of footpaths, which brought protests from the residents of Plaistow whose walk to the station at Mason's Hill was increased as a result of the closures.

On 26 June 1874 the Bromley Direct Railway Bill passed the Lords, and discussion began as to the exact siting of the station.[41] Although progress was being made the inadequacy of the existing rail service was evidenced by the fact that on 8 June 1874 a new coach service had begun from the White Hart Hotel in Bromley to the Royal Exchange. It was served by a four-horse coach which departed at 9.30 a.m. each day and returned from the City at 4.30 p.m. Although the journey took 75 minutes the *Bromley Record* believed that the service was viable and this in itself tells us much about the existing slow and inconvenient rail service. On the other hand it may have attracted passengers who had previously used their own transport, rather than the railway.[42] At any rate the timing of the coach indicates that the clientèle must have been drawn from the upper échelons of the City.

By August 1875 work on the railway had begun and the engineers had 'driven in the permanent stumps throughout the centre of the line', whilst notices to landowners had been despatched.[43] However, the prospect of yet another autumn and winter of inadequate rail services led to a letter from Viator to the *Bromley Record*[44] in which he urged people to walk to Grove Park to catch the train. He felt that this would encourage the South Eastern Railway Company to increase the number of trains. In addition he advocated a new omnibus service from the Market Square in Bromley to Grove Park which he felt would be generally supported. Actions such as this plus a memorial from the influential Hon. A.F. Kinnard, M.P. and John Pound, Esq., to the South Eastern Railway Company, led to an increase in the number of trains, by two up and three down. However on 18 November 1875 it was reported that the Bromley Direct Railway Company had applied for an extension of their building time.[45]

It was not until 1 January 1878 that the Bromley Direct Railway Company branch line and station opened, over 14 years after the project had first been mooted, and 20 years after the opening of the first station. The new terminus provided 22 down and 20 up trains each day, with eight down and seven up on Sundays. On most trains a change had to be made at Grove Park and the journey to the City took half an hour. The annual cost of a season ticket was £17 first class and £14 second, which the *Bromley Record* described as 'serious items in a City man's expenditure'.[46] Early reductions were hoped for.

With two railways Bromley now offered the City traveller a satisfactory service. It was almost exclusively one for the middle and upper classes and the time and cost of the journey did much to determine the nature of Bromley's future development. Workmen's returns were resisted in communities such as Bromley and Sevenoaks, whilst their availability in places such as Penge and Tottenham led to the development of areas where low paid clerks and other workers could live. By contrast Bromley's lower paid occupations developed largely as service groups to the middle classes, who alone worked in London.

Despite these developments the horse still continued to be the main form of transport and the stations became the focal point for omnibus and carrier services. Unlike Camberwell, Bromley was too far from London for the commuter to walk each day, but many now walked to the station. One of the predominant features of the housing advertisements came to be the walking distance from the station, and up to 15 minutes, or about a mile, was a regular selling feature.

2   The pattern of landholding and estate development

The tithe award of 1841 showed that whilst the parish of Bromley was divided among 178 separate landowners, ownership was concentrated in the hands of four individuals, who between them owned 64.6 per cent of the total acreage. In addition to these, another four landowners owned over 100 acres each. Thus a very small minority, only 4.5 per cent of the total number of landowners, owned over 75 per cent of the land. Over the following years only Sir Samuel Scott of Sundridge Park and George Warde-Norman of The Rookery, Bromley Common were able to retain their estates intact and in the hands of their family. We have seen that Scott was one of the opponents of the branch line from Grove Park to Bromley in the 1870s, and the argument put forward by the promoters of the line that the route along the edge of Scott's estate would not entail the destruction of any property is indicative of the still rural nature of the area and the success of the Scotts in withstanding development. Table 2 shows that Scott occupied a greater percentage of his land than the other three landowners, which may well indicate that he was not development-minded. To the south of the parish, G.W. Norman pursued a policy of steady accretion and by 1877 had accumulated a total of 2,446 acres, over half the total acreage of the parish. In Bromley, Norman essentially followed his father's policy of consolidation for income, combined with the desire to preserve the quality of the area. Several farms on, or near, Bromley Common were bought, and though he was not averse to erecting cottages, he did not embark on any extensive villa development on his land.

Thus to the north and south of the parish there were stable landowners who sought to retain the character of their property.

Table 2   The leading landowners in Bromley parish, 1841

landowner	land held (whole acres)	% of parish	land occupied by the landowner (whole acres)	% of land held in hand
G.W.Norman	719	15.5	336	46.7
Bishop of Rochester	691	14.9	175	25.3
S. Scott	699	15.0	599	84.3
J. Wells, Snr	885	19.0	570	64.4
Land held by four landowners	2,994	64.4	1,680	
Parish as a whole	4,646	100.00		

Source: Apportionment of the Rent Charge in Lieu of Tithes in the Parish of Bromley in Kent. Agreed 28 January 1841. (See fig. 1 for the location of these estates.)

This was in part because both the Scotts and the Normans enjoyed incomes over and above what was derived from their Bromley estates. Scott was an important banker whilst G.W. Norman was in banking and commerce.[47]

By contrast with the stability of these estates, two events in 1841 were to begin a sequence of events which were to alter radically the estates of the Bishop of Rochester and John Wells of Bickley, and clear the way for subsequent building development. These were firstly the reorganization of the Rochester diocese, by which the parish of Bromley was transferred to Canterbury, whilst the Bishop moved to a new palace at Danbury in Essex, with the consequent sale of the Bishop's estates in Bromley. Secondly, there occurred the bankruptcy of John Wells of Bickley Hall who held land not only in Bickley, but also in Widmore, on Bromley Common, and adjacent to the Bishop in Bromley. Wells not only owned land bordering that of the Bishop, but also in 1834 he had become a substantial lessee of the Bishop.

G.W. Norman suggested in his memoir that the Bishop's holding was a substantial handicap to the development of Bromley for 'its subsequent increase had been less than in most towns, owing to it being surrounded by Church Property which could neither be sold nor let for building purposes'.[48] In addition, the lengthy sale negotiations of the Bishop's estate which in the main were not completed until 1846 had, as we have seen, a depressing effect upon the town, as for several months the Bishop's Palace was unoccupied, to the detriment of the local shopkeepers and suppliers.

Thus in their different ways the decision to sell the Bishop's estate in 1841, and the bankruptcy of Wells in the same year, were of considerable significance, and rather than seek to survey the whole of Bromley's estate development over a 40-year period, these two estates will be considered in some detail. In addition two other estates, both centrally situated, the Bromley Lodge and the Bromley House estates will be discussed as examples of the important development of the smaller estates.

a. The Bickley Manor Estate
The Wells family had held land in Bromley since 1759 and John Wells had made money in shipbuilding at Deptford before he bought the Bickley Estate from his

brother in 1812. The tithe award showed John Wells Senior to be the largest landowner in Bromley, apart from the considerable holding that he had leased from the Bishop. In order to provide a career for his second son, Wells joined the Maidstone banking firm of Whitmore and Co. as a sleeping partner.[49] However, in the financial crisis of 1841 the firm failed and Wells had to either sell the estate or put it into the hands of a receiver. Fortunately, some years before he had made over part of his property, including Southborough Lodge, to John Wells, junior, which thus remained in the hands of the family after the crash. The remainder of the land was put up for auction on behalf of the creditors of Whitmore and Co. in October 1841. It was described as the Bickley Park Estate and was offered in 23 lots. Lot 1 which comprised the main estate at Bickley was 1,200 acres in extent and the sale catalogue described it as follows:

> This lot comprises a valuable and highly important landed estate known as BICKLEY PARK, for many years the much admired and favourite residence of JOHN WELLS, Esq., it is situate about 11 miles S.E. of London, within 1 mile of the Town of Bromley, in the immediate neighbourhood of the residences of some of the most distinguished noblemen and gentlemen of the country. This beautiful Estate, which has taken the Proprietor many years in bringing to its present compact state, is now with a Ring Fence, and has within the last 20 years been considerably improved by the formation of New Roads, and the reformation of many of the enclosures, and it may now be considered as one of the gems in the favourite County of Kent, every part of the Property is in the highest order and perfection, and is replete with every possible convenience.[50]

Here accessibility to London and Bromley was combined with the appeal to a gentleman seeking a well-laid out estate in a favoured situation. In addition 'fox hounds and harriers are within reach, and the roads in all directions are capital, and within one hour's ride of the Metropolis'.[51]

In contrast to the Bishop of Rochester, Wells had improved and developed his estate up to the time of his bankruptcy, and the sale catalogue of 1841 stressed consolidation and improvement. The first survey of the Bishop's lands in the same year merely pointed to the potential and possibilities for improvement.

The remaining 22 lots comprised outlying land in various parts of the parish. There was a substantial holding at Widmore, adjoining Bromley town, and near Bromley Common, and the lands listed contained houses, cottages and several farms.

In 1834 John Wells Senior had leased a substantial amount of land from the Bishop.[52] This was known as the Bromley Manor Estate and adjoined the Bishop's demesne land near Bromley town. It was this lease, along with John Wells' freehold Bickley Estate, which were sold to John Wright Nokes,[53] as a result of the above sale. It is difficult to ascertain the particular relationship of Nokes to the creditors of Whitmore and Co. It would appear that Bickley Park was bought by the latter and later rented to an Austrian-born merchant, Edelman, for his daughter. Mrs Chalmers wrote 'We came to Bickley in 1844 . . . renting it from a man named Noakes; who was I think, a sort of manager for the creditors of the Wells Estate.'[54]

The estate was now divided and John Wells Senior moved to Southborough Lodge to live with his second son, with whom he died in 1848. The freehold Bickley Park had been bought by Nokes, and rented to Edelman, whilst the leasehold of most of the important Bromley Manor Estate,[55] had also been purchased by Nokes.

When the Bishop of Rochester's lands were put up for sale Nokes was offered and purchased the reversion of the leasehold of the Bromley Manor Estate on 8 June 1846.[56] He wasted little time for on 31 July 1846 this detached portion of the Bickley Estate was put up for auction.[57] The sale plans show that much of the land offered was that which had been put up for sale five years previously. However, the land was now more attractive on two counts. Firstly, the land was now freehold and secondly, there was the prospect of a railway, both of which points were stressed in the sale particulars.

> The following, important and valuable freehold property, offering most eligible sites for building, situate in or near the Town of Bromley in a fine healthy neighbourhood, long celebrated for the beauty of its scenery and with the immediate prospect of the Mid-Kent Railway passing through the Town, where there will be a station, affording constant and easy access to all parts of the Metropolis, within 15 to 20 minutes.[58]

The emphasis with many of the lots was on speculation. 'In an admirable situation for building' was a common theme, and several of the lots offered in 1841 had been subdivided into smaller units for future building development.

However, the projected railway did not materialize for another 12 years, but nevertheless land, which previously had been frozen under complex and restrictive leases held by the bishops of Rochester, had been sold at auction as freehold land. The land was now ripe for development, in anticipation of a railway, and whilst some building took place prior to 1858, other land was available for subsequent development. Thus on the one hand whilst the population of the Parish between 1841 amd 1851 remained static, fundamental changes were taking place in landholding which were to determine and facilitate the future development of the Parish.

As the Bishop found to his cost, Nokes was a bad paymaster. In order to purchase the Bickley Estate he had obtained a mortgage for £50,000 from J. Gurney of Easton, Norfolk and when Nokes defaulted Gurney sold off some of the property.[59] In this way G.W. Norman was able to enlarge his holding at Southborough in 1851 by purchasing 18½ acres of land for £1,100 and later further land for £3,130.[60]

Meanwhile the Edelman family remained at Bickley Hall until 1852 when it was sold to William Dent 'over my father's head for an extra £500 which he wld. willingly have given, as he wished to remain, and thought he had the place, when he suddenly discovered it had been sold privately to Mr Dent.'[61]

William Dent had been a director of the East India Company and in 1856 became the Chairman of the Mid Kent (Bromley to St Mary Cray) Railway Company. Along with Coles Child he was instrumental in bringing the railway to Bromley in 1858 and then to Southborough Road, Bickley, which enhanced the building potential of his estate.

On 7 May 1856 Dent gave evidence before the Select Committee on Private Bills.[62] He was closely questioned, for most of the opposition to the line came from among the tenant farmers of the area who felt that their livelihood was threatened. Dent's argument was that 'it is utterly hopeless to prevent railways coming to Bromley and the district within 12 miles of London; it is much better that landowners and others should take an interest and endeavour to make them as little inconvenient as possible to the neighbourhood than that they should punish strangers to come into the County.'[63] However, Dent did not stay to see the development which he had initiated because in 1861 he sold the estate to George Wythes, a wealthy contractor. Thus in 20 years the Bickley estate had passed from an improving landowner to a businessman interested in bringing the railway to the area and encouraging development, to George Wythes who, during the following years, maintained the mansion, but developed the remainder of the estate. Within a year of his arrival a new road had been cut through the whole length of Bickley Park from near Bickley station to the crest of Chislehurst Hill whilst gas pipes were laid from Bromley to Bickley.[64]

Wythes built only large detached villas and attracted many city merchants, bankers, and professional people to the area.[65] Two- to five-acre plots were laid out, and the census returns of 1871 indicate that many of the houses had lodges and stabling, and three or more servants. The stations at Bickley and later Chislehurst were close by, and Wythes gave £12,000 for the Church of St George which was consecrated in July 1865, 'a handsome modern building of stone, with a lofty spire, neatly pewed, and has accommodation for 820', the living being 'a vicarage in the gift of George Wythes, Esq. of Bickley Hall'.[66] In addition to the church a part of the park was laid out for a cricket ground and by 1870 'contained many first class houses, and is studded with modern villas'.[67]

Not only had a new population come to Bickley but also Wythes as a contractor, was a substantial employer. In 1865 a committee was formed to establish a Working Men's Institute and Reading Room at Widmore 'in order that there may be a suitable resort for the largely increasing population of this class.'[68] Amongst those elected to the committee were the foremen of Wythes' carpenters, bricklayers, masons, plumbers and plasterers. The size of Wythes' business is to be judged by the fact that at his death at Bickley Hall in 1883 he left 1.5 million pounds.[69]

b. The Bishop of Rochester's Estate

The first direct evidence of the intended sale of the land held by George Murray, Bishop of Rochester,[70] came in a survey commissioned by the Bishop and completed by Adam Murray on 29 June 1841.[71] This was primarily concerned with the freehold land held by the Bishop, most of which consisted of his palace and the surrounding land which lay close to Bromley town. The survey shows that the demesne land had not been well-farmed, and it contained several references to the condition of the fields and the need for improvement. Three fields were in need of lime, one required top dressing, whilst others had been neglected or badly farmed.

The surveyor concluded by outlining the favoured situation of the estate before the curtailment of the long-distance coach trade '9½ miles from London and close to the Town . . . where coaches pass to and from London nearly every hour of the day, it is within 3 miles of the Croydon railway and possesses every facility of getting to London and from it, for a Merchant or Banker.'[72] Murray further noted 'the pleasant and agreeable neighbourhood [which is] surrounded by gentlemen's seats and good roads and a healthy country'.[73] Nevertheless he felt that the property was 'capable of great improvement', not only in terms of agriculture, but also by stopping some of the footpaths and building a porter's lodge at the gate.

The Bishop's property was undoubtedly attractive, although the estate had not been managed efficiently and the Diocese of Rochester, though relatively poor, had never exploited the estate on a thoroughly commercial basis. This may have been because a bishop could not provide the continuity possessed by a family estate.

This initial survey was concerned with the freehold land held in hand, and it was recommended that the demesne and the Manor should be sold in one lot, and the woodland and meadow at Bromley Common in two others. By this procedure it was hoped that piecemeal sales would be avoided, with the possibility that the less desirable lots would be left unsold. However, the survey was not acted upon and it was not until March 1845 that the matter was re-opened by the Bishop when he wrote to the Ecclesiastical Commissioners saying that 'the manor might at present be sold, with advantage to the See of Rochester'.[74]

The second survey was concerned with the Bishop's leasehold land known as the Bromley Manor Estate, and was prepared by Robert Wm. Clutton[75] and presented to the Bishop on 20 May 1845. This showed that the leases, which had been purchased by John Wells and later bought by Nokes, comprised approximately 279 acres of the total area of 375 acres. The surveyor recommended that the Palace and estate should be sold if possible to Nokes, it being agreed that the value of the property would be increased if the lessor and lessee's interests could be united. Clutton also commented that the proposed Croydon and Orpington Railway was scheduled to pass through some of the land, adding that 'This Railway would injure the Palace as a Residence for your Lordship, but as a favourable site for Building operations it would be benefited and the Estate . . . would be increased in value.'[76] Here was the classic dilemma for the landowner, for clearly the railway would have brought increased land values but also social inconvenience. In this case the Bishop was able to take advantage of the former without having to stay to experience the latter.[77]

A factor which militated against development was the complicated system of leasehold, with many of the leases being held for three lives. The surveyor argued that an auction would have been desirable if the land had been held in possession, but in the circumstances 'no speculative builder or other person would be found to give any sum beyond the present dry value of the conversion'.[78]

In July 1845 an updated report on the Bishop's freehold property was submitted.[79] The proximity of the Palace both to Bromley and to London was further stressed, rendering 'it peculiarly eligible as a Residence or as an investment'.[80] The demesne lands and the Palace, a 'double fronted and two stories high building' were thought to contain 'ample accommodation for a family of rank'. The quality of the park, the excellent views and the magnificent timber were emphasized, and the remainder was seen as 'most eligible' for farming and 'with little expense' could be improved. In addition the Palace farm was seen as presenting several 'very eligible sites for the erection of villas without inconvenience to the mansion'.[81]

In conclusion it was recommended that the Palace and demesne held in hand and the adjoining land leased by Nokes should be offered to him, whilst all the detached portions of the estate 'should be offered to the parties beneficially interested'. In the event of their refusal the plots were to be included in the sale of the palace and demesne land in hand. Clearly the Ecclesiastical Commissioners did not wish to be left with any unsold land.

Clutton also noted that an increase 'in the demand for Residential Property of the class of His Lordship's Palace has taken place, as well as the fact of the 3 per cents'[82] since Murray's report of June 1841. The latter had estimated the annual value of the demesne land at £365 16s. 4d.; the revised estimate was £650, a rise of 56 per cent.[83]

In normal circumstances the sale to Nokes would have been a straightforward arrangement mutually desirable to both parties. However, Nokes was known to be 'a very litigious person' and Clutton warned the Bishop to exercise great caution in dealing with him.[84] He could not conceive that Nokes was more than an agent for some other person, and noted that he was said 'to have passed a considerable portion of his time in a prison for Debtors . . . and to be a very bad Paymaster'.

Clutton's fears were amply justified since Nokes's delaying tactics meant that the sale was not completed until 30 September 1846. It then appeared that Nokes had been no more than an agent for a third party, Coles Child of Greenwich, who purchased the Palace and demesnes, together with the market tolls and quitrents, for £20,525.[85]

The new owner was to be partly instrumental in bringing the railway to Bromley in 1858. As we have seen he was a director and a major shareholder of the Mid Kent (Bromley to St Mary Cray) Railway Company and strongly influenced the choice of the site of the station at the southern approaches to the town, sufficiently far from the house not to be inconvenient especially as the line was masked by a steep gravel escarpment. In the succeeding years Coles Child maintained and improved the house and pleasure grounds and set the Palace Farm on a sound commercial basis. The *Bromley Record* proudly announced on several occasions that the hops from the Palace Farm were the first Kentish hops to reach the London market; an indication too that in the 1850s and 1860s Bromley was still on the rural fringe of the metropolis.

Coles Child came to personify the spirit of improvement in the town. He provided land for the first Local Board offices, and also demolished the weather-boarded market-house in the Market Square replacing it by a new Gothic Town Hall. Many saw Coles Child's offer to build at his own expense as a public-spirited gesture, but it is probable that he had seen the potential value of this central site in a town which had recently acquired a railway. The new structure, 'the Board's Palace', was opened in 1865, and consisted of a basement containing a covered market, and above that offices, a police station, an estate agent's office, the London and County Bank and the Literary Institute. In addition there was a spacious hall. Coles Child had in fact built not only a Town Hall but a lucrative piece of real estate. Thorne described it as 'a showy red brick Gothic Town Hall, emblem of prosperity and modern gentility, as the plain shed-like building, perched on wooden columns, which it has supplanted, seemed to be of the old-fashioned, tradesman-like thrift and humility.'[86]

The local traders were worried by the size of the new building, but the *Bromley Record* saw the new Town Hall as a portent of future developments.

> To take a prospective view of what the general appearance will be when the new Town Hall is complete, we need only imagine Mrs Grundy having purchased a spic and span new China tea-pot all gilt and ornament, and placing it for the first time on her board amongst a motley lot of odds and ends of ancient common household porcelain. It will not match at all. That will have to be remedied afterwards.[87]

Coles Child had certainly followed Sir Charles Barry's precept that a town hall 'should, . . . be the most dominant and important of the Municipal Buildings of the City in which it was placed . . . [It should serve] as it were, as the exponent of the life and soul of the city.'[88] On the other hand, Coles Child retained the estate virtually intact and only at the fringes did building development take place. To the east of the town approaching Widmore, Tynley Road was developed in the late 1850s, and to the south Brick Kiln Lane was developed by him close to the land which he sold for the site and the new gas works in March 1869. In the main his building was not of the villa type, but rather low rent, cheaper housing. The land which he made available was well away from the house, no longer entirely rural, and came to accommodate brick works, and gas works, with the result that the cottages which were built around them tended to be for the working classes.

Both the Vestry and Local Board minutes indicate some examples of friction between the local residents and Coles Child. He was a magistrate and public benefactor in the town, identified with its development, and the local people had grown accustomed to using footpaths across his land, a practice which increased with the building of the station in 1858, and the development of New Bromley and Plaistow. However, on several occasions he had stopped or diverted footpaths, often for his own privacy, but in 1871 in order to facilitate his own building projects.

The sale of the Bishop's estate in 1846 was of major importance. On the one hand Coles Child purchased the freehold land and maintained intact the Bishop's demesne land, thus adding to the character and status of the area. Equally, much of the leasehold land passed into the hands of those who placed no constraints upon building, and the rapid development of Bromley New Town was a direct result of this. The Palace Estate remained as a private residence until the First World War after which it was bought by a Mlle Rossignon and the Palace was used as a girls' school. She also began to sell off much of the surrounding land for development. In 1927 the Palace Farm was demolished, and inter-war semi-detached houses were built within the former boundaries of Wanstead Road, the railway line, Widmore Road and Love Lane. Nevertheless in spite of the maintenance of the estate as a unit the gross estimated annual rental appreciated, a clear indication of the importance of this central site and the rising land values. In spite of the varied nature of the sources and the minor differences in acreage the overall trend is clear. Between 1841 and 1863 there was a 60 per cent rise in average rental per acre, but in the next decade the value trebled, no doubt reflecting the building which had taken place, but also the overall potential value of the land.

Table 3   The growth in value of the Bromley Palace Estate, 1841–73

year	acreage	gross annual rental (£)	average rental per acre (£)	% rise per acre (1841 = 100)
1841	286	619	£ 2.2	100
1863	235	845	£ 3.6	160.0
1873	259	2,885	£11.1	515.7

Sources: 1841: survey of Adam Murray; 1863: BPL L43.1a. *Bromley Parish Valuation Lists*, April 1863 (manuscript); 1873: Return of the Ownership of Land in Kent, 1873; this was compiled by the Local Government Board (PP 1875).

c. The Bromley Lodge Estate

The Bromley Lodge Estate was situated at the southern end of Bromley High Road, and before the building of the station in 1858, Bromley Lodge was the last residence on the eastern side of the road before Mason's Hill (see fig. 5). Even though the estate only occupied 30 acres it was nevertheless strategically placed and its development provides a good example of the mechanics of estate development.

The main part of the estate, which contained the house and park, was bounded by the High Road to the west, and the town to the north, and contained roughly 20 acres. The remaining ten acres were on the other side of the High Road, adjoining the Bromley House Estate. The estate had been leased for three lives by S.E. Rolland of Victoria Street, Westminster, Middlesex from the Bishop of Rochester, on 1 March 1842. Rolland continued to live in London, renting the estate to tenants, but when the Bishop's leasehold property came up for sale in 1845 Rolland sought to purchase the reversion of the lease at as low a price as possible. However, as the estate formed a valuable frontage and means of approach to the demesne land, which was then under contract to Nokes, negotiations with Rolland were suspended. The price which had been asked for the reversion was £1,496 and Rolland had offered £1,250.[89] In September 1846 the freehold lands of the Palace Estate were sold to Coles Child, but as late as January 1847 Murray was still recommending that a decision over the Rolland lease should be delayed until the future of the railway was clarified.[90] Meanwhile Rolland's solicitors pressed for a decision, arguing that their client was now in a very difficult position as the mansion was in a state of decay because of the uncertain state of the tenure.[91] They clearly felt that the Ecclesiastical Commissioners wanted a speedy sale and further pressed their case by referring to the financial crisis of 1847 and the subsequent 'decline of Public Funds which have been about £6 per cent' and suggested a reduced figure of £1,200'[92]

When it was known that the rail application had failed, Rolland's solicitors increased the pressure. They suggested an even lower price 'due to the decline of Public securities, the 3 p.c. consols which are now 12 per cent lower.'[93] The Ecclesiastical Commissioners, realizing that they were now in a weak position, offered the reversion to Rolland for £1,250.[94] Thus his original offer was accepted and on 4 June 1847 the sale was finally completed.

The steady level of rents before the coming of the railway in 1858 is reflected by the rateable value of the property. The lessee in 1843, William Pott, a London vinegar maker, paid £198 on the house and £28 on the park. Twelve years later in 1855 Charles Devas was paying the same.[95] Devas was a copper smelter,[96] who had played a prominent part on the Vestry and he was to become Chairman of the first Local Board. He had first leased the property from Rolland in 1853,[97] and he occupied Bromley Lodge, the Park, the Park Meadow, meadow by the Gravel Pit, and a meadow on the other side of the High Road. The rent for the whole property was £250 per year.

In the years between 1854 and 1866 Rolland raised four separate mortgages to the value of £1,900 on the Bromley Lodge Estate. His precise motives are unclear, but they were probably for the further acquisition of property outside Bromley. Meanwhile, by the mid-1860s property values were rising in Bromley and in 1868 Devas paid Rolland £14,500 for the freehold estate.[98] Devas raised a £1,000 mortgage for the property from Charles Druce of Billiter Square, London and John

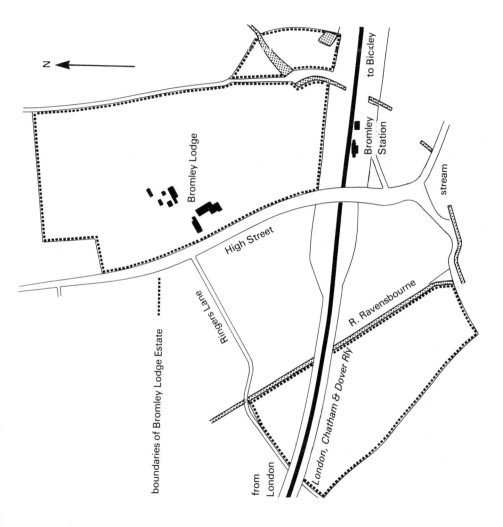

Figure 5. The Bromley Lodge Estate, 1869. To the east of the High Street was the main estate and house. To the west and traversed by the railway was the detached portion of 10 acres. The two sections were separated by the Bromley House Estate (see fig. 6). (Source: BPL 40/2, sale catalogue.)

Nix of The Hall, Worth, Sussex. The money was loaned at 5 per cent interest and was repayable within six months.

Devas had bought the estate in order to benefit from the rising property values and in 1869 the Bromley Lodge Estate was put up for auction.[99] It was described as 'A Freehold Mansion of 23 acres . . . a highly Profitable Building speculation'. In addition the 10 acre site on the other side of the High Road was included as 'Freehold Building Land' (see fig. 5). However, Devas withdrew the estate at £17,400,[100] £1,900 more than he had paid for it a year before.

Devas's land speculation was a factor in the affairs of the Local Board and his position came increasingly under attack until in 1870 he resigned, and moved to Pickhurst Manor, only two miles away, but outside the Parish. Bromley Lodge was sold to Sir Eardley Wilmot Bart., M.P., J.P.,[101] while part of the grounds fronting the High Road nearest the town was sold for development.

Two years later, in August 1872, Devas sold the remainder of the estate to W.J. Adams of St Benets Place, Gracechurch Street, London, for £17,500, retaining only the ten-acre meadow on the other side of the High Road. Adams appears to have been yet another city speculator. Devas had already granted building leases to Adams, for the Local Board had received an application from Baxter and Payne, local estate agents, on behalf of Adams. Proposals were put forward for two new roads, Holwood and Elmfield Park Roads, and these were agreed in June, two months before the sale.[102]

By the terms of the sale contract Devas kept part-possession until Lady Day 1873.[103] Adams gained the right to sell parts of the estate during his mortgage, but the Lodge and the grounds were not to be sold for less than £6,000 and the Moat Field for less than £1,000. Building leases also stipulated ground rents based at a fixed price per square foot which ranged from 4s. to 6s. according to situation. The projected development was for large villas and the proposed plots were substantial, with frontages between 100 feet and 140 feet, with similar depths. The gravel embankment disguised the railway line, and the size of the plots, the largely well drained soil, access to London by rail and a site which was within a few minutes from Bromley's shops, made the prospects look good for development.

However on 1 February 1873 Adams was declared bankrupt and in 1874, as he had defaulted on his mortgage repayments, Devas issued a Bill of Complaint. The result was that Devas was granted foreclosure on his return of £450 to Adams, in lieu of his mortgage repayments to that date. Later in the same year Devas paid Druce (heirs) and Nix £2,540 of his outstanding mortgage repayments and received the freehold of the estate.

Devas was now in a very favourable position. He had left Bromley Lodge and the Chairmanship of the Local Board in 1870 and was thus able to sell off the remainder of the estate for development free from the personal infighting and criticism to which he had been subjected. Development proceeded at a rapid pace and between 1875 and 1881 the part of the estate which lay on the eastern side of the High Road was divided into building plots and sold.[104]

In the deeds of covenant between Devas and the prospective purchasers certain stipulations were laid down which were primarily concerned to establish a development of a certain character. The most expensive property was immediately surrounding the Lodge where houses were not to be less than £1,000 if detached and £1,200 if semi-detached.[105] The lowest were those on the northern edge of the estate bordering the town and the White Hart Hotel which were to be £600 detached

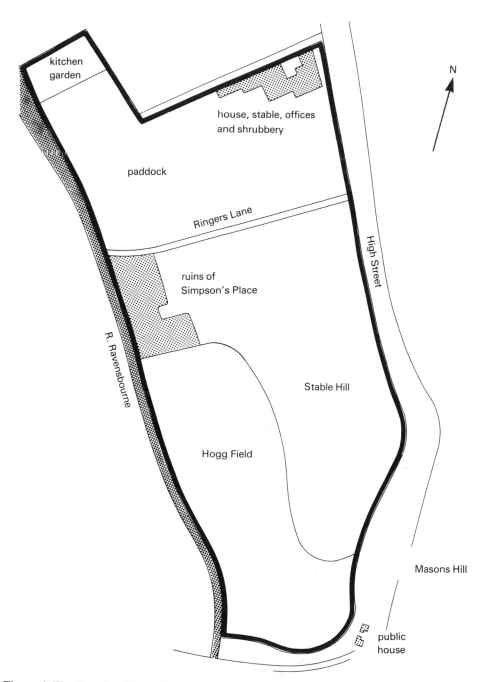

Figure 6. The Bromley House Estate, 1855. The map shows the estate prior to the railway which, as fig. 5 shows, divided the lower portion of the estate. The estate was purchsed by the British Land Company in 1868 and on the southern portion Hawksworth and Simpson's Roads were laid out. (Source: BPL 48/1, abstract of title of the British Land Company, 1868.)

and £800 semi-detached, whilst upon certain plots close to the station no restrictions were placed. The size of the frontages was also stipulated.

The speed of change was evidenced by Bromley Lodge. When Wilmot had lived there the house had spacious and well laid out gardens. He was succeeded by a developer Samuel Cawston who lived there from 1880 to 1883. When he moved to Bromley Hill, the Lodge became the headquarters of the Conservative Club, and the gardens fronting the High Road were sold for shop development.

Devas had benefited from the return of the remainder of his estate after Adams' bankruptcy, at a time when Bromley's position as a residential area was well-established.

d. The Bromley House Estate

To the west of Bromley High Road the land fell sharply towards the Ravensbourne Valley, where there were problems of drainage and flooding from the river. It had been an area of some natural interest, but one which in its lower reaches was less desirable for building. This estate of approximately 18 acres had formerly been part of Simpson's Place, a moated manor house, though little remained by the middle of the nineteenth century but ruins amongst which the children played, whilst the moat had been transformed into ornamental gardens. On the higher ground on the northern edge of the estate fronting the High Road Bromley House had been erected, with gardens which ran down the slopes towards the river. To the south lay water meadows and grazing land. The estate had been leased by H.G. Veitch, a Naval Lieutenant of Woolwich, to his brother-in-law George Tweedy, a colonel in the East India Company. In 1855 Tweedy paid £3,000 for the reversion of the lease[106] (see fig. 6). When the railway line was extended from Shortlands to Bromley it ran along the Ravensbourne Valley and cut across the lower third of the estate to go under the High Road to the new station (fig. 5). Colonel Tweedy was involved in a long battle with the Mid Kent (Bromley to St Mary Cray) Railway Company over the price to be paid, and in 1859 he repurchased his unused land from the company for £1,300. Following his death, and subsequently that of his wife Violet, in 1865 the estate was sold by the Trustees to the British Land Company for £17,000.[107]

The future development of the estate was determined by the route of the railway line, which allied with the natural features of the estate, led to development of two very different kinds. Before 1850 Bromley House was the last building on the western side of the High Road before Mason's Hill, but by the 1870s several large villas had been erected, the ruins of Simpson's Place had been demolished in 1868 and 1869 and three new roads cut across the estate.[108]

John Richardson erected a large villa called Ravensfell, alongside Bromley House in 1858 and then in 1875 purchased Bromley House from the British Land Company for £5,000. Thus the land on the higher ground towards the north was opened to villa development, whilst three roads had been cut for middle class housing.

To the south of the railway line the development was of a very different character. Within the triangle of land enclosed on two sides by the river Ravensbourne and the railway line was four and a half acres which the British Land Company developed as Simpson's and Hawksworth Roads in the years after 1868 (see fig. 5). In contrast to the land to the north, and across the High Road on the

Bromley Lodge Estate, this was essentially artisan housing, with frontages of between 16 and 20 feet.[109]

R.C.W. Cox has suggested that 'the timing of the process of sale for building is largely a matter of chance'.[110] Certainly local factors played a part in the subsequent development of the estates under consideration. The bankruptcy of John Wells in 1841, and the coincidence of the sale of his estate with the decision to sell the Bromley Palace Estate brought on to the market two estates which together formed a substantial acreage of land in a prime area. The length of the sale negotiations resulted partly from the failure to achieve a railway in the 1840s Nevertheless, as a result of their sale both estates passed into the hands of those who were not against development and were improvement-minded. In the case of the Bickley Estate the development of the freehold land in Bickley attracted the prosperous upper classes, particularly those from London. It also freed land leased from the Bishop which developed as Bromley New Town. On the other hand, the Palace Estate, shorn of its leasehold lands at Bickley, Bromley Common, and north of Widmore Road remained a substantial working estate. Its proximity to the High Road and Market Square enhanced Bromley's attractiveness to the middle classes as instanced by an advertisement by G.B. Baxter in 1859 'substantial and modern brick-built RESIDENCE, with large garden and lawn, situate in the Widmore Road, with commanding and extensive views looking over the Palace Estate, in this much admired and sought for neighbourhood'.[111]

The development of the Bromley Lodge Estate was no doubt enhanced by having the convenience of a station on the one hand, the High Road nearby with its shops and other amenities, and the Coles Child estate providing permanence and stability on the other. Similarly to the north the Scotts of Sundridge Park, and Bromley Hill, and the Normans to the south helped to give Bromley its particular character. The local residents were faced with what seemed to them a crescendo of building as H.G. Wells described in *The New Machiavelli*,[112] whilst several complained in the local press of the break-up of the estates. However, to the middle classes moving from London, Bromley offered the convenience of a rail link with London which they sought in a suburban home, allied to a semblance of stability and low-density building. For many of the middle classes and for those occupied in the service industries further development and the closing of footpaths as new roads were cut, created tensions which were brought to a head over the question of drainage and led to bitter conflict with the Local Board.

3 Housing developments

Having considered the steps by which certain estates were made available for development, this section will be concerned with the various groups involved in the purchase of the plots, the building and the eventual ownership of the houses, whether for occupation or investment. Three case studies will be taken in the initial section. The first emphasizes the purchase of land for speculation by private individuals on the Bromley Lodge Estate; the second emphasizes the role of a freehold land society in Plaistow and the third the actual builders and the heads of household in Hawkesworth and Simpson's Road. In conclusion more general considerations and trends in Bromley and the surrounding area will be discussed.

Figure 7a. The erection of Ravensfell, Lower High Street, 1858. The first owner was John Richardson, an Australian merchant, born in Camberwell. In 1861 he had nine domestic servants. Note the rutted road surface and the tenth milestone to London Bridge on the left.

Figure 7b. View of New Bromley, looking north-east up Park Road, with Rochester Villas to the right on the north side of Widmore Lane, with Palace estate on the south; the Baptist church is to the left.

54

Figure 7c. Rochester Villas, Widmore Road. The Bishop had restricted building to beyond 469 ft of his property and this land only became available for building after 1846. In 1861 none of the householders of these villas were Bromley-born, and their occupations were house proprietor, private school owner, wholesale clothier, fundholder and historical engraver, with two retired.

Figure 7d. Palace Road, New Bromley. Plots of land were bought for speculation and many were later individually advertised in the *Bromley Record*. Consequently development was piecemeal and in this short section of road four separate developments can be identified.

a.   The development of two Bromley estates

i.   The Bromley Lodge Estate – Elmfield and Holwood Roads
Following the bankruptcy of Adams in 1873 and the return of estate land surrounding Bromley Lodge, Devas began the process of selling off the property. The earliest plans of 1869 had envisaged the cutting of two roads and this had first been pursued by Adams, who had submitted plans to the Local Board, and later by Devas in 1875. The first road, Elmfield, led eastwards from the High Road separating the kitchen garden of the lodge from the Home Field on which some development fronting the High Road had already taken place. The road then curved round the boundary of the Park southwards to the station. To the north Holwood Road ran along the boundary of Home Field and the Park and then curved eastwards to join with the Coles Child estate and Love Lane. The latter was the boundary between the two estates and also an important right of way, much used by foot-passengers to the station.

The deed of covenant between Devas and the prospective purchasers of plots in these two roads was drawn up in November 1875,[113] and the land was frequently advertised in the local papers as being suitable 'for builders and speculators'. It was divided into 24 lots which were sold over the next six years, the last plot being disposed of in October 1881. The lots were acquired by 16 separate purchasers. No pattern of sale can be identified, although amongst the first to be sold were two plots fronting the High Road between the Lodge and the station, and another two adjoining the latter. The last remaining lot comprised virtually the whole of the southern side of Holwood Road, which was designated for smaller villa development (see fig. 8).

An analysis of the addresses given by the purchasers shows that 11 had Bromley addresses and the remaining six were from London, some purchasing more than one plot. Two-thirds of those listed described themselves as gentlemen, six from Bromley and two from London. In addition there was an engineer, a builder, and a manufacturer with London addresses, whilst a surgeon and a farmer[114] had Bromley ones.[115] Only five of the purchasers of land eventually lived in the houses which were built[116] suggesting that the majority of plots had been purchased by developers or for speculation. Two London gentlemen had houses built for themselves, whilst a London manufacturer built a substantial villa, 'The Hawthorns', on his plot in 1876 and then purchased the two adjoining plots for development. Similarly G.F. Fertel of Bromley in association with a Middlesex gentleman purchased a plot in 1877 and then in May 1880 purchased the adjoining one. The house built on the first, 'Holmcroft' in Holwood Road, was occupied by the Fertel family, and his wife ran a private school, on the premises.

Whilst the total numbers involved were small, one is impressed by the number who purchased plots for speculation. Excluding the three builders, four owners of nearby property bought plots and another four bought plots adjoining their existing residences. None of these were purchased in order to extend their gardens and can only have been for speculation, or perhaps to control the type of development which would take place. One of the most significant purchases was by Samuel Cawston who had acquired Bromley Lodge in 1879. In November 1879 and April 1880 he purchased two substantial corner sites in Elmfield Road. Part of one of these he sold to Thomas Jones, a local builder of West Street, Bromley in 1884 for £1,062 10s.[117] Jones had already built at least two of the Elmfield Road villas,

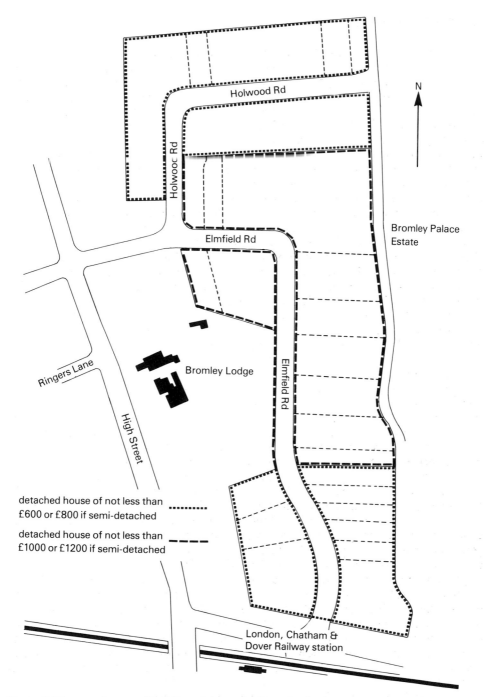

Figure 8. The purchasers of building plots on the Bromley Lodge Estate, 1875–81. (Source: BPL 40/4, B225, deed of covenant, 30 November 1875, between C. F. Devas and the purchasers of land (see fig. 5).)

'Claire Croft' and 'Lyndon Lodge', but in the following year 1885 he was declared bankrupt. Meanwhile in 1883 Cawston had sold Bromley Lodge, moving to the Bromley Hill Estate on the Bromley–Lewisham boundary where he initiated further building developments.

By 1885 16 large villas, each individually named, had been built in Elmfield Road and 14 slightly smaller ones in Holwood Road, whilst infilling had begun to take place along the High Road, with the erection of a terrace of shops in front of Bromley Lodge, the new premises of the Conservative Club. Another feature of the development was that three schools were opened. Two of these were in houses in Holwood Road, reflecting the growing demand in the area for the private education of the middle classes. The third, opened in 1883, was in new and purpose built premises, by the railway. This was the Bromley Girls' Public Day Trust school which was erected on the land originally purchased by Mr Lansbury, the farmer from Bromley Common in 1876; a clear case of land speculation on his part.

ii.   The Plaistow Estate: the work of the People's Freehold Land Society in Crescent, Cambridge and Bromley Roads

The operation of building societies and freehold land societies was one of the principal means of financing development by advancing money to builders and potential house owners. Professor Dyos estimated that there were over 60 societies in London and the suburbs by 1854,[118] whilst the Royal Commission on Friendly Societies calculated that by 1869 there were 2,000 building societies with a total of 800,000 members in the country as a whole.[119] Although the origins of these two types of society were different, by the middle of the nineteenth century their functions were essentially similar, as the freehold land societies were no longer primarily concerned to create 40-shilling freeholds for voting purposes. The 1867 Reform Act took away the need for freehold creating societies, and from the 1870s they increasingly served the middle classes.

The People's Freehold Land Society was active in Plaistow, a hamlet some half a mile north of Bromley town, which had increased in population with the coming of the railway and where in 1863 St Mary's Church had been consecrated. The Society, which had its headquarters in London Street, Greenwich, had bought land from Robert Boyd on the Plaistow Lodge Estate, which in the late 1850s and early 1860s was being developed on its southern boundaries.

An undated map[120] published at this time for subscribers to the Society showed the location of the estate and the details and prices of the plots. The estate was shown to be a mile from the proposed railway station on the Mid Kent line and as this is sited on the map where Shortlands Station was built one can fairly accurately date the map to between 1856, when the Mid Kent (Bromley to St Mary Cray) Railway Company was founded, and 1858 when the station at Shortlands was opened. In all there were 143 separate plots which varied in price between £43 and £70, of which 11 cost £43, 15, £45 and 20, £50. Members who had paid up the full amount of their subscription were able to choose from 38 selected plots, whilst those entitled to rights by rotation and ballot could choose from the others. In the conditions of sale, the semi-detached houses which were to be built on plots in Cambridge and Bromley Roads[121] were not to be of a value lower than £600 per pair (see fig. 7a), and the remainder were not to be less than £450 per pair. They were thus intended for the middle classes and prosperous tradesmen and shopkeepers, and support the view of Gosden that the subscriptions to the societies were not suited to the working classes and that the societies 'attracted strong support among tradesmen and other members of the lower middle classes'.[122] The prices contrast with the conditions for housing on the Bromley Lodge Estate where the lower priced semi-detached houses were not to be of a lower value than £800 per pair.[123] The majority of houses on the Plaistow Estate were in the £450 per pair category. Certain restraints were placed forbidding commerical development, apart from certain shops which were allowed on particular plots in Bromley Road, and a corner site at the junction of Crescent and Cambridge Roads which was set aside for a tavern,[124] itself indicative of the type of development envisaged.

The development of the estate was slow. The Ordnance Survey map of the area for 1862[125] shows a number of plots laid out in Cambridge Road, Crescent Road, and Alma Grove, but only one house built. By 1873 Cambridge Road still had only five houses and Crescent Road 11,[126] and the secretary of the company, Wm. Gurley-Smith, distressed at the slow progress, was active in seeking a branch line for Bromley, which in 1873 seemed to be yet again on the point of failure. His criticisms of the existing service and his appeal to both landowners and the major companies met with general support.[127] However, without the branch line the Plaistow Estate did not develop very quickly, for since the opening of the first station in Bromley in 1858, there were other building developments in the town within a similar price or rental range, which were nearer the station. In a broader context Bromley's rail service with London was inferior to other growing suburbs such as Beckenham, which were the same distance from London and where similar properties were available for purchase or rent. The opening of Bromley North Station in 1878 gave a boost to development north of the town for not only was the new station much nearer, but the service was at last competitive with that of other areas. In fact as early as 1861 the plots in Plaistow were being advertised to the public at large,[128] and by 1880 Crescent Road had 16 houses,[129] whilst the area between the estate and the new station was opened up for building, with the result that by the late 1880s the whole area to the north had been developed, and Plaistow had become part of urban Bromley.

iii.   The Bromley House Estate

The development of the Plaistow Estate had been conceived of as a compact unit with the houses within a fairly similar price range. By contrast the Bromley House Estate which had been purchased by the British Land Company in 1868 offered, and necessitated, two contrasting forms of development.[130] The river and the railway line roughly divided the estate, and on the higher ground along the High Road and on the three new roads to the north, villa development took place in

Table 4   Occupations and place of birth of heads of household in selected villas on the Bromley House Estate, 1871

name of villa	occupation	place of birth
Ethelbert House	gold manufacturer	Brixton, Surrey (London)
Thornet Lodge	carriage builder	Margate, Kent
Brunswick House	civil engineer	St Pancras, Middlesex (London)
Argyll House	auctioneer	St James, Middlesex (London)

Source: Census enumerators' returns, 1871.

Figure 9a. The Plaistow Estate. Sketch of two substantial semi-detached villas included in plans for the proposed estate purchased for distribution to members by the People's Freehold Land Society prior to 1858.

Figures 9b and c (far right). The Plaistow Estate. Two substantial houses in College Road (nos. 104 and 106/8), formerly Plaistow Lane or Bromley Road, opposite St Mary's Church. Houses were to be built which were not less than £600 per pair but these are the only houses which bear any similarity to the original plans, as the estate was completed over a much longer period of time than at first envisaged.

Figure 9d. The Plaistow Estate. Houses in Crescent Road were to be not less than £450 per pair. These more modest villas were enhanced by the classical stonework and facing around the windows and doorways which gave an added veneer of respectability and prestige.

which two local builders, Thomas Presland and Frederick Pearce[131] were chiefly involved.

The occupations of the heads of household in 1871 indicate the type of person who acquired the prime property fronting the High Road, below Bromley House.

By contrast the development of the land to the south of the railway was quite different. On this small site of only four and a half acres the British Land Company laid out Simpson's Road in 1868 and Hawksworth Road in the 1870s. The evidence available is fragmentary but from what remains one can trace the slow development of the southern side of the roads over approximately a decade and it was not until 1877 that the southern section of Hawksworth Road was divided into plots and put up for sale.

In the initial sale of land by the British Land Company in 1868 four local men were involved. These were Arthur Pearce of Mason's Hill, plasterer; John Rump of Cage Field, builder; Samuel Rump, 10 Henry Street, carpenter and plasterer, and Thomas Presland, the builder who had figured prominently in the villa development on the northern part of the estate. In addition a fifth builder, William Humphries of Bermondsey, was involved. In most cases the procedure was for a builder to buy the land from the British Land Company and then build a house on the plot which he would either then sell, or retain, in order to rent or lease. For instance Arthur Pearce bought plot 130 and in July 1869[132] sold the house he had constructed to George Bishop, railway porter for £210. Two years later in December 1871 Bishop sold the house to James Harding for £205. At the same time Arthur Pearce sold Harding the adjacent house on plot 131 for the same amount. There is no evidence of Harding having occupied either house, and he no doubt had bought both properties for investment. Arthur Pearce for his part appears to have been able to purchase the plots without recourse to mortgages, for he was one of the largest builders in Bromley, employing 12 men in 1871, and sufficiently large to buy fresh land from capital.

Smaller men such as the Rump brothers frequently used building societies for mortgages. Each obtained a separate mortgage in September 1869 from the Frome Building Society for plots 132 and 133 and the erection of two houses. On one £170 was loaned, whilst on the other £60. Interestingly it was Arthur Pearce who loaned the other £110. Six months later, no doubt after a house had been built and sold, Samuel Rump obtained a further mortgage on another plot from the Frome. This building society based in Frome, Somerset[133] supplied several of the mortgages, whilst others came from the National Freehold Land Society and the People's Co-operative. In some cases private loans were obtained. William Carter, plumber of Bromley, bought two plots in July 1870 and William Horsley of Regent's Park, Middlesex loaned him £300 on security of the land. The loan was for one year at an interest of 5 per cent and if Carter defaulted, the house and land could be sold by Horsley. The partnership worked well, for on a number of occasions Carter's name appears, with the mortgage supplied by Horsley.

By 1871 there were 35 houses in Simpson's Road, only two of which were unoccupied.[134] There were still 49 empty plots which were developed over the next decade. An analysis of the 42 householders living in the 35 houses indicates that the majority were in social classes III and IV, with the larger number being in the skilled occupations, and none in the professional occupations of class I. The social classification of the non-heads of household follows closely that of the heads of household. The industrial classification of the heads shows that they were fairly evenly distributed between the building, agricultural, manufacturing and dealing sectors, with many employed as skilled or partly skilled craftsmen. This evidence conforms to what one would have anticipated, but one is impressed by the fact that only 12 of all those employed were Bromley born, and only four of the 42 heads of household had been born in the parish. The numbers born in Bromley, Kent and London are roughly equal, but in total they only account for 41.3 per cent of the whole, and 38.1 per cent of the heads of household, suggesting that houses such as these, the majority of which were rented, provided accommodation for many of the growing number of skilled and partly skilled workers moving into the parish.[135]

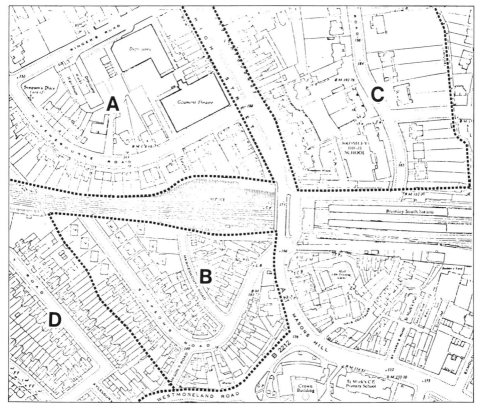

A   Bromley House Estate: Ravensbourne and Ringers Road
B   Bromley House Estate: Hawksworth and Simpson's Road
C   Bromley Lodge Estate: Elmfield section
D   Bromley Lodge Estate: detached section

Figure 10. Contrasting building densities in Bromley, 1960. On the higher land to the north of the railway large villas were built, increasing in size with distance from the line. On the lower land to the south densities were higher, though the development of the northern section of Simpson's Road did not take place as planned. Note how access to Westmoreland Road was gained at the cost of two building plots. (Source: Ordnance Survey Plan TQ 4068, 1960, Crown Copyright reserved.)

In 1877 the British Land Company put up for sale the remaining portion of land[136] (fig. 10). In this triangular piece of land no houses of less value than £150 were to be built on the plots on the southern side of Hawksworth Road (plots 211–18) and no house of less value than £200 on the plots from the remainder of Simpson's Road. The belief that this difficult shaped and badly-sited piece of land could not be retained for long purely as residential property was indicated by the fact that the building restriction prohibiting shops, workshops, warehouses, factories and inns was for the first period of ownership only. In all 11 different purchasers bought the 19 plots, four of whom were builders, including Thomas Presland and Arthur Pearce who between them bought 10. Another local builder, Arthur Jayes of East Street, purchased five. Two of the purchasers cannot be identified from the Bromley directories and presumably lived outside the Parish as did George Bodley, an ironmonger from Greenwich. Amongst the non-builders were a publican, grocer, fruiterer and the bailiff to G.W. Norman. However, of the 11 purchasers of the plots only one ultimately lived in the house which was built and that was Thomas Presland, who moved into one of his newly built houses.

Once again the money for the purchase of the plot and building was obtained from a variety of sources. From the five remaining deeds,[137] it is recorded that Edward Unstead, grocer and cheesemonger of Mason's Hill, held shares to the value of £100 in the Penge Perseverence Permanent Building Society and was therefore entitled to an advance of £400. The aim of the society was to promote building but as one of the trustees was a builder one wonders whether he gained the building contract as well.[138] In 1882[139] the mortgage was repaid and Unstead gained the freehold. There is no mention of him in the local directories and one must assume it to have been a case of property purchased and then directly rented for income. Other societies named included the Bromley Mutual Benefit Investment and Redemption Society which advanced a further £100 to a member who already held two £50 shares; a £150 mortgage for 16 years for Daniel Darnell, greengrocer from the People's Co-operative Permanent of Greenwich and the National Freehold Society which Presland continued to use. Presland in turn sold one of the three houses he had built to a coachman who obtained a mortgage from the National Permanent Mutual Building Society.

From this very small sample one is impressed by the number of societies which were in operation, all of which, with the exception of the Frome, were locally based. Not only did they provide loans to builders, but also to would-be purchasers, who had diligently saved with the society until they had sufficient shares to qualify for a mortgage to purchase the land, which in this case the British Land Society had brought on to the market. In many cases the mortgages were to be no more than a means towards acquiring a house, as an investment, rather than for direct occupation.

b. General considerations

Between 1858 and 1881 the various Bromley newspapers, and the *Bromley Record* in particular, carried a large number of advertisements for land and property. In addition a random selection of sale catalogues and conveyances have survived. This evidence is therefore fragmentary; the newspaper advertisements give no indication of the price received, only the asking price, and they often omit the name of the vendor. Bearing in mind the limitations of the evidence, a few tentative points

Table 5   The social and industrial classifications and place of birth of all those employed living in Simpson's Road, 1871

A. SOCIAL CLASSIFICATION[a]

class	heads of household	others	total
I professional, etc. occupations			
II intermediate occupations	3	1	4
III skilled occupations	19	20[b]	39[b]
IV partly skilled occupations	11	13[c]	24[c]
V unskilled occupations	5	4	9
total	38 (+4)[d]	38	76 (+4)[d]

[a] The Social Classification of 1951 has been used. See A. Armstrong, 'The use of information about occupation', in *Nineteenth-Century Society: essays in the use of quantitative methods for the study of social data*, ed. E.A. Wrigley (1962), 198–225.
[b] Includes 8 females.
[c] Includes 10 females.
[d] 4 female heads were either annuitants or with house property.

B. INDUSTRIAL CLASSIFICATION

industrial sector	heads of household	others	total
agriculture and breeding	6		6
mining		1	1
building	7	4	11
manufacturing	6	13[e]	19[e]
transport	7	3	10
dealing	8	4	12
industrial service	4	3	7[f]
public and professional service		1	1
domestic service		9	9
property owning and independent	4		4
total	42	38	80

[e] Includes 6 females engaged as needlewomen or seamstresses.
[f] Includes 6 male general labourers.

C. PLACES OF BIRTH

place	heads of household	others	total
Bromley	4	8	12
remainder of Kent	8	2	10
London	4	7	11
elsewhere	26	21	47
total	42	38	80

Source: Census enumerators' returns, 1871.

will be made as to how, after the break-up of several of the larger estates, the smaller parcels of land became available for building development.

i. The vendors of land

Earlier in this section the work of the British Land Company and the People's Freehold Land Company has been discussed, making plots available not only to their members but also to the general public. In the case of the latter company, the *Bromley Record* in July 1861 carried an advertisement in which they offered 26 plots for sale in Plaistow which they suggested would bring rents of £30 per year. The Society offered not only land for sale, but also mortgage arrangements, confirming the view expressed earlier that their appeal was to rentiers as well as owner-occupiers.[140] Baxter and Payne, the town's largest estate agents and auctioneers, frequently advertised for 'housing and land, large houses, farms of 100 acres, mostly grass, etc.'[141] which they either sold intact to purchasers, or divided up into more convenient units.

Land was also offered by individuals who had kept it until the market seemed opportune. For instance, after the opening of the station in 1858 and the development of New Bromley, Mr Fitzhe offered land 'ten minutes away from the station' at £2 10s. per foot for plots which were 132 feet in depth. Fitzhe had earlier bought his land for re-sale, but there were instances of owner-occupiers, seeing the potential of the land, offering it for sale. Richard Cooper, corn-, coal-, and seed-merchant of Bromley Common, offered 17 acres of his land for building, in the year following the opening of the station.[142]

Yet another type of land development was that carried out by the Bromley Cottage Improvement Company Limited on land made available by Coles Child on the southern fringe of the Bromley Palace Estate. The Company was established at a public meeting in Bromley in 1868, when it was argued that hundreds of dwellings were empty because of high rates. The Company was modelled on a similar association in Penge which had built Alexandra Cottages. A committee was elected to collect subscriptions and the aim was to erect workmen's dwellings. They were to have three bedrooms and a sitting room, a wash house, and a small garden, and were to be let at 5s. 6d. per week.[143] The scheme was supported by the Vicar of Bromley for 'by improving the dwellings of the labouring classes you at the same time greatly assist in improving their moral condition'.[144] At the first meeting three subscriptions of £250 were offered, one by William Starling, a developer and Local Board member. At a subsequent meeting in 1869 a limited liability company was approved with shares set at £5 each, and an upper interest rate of 6 per cent.[145]

By February 1878, 27 cottages had been built in Homesdale Road. The land was low lying, adjoining the railway, brickworks, and the new gas works. The rents varied from 3s. 6d. per week for two-bedroomed cottages to 5s. 9d. per week for three bedroomed ones. The company had also purchased the nearby road leading to the new gas works. Here in Waldo Road, an attractive development took place around a central green.

ii. The appeal of the property advertisements

In nearly all the advertisements at least one of the following points was empha-sized. Firstly, that the estate, property or plot was well situated. This would vary according to price level; in some cases the fact that the property was nearby an existing estate was used; in others that the railway was only a few minutes away.

Secondly, if the property was freehold the prospect of a vote was offered, but this soon lost its significance. Finally, the property was offered as an investment.

A favoured situation   For the middle classes seeking a suburban home the status and character of an area were powerful selling features. The density of houses to the acre varied according to the type of development, but whether it was low density as on the Bickley Park Estate,[146] or higher as on the Plaistow Estate, appeal was made to the established features such as the house or park of the estate, which was often built into the name of the district. Other features were looked for and offered by the advertisers. For instance, 'Gyah Lodge' on Bromley Common was 'near the new Church' whilst St Mary's Church enhanced the appeal of Plaistow. Similarly George Wythes erected St George's Church on his estate at Bickley, as the existing parish churches at Chislehurst and Bromley were too far away. Samuel Cawston did the same when he began to open up the southern part of the Bromley Hill Estate erecting not only Christ Church on Highland Road, but also a children's church.

The proximity of the station and good services to London   Many of the times to the station listed in the advertisements could only have been achieved by fast walking, and also through the continued access to the various rights of way across the fields, which were increasingly being stopped as new roads were cut. The opening of the second station at Bromley North in 1878 was met with relief by the traders and the travellers desiring a better service. On the other hand protests at the stopping of several footpaths led to bridges being built across the new line, and the continuance of several paved rights of way which have remained to this day, in the built-up area of Bromley.

When the South Hill Estate to the west of the town came on to the market in October 1878 reference was made not only to its splendid position close to the station and 'commanding extensive Panoramic views, and now ripe for building thereon gentlemen's residences',[147] but great stress was also laid on rail access and the new link with Cannon Street. Bromley, it was said, 'has the best train service in the vicinity of London . . . and . . . the properties are only 10 miles from London'.[148]

Investment potential   It was felt that the attractiveness of the South Hill Estate and others put up for sale in 1878 would 'most certainly enable builders or owners building upon the estates to command tenants or purchasers for houses which they may erect; and these advantages make the land well worth while the consideration of builders and speculators, or Investors wishing to create ground rents.'[149] In many ways this third category of appeal, that of investment, was the most important, though the auction and sale of the larger properties and holdings were usually held in London.[150] Thus the South Hill Estate and the Bromley Lodge Estate attracted purchasers from outside the town. Conversely many of the advertisements in the *Bromley Record* appealed to the local builder or investor.

iii.   The local speculators and investors
The development of four roads on Bromley Common provides a useful illustration of how the small builder or tradesman disposed of the house he had built and of the local people who acquired them for investment. Pope, Chatterton, Walpole, and

Figure 11a. Walsham Cottage, 31 Bromley Common. In 1861 it was occupied by the chief clerk to an East India merchant and in 1871 by a London-born ship's insurance broker. The appellation 'cottage' symbolized the attractions of Bromley: relatively rural yet in this instance within walking distance of the station.

Figure 11b. 35 Bromley Common, which in 1871 was occupied by a tea dealer. This semi-detached villa illustrates the hierarchy and segregation of the Victorian household, with the ground and first floors being occupied by the family, the attic and basement being for the servants.

Figure 11c. Sparke's Cottage, Mason's Hill. In 1673 it was the farmhouse of Stubberfield's Farm. Two hundred years later the farm had gone and the buildings were in multiple occupancy, with a reputed rent of 2s. 6d. per week. In 1871 the occupants were a labourer, a letter carrier and a gardener, whilst the sign above the door reads: 'Mangling done here'. The property was demolished in 1877 and the site redeveloped, ridding the area of what the residents of the nearby villas probably regarded as rural squalor.

Figure 11d. Plymouth (formerly Campbell) Road, New Bromley, adjoining Henry Street. These two roads exemplified the demand for low-rental cottage accommodation in the 1860s and 1870s by the new unskilled migrant. Only 7 out of the 54 in Henry Street, and 11 out of the 41 employed residents in Plymouth Road in 1871 were Bromley-born. Of the 95 employed, the majority was unskilled, 23 being labourers, 10 gardeners, and 10 laundresses.

Johnson Roads developed in a piecemeal fashion in the late 1860s and 1870s after the first railway, providing homes for many artisans and those employed in service industries, and were an ideal type of investment for the small man. The freehold land from which these roads were cut came on to the open market in 1867 when the British Land Company offered plots with 90 per cent mortgages, with 5 per cent interest which was repayable in half-yearly instalments over nine years.[151] In May 1870 two freehold, six-roomed cottages in Walpole Road which had been let at £20 per year were offered for sale, whilst a seven-roomed house in Pope Road was offered for rent at £19 per year. Several other properties which had been purchased with a view to early renting by the owner soon appeared in the advertisements: for instance, a local plumber, William Satchell of the High Street, advertised a '6 roomed cottage, Pope Road. No water. To let £15', and '6 roomed houses Chatterton and Pope Roads. 6s. per week'.[152] The advertisements contain many examples of local tradesmen dealing in property as well as builders who were seeking a quick disposal of their newly built houses. For instance, S. Rawlinson, bricklayer of the Market Square, frequently advertised brick-built cottages in 1860 and 1861 and A. Bulleid, another Bromley builder advertised the sale of '2 6 roomed houses. 99 year lease. £430' in May 1867.[153] Three months later he was advertising another four. This time the wording of his advertisement was changed to stress the letting and investment potential 'letting at 10s. p.w. Leasehold at ground rent of £3 4s. each. Freehold may be purchased for £900; part mortgage if necessary. A. Bulleid, Builder, Tynley Road.'[154] By November the wording of the advertisement had changed yet again for now six houses were offered 'Freehold or leasehold. Lease 99 years. G.R. £3 4s. Producing £156 p.a. price £1,350.'[155] It is quite possible that the six houses were the same as advertised in May and August for the total price was similar and the aggregate rent of £156 was probably thought more attractive than 10s. per week. If the houses first advertised had been disposed of, then one feels that Bulleid would have kept to the same formula.

iv.   Particular examples of property accumulation

Either through piecemeal buying, or through those with capital buying a number of adjoining houses, some impressive accumulations took place. The advertisements stressed the stability of the tenants or that the need for their particular type of property for disposal exceeded supply. For instance in 1866 'Investment – to pay nearly 9% for disposal – 12 modern leasehold houses to good paying tenants, and always sure to be occupied. Rents £218. Price £1,800.'[156] It was not uncommon to find a retired tradesman or builder erecting or buying a terrace of cottages and living in one of them. Several of these terraces bore the name of the owner, such as Sinclair's or Heaysman's Cottages. On the death of the husband the widow was left with a home and she was able to use the rents from the others as income.[157]

However, some accumulations were on a larger scale. The Bromley valuation lists for 1863 and 1872[158] provide evidence of ownership and form the basis of the evidence for the three case studies which follow of local men who developed a considerable holding of property.

Richard Barrett, builder[159]   Barrett was probably Bromley's most successful local builder. In the tithe of 1841 he was listed as owning 21 houses and during the next 20 years he almost trebled his holding. In the 1863 valuation lists he was shown to be the owner of 62 house properties, two of which had stabling, one public house, one shop and a building plot. Most of his holdings were on Mason's Hill, the remainder being on Bromley Common and along Widmore Lane. Over half the property was of the cottage type and on 32 of the cottages the estimated rent was £12 per year or less, or 5s. per week, with 26 of these being £8 5s. per year or less. The remainder of his property was of a higher value, 23 houses brought an estimated rental of between £30 and £55 per year, whilst a further one brought £84 and two £105. In all his gross estimated rental was £929. By 1872 Barrett had died but his executors were listed as owning five acres of land and property which brought in £1,835.

Charles Muffett, builder[160]   Muffett owned 54 houses in 1863 which brought in a gross estimated rental of £926. All but one of these properties were in Bromley New Town and only six were of the villa type with rentals ranging between £38 and £45 per year. Conversely table 6 shows that 43 of the properties had rentals of £14 or below and as all but one of these properties were in continuous rows it indicates that Muffett was active in developing low income housing in Bromley New Town. In the 1872 valuation lists he was listed as owning four and a half acres which brought a gross estimated rental of £837. Muffett by this time had retired and was living on his rents.[161]

Table 6   Cottage property owned by Charles Muffett, builder, in 1863

number of properties	gross estimated rental per year	rent per week
10	£ 9	3s. 6d.
8	£10	3s. 10d.
1	£10 10s.	4s. 0d.
6	£12	4s. 6d.
18	£14	5s. 4d.
1	£20	8s. 8d.

Source: Bromley Valuation Lists, 1863.

William Morum,[162] *builder and brickmaker*   Morum was a builder and brickmaker whose five acres of land in 1863 were described as 'meadow land and brick fields and near the gas works'[163] and for which the gross estimated rental was £40 10s. A year later a new and larger gas works was built off Homesdale Road to cope with the rising population. Morum benefited as a result of both these events, for there was a demand for building land fairly centrally situated and his land was enhanced by the removal of the gas works to a new site. His major development was Mooreland Road, off Farwig Lane in which he erected terraced cottages in the mid 1860s. Only three years later in 1868 the Local Board, faced with a public health crisis in the town, resulting from the increasing density of the population, received a report on the unsatisfactory state of the water supply in areas where pumps and wells were the only source of drinking water. In this it was stated that in Mooreland Road, all the 59 houses were tenanted, and several in multiple occupation, increasing the danger to health. All but four of these houses were owned by one man, William Morum.[164] By 1872 Morum had retired and was living in Park Road, New Bromley. He owned approximately three acres of land, but with high density cottage development such as Mooreland Road his gross estimated rental had risen to £505 5s.

Thomas Wells, grocer and wine merchant   The will of Thomas Wells, a grocer and wine merchant of Bromley High Street, provides an insight into the property accumulation of a successful Bromley tradesman.[165] Only once did his name appear in a local property advertisement, when in June 1867 he advertised a detached four bedroomed cottage in Plaistow for rent at 36 guineas per year.[166] However, his will showed that he owned a large amount of property and land in Bromley, listing 17 freehold houses, two leasehold ones and five pieces of land. These had been acquired over a period of 30 years, beginning with the purchase of two plots of an unstated area in Plaistow in 1856,[167] probably from the People's Freehold Land Society, which was followed by the purchase of two further plots in the same district. He also owned two houses in Cambridge Road, Plaistow, living in one and renting the other. In addition he owned four houses in Simpson's Road, which he had bought from the British Land Company and had been built by the builder, William Carter. Similarly he purchased two leasehold houses, again built by Carter, in Palace Grove, New Bromley in 1867 on land purchased from William Horsley.

After the opening of the second station in 1878 and the development of East Street he purchased a house and a shop from the Coles Child Executors in 1882, and land to the rear of East Street four years later. Finally, in 1887 he purchased nine houses in the newly built Park End from Samuel Cawston who had begun to develop the southerly part of his Bromley Hill Estate. No evidence of further purchases of property after 1887[168] is available, but the state of his holdings at that time illustrates how an astute local trader was able to respond to the development of the Parish by the purchase of property and live off the rents after his retirement.

v.   The motives of a Bromley investor: Martha Ann Howlett[169]

In her memoir Martha Ann Howlett records in detail her property and investments, and whilst she was atypical, in being a governess who spent much time away from Bromley in private employment, her problems and the conflicting arguments which she discusses, throw light on the situation of many females, either widowed or unmarried, who without an adequate inheritance, were forced to seek the best possible investment for their capital, in order to maintain what they considered to be their position and status in society.

In 1867 the Howlett family moved into the newly developing area of New Bromley and rented for three years 46 Palace Grove, a semi-detached villa for which they paid £70 per year. The family had engaged one servant, but soon came to justify another as the social round developed. In addition 'the water was not laid on to the house, and every drop had to be pumped from a well or from a soft water tank. Sometimes I had to help . . . her'.[170]

In January 1874 Martha's father died and she 'set to work to retrench in every way'. The rent of the house in Palace Grove was now too much, and so a tenant was found and a smaller house in Widmore Road was taken for £35 per year.[171] In this Martha, her sister, and an orphaned nephew, a day boy at Dulwich College, set up home. Meanwhile, Martha was in a post in Maidstone and contributed out of her earnings to the upkeep of the Bromley home. In 1876 her sister Mary bought the rented house and also the adjoining one.[172] In time her sister came to regret the purchase, but Martha justified it as Mary was unable to work and therefore had to obtain an income. The houses, which were leasehold, cost about £700[173] and 'they yielded £70 per annum gross income at the least. The ground rents being £12, I reckoned that with the deduction of £20 for insurance and repairs, she would still reap 5½ per cent by the investment which would be less risk than foreign bonds for which we had no secure place of deposit.'[174] Not only was house property regarded as a more secure and profitable investment than bonds, but also at the age of 36 Martha felt that

> the purchase of an annuity would have been a pity as it would have cost at the rate of £20 for every £1 of income, or roughly speaking the £700 paid for the houses would have procured an annuity of £35 per annum. The fact was that the £1,500 we had each inherited was utterly insufficient to maintain us even with the strictest economy, in the manner and in the society in which we had been brought up . . . I foresaw at 50 years of age, I could not look forward to obtaining a salary much longer.[175]

Martha appears to have borrowed £800 for a house mortgage, for in 1877 the ground landlord required her lease for alteration, and against her solicitor's advice she refused to hand it over. In addition she had some bonds, and recounts that in 1876 she had lost £35 on £250 worth of Russian bonds due to the scare over the Russo–Turkish war. She also lost £15 on £75 worth of Egyptian stock. Clearly, at this time, she was uncertain about her future, and at one point considered the purchase of a school, which could be used as their home. Meanwhile the houses in Bromley had been let, and when Martha and her sister visited the town they usually took three small rooms for which they paid 21s. to 25s. per week.

In 1879 the mortgage loan from which Martha had received £44 per year was paid off and the £800 was paid into her bank.[176] She obviously regretted this, regarding the interest from the loan as a sound and safe investment, better than the £36 per year which she estimated she would get elsewhere. For her, houses were not regarded as assets which would appreciate in value, but as investments which would bring a reliable income either from rents or in mortgage repayments each year. If the value of the house appreciated this was to be regarded as a bonus. The other £700 of her inheritance was invested in shares and Portuguese bonds and brought in £35, the shares bringing in over 5 per cent in interest. Nevertheless, Martha was hesitant, fearing a possible loss, by theft, of her securities. Her brother, who lived locally,[177] had recently deposited several hundred pounds worth of securities at the Bromley branch of the London and County Bank in the Market Square. Martha's confidence was not enhanced by the fact that a clerk in this bank was later charged with embezzlement.

The desirability of property and doubts about securities led Martha to look for a house in Bromley. In 1880 she bought a pair of houses in Widmore Road from Charles Devas. The asking price was £1,800 but as they were in poor condition she was able to purchase them for £1,600.[178] Later she regretted that she had not held out for a lower price, but she did not wish her money to lie idle, and was also at the disadvantage of being in work in Weymouth.

Her income, with the acquisition of the houses, was £105 per year but the conveyance of the house cost £20, blinds another £9, and £50 was set aside for doing up Number 30.[179] In order to pay the expenses she borrowed, and realized one of her sister's bonds. In her Memoirs, written around 1905, Martha argued that the only alternative to property was consols, but regretted that in the ensuing years 'the rate of interest has gone down, while workmen's wages have risen in that time. Thus I am beggared by the cost of repairs, as well as being obliged to lower the rents.'[180]

c. General trends in Bromley

We may conclude that a wide spectrum of interests was involved in housing development in Bromley. The activities of the estate owners themselves and the numerous London gentlemen who were ready to put forward money for larger mortgages or in order to acquire the ground rents on the leasehold properties have been discussed. In terms of building one is impressed by the number of local builders and craftsmen involved, who borrowed in order to build, and if successful retained a number of properties in order later to live on the rents.[181]

Finally there were those who saw land and property as a means of investment, ranging from the Cawstons and the Starlings to the prosperous tradesmen who judiciously built up an impressive array of property and land,[182] taking the opportunities afforded by the growing population not only to increase their trade and business but also to invest their surplus in the local property market. At a different level again were the widowed or the single such as Martha Howlett who regarded property as a safe investment which afforded more security in terms of a fixed return and safety, than stocks and shares or an annuity. There were in fact two different types of investor. On the one hand the speculative builder who was affected by wages and costs, by interest rates and loans, and on the other hand the investor–house owner who, as Gauldie says, was 'affected by the comparative return from housing and other sources of income.'[183]

i. Rentals and land values

It is difficult to assess the difference in house prices and rents between the various districts of Bromley because of the limited nature of the evidence and the ambiguity of nomenclature of the terms house, villa, and cottage. Nevertheless, the influence of the station upon the value of houses has been noted, though as Dr Kellett stated there was usually an inner band around the station where noise and inconvenience led to the development of lower priced housing.[184] Certainly land immediately adjoining the station on the Bromley Lodge Estate was valued less than land a few hundred yards further away, which had convenience without distraction. Similarly, land which was badly sited, and low-lying was often developed with fairly low-cost housing. For instance, Hawksworth Road, between the railway line and the river, was constructed out of a difficult and relatively small triangular piece of land. Equally, land near the old gas works at Farwig saw cottage development by William Morum, as did that near the new one in Holmesdale and Waldo Roads.

According to situation cottages were advertised for letting at between £15 and £25 per year between 1858 and 1870 and for sale between £150 and £215 in the same period. Significantly, in the decade 1871–81 there were several instances of cheaper cottage development for either sale or rent. Many of these were in Bromley New Town where new slate roofed cottages, usually 'two up and two down', were advertised in such roads as Campbell Road and Henry Street (see fig. 11d). These were houses constructed with scant attention to drainage and sewerage and were built to meet the relatively small but significant demand for low-cost rented accommodation. Similarly, cottages were erected in Holmesdale Road and Church Terrace for £11 per year rent, and were usually occupied by unskilled workers. Slightly larger houses such as those in Pope, Chatterton, and Walpole Roads, with two or three bedrooms were rented at approximately £15 per year.

At the next level were three-bedroomed villas in areas such as Plaistow or on Bromley Common which remained at a steady £30 to £40 rent or sold at approximately £400 to £500, but in the late 1870s, with the opening of the second station in 1878, there was a growth in the number of larger villas offered in such areas as London Road and Hope Park to the north of the town. Prices were approximately £500, renting at £65. Five and seven-bedroomed houses were erected in Hope Park, where the rentals were in the range of £80 to £90 per year for the former and £105 for the latter.

The overall impression drawn from the advertisements is that of properties for sale with a view to renting, and this is confirmed by the annual directories for roads such as Simpson's Road where it is possible to check the name of the householder against the owner.[185] In this particular case the majority of the houses were rented as they had been bought for investment. Whilst money incomes and real incomes rose by one half to one third in the last 30 years of the nineteenth century average rents rose by $12\frac{1}{2}$ per cent nationally, and the proportion of income spent on accommodation also tended to rise as income levels rose.[186] Nevertheless, there were few who could become owner–occupiers in the nineteenth century. Professor Dyos estimated that 75 to 85 per cent of residential property in Camberwell was rented in the nineteenth century;[187] in contrast to Bromley though, Camberwell contained more lower grade London workers, such as clerks, who could walk into London. It may also have been related to attitude, for owning ones' home was not then an accepted cachet of the middle classes, as it has become in the twentieth century. Equally the shortness of the mortgage period referred to in the Bromley advertisements, where nine years seems to have been the norm, implied a much higher annual repayment than in the longer term mortgages of today. Finally, in the properties where there was sub-letting by the tenant, or by the landlord, the inter-censal mobility of the householders was considerable. This was the case in the courts and yards off the Market Square which contained the most transitory population where the rental was by the week, and often by the night, without longstanding agreements. Mobility was also common in areas which one would have thought to have been more settled. For instance, of the 91 heads of household in Farwig Lane in 1861 only 29 were still living there in 1871.[188] There were also five other cases where the surname was the same, but the relationship was not proven. Thus approximately two in every three houseolds had moved from their original house, on occasions to other more suitable rented accommodation nearby. Mobility within the parish, and even within a particular district would seem to have been common.

ii.   House building

Whilst the newspaper evidence is at best impressionistic,[189] the census provides one with the total number of occupied and unoccupied houses in the parish. Table 7 shows that there was little growth between 1841 and 1851, although the fact that there was an increase at all confirms the view that the small fall in the population of the Parish during this decade owed more to the closure of the four schools and the removal of the workhouse to Farnborough than to migration. The

Table 7   The decennial increase in the number of occupied and unoccupied houses in Bromley parish, 1841–81

year	no. of occupied houses (A)	no. of unoccupied houses (B)	total no. of houses (A + B)	% of houses unoccupied	% increase in total no. of houses between decades
1841	793	49	842	5.8	
1851	848	58	906	6.4	7.6
1861	1,090	33	1,123	2.9	24.0
1871	1,946	146	2,092	7.0	86.3
1881	2,684	150	2,834	5.3	35.5

Source: Census tables, 1841–81.

increase in the next decade was 24 per cent, but the effect of the first railway in 1858 is to be seen between 1861 and 1871 when the increase was 86.3 per cent. In 1871 146 houses were unoccupied, representing 7 per cent of the total. To a point this indicates a certain level of building activity but on the other hand the *Bromley Record* in the 1870s complained of houses standing empty, and the pressure for a second railway in that decade sprang not only from a desire for a better service from the commuters, but from the local builders, traders and investors seeking a means of stimulating demand for houses, as neighbouring parishes such as Beckenham forged ahead.[190]

Parry-Lewis has pointed to the regional nature of the building industry in the nineteenth century and suggests that within any region local and national forces were at work.[191] Firstly he argues that credit for house building was local, and the part played by local people and by local building societies has been noted. Secondly, the national bank rate was influential in determining alternative forms of investment. Similarly the price of food determined the amount of money which was available for accommodation and thus the consumption theory is significant.

It is difficult to fit Bromley into even a regional pattern, though as the level of migration into the parish increased, employment levels and the general level of prosperity of those from London who were seeking a home, but not employment, in Bromley grew in importance. Their decision in turn increased the job opportunities in the parish and thus helped to enhance the attractiveness of Bromley for those seeking employment and a home in the parish. In this sense Bromley was influenced by the general trend of economic development in London and the country as a whole.

Parry-Lewis describes the prosperity of building enterprises in 1853–5 which drew many workmen to London. Overbuilding resulted and by 1857 the building industry in London was in a depressed state. By 1863 an upswing had occurred. In July 1863 the *Builder* wrote of suburban development: 'In suburbs acres of ground are in these summer months built upon, and in all directions spacious and substantial churches, chapels and schools are being erected.'[192] This upswing lasted until roughly 1868 and then the building industry fell into a trough in the early 1870s, until a further boom in the late 1870s.

Table 8 shows that there were only three new roads in Bromley between 1851

Table 8   The number of roads in Bromley parish, 1851–81

year	no. of roads	% increase between decades
1851	29	
1861	32	10.3
1871	54	68.8
1881	83	53.7

Source: 1851, 1861 and 1871 Census enumerators' returns; summary of houses and roads included in description of each enumeration district; Strong's *Directory of Bromley*, 1881.

and 1861, with the greatest increase coming in the decade which followed the railway. To this extent the decennial number of roads adds little new information to the number of houses which has already been discussed, except to show where the development was taking place. However, with the use of the annual directories which are continuous from 1869, it can show far more precisely when the roads were first begun, bearing in mind that the opening of new roads is a very crude indicator. Several may not have contained many houses at first and their development may have been by stages over several years. In addition several roads were un-named, whilst rows 'at the back of' or described as an individual's villas or terrace, may have contained as many houses as other roads which came to be described as such. Nevertheless, the very fact that the road was begun and came to be included in the directory is an indication of confidence and the belief that development would in time take place.

Between 1851 and 1868 nine new roads were added, but it was in the years, 1869, 1870, and 1873 that the greatest increase took place when 27 new roads were begun. After 1873 progress was slow, perhaps reflecting the decreasing attractiveness of Bromley, but in 1877 – possibly in anticipation of the second railway – four more were opened and then in 1879, 1880, and 1881 another 11. On this evidence Bromley seems to have lagged behind the pattern described by Parry-Lewis. Bromley's boom seems to have continued throughout 1869 and 1870, but after two fallow years, which kept in step with the region, 1873 saw the opening of 11 new roads. Finally, between 1879 and 1881, 11 more new roads were opened and these were clearly related to the opening of the second railway station and support Parry-Lewis's suggestion that renewed transport developments were a major factor in the boom of the late 1870s. Certainly the opening of Bromley North station had an immediate effect upon Bromley.

d.   The development of the surrounding area

The development of the parishes adjoining Bromley illustrates the dangers of generalizing even about a relatively small geographical area. The number of houses in Beckenham rose dramatically, trebling between 1861 and 1871 and then doubling again in the next decade. This was directly related to the coming of the railway and the nature of suburban growth. In 1876 Thorne described Beckenham as a 'pleasant suburban village but [it] has lost much of its old-fashioned rusticity since the coming of the railways',[193] whilst New Beckenham, half a mile north-west of the town was 'a village of villas, many of superior class, which have sprung up in proximity to the New Beckenham Station of the Mid Kent'.[194] By 1876 Croydon, seven miles to the west of Bromley, had eight railway stations with 300 trains daily. Thorne wrote that

> vestiges of antiquity are . . . diminishing. Lecture rooms, shops with showy plate-glass windows, and joint stock banks in the latest architectural mode are occupying all the available sites in the leading thoroughfares. Monotonous streets and lines and lines of villas are fast encircling the town, the neighbourhood of which being pleasant and picturesque, and within easy reach of the City, is a favoured residence for men of business, who may be seen flocking to the morning train in surprising numbers.[195]

Bromley, Beckenham, Chislehurst, and Croydon all developed from existing villages. Croydon and Bromley were both market towns and each had a long tradition of being centres for the outlying parishes. All four were to be boosted by the railway, and with healthy, elevated sites were to develop as areas of substantial suburban growth which were much favoured by the city worker or businessman, who was able to afford not only a house, or rental, but also the cost of travel, and whose job would allow the time for travelling in each direction. The character of the suburb thus came to be determined by the middle- and upper-class traveller to London, though not all the development was of the villa type. Indeed Croydon, Bromley, and Beckenham suffered considerable public health problems, arising from the rapid rise in population in the densely populated service areas.

Not all those travelling into London were the middle classes. Many areas such as Tottenham owed much to workmen's fares. Bromley had opposed such concessions, but nearby Penge, between Bromley and Croydon, developed as a result of them. Thorne related that, 'Fifty years ago Penge was only spoken of as a common and the maps show hardly a house upon it'. Then after the old Croydon Canal was converted into a railway in 1839, and a station built at Penge Common for Norwood and Beckenham 'the plague of building lighted upon it. Now Penge is a town in size and population . . . in appearance a waste of modern tenements, mean, monotonous and wearisome. It has three churches, many chapels, schools, taverns, inns, offices of all sorts, shops, four or five Railway Stations, and whatever may be looked for in a new suburban railway town.'[196]

Penge's development was in direct contrast to that of Beckenham, Chislehurst, and Bromley. In the parishes to the south of Bromley, beyond the growing suburban fringe, development was much slower. Neither of the two decades (1861–81) in which Bromley and Beckenham saw their greatest growth did the three rural parishes of Cudham, Downe, and Keston witness an increase in the number of occupied houses of more than 8.5 per cent. However, they were changing, not in terms of an increase in either population or building but rather in terms of land use. Cudham was no longer 'wild and solitary'; by 1876 'there were cornfields, and fields of strawberries and raspberries'.[197] Soft fruits were largely grown at Cudham and Farnborough for the London market, and no doubt the local producers found a ready market for their produce in the expanding parishes to the north, such as Bromley, Chislehurst, and Beckenham.

4 Conclusions

The decision in the seventeenth century of the Bishops of Rochester to use the Palace in Bromley as their major residence not only conferred prestige on the town but symbolized a decision which was later to be taken by many other wealthy individuals for whom proximity and ease of access to London was important. Even before the extension of the railway into Kent, Bromley provided an ideal place of residence, with frequent coach services passing through the town and a well-maintained turnpike road. The county historians Hasted,[198] Ireland, and Greenwood[199] all commented on 'the opulent gentlemen's families'[200] and the favourable situation of the Parish, though much of the soil was thin and poor and 'much inclined to gravel'.[201] These Blackheath pebble beds were later to provide excellent, well-drained land for building, and in time there came to be a close relationship between height and the value of the land. Waugh has illustrated this by contrasting land values in the elevated, well-drained areas of Bickley and Chisle-hurst with the low-lying land in Shortlands.[202] Similarly the earlier discussion on the Bromley Hill Estate showed how differing housing densities could occur in fairly close proximity. Fig. 10 shows the variety of housing densities before the recent redevelopment of much of this part of Bromley.

During the 1840s the particular circumstances of the bankruptcy of John Wells, the departure of the last Bishop, and the long drawn out sale negotiations, which in part were related to the possibility of a railway, and the effect this would have had upon land values, had a depressing effect upon the trade of the town. Nevertheless, the sale of these estates and their possession by two landowners who were 'improvement-minded' were significant harbingers of change. Poor communications may well have deterred would-be residents during the 1840s and 1850s, although during the second of these decades signs of incipient suburbanization were already noticeable.[203] This was reflected in the small, but significant number of residents in commerce and the professions living in the parish, who worked in London, for whom the time and the cost of the journey to their place of employment were not the sole determining factors in choosing a home. With the coming of the railway in 1858 a much broader spectrum of the middle classes was attracted for whom journey-time was an important criterion. The villa development which ensued was facilitated by the changes in landownership which had already taken place. In addition sufficient estates remained to ensure that the attractiveness of the area continued.

From 1858 Bromley had rail access to London, but its position on the outer fringe of the metropolis, some ten miles distant, led to rail fares which placed the parish outside the range of all but the substantial middle class traveller. Thus there developed a middle- and upper-class group which worked outside the parish in London, who though they often complained of the high fares were not deterred by them. However, during the late 1860s and 1870s other places such as Chislehurst and Beckenham acquired a rail link with much faster services than from Bromley. The result was that pressure began in Bromley in the 1870s for a second station, which linked the interests of the existing middle class travellers with the tradesmen, the property developers and builders who saw that future development lay in improved communications. With the opening of a second station in 1878 Bromley once again became competitive with the other developing residential areas at an equal distance from London.

Bromley's position outside the Metropolitan Counties gave the parish a certain cachet which from the 1870s the town sought to maintain. The parish was well beyond walking distance of the capital and successfully resisted the introduction of workmen's cheap fares. Bromley's development was thus unlike that of Camberwell which became a residence for clerks, or Penge where workmen's fares were introduced. Similarly, at a later date Bromley was able to resist the extension of the tramway to the town. Thus by the late 1870s, and increasingly in the 1880s, Bromley had become a wealthy middle class Kentish suburb with many of its middle classes working in London. Whether the figure amounted to the 10 per cent suggested by Waugh as a criterion for a suburb is difficult, if not impossible, to assess accurately at this time.[204]

The analysis of the variety of building development which took place not only highlighted the range of house sizes, but also pointed to the dangers of concentrating exclusively on the middle class commuters. Cox has reminded us that the majority of the London suburbs started from well-established bases and both Bromley and Croydon were medieval market towns.[205] Bromley in 1841 was an important centre for the surrounding hamlets and villages, with a well-developed town which provided a wide range of services. In spite of the decline of the long distance coaches, trade and passenger transport over a shorter distance continued to flourish, especially after the arrival of the station, which became the focal point for the carrier and the omnibus. Fig. 12 shows the strength of the manufacturing, dealing and transport sectors in Bromley Parish in 1851, which together totalled 38.1 per cent of the occupied male population. These provided a firm basis for the future, providing local initiative and the capacity for adaptation to changing circumstances. Equally, the decline in the agricultural sector from 35.8 to 15.2 per cent between 1851 and 1871 reflected the transition of a parish in which this sector had been dominant, but which only 20 years later was ranked fourth behind building, industrial service, and dealing. The change from 'rural' to 'urban' had taken place at a much faster rate than in the nation at large. Rising land values had transformed a good deal of agricultural land into building plots, but within the parish and certainly the larger Registration District changes in agricultural land-use had taken place. Market gardening and soft fruit farming had developed with improved communications, and the population of London together with the growing local population provided a ready market for both the more expensive soft fruits and the more essential vegetables which had often been grown on cottage plots. In addition the larger houses erected in areas such as Bickley had large gardens which required cultivation, with the result that by 1871 gardeners in the Parish outnumbered agricultural labourers by practically 2:1. Thus by 1871 the industrial classification showed that the manufacturing, dealing, and transport sectors had kept pace with the rise in population, whilst the building sector had replaced agriculture as the major sector, giving employment to one in every seven males. Female employment was dominated by domestic service, and in 1871 four out of five women were in this sector; yet another indicator of the nature of Bromley's development. It is likely that many of the indoor domestic servants had accompanied their employer when the family had moved to Bromley, but many others were recruited to specific jobs in Bromley, and the parish provided a considerable attraction to those who were seeking jobs rather than housing. Besides domestic servants, many in the building trade and unskilled general labourers were drawn by job opportunities and wage rates which were competitive, if not equal, with those of London. Hunt's study of regional wage variations[206] has a particular relevance in showing that higher wage rates were paid within the proximity of large towns and cities. The building industry's demand for labour, and the rates of pay which were higher than in the rural areas, must have been an important factor in nineteenth-century migration. Development was not only of substantial villas and detached houses for the middle and upper classes, for many of those who lived in the more modest properties or in the terraced roads worked in the parish, and there was an increasing number of people employed in the service occupations. All these supporting services were stimulated not only by the growth and demands of the middle class consumer and the continued building, but also by Bromley's development as the centre for the surrounding parishes, whose population was increasingly drawn to the shops and services offered by the town.

The places of birth of the occupied population (fig. 13) warn against the dangers of supposing, that London was the only attractive force or that only those from London settled in the suburbs. As Waugh[207] has pointed out, it was in the suburbs that the inward move from the countryside to the town met the outward movement from the city to the suburb. Evidence from the census enumerators' returns confirms the attractiveness of Bromley for migrants not only from Kent but also from a wide range of places outside the Home Counties, so that by 1871, 30.6 per cent of the occupied males and 37.4 per cent of the occupied females were born in other parts of the country. The relationship between the place of birth and occupation indicates that in 1871 the migrant born in London was likely to be a member of the middle classes seeking a suburban home in more attractive surroundings where the housing densities were lower, whilst the indigenous group, and those from Kent, tended to be found in the unskilled occupations.[208]

In spite of the mixed social composition of the parish, distinctive areas began to develop, and it is significant that it was only in New Bromley, the first new area of intensive development, that a wide variety of housing types and sizes were to be found in close proximity one to another. Thus the protest concerning drainage and public health in New Bromley came from the middle class residents who lived in close juxtaposition to those with inadequate sanitation. Later building developments were to take on a more distinctive character and the formation of the Local Board in 1867 with the specific task of improving the public health of the parish, provides an interesting example of local politics. This was mirrored in many other parishes where both high and low density developments not only separated many of the ratepayers from the problems of the parish, but also disguised the extent of the problem by providing a tolerable average death rate for the parish as a whole. The politics of the Bromley Local Board also illustrate the prevailing attitudes towards development and show the variety of alignments which took place on a wide range of issues.

Between 1841 and 1881 Bromley underwent not only growth but change. The phasing of growth was frequently subject to local circumstances but Bromley's growth was similar to that of several other small towns on the outer fringe of London. The parish in 1881 was far removed from that of 40 years before. By 1881 the middle classes were firmly entrenched on the Local Board and much of the parish had become suburbanized with many of the professional and commercial groups working in London. Rapid changes had certainly occurred and the population of the parish had practically quadrupled between 1841 and 1881 (table 1). Nevertheless several of the major estates remained, some reduced in size, but

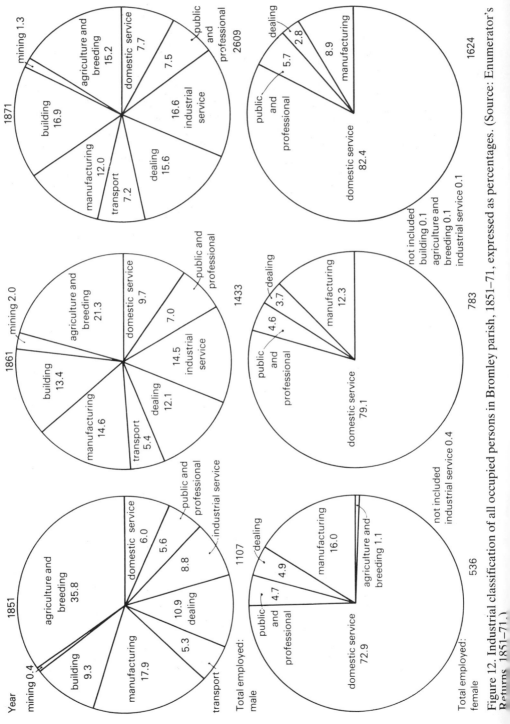

Figure 12. Industrial classification of all occupied persons in Bromley parish, 1851–71, expressed as percentages. (Source: Enumerator's Returns, 1851–71.)

Bromley: Kentish market town to London suburb, 1841–81
J.M. RAWCLIFFE

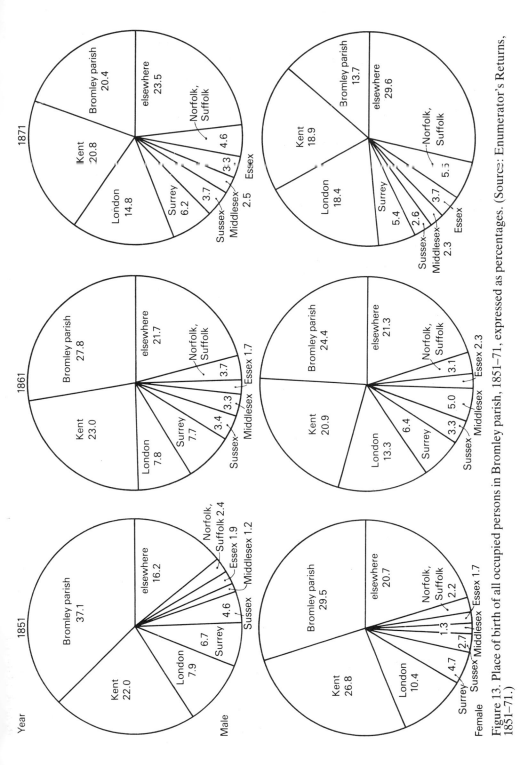

Figure 13. Place of birth of all occupied persons in Bromley parish, 1851–71, expressed as percentages. (Source: Enumerator's Returns, 1851–71.)

still important. Ribbon development had taken place along the main road from Bromley to Lewisham, but there was still a recognizable division between the two, and as late as 1921 the Ordnance Survey map showed a roughly similar stretch of open land, so that Bromley was visibly set apart from the urban area of London. Bromley was still in Kent rather than London, and even today retains a Kent postmark, though administratively part of the Greater London Council. By 1881 Bromley still retained a degree of separation from London, and was not administered by or subject to it, though it had an important group within its population which travelled into London to work. These commuters gave Bromley many of its recognizable characteristics, living in areas where the houses were at a low density per acre, and sufficiently powerful by 1881 to develop parks, maintain much of the common land, and basically retain much of the rural character of the parish albeit in a suburban form. In this they were aided by the existence of still rural parishes to the south, where much of the land has now been preserved as Green Belt. Thus by 1881 Bromley bore the hallmarks of a Victorian suburb deriving its 'essential characteristics from the nature of its resident population rather than from the jobs located in it'.[209]

After 1881 population growth never again approached the peak rate attained in the decade 1861–71 of 93.9 per cent (see table 1). Whereas the population of Bromley parish virtually doubled in those ten years, the next doubling, to 21,684 in 1891, took 20 years, and a further doubling, to 45,374 in 1931, almost 40 years; by 1961 the population had risen by half again, to 68,169. Decennial growth rates eased off from the explosion of the 1860s and the high 40 per cent rates of the 1870s and 1880s, to levels around 15 per cent in the twentieth century, and on average total population continued to increase by about 6,000 each decade. It is indeed possible to view these figures from the other end, and point out that since the 1911 population was less than half the size of the 1961 population there has been massive physical growth in the twentieth century. This growth, much of it in the interwar period and particularly in the 1930s, quite largely took place on estate land, such as the farms owned by the Bickley and Bromley Manor estates. Post-1945 development has seen some encroachment on new land, but mainly it has been at the expense of the larger houses, with their outbuildings and large gardens. Nevertheless, while the density per acre has increased, the high cost of land and houses has meant that Bromley has remained a wealthy suburb. Building land has become so scarce in the 1970s that many of the terraced houses in areas such as Bromley New Town, which were built specifically for the service groups, are now being modernized and bought by the middle classes, many of whom work in London. Hence Bromley has retained the main features of a prosperous Victorian suburb, the foundations of which have been described in this chapter.

NOTES

1 Based on J.M. Rawcliffe, 'The social and economic development of Bromley, 1841–81' (M.A. thesis, University of Kent, 1976).
2 S. Bagshaw, *History, Gazeteer and Directory of the County of Kent*, II (1847), 634.
3 *Cenus of England and Wales, 1841*. Abstract of Answers and Returns: Enumeration Abstract, Part 1.
4 *Ibid*.

5 Bagshaw, *op. cit.*, 636.
6 BPL, *Apportionment of the rent charge in lieu of Tithes in the Parish of Bromley in Kent*. Agreed 28 January 1841.
7 BPL, original notebook of G.W. Smith, Flint Cottage, Bromley Common entitled *Notes on Bromley for Mr Norman's History* (dated May 1908), 10.
8 C. Freeman, *The History, Antiquities, Improvements, etc. of the Parish of Bromley, Kent* (1832), 16–17.
9 A very useful summary of the guides and directories providing coaching information for Bromley is given in B. Taylor, 'Bromley, Beckenham, Penge, Kent, since 1750. A comparative study of the changing geography of three towns on the southern fringe of the metropolis' (Ph.D. thesis, University of London, 1965), 831–2.
10 Freeman, *op. cit.*, 20.
11 BPL, evidence of William Hawley, Minutes of Evidence given before the Select Committee of the House of Commons on Railway Bills (GroupA). The London and Croydon, Chatham and Gravesend Railway Bill, 23 June 1845 (PP 1845), 463. Hawley is clearly a typographical error as the evidence was given by William Pawley.
12 *Ibid*, 466. Another witness John Ward of Holwood, Keston said that there were only 'one tenth of the number of coaches that we had before the S.E.R. was formed': *ibid*, 455.
13 *Ibid*, 467. Evidence of W.R. Ray, corn factor and coal merchant.
14 *Ibid.*, 466.
15 *Ibid.*, 463.
16 *Ibid.*, 462.
17 BPL, *anon, A History of Bromley, in Kent, and the surrounding neighbourhood*; E. Strong, *Bromley* (1858), 6.
18 Freeman, *op. cit.*, 23.
19 Bagshaw, *op. cit.*, 635.
20 *A History of Bromley*, 7.
21 Minutes of Evidence House of Commons Select Committee on Railways Bills (Group A), 468.
22 PRO, Rail 478/1, Mid Kent Railway Company Minute Book, 21 June 1858, 262.
23 *Ibid.*, 30 June 1858, 269.
24 *A History of Bromley*, 2.
25 The letter was reprinted in the *BR*, 1 February 1864, 13–14.
26 *BR*, 1 December 1863, 202.
27 *Ibid.*, 203.
28 *Ibid.*, 1 August 1864, 78–9; report on a meeting of the South Eastern Railway Company, 22 June 1864.
29 *Ibid.*, 1 December 1872, 233.
30 *Ibid*, 1 October 1873, 45.
31 *Ibid.*, 49. The landowner in opposition was Sir Samuel Scott, a banker of Sundridge Park. He was also a director of the South Eastern Railway Company and may well have been bringing pressure to bear on the Company. William Gurley Smith was the Secretary of the People's Freehold Land Society which had been active in Plaistow.
32 *Ibid*.
33 *Ibid.*, 1 February 1874, 90: letter to the Editor, from the solicitor of the Bromley Direct Railway Company.
34 *Ibid.*, 1 April 1874, 103–4.
35 The journey from Chislehurst to Cannon Street took 22 minutes by the South Eastern Railway Company.
36 *BR*, 1 April 1874, 103–4.
37 For the population of Bromley see table 1. Beckenham's population for the years 1841–81 from 1608; 1688; 2,124; 6,090 and 13,045.
38 *BR*, 1 April 1874, 103–4.

39 *Ibid.*

40 *Ibid.*

41 *BR*, 1 July 1874, 132.

42 *Ibid.*

43 *BR*, 1 September 1875, 258.

44 *BR*, 1 September 1875, 260. Viator was William Gurley Smith of the Firs, Bromley.

45 *BR*, 1 December 1875, 286.

46 *BR*, 1 January 1878, 206.

47 G.W. Norman dealt heavily in property speculation outside the Parish having expended a total of £50,000 by the mid 1860s. He also sold St Ann's Wharf, Blackfriars to the London, Chatham & Dover Railway Company for £12,000. See G.W. Norman, *Memoranda Regarding Bromley and its neighbourhood during the Residence of our Family there* (c. 1857–80), 40.

48 *Ibid.*, 6.

49 E.L.S. Horsburgh, *Bromley, Kent from the Earliest Times to the Present Century* (1929), 204.

50 BPL, 81 a.b., sale catalogue of the Bickley Manor Extate, 1841. The sale was conducted by F. Fuller, auctioneer of 32 Poultry and Croydon, at Garraway's Coffee House, Change Alley, Cornhill on 8 October 1841. It was conducted by the assignees of Messrs Whitmore. The particulars are from the sale catalogue.

51 *Ibid.*

52 EC 5798. Survey of the Bishop of Rochester's leasehold land entitled 'The Bromley Manor Estate', 20 May 1845, 1.

53 J.W. Nokes of Abingdon Villas, Kensington, Middlesex.

54 Horsburgh, *op. cit.*, 204. Regrettably the book has no references and the original letter cannot be traced.

55 The Bromley Manor Estate was the name given to the Bishop's leasehold land. 279 acres of this were leased to Nokes, of which 89 acres were adjacent to the Palace, though he was restrained from building within 469 feet of the Bishop's boundary. The remainder of this estate consisting of another 95 acres was leased by the Bishop to other tenants.

56 EC, 2146/46: Murray to Rochester, 9 June 1846.

57 The auction was conducted by Hoggart and Norton at The Auction Mart, Tokenhouse Yard, London, where Professor Dyos states that many suburban auctions were held.

58 BPL, 81 c and d: sale catalogue, p. 2, published by Messrs Hoggart and Norton, 31 July 1846.

59 BPL, 68/11 M.225.

60 Norman, *op. cit.*, 40ff.

61 Horsburgh quoting Mrs Chalmers, *op. cit.*, 205.

62 HLRO, Vol. 35, Group M.2. 6, Select Committee of House of Lords on Private Bills: Mid Kent Direct Railway (Bromley to St Mary Cray), 7 May 1856.

63 *Ibid.*, 85.

64 *BR*, 1 July 1862, 13.

65 Examples from the Enumerators' Returns for 1871 include:

address	occupation	place of birth
10 Page Heath Lane	Deputy Secretary, Bank of England	Herts.
2 Lower Camden	architect, Poor Law Board	London (Mx)
Bullers Wood	Cape merchant (member of Lloyds)	Cape of Good Hope
The Firs, Bickley	Stock Exchange	Surrey
Thornton House	chief cashier, Bank of England	Scotland
Annandale	proprietor of *Daily Standard*	London

66 Kelly's *Post Office Directory*, 1870, 1044.

67 *Ibid*. In the 1871 census, enumeration district 13 had 64 unoccupied houses and 175 occupied. 52 of the vacant ones, a third of the Parish total, were in Bickley.
68 *BR*, 1 October 1865, 226.
69 Horsburgh, *op. cit.*, 204. BPL holds a proof copy annotated by the local historian, William Baxter, who added that Wythes was born in 1811 and was the son of Thomas Wythes of Worcester.
70 George Murray, Bishop of Rochester (1827–60). The diocese was a poor one, and Murray was also Dean of Worcester. The Bishop received the tithes as Rector of Bromley but had leased them to Wm. Leigh of Mount Radford, Exeter. In the tithe apportionment of 1841 Leigh was to receive £1,000 per year until the termination of his lease.
71 The survey was prompted by the restructuring of the diocese of Rochester, and the eventual purchase by the Bishop of Danbury Park in Essex.
72 EC, 3074/45.
73 *Ibid*.
74 EC, 1274/45: Rochester to Murray, 29 March 1845.
75 Of 8 Whitehall Place, London.
76 EC, 5798/45, 12.
77 Both the railway lines mentioned in the survey by Clutton and the one in the following year in the sale catalogue for the freehold sale by Nokes failed to materialize at this time. The importance of a rail connection with London is shown in that even the prospect of one was regarded as a selling feature.
78 EC, 5798/45, 12.
79 EC, 2969/45 2a: report by Wm Clutton, 9 July 1845.
80 *Ibid*.
81 *Ibid*.
82 *Ibid*. '3 per cents' refer to consolidated stock which gave a nominal rate of interest of 3 per cent from 1756 to 1888. In 1845 the yield from consols was 3.1 per cent and hence Clutton's suggestion that land was a better investment: B.R. Mitchell and P. Deane (eds.), *Abstract of British Historical Statistics* (1962), 455.
83 In 1841 the years purchase had been 28 years, in 1845 it has been reduced to 26. Thus the annual value of the fee simple was now £650 annual value × 26 years purchase giving a sum of £16,900, an increase of 65 per cent over the 1841 estimate.
84 EC, 5798/45, 16.
85 EC, 3521; White and Murray to Rochester, 3 October 1846. The purchase price was comprised as follows: Purchase of the Palace and Demesne £20,000, Market and Tolls etc., £275, Quit rents £250.
86 J. Thorne, *Handbook to the Environs of London* (2 vols., 1876, repr. 1970), 61.
87 *BR*, June 1863, 141.
88 Quoted by A. Briggs, *Victorian Cities* (1963), 159.
89 EC, 4461/45. The documents indicate that the reversion was calculated by the difference between the value of the fee calculated as if the estate was actually held in possession, and the value of the leasehold interest over 30 years.
90 EC, no reference number: Murray to Clutton, 15 January 1847.
91 EC, 265.2b/47; Tustin and Barlow to White and Murray, 1 February 1847.
92 *Ibid*. Between August 1846 and January 1847 the Bank of England's bullion reserve fell from £10 million to £7 million and by April 1847 was barely £3 million. F.W. Fetter, *The Development of British Monetary Orthodoxy 1797–1875* (Harvard, 1965), 204.
93 EC, 1536.2b/47; Tustin and Barlow to White and Murray, 4 May 1847. Both consols and railway shares had shown short-term fluctuations in February 1846, and April and October 1847 which corresponded with periods of stringency in the money Market: C.N. Ward-Perkins, 'The commercial crisis of 1847', Oxford Economic Papers II (1950) reprinted in *Essays in Economic History*, ed. C.M. Carus-Wilson, III (1966), 278.
94 EC, 1505: Murray to Tustin, 21 May 1847.

95 Horsburgh, *op. cit.*, 423.

96 Census enumerators' returns, 1861.

97 BPL, 40/5 M234: Abstract of Title of C.F. Devas to remainder of (Freehold) Bromley Lodge Estate 1878. This contains a summary of the leases.

98 *Ibid.*, S.F. Rolland to C.F. Devas, 29 August 1868.

99 BPL, 40/2. Significantly the catalogue which was dated 1869 was the second edition. The sale was conducted by Norton, Trist and Watney and Co. of 62 Old Broad Street, Royal Exchange.

100 *Bromley Telegraph*, 5 June 1869.

101 Wilmot lived at Bromley Lodge from 1870 to 1879.

102 BPL, Bromley Local Board Minutes, 5 June 1872, 194.

103 BPL, 40/2 F122, 15 April 1872. The contract was finally signed on 24 August 1872.

104 Details of the building development are given on pp. 56–8.

105 BPL, 40/5 F122.

106 BPL, 48/1 M107, Abstract of the Title of the British Land Company Limited to Freehold Land situate at Bromley in the County of Kent 1868.

107 The British Land Company was formed on 14 March 1856. It was a joint stock company with limited liability. Its stated object was to purchase land and improve the same by roads, drainage and houses.

108 The new roads which led off the High Road were Ringers, Ethelbert and Ravensbourne Roads. The first application to the Local Board had been made on 23 Match 1868.

109 The sale of the plots by the British Land Company is discussed on pp. 61–4.

110 R.W.C. Cox, 'Some aspects of the development of Croydon 1870–1940 (M.A. thesis, University of Leicester, 1966), 138–9.

111 *BR*, May 1859.

112 H.G. Wells, *The New Machiavelli* (1911; Penguin edn, 1966), Book One, chapter II, 'Bromstead and my Father', contains a good description of Bromley in the 1860s and 1870s.

113 BPL, 40/4 B225: Deed of Covenant, 30 November 1875 between Charles Frederick Devas of Pickhurst Manor, Hayes and the purchasers of plots of land on the Bromley Lodge Estate.

114 In Kelly's *Directory* for 1874, he was similarly described as a farmer residing at Hook Farm on Bromley Common. In the 1878 directory he is listed as a road contractor.

115 The final lot went to Messrs J.W. Smith and Broadley for whom neither address nor occupation was given. They do not appear in any of the Bromley directories, and one must assume they were from elsewhere.

116 The evidence for the year of the building of the houses and their occupiers is derived from *Directory of Bromley*, E. Strong, Bromley. This was published annually from 1864 and will be referred to as Strong's Directory.

117 BPL, 51/1 M47: Indenture between Samuel Cawston and Thomas Jones, 25 September 1884.

118 H.J.Dyos, *Victorian Suburb. A Study of the Growth of Camberwell* (1961), 115.

119 *Royal Commission on Friendly Societies* (PP 1872, XXVI), 2nd Report, para. 24. Quoted by P.H.J.H. Gosden, *Self Help: Voluntary Associations in the Nineteenth Century* (1973), 152.

120 BPL, Map 38 (undated): The Plaistow Estate – purchased for distribution among the members. Inset in the corner of the large-scale map is a smaller one showing the location of the estate.

121 Bromley Road by 1862 was called Plaistow Lane and later after the opening of Bromley North Station when a road was cut through the glebe land it was renamed College Road.

122 Gosden, *op. cit.*, 143.

123 See pp. 56–8 above.

124 The directories indicate that a tavern was never built, and the house on this site bears the date 1880, in blue brick, on its side wall.

125 25 inches to the mile, Ordnance Survey Map, 1862.
126 Amongst the occupations listed by the heads of household in the 1871 census enumerators' returns were retired builder, merchant, homeopathic chemist, traveller and annuitant.
127 Extracts from his letter to the *BR*, p. 38 above.
128 The advertisements appeared in the *BR*.
129 Strong's *Directory of Bromley*, 1880.
130 The topography of the Bromley House Estate is described on p. 52.
131 Their names appeared most frequently in applications for planning permission to the Local Board for the erection of houses in Ringers, Ethelbert and Ravensbourne Roads. Houses in these roads were first advertised in the *BR* in May 1871.
132 BPL, 49/13, various contracts and agreements. These form the basis of the evidence for the ensuing discussion.
133 One of the occupants of the newly built houses came from Frome, but this was probably no more than a coincidence.
134 Census enumerators' returns, 1871.
135 For the industrial classification and place of birth of all occupied males and females in Bromley Parish 1851–71 see figs. 12 and 13.
136 BPL map (no reference number) of Freehold Building Land, Hawksworth and Simpson's Road, 5 June 1877. Sale by auction in 19 lots by W.H. Collier at the White Hart Inn, Bromley.
137 BPL, 48/2 M54. The five deeds were of houses which were later acquired by Bromley Council through compulsory purchase for road widening.
138 BPL, 48/2 M54: mortgage dated 19 September 1878. The trustees were named as J. Verinder, 14 Sun Street, Finsbury, Middlesex, oil and colour merchant; J. Johnson, Jasmine Grove, Penge, builder; and J. Cooper, Weighton Road, South Penge Park, gentleman.
139 *Ibid.*, 30 June 1882.
140 *BR*, July 1861. 95 per cent mortgages were offered over nine years at 5 per cent interest.
141 *BR*, July 1873.
142 *BR*, June 1859.
143 *BR*, November 1868, 46–7: report of a meeting held in the Iron Room, Bromley, 10 October 1868. The majority of houses of this type in Bromley were two up and two down.
144 *Ibid.*
145 *BR*, January 1869, 64.
146 The Bickley Park Estate and the work of George Wythes have been discussed earlier: see p. 44 above.
147 BPL, Sale Catalogue no. 84: Baxter Payne and Lepper, 16 October 1878.
148 *Ibid.*
149 *Ibid.*
150 Several of the major auctions of land in Bromley were held in London. The auction of part of the Bickley Park Estate in 1846 was held at The Mart, Tokenhouse Yard. Baxter and Payne frequently auctioned their more important properties there, and usually attracted a London purchaser.
151 *BR*, March 1867.
152 *BR*, May 1871.
153 *BR*, May 1867.
154 *BR*, August 1867.
155 *BR*, November 1867.
156 *BR*, June 1866.
157 E. Gauldie, *Cruel Habitations: a history of working class housing, 1780–1918* (1974), 182. The local evidence is similar to that found by Gauldie.
158 BPL, L43.1a, 1863 Bromley Parish Valuation Lists 1863 and 1872; and W.E. Baxter,

The Domesday Book for the County of Kent being a return of the owners of land (1877). This is based on the returns of the owners of land in 1873, which were taken from the 1872 returns collected by the Clerks of the Guardians in September 1872. It contains several inaccuracies. The returns made to the Local Government Board were published as *Returns of Ownership of Land in Kent 1873* (PP 1875).

159 In the 1851 census enumerators' returns Richard Barrett described himself as a builder, born in Philbourne in Kent. He lived in the High Street with his wife and one 16-year-old domestic servant.

160 In the 1851 census enumerators' returns Charles Muffett described himself as a master carpenter, employing 14. He was Bromley-born, aged 35 and had one 16-year-old domestic servant.

161 1872 valuation list.

162 In the 1851 census enumerators' returns William Morum described himself as a builder, born in Bromley. In 1851 he was 48 and had one son apprenticed to him. He lived in a small terraced house in Centenary Place.

163 1863 valuation list.

164 *BR*, April 1868, 229. Report of the meeting of Bromley Local Board, 25 March 1868. The newspaper accounts were often in far greater detail than the Local Board minute books.

165 BPL, 61/M202: will of Thomas Wells, dated 24 October 1887. Wells died in 1901.

166 *BR*, June 1867.

167 Will of Thomas Wells.

168 The will had no additions after it was first drawn up in 1887.

169 *Memoir of Martha Ann Howlett* (c. 1905), in private hands.

170 *Ibid.*, 337.

171 *Ibid.*, 349.

172 *Ibid.*, 362.

173 *Ibid*. In 1901 they were sold at auction and fetched £695 for the pair.

174 *Ibid*.

175 *Ibid*.

176 *Ibid.*, 404.

177 He rented 2 Palace Grove for £60 *per annum*.

178 Howlett Memoir, 406. A marginal comment by a relative after Martha's death in 1913 added that in 1920 the family sold one of these houses, which was in a poor state of repair for £700, and the other for £1,135 in 1923.

179 *Ibid.*, 407. In a later renumbering no. 30 became no. 83.

180 *Ibid.*, 408.

181 In Camberwell, Professor Dyos found that approximately 90 per cent of the houses were built by speculative builders. Dyos, *op. cit.*, 137.

182 The individuals cited were only examples. Others included Richard Eaton, butcher, who in 1872 owned 14½ acres which brought in a gross estimated rental of £357 and Thomas Satchell, plumber whose acre of land in Chatterton and Pope Roads was worth £245 in estimated rental: valuation list 1872.

183 Gauldie, *op. cit.*, 182.

184 Kellett, *op. cit.*, 393.

185 Strong's *Directory of Bromley* was published annually between 1864 and 1897 but no copies of the issues for 1865, 1867, 1868, 1871, 1872 have survived. The 1871 census enumerators' returns give all the occupants of the houses. Both sources reflect occupancy rather than ownership, but for certain roads such as Simpson's Road deeds remain which enable one to confirm the latter.

186 Kellett, *op. cit.*, 409.

187 Dyos, *op. cit.*, 90.

188 Census enumerators' returns, 1861 and 1871. R.S. Holmes, 'Ownership and migration from a study of rate books', *Area*, v (1973), 242–51, has shown that in the early 1850s

one-third of the houses in Ramsgate had a change of occupier every two years.

189 At times it did not represent the developments which were taking place. For instance no houses in Bickley were advertised in the local newspapers though the district was developing rapidly. This no doubt reflects the fact that certain districts were attracting people from outside the parish, who did not get their information from the local press, which concentrated naturally on opportunities for local people.

190 The total number of houses in Beckenham was as follows: 372 in 1861; 1,099 in 1871; 2,170 in 1881.

191 J. Parry-Lewis, *Building Cycles and Britain's Growth* (1965), 101.

192 *Ibid.,* 100.

193 Thorne, *op. cit.*, 36.

194 *Ibid.*, 37.

195 *Ibid.*, 125–8.

196 *Ibid.*, 467.

197 *Ibid.*, 132.

198 E. Hasted, *The History and Topographical Survey of the County of Kent*, I (1797), 550–70.

199 C. Greenwood, *An Epitome of County History,* I; *County of Kent* (1838), 34ff.

200 W.H. Ireland, *A New and Complete History of the County of Kent*, IV (1830), 623.

201 *Ibid.*, 622.

202 M. Waugh, 'Suburban growth in North West Kent 1861–1961' (Ph.D. thesis, University of London, 1968), 95.

203 An excellent discussion of suburban growth is provided by D. Mills in *The Spread of Cities* (DT 201, Unit 24, Open University, 1975).

204 Waugh, *op. cit.*, 25.

205 R.C.W. Cox, 'The old centre of Croydon. Victorian decay and redevelopment', in *Perspectives in English Urban History*, ed. A. Everitt (1973), 186.

206 E.H. Hunt, *Regional Wage Variations in Britain, 1850–1914* (1973).

207 Waugh, *op. cit.*, 88.

208 See chapters 3 and 4 of Rawcliffe, *op. cit.*

209 Waugh, *op. cit.*, 25–6.

Suburban development in outer west London 1850–1900

MICHAEL JAHN

Suburban development in outer west London, 1850–1900[1]

MICHAEL JAHN

During the last half of the nineteenth century the population of London increased from some 2.3 to 6.6 million. In 1850 the edge of the urban area beyond which building extended along many of the main roads, lay about three miles from Charing Cross. Fifty years later the outer margins of London were from five to ten miles from the centre. To the west the suburban frontier had advanced from Kensington and Hammersmith to beyond the river Brent, and the hitherto largely rural communities of the area had almost coalesced to become residential districts of London.[2] This study examines the process of suburban development in Acton, Chiswick, Ealing, and Hanwell.

The outer western suburbs were sufficiently far from inner London for the nature of railway services to have been a significant influence on the course of residential building. Recent work has emphasized the importance of local employment opportunities in accounting for suburban population increase, and of means of transport other than the railways in the development of inner London suburbs and those of provincial cities.[3] For the outer metropolitan districts, however, the railway was, before the advent of electric tramways, the only effective means of transport for most daily travellers to inner London. By 1900 outer west London was traversed by two main-line companies (the Great Western and London & South Western) and two (the District and North London) whose operations were confined to the metropolitan region. The varying responses by landowners and developers in different parts of the area to the opportunities for suburban development will be discussed in the context both of the policies of railway and tramway companies and of the London building cycle.

Building in outer west London took place under differing forms of tenure. On the Wood property in north Ealing, on the Goldsmiths' Company's East Acton estate, and to a large extent on the lands of the Dukes of Devonshire and the Ecclesiastical Commissioners at Chiswick, for example, development was by means of 99-year leases. Much building land on adjacent properties was sold freehold and extensive tracts, particularly in Acton, were acquired by land companies for subdivision and resale. By the end of the century the various districts of the area

94

Table 9 Population growth in outer west London, 1841–1911

	(1) Acton	(2) Chiswick	(3) Ealing	(4) Hanwell	(5) (1) to (4)	(6) Brentford	(7) (5) + (6)
1841	2,665	5,811	3,349	1,469	13,294	7,232	20,526
1851	2,582	6,303	3,771	1,547	14,203	8,120	22,323
1861	3,151	6,505	5,215[a]	2,687	17,558	8,743	26,301
1871	8,306	8,508	9,959	3,766	30,539	10,273	40,812
1881	17,126	15,975[b]	15,764[c]	5,178	54,043	11,810	65,853
1891	24,206	21,963	23,979	6,139	76,287	13,738	90,025
1901	37,744	29,809	33,031	10,438	111,022	15,171	126,193
1911	57,497	38,697	61,222	19,129	176,545	16,571	193,116

[a] Population of Ealing Local Board area (1863–73): 4,954 in 1861; 9,959 in 1871.
[b] Including detached portion of Ealing at Bedford Park, transferred to Chiswick 1878.
Population within 1871 boundaries: 15,663.
[c] Less detached portion mentioned in b. Population within 1871 boundaries: 16,076.

Table 10 Population in outer west London: decennial percentage increase

	(1) Acton	(2) Chiswick	(3) Ealing	(4) Hanwell	(5) (1) to (4)	(6) Brentford	(7) (5) + (6)
1841–51	−3	8	13	5	7	12	9
1851–61	22	3	38	74[a]	24	8	18
1861–71	164	31	91	40	74	17	55
1871–81	106	88[b]	58[b]	37	77	15	61
1881–91	41	37	52	19	41	16	37
1891–1901	56	46	38	70	46	10	40
1901–11	52	30	85	83	59	9	53

[a] Increase mainly attributable to opening of Central London District Schools.
[b] Within 1881 boundaries (see footnotes b and c to table 9).

Table 11 Houses in outer west London, 1841–1911

	(1) Acton	(2) Chiswick	(3) Ealing	(4) Hanwell	(5) (1) to (4)
1841	497	1,114	657	263	2,531
1851	537	1,184	711	306	2,738
1861	649	1,265	1,007	335	3,256
1871	1,863	1,627	1,885	518	5,893
1881	3,236	3,057[a]	2,861[b]	809	9,963
1891	4,461	4,021	4,481	1,173	14,136
1901	6,540	5,308	6,435	2,025	20,308
1911	9,935	7,079	12,959	3,605	33,578

[a] 2,955 within 1871 boundaries.
[b] 2,963 within 1871 boundaries.

Table 12   Houses in outer west London: decennial percentage increase

	(1) Acton	(2) Chiswick	(3) Ealing	(4) Hanwell	(5) (1) to (4)
1841–51	8	6	8	16	8
1851–61	21	7	42	9	19
1861–71	187	29	87	55	81
1871–81	74	88[a]	52[a]	56	69
1881–91	38	32	57	45	42
1891–1901	47	32	44	73	44
1901–11	52	33	101	78	65

[a] Within 1881 boundaries (see footnotes b and c to table 9).

Note to tables 11 and 12
The increase in the number of structurally separate dwellings is greater than shown here, particularly after 1881, since flats are not separately enumerated.

Table 13   House building in outer west London, 1870–1900

Year	Acton (1)	Ealing (2)	Ealing (3)	Ealing (4)	Wood estate (Ealing) (5)
1870		84			
1871		61			
1872		82			
1873	41	75			
1874	17	47			
1875	47	54			8
1876	85	30			8
1877	115	52			42
1878	151	178			49
1879	349	170			37
1880	295		121		46
1881	111		214		83
1882	115		125		49
1883	65		256		40
1884	60		184		72
1885	69		174		48
1886	79		134		30
1887	111[a]		124		20
1888	55		174	106	
1889	58			110	
1890	69			108	
1891	234[b]			50	
1892	130[c]			102	
1893	130			131	
1894	128			133	
1895	103			144	
1896	311			240	
1897	473			396	
1898	307			495	
1899	507			526	
1900	300			522	

[a] Includes permit for 14 houses to be built by Atlas Brick & Tile Co. near Willesden Junction.
[b] Includes permit for 36 houses to be built by London & North Western Railway near Willesden Junction.
[c] Includes 13 railway cottages.

(1) Building permits for houses: Acton plans registers (1873: from April).
(2) Houses built: *Middlesex County Times*, 28 August 1880.
(3) Building plans for houses: Ealing plans register. It is not clear whether entries are for plans deposited or only for approvals. The register from which the series was compiled was not available for the original transcription made for my thesis to be checked.
(4) Building permits for houses: J. Parry Lewis, *Building Cycles and Britain's Growth* (1965), 311, based on annual reports of Ealing Surveyor, from which 1900–1 figure obtained. Figures are for the period from 1 April to 31 March of the following year (cols. 1–3 and 5 are for calendar year).
(5) Leases granted: Middlesex Land Registry 1888/6/784. 29 leases granted between 1852 and 1868 are also recorded.

Note to cols. (1) and (3)
These figures have been presented to give an approximate idea of the level of building, and should not be regarded as exact. Plans for some houses, for instance, may have been approved more than once, and it is not always possible to distinguish between shops and houses.

under consideration had acquired distinct social characteristics. The following account is an attempt to outline by means of an examination of changes in transport facilities and in the nature of building on individual estates how this social differentiation came about.

1 The transition towards a suburban environment

By the early nineteenth century the pattern of land use in west Middlesex, between seven and eleven miles west of the City, already reflected the influence of the metropolis. The terrace gravels and brickearth on the north bank of the Thames were mostly occupied by orchards and market gardens, together with the parkland of private estates.[4] A contrast in the pattern of land ownership was evident between the small properties in the market garden area and the large, compact estates on the clayland north of the Uxbridge Road. The principal exceptions were the estates surrounding such villas as Ealing Park, Boston House and Gunnersbury Park in the south of the area; in Chiswick the Devonshire estate around Chiswick House comprised over half the parish. On the northern claylands and the Hanger Hill ridge the Wood family, whose principal property was in Corve Dale, Shropshire, owned over 920 acres in Ealing and north-west Acton. Some 750 acres of this formed a compact estate.[5] The land ownership pattern was of fundamental importance in determining the course of suburban growth. Low-density development by building lease was particularly characteristic of large estates whose owners had the resources to undertake the gradual and controlled transformation of their properties into middle-class residential districts. Some of the problems involved in this process will be illustrated from the records of the Goldsmiths' Company relating to its East Acton estate.

The only community of urban rank within the area at the opening of the century was Brentford. One of its principal industries was brewing, and in the 1840s there were also timber yards, a soap factory, and a gas works.[6] Throughout the nineteenth century the town retained its industrial character, and as such failed to become a focus for the middle-class building typical of neighbouring centres such as Ealing and Turnham Green. Like Brentford, the latter were both situated on a main road leading westwards from London, Turnham Green on the turnpike to Staines and Ealing extending southwards from that to Uxbridge. Although in 1838–9 there were fewer than ten omnibuses and short-stage coaches licensed to ply between Ealing and the City, some 40 were operating between Turnham Green and

London.[7] By 1850 the succession of buildings, on one side or another of the road, approached continuity from the margins of London at Notting Hill through Hammersmith and Turnham Green to Brentford, while in both Chiswick and Ealing the beginnings of suburban building were becoming apparent.

The two latter parishes in particular had already by the opening of the century come to be regarded as desirable locations for residences within easy reach of London. Chiswick House was the most architecturally distinguished of numerous country villas built in this part of Middlesex before the suburban era. Its park was adjoined by the grounds of smaller mansions such as Corney House and Sutton Court. The Georgian terraces along the Thames at Hammersmith are continued westward by building from the same period on Chiswick Mall and near the parish church. Substantial houses from the late eighteenth and early nineteenth centuries still front parts of Ealing Green, where in 1800 Pitzhanger Manor was bought by the architect John Soane and then rebuilt for his own use. Early in the nineteenth century the Duke of Kent, father of Queen Victoria, resided at Castle Hill Lodge on the southern slopes of the Hanger Hill ridge, while to the south-east of the village centre Elm Grove was occupied in the first decade of the century by the prime minister Spencer Perceval. Gunnersbury Park, a royal residence in the eighteenth century, was acquired in 1835 by a branch of the Rothschild family. In 1840 the tithe report for Ealing noted the 'considerable breadth of Villa and Park like grounds' in the parish.[8]

Although the villages of Acton and Hanwell were by the earlier nineteenth century both adjoined by the grounds of several residential properties, neither parish was regarded in contemporary accounts as possessing the social or topographic advantages of Ealing and Chiswick.[9] Hanwell's prospects for developing in a manner similar to that of Ealing were subsequently regarded as having been compromised first by the opening in 1831 of a large county lunatic asylum immediately to the west, and then between 1854 and 1856 both by the appropriation of land in the parish for cemeteries for Kensington and Saint George, Westminster, and by the establishment of the Central London District Schools, which came to house over one thousand poor-law pupils. At least three attempts were made before the end of the century to rename either the parish or the asylum in the belief that prospective residents of Hanwell were deterred by its associations with the institution.[10] By then the character of Hanwell had in any case been influenced by the building of small houses for local workers, while in comparison with Ealing its communications with inner London had remained much less inviting to middle-class residents.

In 1838 the railway came to west Middlesex with the opening of the Great Western. Eleven years later services began on the London & South Western Hounslow loop, which left the line to Richmond and Windsor at Barnes and rejoined it after passing through Chiswick and Brentford. During the 1840s and 1850s the Great Western, in common with most other main-line companies, made little attempt to develop suburban traffic. For 30 years after the opening of the line Ealing, nearly six miles from Paddington, remained the first station beyond the terminus. In 1850 the first train from Hanwell and Ealing arrived at Paddington (itself nearly four miles by congested roads from the City) at 9.05 a.m., while that leaving the terminus at 7 p.m. was the last of the evening for suburban stations. Trains on the London and South Western loop line were little more frequent: an hourly service was provided from Waterloo between 5.15 and 8.15 p.m. Third class

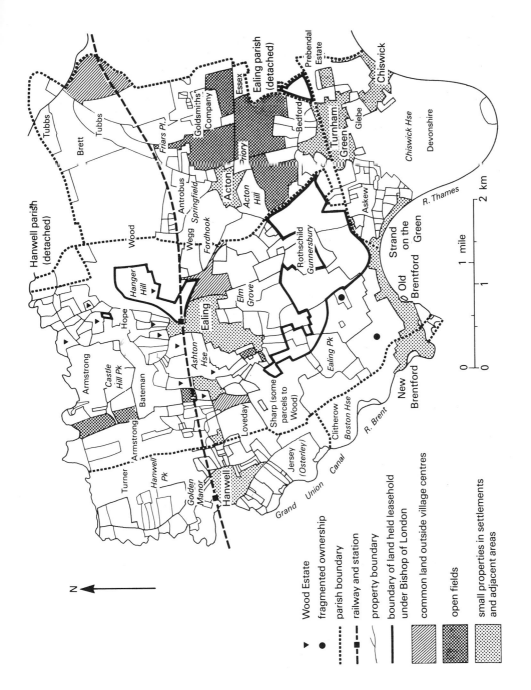

Figure 14. Outer west London land ownership in the 1840s. (Source: Tithe appprtionment surveys: see n. 4.) Dates of apportionments: Acton 1844; Chiswick 1847; Ealing (with Old Brentford) 1841; Hanwell 1838; New Brentford 1839.

accommodation was provided on neither of these Great Western trains and on only some of those run by the London & South Western.[11]

An Act was obtained in 1851 for a third railway across the area, from Willesden on the London & North Western to Kew on the Hounslow loop of the London & South Western. This was the North and South Western Junction, promoted by the two main line companies and opened two years later as a link for goods traffic between their respective systems.[12] An agreement was subsequently made with the North London company (in which the London & North Western were majority shareholders) by which the passenger service of the latter was extended in 1853 from Hampstead Road (Chalk Farm) via Willesden over the North & South Western Junction to Kew. The North London had originally been promoted to provide access from the London & North Western to the London docks, and until its new terminus at Broad Street was opened in 1865 the railway suffered the disadvantage of a very circuitous approach to the City. Only a few carriages ran through from Kew and Acton to the terminus at Fenchurch Street. It was usually necessary to change at Hampstead Road and subsequently at Camden Road, following the diversion of the service in 1860 on to the newly-opened Hampstead Junction Railway, a loop line of the North London from Willesden via Brondesbury to Kentish Town. The initial North London service on to the North & South Western Junction was furthermore even less frequent than that provided by the Great Western from Paddington. In 1860 the earliest morning connection for Fenchurch Street did not reach the terminus until 8.55 a.m., the journey from Acton occupying an hour.[13]

By the 1850s the Great Western was realizing the need for a terminus nearer the City. In 1860 the directors observed in reply to a memorial from Ealing residents for an additional train that there was little likelihood of increased traffic until the Metropolitan Railway was completed, when a more frequent service would be introduced. Twenty years later the Great Western's general manager was to concede that 'no doubt . . . for a period of years [none of] . . . the stations near London (say between Paddington and Slough) had anything like the service which they ought to have had'.[14] The Metropolitan was opened in 1863 from Paddington, where a junction with the Great Western was provided, to Farringdon Street (extended to Moorgate Street in 1865). £185,000 of the initial capital had been subscribed by the Great Western under an agreement of 1853, in return for through running of the latter company's trains. The original Metropolitan rolling stock was also provided by the Great Western. Almost immediately after the opening of the railway, however, conflict developed between the two companies as to the number of trains to be run through from the main line.[15] An agreement of 1868 permitted 12 through trains in each direction, of which not more than seven were to be goods trains. In 1872 a total of only about four passenger trains appear to have run daily between the main line and the Metropolitan.[16]

In 1866 the Great Western suburban service compared unfavourably with that on other railways in the area. No suburban train left Paddington between 5.30 and 6.30 p.m., while the first such train in the morning arrived at Farringdon Street at 8.48 a.m., the next following about an hour later. An intermediate train reached Paddington at 8.55 a.m., but the only other Great Western suburban train to arrive in London before 10 a.m. was one on a newly-established service from Southall and Ealing via the West London line to Victoria. In contrast five trains arrived at Waterloo from the London & South Western loop line before 10 a.m., while the

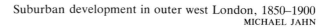

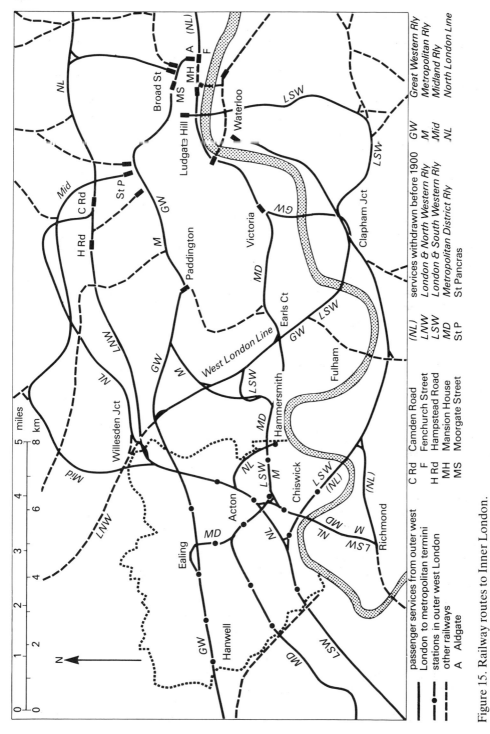

Figure 15. Railway routes to Inner London.

North London introduced a 30-minute interval morning and evening service following the opening in 1865 of its Broad Street terminus.[17] This frequency was doubled on the section between the City and Willesden. The improvement to the North London Service to Acton coincides with the first local boom in speculative building during the 1860s.

It was during the 1850s that the sale and lease of land for building began to alter the character of Ealing from that of an essentially rural community, even if influenced in its landscape and social composition by proximity to London, to that of a predominantly middle-class residential suburb. Early in the decade the Conservative Freehold Land Society purchased the Ealing Rectory estate.[18] Situated near the southern extremity of Ealing village, this was about 15 minutes' walk from the Great Western station. In 1853 the society unsuccessfully applied for season ticket concessions to be granted to purchasers of plots on the estate. By the mid 1860s five roads had been constructed across the estate, but only about twenty houses completed.[19] These were mostly detached or semi-detached villas on frontages of about 30 feet, and assessed in 1870 at between £30 and £50. To the north of Ealing station, some five acres of land at Castlebar Hill was sold in 1852 for about £255 per acre.[20] Most had been let for building by the end of the decade in plots from 40 to 50 feet wide. Within the old village, The Park was laid out as a residential street in 1846 by the architect Sydney Smirke,[21] while the development on 99-year leases of part of the Ashton House estate, to the west of the village centre, began the same year. Here large villas were built on frontages of up to 50 feet along Uxbridge Road and Mattock Lane.[22] The character of the new suburban estates in Ealing can to some extent be illustrated from the 1861 census. In Craven Villas, a group of large semi-detached houses on the Wood property along the north side of the Uxbridge Road, the average number of servants per household was 2.5. Of the ten heads of families, half were retired or of independent means, as were nine of 14 householders present on the Ashton House estate immediately to the south.[23] Communications were evidently still inadequate for the needs of most professional people working in inner London.

During the 1850s it was only in Ealing among the parishes of outer west London that the development of building estates for prospective suburban residents began. In Acton and Chiswick, although both were closer to inner London, the sale or lease of property for building on any significant scale did not commence until the following decade. In Acton the sale of land around the village centre and the North London station was hindered by the failure of earlier attempts to enclose the four open fields, while in Chiswick the existence of the 650-acre Devonshire estate effectively prevented building around the adjacent London & South Western station. Towards the end of the decade, however, statutory changes were secured that were recognized at the time as preliminary to the process of suburban development. In Chiswick a local Act of 1858[24] provided for the establishment of a board of Improvement Commissioners to supplement and in part take over the work of the existing parish authorities, while in Acton the open fields were at last enclosed. By 1856 a special committee appointed by the Royal Society was referring to the potential value of its south Acton property as suburban building land. Under the 1859 enclosure award 25 owners secured apportionments, and the number of parcels was reduced from 399 to 50.[25] By 1868 about one third of the 327 acres so enclosed had been sold for building, and the transformation of Acton from village to suburb was rapidly beginning.

2 The first boom, 1860–75

Three distinct cycles of building activity in suburban London have been recognized for the last 40 years of the nineteenth century. Upswings were to about 1868, 1881 and 1899 and downward movements to about 1873, 1891 and during the later 1900s.[26] The suburban boom of the 1860s corresponds to the beginning of development on a significant scale in outer west London. Much of this building took place on leasehold estates, but of equal importance were the properties of freehold land companies. Freehold land societies had originally come into existence as a means of altering the political balance in county constituencies; but by the early 1850s, when over 60 such societies were operating in the London area, estates were being purchased and subdivided essentially as a means of creating suburban building plots. The building operations of those to whom the plots were sold, usually on an initial payment of ten per cent of the purchase price, were then financed by the freehold society through loans on the security of the land and the houses in the course of erection. After 1856 the acquisition and sale of land was carried out for some of the largest societies by an associated joint-stock company, in the case of the National Freehold Land Society by the British Land Company.[27] The role of freehold land societies and companies in the provision of housing in London during the later nineteenth century merits further investigation. Their principal function appears to have become less the promotion of working-class home ownership than the preparation of sites and the provision of finance for speculative building. The social characteristics of particular land company properties were to a considerable extent influenced by the initial plot layout and restrictions on the nature of building, both of which varied from one estate to another. Although most building seems to have been for artisans or the lower middle class, some properties were also developed for low-rental housing and others for middle-class villas.

The British Land Company was the largest such organization operating in the metropolitan area. In the early 1860s it was purchasing estates in towns throughout south-eastern England, but its activities were principally concentrated near London, in districts made increasingly accessible by new railways and improvements to existing services. In the single year 1867, for example, 23 estates were acquired on the margins of London, from Barnet and Enfield to Wimbledon and Dulwich.[28] From a figure of £33,529 in 1857 the expenditure of the company rose to £191,489 in 1867, after which purchases diminished rapidly during the early 1870s. By 1872 the depression forced a general reduction in land prices on the company's estates, and the following year building leases were being granted on its Highbury property as a temporary measure in view of the difficulties in selling land outright.[29] In 1859 the British Land Company acquired its first estate in outer west London, with the purchase of 85 acres at Acton Hill.[30] During the following decade it bought eight other properties in Acton and Chiswick. Building plots on estates in the area were also provided by the Birkbeck Freehold Land Society and, in the 1880s, the National Liberal Land Company. At first, as at Acton Hill and on the Birkbeck Society's land near the North London station, much building was for middle-class occupation. Lower-rental housing subsequently came to predominate on land company estates in the area, and in south Acton a new working-class district was created.

A considerable portion of the Acton Hill estate, including the house itself, was resold without prior division into plots almost immediately after its acquisition by the British Land Company,[31] presumably because the development even of the remaining 50 acres was at this stage highly speculative. Frontages on Mill Hill Road and Avenue Road were mostly of 30 to 40 feet, although the minimum cost of any houses erected was to be only £150. The sale of land began in March 1860 with the auction of 42 plots fronting Gunnersbury Lane and the north side of Mill Hill Road. Most of the property seems to have been sold fairly rapidly, but other auctions of land further from the centre of Acton were less successful. About half the plots on a second portion of the estate were taken at a sale the following month, while in July only seven out of 39 plots were disposed of in an auction of land on the north side of Avenue Road. Most of the purchasers of plots on the estate were local residents, including many tradesmen, particularly those engaged in the building industry. Of 63 plots sold by the British Land Company in 1860, 45 were obtained by residents of Acton and 6 by those of the west London suburbs of Paddington, Kensington, Hammersmith, and Fulham. Thirty individuals bought plots, of whom 16 bought only one each and nine two each, no purchaser obtaining more than ten.[32]

By 1868 a further 89 acres had been acquired in Acton by the British Land Company.[33] The implicit optimism over the possibilities for suburban development in the area is clearly associated with the general London building boom of the period. By 1866 building at Acton Hill had taken place along about two-thirds of the Avenue Road frontage. Most of these houses were semi-detached or even detached villas. On the narrower frontages of Church Road and the Grove House estate, closer to the centre of Acton, building was well advanced, whereas on Park Road East and North, further from the village centre and the station, many vacant plots remained. Although the North London service to Camden Road and Fenchurch Street had been improved during the earlier 1860s,[34] the major shortening of the journey time and increase in frequency did not occur until 1865. It is likely, however, that the prospect of this improvement affected the sale of land from 1861, when the Act for the Broad Street extension was obtained.

To the north-east of the village centre of Acton, mostly on the far side of the North London line and with a frontage on the south to the Uxbridge Road, lay the property of the Goldsmiths' Company. This comprised in 1860 237 acres, of which 228 acres formed part of a trust administered by the Company under the Charity Commissioners.[35] The hamlet of East Acton, part of which was owned by the Company, and which already contained a number of middle-class residents, lay near the centre of the estate. The southern part of the property lay on the well-drained brick earth zone; the northern extended over the London Clay. Less than three years after the 1859 enclosure award part of the former Church Field, near the North London station, was bought by the Goldsmiths' Company for about £450 per acre.[36] This land was the first portion of the East Acton estate to be laid out for speculative building, the beginning of a gradual process of transformation from agricultural land to residential district that was to last until well into the following century (fig. 19).

A draft plan of 1864 provided for 81 houses to be built on three roads cutting across the 15-acre site in a simple rectangular pattern. There was to be a graduated rental scale while building was in progress, ranging from £50 in the first and second years to the full rent of £400 in the eighth and successive years. The scheme was scheduled for completion within six years, a stipulated number of houses to be completed each year.[37] This first attempt by the Company to secure the develop-

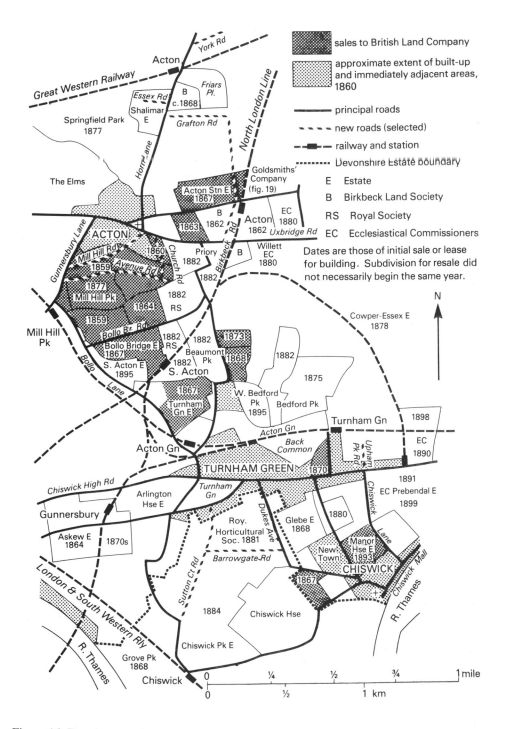

sales to British Land Company

approximate extent of built-up and immediately adjacent areas, 1860

—— principal roads

– – – new roads (selected)

–■– railway and station

········· Devonshire Estate boundary

E   Estate

B   Birkbeck Land Society

RS   Royal Society

EC   Ecclesiastical Commissioners

Dates are those of initial sale or lease for building. Subdivision for resale did not necessarily begin the same year.

N

Figure 16. Development in Acton and Chiswick.

105

ment of part of its estate was unsuccessful. Negotiations with the prospective lessee broke down, possibly over a problem that was to hinder the progress of building throughout the next 25 years: that of obtaining adequate main drainage. The Company's surveyor, the architect Philip Hardwick, advocated laying a sewer eastwards along the Uxbridge Road to join the London main drainage system within the Metropolitan Board of Works area. This would meet the immediate needs of the Churchfield land and permit the eventual development of 70 acres fronting the road.[38] In 1865 the application was rejected by the Board on the grounds that it had always refused to drain beyond its boundary.[39] It suggested instead that the Goldsmiths' Company obtain an Act for the inclusion of its estate within the Metropolitan Board of Works area.

By 1868 the Company had come to a fresh agreement for the Churchfield site. Its new lessee was George Smith, a Kensington builder who had been engaged in operations on the Cromwell Road.[40] The revised layout was slightly more imaginative than in the 1864 scheme, detached houses being intermixed with semi-detached in a curving rather than rectangular road pattern. As in subsequent building agreements on the East Acton estate, roads and sewers were to be made by the lessee. Concern by the Goldsmiths' Company to control the character of the estate is evident: no terraces were permitted except in the case of shops and stables (which were carefully segregated), while the minimum value of detached houses was to be £800 and of semi-detached £600.[41] Simultaneously the Company purchased to the north of the main line from Paddington the 12-acre Friars estate which was immediately made the subject of an agreement with the same lessee for an ambitious building scheme. The Goldsmiths' Company paid £8,000 for the site, which was adjacent to the Great Western station for Acton opened the same year. This price was double that for which the property had changed hands 16 years before.[42] It was at this period also that the Birkbeck Land Society purchased its Horn Lane estate to the south of the station and that building projects at Leamington Park and York Road and the development of the nearby Shalimar estate were begun.[43] From the terms of the Friars estate agreement the Goldsmiths' Company appears to have had very optimistic expectations as to the possible progress of building. The lease applied to the entire site with the exception of the mansion and immediately surrounding grounds, and the conditions were even more rigorous than in the new Churchfield agreement. Only private residences were permitted, and the values of the semi-detached and detached houses to be built on the 11 acres were respectively to be not less than £700 and £900. Development was to be completed in six years.[44]

Building on the new estates can hardly be considered to have been actively encouraged by the train service for Acton provided by the Great Western. In 1871 there were only two trains for Acton leaving Paddington between 4.30 and 7 p.m., in contrast to seven leaving Broad Street for Acton on the North London during approximately the same period.[45] Within one year of the commencement of the Friars agreement it had become obvious that the lessee would be unable to carry it out. His mortgagees (James Wright and G.L.P. Eyre) submitted proposals to the Goldsmiths' Company for the assignment to them of the agreements. Wright and Eyre evidently regarded the continuation of building at the Friars as hopeless, and stated that they wished to confine their interests to building and brickmaking on the Churchfield site, where six pairs of houses had been erected. The latter estate was accordingly relet in 1870, the third building agreement for the site in six years. The terms were generally similar to those of 1868, with a slight reduction in the ultimate ground rent, from about £40 to £38 per acre.[46] Meanwhile the Goldsmiths' Company had apparently concluded that the attempt to develop the Friars site had been premature. In 1870 it was relet for 14 years together with the mansion, although the lessors were to have the option of resuming possession of about half the estate after seven years, in case the prospects for building then looked more promising. In fact the property was relet in 1884 for a further seven years and eventually was sold to Acton Council for £13,400 in 1902 for use among other purposes as an isolation hospital, despite protests that this would depreciate the value of adjacent land.[47] By then it seems that the Goldsmiths' Company had become sufficiently disillusioned by its experience in attempting to develop other portions of its estate to be glad of the chance of disposing of the site on reasonable terms.

In the view of the Goldsmiths' Company it was the kind of development permitted on some land company estates that was one of the principal obstacles to progress on its own property. At auctions from 1862 onwards land south of Acton Hill was sold by the British Land Company in plots with 15-foot frontages to Enfield Road and the western part of Osborne Road,[48] while even on 30-foot plots much building in this locality was of a different standard from that on most estates of significant size developed hitherto in outer west London. In 1866 the Acton Local Board was constituted, principally to secure some control over new building and to provide for an adequate drainage system. Three years later it appointed a committee to investigate conditions on the South Acton estate of the British Land Company.[49] Laundering was one of the first industries to develop in the area, possibly in part to supplement seasonal fluctuations in the earnings of families where men were employed in the brickfields and building trade. In 1872 over 60

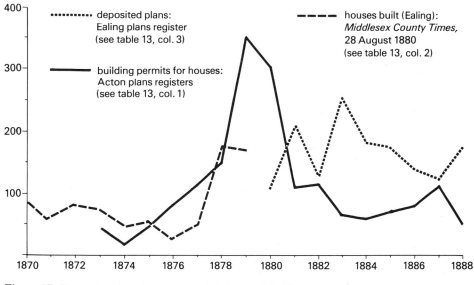

Figure 17. House building in Acton and Ealing, 1870–88.

laundries were established in South Acton, most being on the premises of private houses, and by the end of the century Acton contained between 200 and 300, the industry giving employment to over 3,000 residents of the suburb, of whom four-fifths were women.[50] The cause of concern to the Local Board was not the laundries but other establishments such as slaughterhouses in what was becoming a densely populated residential district. By 1881 it was reported to the council that nearly 1,200 pigs were being kept in the area. Numerous objections had been received over the maintenance of manure heaps and the boiling and crushing of bones. A prosecution for the latter nuisance seems to have resulted in the removal from the area to Northolt of at least one such works.[51] In 1877 the British Land Company property at south Acton was described as

> all cut up into small plots of 20 feet frontages . . . let out without any restrictions or covenants as to the class of buildings that may be put upon them, or the use to which the land may be applied. Among the buildings upon that land there is a considerable quantity of laundries . . . There is a dye works also; there is a pig slaughterhouse, and there are bone manure crushers, and any of the vacant land may be had for factories.[52]

In 1867 the Goldsmiths' Company came to be more directly affected when 19 acres of the recently-enclosed land west of the North London line was bought for £15,270 by the British Land Company and rapidly developed during the subsequent seven years as the Acton Station estate.[53] Frontages were mostly of 20 feet, and the plots were sold subject to a minimum building cost of £150. In contrast to the Company's estates in south Acton no trades or manufactures were permitted. Although the last plot on the estate was not sold until 1874, all but a few had been disposed of by the end of 1869, by when receipts from sales amounted to £19,723.[54] By 1871 119 houses on the estate (a figure which excludes shops and houses on Churchfield Road along its southern margin) were occupied by 138 households of which 22 per cent were headed by clerks, many of whom probably used the North London line. The railways themselves provided employment for 26 household heads on the estate. Seventeen per cent of households employed a servant, in no case more than one. This proportion contrasts both with parts of the Acton Hill estate, where for instance in the part of Avenue Road east of Park Road two-thirds of houses contained resident servants and nearly one-quarter more than one, and with Birkbeck Road, adjacent to the North London station and developed by the Birkbeck Freehold Land Society, where all eight inhabited houses each contained one servant. On the British Land Company's Bollo Bridge estate in south Acton, on the other hand, virtually none were recorded in households in Osborne, Enfield, Hanbury or Packington Roads.[55]

These differences suggest that from the outset the various land company estates came to acquire distinct characteristics. Social differentiation is evident not only between middle-class properties (mostly leasehold) on the one hand and many of the estates divided into freehold building plots on the other, but also between different estates of the same land company. Since the development of the latter took place in most cases over a considerable period and was undertaken by a large number of small builders complete uniformity of house type on any one estate would not be expected. Although the Acton Station estate, for instance, comprised mostly two-storey terraced houses some three-storey semi-detached villas were also built. But the nature of building on particular land company estates was in general broadly similar, determined within the context of the local demand for housing by plot layout, building conditions, and the nature of nearby transport facilities.[56]

The fact that building on the Acton Station estate was for artisan or lower middle class occupation was not welcomed by the Goldsmiths' Company. Within two years of the commencement of the third Churchfield agreement, the Company was forced to recognize that its expectations as to the rate of building had again been too optimistic. In 1871 a reduction was approved in the brickmaking royalties, and the following year the Company consented to a reduction of £100 per annum in the ground rents payable during the next four years.[57] The impracticability of carrying on brickmaking and building on the same site was becoming apparent. A neighbouring property owner subsequently claimed that

> there can be nothing more objectionable than the neighbourhood of brickfields with their accessories of brick burning – rubbish heaps of filthy composition, ashes, etc. – injuring health and vegetation by unwholesome fumes and exhalations – to say nothing of the wholesale addition of 'roughs' to a quiet village population.[58]

One of the Goldsmiths' lessees, James Wright, commented in 1871 that

> We have already 6 out of the 10 houses [on Churchfield Road] completed, and unlet mainly from the nuisance of the brick making; this of course is not the sole cause, as you can see that unfortunately the style of small house built on the opposite side of the Railway will for some little time operate against the better style of house we intend to erect.[59]

The Company was obliged to accept that brickmaking rather than building provided the only immediate source of profit to its lessees. In 1878 the limit within which the extraction of brick earth was permitted was extended northwards to a distance of up to 500 feet from the Uxbridge Road. The Goldsmiths' Company also agreed to provide loans to Wright and Eyre to finance building operations, amounting by 1877 to £8,000.[60] Yet despite these advances and the modification of the building agreement, the development of the site made little progress. Only four more houses appear to have been completed during the entire decade.

An example of more successful development is provided by the Duke of Devonshire's estate at Chiswick. The first building in what was to become the new suburb of Grove Park took place from 1868 on land around Chiswick station, opened 20 years before. By the middle of the following decade some 50 houses and a church had been completed. The initial impetus to building seems to have been given by the boom of the mid-1860s and what was for the time the relatively frequent service on the London & South Western loop line. The social character of the district is shown by the fact that frontages, few of which were of less than 35 to 40 feet, ranged upwards to between 60 and 90 feet. Much of the early building was on a leasehold basis, but the freeholds of many houses, as well as of individual vacant plots, appear to have subsequently been sold outright. During the 1880s large parts of the estate were sold for building without prior subdivision into plots, although with covenants governing the type of housing that would be permitted.[61]

Rapid development also took place during this period on the Askew property between Kew Bridge and Turnham Green. Already in 1846 a private Act had removed the legal obstacles to the granting of building leases on the family's estates in Hammersmith and Chiswick.[62] Building on a significant scale, both here and on the Arlington House estate to the east, did not, however, begin until the 1860s. In this period considerable improvements were made to the North London service and in 1869 the London & South Western route from Hounslow and Richmond via Turnham Green to Waterloo was opened, five years after parliamentary sanction was secured.[63] In the parliamentary session of 1864 four rival Bills had been deposited for railways in the area. Apart from the successful London & South Western Bill, one was promoted by the North & South Western Junction for a direct extension to Richmond; hitherto North London trains had reached the latter town over the London & South Western via Chiswick and Barnes. The Metropolitan proposed that its Hammersmith and City line, opened the same year, be extended, while a fourth project was for a line between Hammersmith, Turnham Green and Kew Bridge. The North London and Metropolitan (and the District in the next decade) were eventually granted running powers over the London & South Western line, which linked the West London railway at Kensington with the Windsor line at Richmond. The possibilities of creating suburban traffic were clearly being recognized. The Metropolitan, having successfully promoted the Hammersmith & City line across what were then fields west of Paddington and north of Kensington, claimed that between Hammersmith and Kew the entire district would 'be crowded with a population who would require to go to the City and return'.[64] The example of the growth of building and suburban traffic along the North London was cited at the committee stage of the Kew, Turnham Green & Hammersmith Bill, as was the development of the Askew estate.[65]

Both the North London and London & South Western services could be used from the new Gunnersbury station, opened in 1869 (as Brentford Road) and close to the Askew Estate. A year after the opening of Turnham Green station on the same line the British Land Company purchased an adjacent four-acre estate on which all plots had been sold by 1873. Early in the 1870s Upham Park Road, off the High Road near Turnham Green station, was developed with seven-room houses each of an estimated value of £36.[66] The first leases on the main part of the Askew estate in Chiswick date from 1864, and apply to houses on the south side of the main Bath Road. The same year a building agreement was apparently concluded for land immediately to the south: here frontages on the side roads were rather less than on comparable middle-class estates, most being between 20 and 25 feet. The remainder of the property west of the North London extension line was covered by a building agreement made three years later. Building continued steadily for the remainder of the decade, and in 1872 a further agreement was made for the land east of Gunnersbury station, at a time when the suburban building boom was well past its peak.[67]

The Askew property was by the 1860s clearly ripe for development. In contrast the Castle Hill area of north Ealing was still well beyond the suburban frontier. Here one of the most remarkable speculative building projects begun in outer west London during the nineteenth century was undertaken. In 1862 Henry de Bruno Austin concluded agreements with C.P. Millard, who six years previously had purchased over 420 acres in north Ealing, for a building lease covering 107 acres, with provision for subsequent sale. Two years later Austin made a similar agreement relating to the 65-acre Swinden estate between Castlehill Park, of which he was the lessee, and the Great Western railway. By 1866 Austin had secured possession for building of nearly 230 acres between the main line in the south and the river Brent in the north, on the slopes of the western part of the Hanger Hill ridge.[68] The scale of the enterprise illustrates the optimism with which the prospects for suburban development in an area eight miles from central London could be regarded as early as the 1860s. By the middle of the decade new 50-foot roads had been built across the property and several others were projected or in the course of construction; gas and water mains had already been laid to Castle Hill by 1862.[69] Twenty-three houses had been completed, of which six were large detached villas in half-acre grounds. The intended character of the new suburb is illustrated by the fact that in 1868 houses were being advertised at rentals of from £150 to £250 per annum; semi-detached houses in Kent Gardens and villas in Cleveland Road each contained eight and ten bedrooms respectively.[70] In 1900 the average rateable value of the nine Cleveland Road houses was £143.

Five years after the beginning of the project it was becoming evident that the initial expectations had been far too optimistic. From 1867 the estate was administered under the Bankruptcy Act, and a year later foreclosure was decreed. Austin, who also possessed property in Kensington, had a certified debt of over £47,000. In 1872 he was adjudged bankrupt.[71] The southern part of the estate, near Castle Hill station (opened in 1871 on the Great Western main line) was eventually sold to a land company, and was auctioned with some success from 1882 in 20-foot plots.[72] But elsewhere on the property scarcely any houses were completed for the rest of the century. Several attempts were made to auction land in the 1870s and early 1880s, apparently without success.[73] In 1876 St Stephen's church was consecrated in the centre of the estate, but in the mid-1890s it remained in isolation at the intersection of two of the principal estate roads constructed 30 years before.

Austin's was not the only property in north Ealing on which an attempt was made to sell or lease land during the first suburban boom. On both the Castlehill Park and Castlebar Park estates sales took place in the early 1870s, but little building was accomplished at either. By 1874 St Stephen's Road had been cut across Castlebar Park and a few large villas built. The adjacent 27-acre Castlehill Park property to the north was sold in two parts in 1870 at £555 per acre, one lot comprising the house and grounds. The rest of the estate was intended for subdivision into building plots of 50-foot frontage. The following year most of this part was resold to the purchaser of the mansion, the project having apparently been abandoned.[74] In 1880, during the second building boom and while the District Railway Uxbridge extension Bills were being promoted, 18 acres of the estate, including the house, were sold to the British Land Company at £730 per acre.[75] But here again, with the failure of the Bills and the end of the boom, the hopes of the developers were not fulfilled, even though some building this time took place.

Several reasons may be advanced for the failure of these building projects in north Ealing. One was the initial difficulty of securing adequate house drainage. The boundaries of the Ealing Local Board, of which Austin became a member in 1864, did not at first include the site of the proposed Castle Hill development. It was not until 1873, ten years after its establishment, that the jurisdiction of the Local Board was extended to cover the entire parish of Ealing (except for Old Brentford). Only then could a drainage scheme be prepared for the northern district.[76] In 1875 a report from the Board's medical officer strongly criticized the lack of a proper outfall for the sewerage of houses in the district: for this reason it

111

was fortunate that development had not taken place more rapidly.[77] Although these difficulties, as well as the end of the boom, probably contributed to the halt in building, they were clearly not the sole cause of the failure of the Castle Hill speculation: 25 years later building had still not been resumed. Austin may have been encouraged in his extensive land purchases by the prospect that a station would be opened near Cleveland Road on the projected North Metropolitan Railway, for which an Act was secured in 1866.[78] The line was intended to link the Great Western near Southall and the main lines from the north with the London docks, but was never constructed. Most of the few villas actually built were probably occupied by carriage owners (a mews was also provided), since the centre of Austin's estate lay about a mile from the nearest station, at Ealing on the Great Western Railway. The most successful projects begun in the parish at this time were far closer to stations than this. During the 1860s Oxford and Windsor Roads, immediately south of the station and close to the village centre, were rapidly built up. By 1871 the two roads contained 89 occupied houses, with an average of about 1.4 servants per household. Eaton Rise, off Castlebar Hill and not far from the station, was lined with large villas by the mid 1870s, some seven years after the land had been sold at £500 per acre.[79] At Drayton Green building of a similar nature took place on Argyle and Sutherland Roads soon after they were laid out in 1870, a year after the Great Western had decided to provide a station immediately adjacent to the property.[80]

The Hanwell Golden Manor estate was also situated close to a railway station, in this case opened well before the urbanization of the surrounding district began. The property consisted of slightly over ten acres on the northern edge of Hanwell village. In 1860 it was sold for about £190 per acre, and three years later its new owner, C.S. Mills, obtained its enfranchisement, a preliminary to building operations.[81] In 1866 Mills concluded an initial agreement for the development of part of the estate with a Harrow builder. Its timing may have been influenced by the opening in 1863 of the Metropolitan Railway, which for the first time enabled the Great Western to provide direct rail communication between Hanwell and the City, some eight miles distant. The agreement was similar to those on the Goldsmiths' estate. 99-year leases were to be granted when the houses had been covered in, the plans and elevations to be prepared by the estate surveyor. Only private dwelling houses were to be erected, and leases were to include clauses prohibiting structural alterations or conversion to other uses without the consent of the ground landlord. Relatively high minimum costs were required: of the 31 houses eventually to be built on the estate, seven were to cost not less than £800, twenty £500–600 and only four £300.

Owing to the lessee's failure to fulfil the agreement, fresh negotiations were begun within a year by Mills with other developers. The resulting two agreements provided for the erection by 1872 of from 30 to 47 houses of a character similar to that previously stipulated. As with the Goldsmith's Company, mortgage loans were to be provided by Mills, who also undertook to buy the improved ground rents (where at least 80 years of the term remained) at 20 years' purchase. Under the new agreements a start was at last made on building, but this amounted to far less than was originally anticipated. By 1869 four or more large detached houses and a terrace of eight, most of the latter with 20-foot frontages, had been at least partially completed. This was as far as the project proceeded at the time. In 1870 and 1873 respectively the two agreements were cancelled. Apart from the completion of the

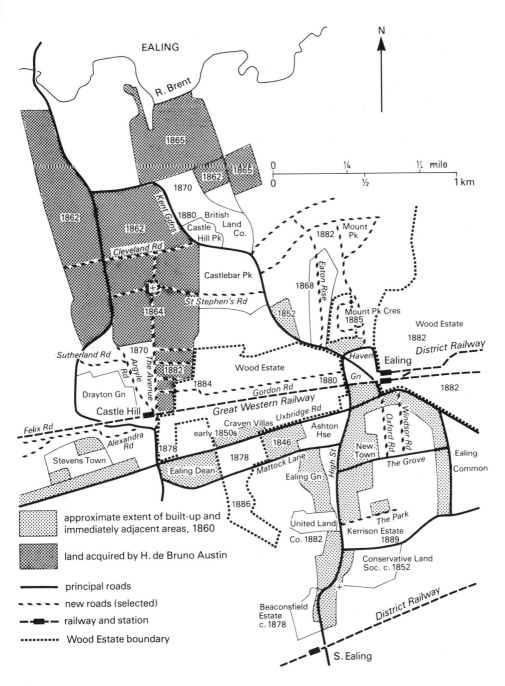

Figure 18. Development in Ealing. Dates are those of initial sale or lease for building.

existing buildings and the apparent erection of another three houses, no further building had taken place by 1886, when the estate, including seven acres of potential building land, was offered for sale.[82]

These examples illustrate some of the features common to most leasehold building estates in outer west London: concern for the maintenance of their middle-class character, the over-optimism of initial development plans, and the influence of the depression of the 1870s. Already in 1871 16 per cent of houses in Acton and 10 per cent in Ealing were unoccupied.[83] With the ending of the boom, it was mainly on those estates close to a significantly improved rail service, as at Turnham Green, that building continued. On others, development to a large extent ceased until the beginning of the second boom in the later 1870s. In 1874 local landowners were among the promoters of an unsuccessful Bill for a line to link the centre of Acton with the western terminus of the District Railway at Hammersmith.[84] New purchases by land companies in Acton ceased during the early 1870s, and available building land was sold with increasing difficulty. That part of the Acton Hill estate resold by the British Land Company in 1860 was unsuccessfully offered in several large lots nine years later and again in 1873. It was eventually sold for building in 1877, the same year that approval was secured for the District Railway Ealing extension, which was to provide a station at Mill Hill Park adjacent to the estate. The purchaser was William Willett, who with his son was to become the largest builder of late nineteenth-century Hampstead.[85] In the following years, during the second boom, the development of Mill Hill Park as an estate of large villas was begun. Willett clearly regarded it as necessary to isolate his estate as far as possible from the land company property to the east and south, with which no direct connection by road was provided. Although about half the frontages on the property had been built on by the mid-1880s, the remainder stayed vacant during the rest of the century. The social character of southern Acton had been determined by the British Land Company during the first boom, a fact that could not subsequently be ignored.

3 The second boom 1875–85

It was during the last years of the 1870s and the first of the next decade that the outer west London suburbs became linked in a continuous urban area, even if considerable tracts of undeveloped land remained. The rapid increase in building towards 1880, common to suburban London, coincided in the west with major improvements to railway services. A new suburban service was introduced on the Great Western in 1878, followed by the opening of the Ealing and Hounslow branches of the District Railway.

During the later 1860s the Great Western came to reconsider its hitherto largely negative attitude towards the development of suburban traffic. In 1869 a limited suburban service between Paddington and Southall was introduced to supplement the meagre provision by main-line trains.[86] The general manager observed in a report the same year that the number of passengers between Ealing and the London termini had increased by 164 per cent in the period 1861–7, while that between suburban and Metropolitan line stations had doubled in the three years after 1864. Traffic from the station opened at Acton had been far less than anticipated – although its distance from the centre of Acton and the infrequency of the train service scarcely encouraged a rapid increase in the number of users. The report stated that the southern lines and the Great Northern provided frequent suburban services. If the Great Western was to compete and attract 'City people' to live on its line, an improved service was needed.[87] Any considerable increase in frequency on the main line was, however, limited by the number and occasional unpunctuality of long-distance trains: thirty years after the opening of the line it still comprised only two tracks. In contrast, when the London & South Western had opened its new terminus at Waterloo in 1848 four tracks had been laid at the outset. The same problem was soon encountered by the Great Northern after its rapid development of suburban traffic from the later 1860s.[88]

In the early 1870s the Great Western decided that the only solution was to double the main line. It was originally intended to carry this only as far as Acton, with three tracks from there to West Drayton, but in 1876 it was decided to continue the extra pair of lines to Slough. In addition the crossing on the level of the main line by the Hammersmith & City service of the Metropolitan was to be eliminated. The new relief lines, which were opened as far as West Drayton in 1878, were to be used for goods as well as local traffic.[89] Unlike the Great Northern, the Great Western postponed the introduction of a more intensive suburban service until after the track improvements had been completed. This resulted in growing criticism of the company during the 1870s from local interests.[90] The effectiveness at parliamentary committees of the promise eventually to introduce higher frequencies was probably somewhat reduced by memories of similar statements made before 1863 of improvements to follow the opening of the Metropolitan. The attitude of the Great Western to the construction of new suburban lines across its territory is shown in a report of 1874 on the projected Shepherds Bush & Brentford Railway. The line was to run from the Hammersmith branch of the Metropolitan to the Great Western at Brentford, with a link at Acton to the North London. It would provide more convenient access to Acton than that from existing routes, and the report warned that for the Great Western to retain its traffic a reduction of fares on the main line would be necessary. Nevertheless it might be desirable for the Great Western to aid in the promotion of the line to prevent its adoption by the Metropolitan, which might subsequently extend it to Windsor, leading to serious competition with established Great Western traffic. If it was decided to support the Bill, it would be with the intention of preventing 'any hostile and unnecessary extensions beyond it'.[91] This attitude was similar to that of the London & South Western, one of whose principal motives for the construction of the Kensington-Richmond line seems to have been to forestall an independent North London line south of the Thames, from which (as with the District line to Wimbledon 20 years later) further extensions into London & South Western territory might be projected. Opposing counsel quoted in committee a statement by the London & South Western directors that they 'were no "extensionsts", and only took up extensions when driven to it, lest . . . a greater evil should befall them'.[92]

The new Great Western service was inaugurated in June 1878. About ten extra trains were provided in each direction, with 13 through trains to and from Moorgate Street in place of the previous seven. Until two years previously the earliest train from Ealing for Paddington had departed after 8 a.m.[93] These improvements were followed in the 1890s by further increases in frequency, the number of trains during the main morning and evening travelling periods increasing from 15 in 1891 to 24 ten years later. It was considered that had it not been for the imminent opening of the District Railway's Ealing extension the improvements of 1878 in the Great Western service would have been far less.[94]

The Metropolitan District Railway was originally promoted as a southern complement to the Metropolitan: a circular line within the inner suburbs was to be created by linking a western extension of the Metropolitan at South Kensington with the City via Westminster and the projected Thames embankment. By 1871 the line was completed as far as the Mansion House station in the City. In the early 1870s the District Railway, as the Metropolitan District was generally known, was considering suburban extension as an alternative to immediate continuation with construction through the expensive City property eastwards from the Mansion House. In 1874 the railway was extended west from Earls Court to Hammersmith. Three years later a short link from Hammersmith enabled the District to extend its service over the London & South Western Kensington-Richmond line. This was the same route that the Metropolitan had secured to Richmond, through the construction from its Hammersmith & City line of a similar link. In 1877 the District Railway sponsored a Bill for a further extension from the London & South Western at Turnham Green to the Great Western at Ealing, with intermediate stations at Acton Green (later Chiswick Park), Mill Hill Park (later Acton Town) and Ealing Common. Although the main aim of the line was to secure the diversion on to the District Railway of part of the present and prospective Ealing traffic, it was also apparently anticipated that the branch would stimulate building in the neighbourhood of the new stations. Three years later the District cited the commencement of building on estates at Ealing Common as evidence of the influence of the new line on suburban growth.[95]

The only major new speculative venture begun in the years immediately preceding the second boom seems to be linked with the arrival of the District Railway in outer west London. In 1875, with the plans for the Richmond extension already known, J.T. Carr began the purchase of land at Bedford Park for what was to become one of the most noteworthy building estates in suburban London.[96] The original estate comprised some 45 acres north of Turnham Green station. Building began in 1876; by March 1877 only some 18 houses had been completed, plans having been made for an eventual total of about 600.[97] Carr subsequently acquired the entire 29-acre detached portion of Ealing, which owing to the refusal of either the Metropolitan Board of Works or the Acton Local Board to provide drainage, was in 1878 amalgamated with Chiswick. After this, at the height of the suburban building boom, progress was far more rapid, special arrangements for drainage eventually being made with the MBW. Nearly 300 houses had been built by spring 1880, most being semi-detached on 50-foot frontages and in the rental range of £50 to £80. By the mid-1880s Bedford Park had been largely completed within its original boundaries, coming to be widely admired as a forerunner in its architecture and layout of the garden suburb.[98] In 1882 a further 22 acres to the west of the original estate were acquired, giving a total for the development of over 100 acres,[99] but for the next 12 years the market gardens so obtained mostly remained as a wedge of open land between the new suburb and the main part of Acton.

By 1877 the second major building boom since suburban development began was becoming evident in outer west London. During the following five years the subdivision of vacant land and rate of building attained a scale that was not again reached until the last few years of the century. A clear example of the revival of confidence is provided by the chronology of building on estates south of the Great

Western line in Acton. The Birkbeck Land Society had bought a nine-acre site near the station about 1868, but no building appears to have taken place on new roads off Horn Lane until 1877, when the first house plans were accepted by the Local Board.[100] Over 70 houses, semi-detached or in terraces, had been approved by 1882. Most appear to have been built by the mid-1880s, after which little further construction took place until the end of the following decade. To the west, the 77-acre Springfield estate changed hands in 1877. By 1880 much of the property, on which the preservation of trees was stressed in advertisements, had been divided into plots of about 50-foot frontage. Houses of five and six bedrooms were being

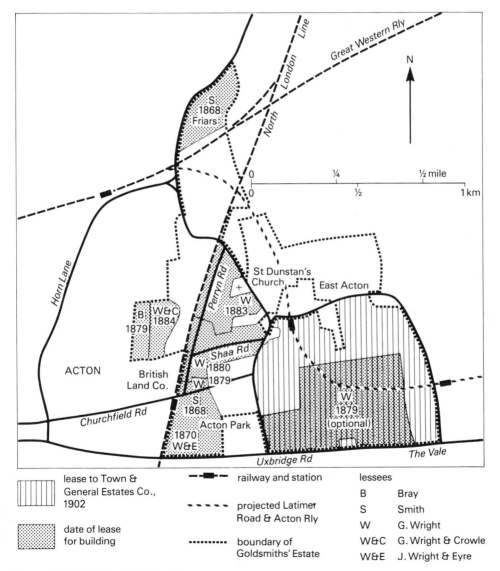

Figure 19. East Acton building leases.

erected on 99-year leases, and let at £70 to £75.[101] Five years later the entire estate was intersected by new roads on which about half the available frontages were occupied by houses.

Over the greater part of the Goldsmith's Company's estate brickmaking and building agreements were substituted between 1878 and 1884 for the original agricultural tenancies. The earlier Churchfield agreement (on the Company's corporate property rather than charity land) may to some extent be seen as experimental, but during the last two decades of the century the essential interest of the Company in East Acton was in the progress of its transformation into a portion of surburban London. Nearly £15,000 was spent by the Goldsmiths' Company on the building of St Dunstan's church, consecrated in 1879 on a site close to that part of the estate now to be developed.[102] In 1878 126 acres were held on an agricultural lease by George Wright, who proposed the granting of a brickmaking agreement for 49 acres of this land, covering most of the south-eastern part of the estate adjacent to the Uxbridge Road. (Wright subsequently became a leading local Conservative. He was twice chairman of the Acton Local Board and was an alderman of the Middlesex County Council).[103] Following the Goldsmiths' Company's earlier experience, its surveyor suggested that it might be preferable for brickmaking to precede rather than accompany building, for which there was still much available land nearer the station. He maintained his conviction that the interests of the Company and charity would in the long run best be served by a scheme for houses of relatively high value at low densities. In a report of 1878 plot sizes of one-quarter of an acre were proposed for most of the site and minimum values for houses of £800, a figure little different from that demanded on the Friars site ten years before.[104]

Yet at the same time it was becoming clear that the development scheme for the Churchfield site would have to be reconsidered. About 1878 James Wright became bankrupt, but negotiations were continued by the Company with Eyre. Two years later the latter asserted that £19,000 had been spent on the estate during the previous decade, but that receipts, including advances on mortgage and income from brickmaking, had amounted to only £13,000. The immediate causes given for 'this disastrous state of affairs' were the absence of demand in the district for the type of house required in the building agreement, and the heavy ground rents. In addition, the houses being built on neighbouring estates were 'of a class calculated rather to hinder than to promote the erection of houses of a good residential character'. Eyre also referred to the adverse effect of the railway services for Acton in comparison with those of other suburbs. While the Great Western service had undoubtedly been inadequate, this was less true of that of the North London, and it seems unlikely that Eyre would have considered this cause a major obstacle to the development of the estate. He concluded by reiterating that although *bona fide* enquiries had been made during the previous year as to building on the property, objections had been made in every instance to the ground rents and to the style and value of the houses required by the Goldsmiths' Company. Rental values of from £40 to £50 were far more suitable for the main part of the estate than villas worth £60 a year and more.[105]

Subsequent negotiations were to show, however, that the Goldsmiths' surveyor (from 1880 J.W. Penfold) was not yet prepared to alter the type of house to be built to the extent wished by Eyre. The surveyor's proposals in detail were for minimum frontages of 35 feet, with 50 feet on the Uxbridge Road as well as on the other margins of the site where plot depths were less than 120 feet. Eyre pointed out in reply that already in July 1877 the Goldsmiths' Company had agreed in principle to the erection of 91 houses with a hotel and blocks of stabling, in place of the 66 houses in the 1870 plan. This had followed representations made by Eyre as early as 1874 that the house types proposed were on too large a scale. In December 1878 Robert Hesketh, the previous surveyor, had consented to plot widths of 27 feet. In other words, what was now presented as a concession was less than had been agreed two years before.[106] Despite the fact that the second suburban boom in Acton was now nearing its peak, no new agreement was concluded. In 1881, 19 years after acquiring the land, the Goldsmiths' Company resumed possession of a 15-acre building site that now contained merely the beginnings of a road system and 14 completed houses.

In 1879 building, not preceded by brickmaking, began on another part of the land held by George Wright. The site comprised little more than one and a half acres, near the North London station, but the building estate was capable of extension northwards if justified by initial success. Twelve houses were to be erected in three years; the terms of the agreement, which provided for an ultimate ground rent of £50 per acre, were similar to those for the Churchfield site in 1870, with 35-foot frontages and minimum house values of £600.[107] This relatively small site was the beginning of what was to be the main building development on the East Acton estate that had attained any degree of success by the end of the century. One other portion of the estate was let on a building lease before the end of the decade. A local builder offered to take an agreement for the road frontage of that part of the estate west of the North London line. Twenty-two houses were to be built at the rate of four per year. The agreement included a clause which evolved into a standard safeguard in Goldsmiths' leases against overbuilding. (In this instance it was less favourable to the builder than in subsequent cases). It provided that after 16 houses had been built, if more than three remained unoccupied, no further building would be required until two of these had been let. The ground rent was at the rate of £40 per acre, but the conditions imposed on the type of building were similar to those demanded before. The minimum frontages of 30 feet, although less than had been required on other parts of the Goldsmiths' estate, still contrasted with those permitted on the adjacent British Land Company estate to the south.[108] All 22 houses had been completed by the middle of the decade, when building in East Acton had come to a virtual halt.

The one and a half-acre building lease to Wright of 1879 was evidently considered sufficiently promising to justify its extension, since the following year an agreement was made applying to a further 14 acres. The site was to be intersected by two new roads (subsequently Perryn and Shaa Roads) and the full rent was to be payable in the seventh year. Wright was also given the option of taking within two years another building lease for 14 acres to the north. In 1883 he contracted to erect by 1889 on this third section of the site an additional 91 houses of the same character.[109] One further building scheme on the estate was begun before a long period of stagnation set in. Its site was immediately south of land bought by Wright on the west of the North London line. In 1883 he suggested that the Goldsmiths' Company could aid the development of this site, on which he intended to erect houses in the rental range of £40 to £50, and its own property, by permitting the construction of a new road across both sites to link the North London and Great Western railway stations. Wright offered to contribute towards the cost of the roads over the Company's land and to take a building lease of the portion of the Goldsmiths' estate in question. A guarantee would also be given that the value of the houses to be built on the continuation of the road through his own land would be at least £500 each, the proposed minimum cost of these on the Goldsmiths' site. As a further safeguard the Company was to have powers to close its portion of the road in case these conditions were not fulfilled. In 1884 Wright, with a Kensington builder, J. Crowle, accordingly contracted to erect on the Goldsmiths' land a further 57 houses within the next six years.[110] This brought the area covered by building leases granted by the Goldsmiths' Company between 1879 and 1884 to about 40 acres. The principal lessee, George Wright, was under contract to build 247 houses on 35 acres. About another 60 acres were occupied by two brickfields. Most of the houses ever completed under the agreements were built between 1879 and the mid-1880s. Seventy-three of the 121 houses required on three sites begun in 1879 and 1880 had been built by 1886.[111] But in common with other landowners, the Goldsmiths' Company was to find that the optimism of its lessees during the early 1880s was followed by complete failure to carry out the stipulated building programme in subsequent years.

South of the Uxbridge Road building now took place on most of the remaining land enclosed in 1859. Already by 1873 the Royal Society was considering the development of its 32-acre estate on 99-year building leases, but during the subsequent depression no further attention seems to have been given to the matter. In 1879 the prospects for building were again reviewed, and three years later the estate was sold for about £32,000.[112] By the mid-1880s all but the nine acres to the south of the North London line, on which an adjacent station was opened in 1880 after considerable local pressure, had been laid out for building as the South Acton Station estate.

The layout was clearly influenced by the existing character of those parts of South Acton which were developed during the first boom 15 to 20 years before. Subdivision was into plots of 16- to 18-foot frontage, which were offered on what were by then the normal land company terms. A ten per cent deposit was required with a nine year period for repayment of the remainder at five per cent interest, or three-quarters of the cost to remain on mortgage at four and a half per cent. All but one of the lots offered at the first auction in 1882 were sold within a month.[113]

On the adjacent Beaumont Park estate of the National Liberal Land Company the disposal of land was at first similarly rapid. All 70 of the plots (fronting roads already kerbed and drained) offered at the first auction in 1882 were sold immediately. The land was to 'be sold as free as possible from all restrictions, except as regards noxious trades and [with] a low minimum building value'.[114] The third major property in Acton south of the Uxbridge Road to be sold for building at this period was the 12-acre Berrymead Priory estate immediately south-east of the village centre. In 1882 this was bought for subdivision by the Reading Land Company (subsequently the Berkshire Estates Company) for £23,000, a bid by the Acton Local Board, which intended to use the well-wooded grounds as a public park, being insufficient.[115] The ending of the building boom and the delay in completing a drainage scheme for Acton, until when cesspools were to be permitted on the estate,[116] prevented any rapid disposal of the available building plots. After an initial and quite unsuccessful auction in 1883 roads were constructed across the estate, but at an auction of 91 plots three years later none were sold.[117]

The refusal of the Metropolitan Board of Works to continue accepting drainage into its sewers from new houses built beyond its boundaries precipitated the collapse in Acton of the building boom. In 1877 the Board brought an action against the Acton Local Board, and secured a restraining injunction five years later. Work on a new drainage scheme for Acton was not begun until 1885.[118] Already in 1879 the Local Board refused permission for a proposed building estate of 143 plots at Leamington Park, north of the Great Western line, on the grounds that the drainage system was not large enough to carry another such estate.[119] On the 130-acre Cowper-Essex property in Acton Vale building agreements were concluded between 1878 and 1882 for the construction of over a thousand houses,[120] but by 1885 scarcely any had been erected except along the Uxbridge Road frontage. Representations were made to the council as to the urgent need for a new Acton sewerage scheme by the property's owners as well as by the developers of the Priory and Beaumont Park estates: in the case of the latter it was claimed in 1883 that building operations had entirely ceased. Two years later the same reason for failing to begin building was given by William Willett, holder of a building agreement granted in 1880 for three acres of land belonging to the Ecclesiastical Commissioners on either side of the Uxbridge Road at East Acton.[121]

In Chiswick and Ealing the impact of the second boom was as definite as in Acton. Much of the Devonshire estate in Chiswick, following the gradual development in the 1870s of the section south-west of Chiswick station, was now offered for building. That part around the Royal Horticultural Society's grounds, south of the built-up area in Turnham Green, was sold in large lots of several acres each between 1879 and 1881.[122] By the mid-1880s much of this land had been covered with high-rental housing similar to that of Grove Park. In 1882 over £1,600 per acre, said to have been the highest price yet paid in the neighbourhood, was obtained for land fronting Duke's Avenue. Two years later 80 acres of the Devonshire property, comprising what came to be known as the Chiswick Park estate, were bought by Thomas Kemp Welch at a price of £70,000 for development on lines similar to Bedford Park.[123]

The rapid increase towards the end of the 1870s in the number of houses built annually in Ealing came partly from an extensive development programme for the 540-acre property of the Wood family. In 1878 the total completed in Ealing was over three times that for the year before, and six times that for 1876, at the trough of the preceding depression.[124] Between 1876 and 1880 roads were laid out and building leases granted for virtually all parts of the Wood estate close to the existing built-up area or to railway stations; the areas remaining undeveloped at this period were largely those on the clayland to the north. A comprehensive plan had been formed by 1877 which included the provision of six through roads, but its implementation was in part delayed for over three years owing to a dispute with the Local Board over some of the parish common land to be taken by new roads.[125] During these years, which coincided with the approval of the District Railway's Ealing extension in 1877 and its opening two years later, the Christ Church end of central Ealing finally lost its rural aspect. Building took place on all the vacant Uxbridge Road frontages of the Wood estate from Ealing Dean in the west to the Common, near the new station on the District Railway, in the east. Houses were also built to the north of Ealing station around Haven Green, and in 1880 the Wood estate purchased a further 18 acres between the latter and the new suburban district north of Castle Hill station. This land was almost immediately laid out for building.[126] Most of the plots on the Wood property were offered on 99-year leases, primarily for middle-class villas. Frontages were often somewhat less than in the 1850s, as with those of 25 to 30 feet on the west side of Haven Green and between Uxbridge Road and Mattock Lane. A few sites, close to terraces of cottages that dated from before the suburban era, were developed at higher densities on frontages of less than 20 feet. The most notable example was to the east of Stevens Town in west Ealing, adjacent to an estate developed for working-class housing.

Stevens Town had come into existence by the mid 1860s, and consisted of cottages mostly rated in 1885 at only £6. A survey in 1877 criticized as defective the drainage of about one-sixth of the 126 houses inspected.[127] During the second boom the land between Stevens Town and the railway, not far from Castle Hill station, was laid out for building. Plots with 15- or 16-foot frontages to Eccleston, Felix and Endsleigh Roads were offered at auctions between 1882 and 1885 as 'suitable for the erection of Workmen's Houses of about 8s per week rental value'. Low minimum values of £180 to £200 were permitted. It was claimed with only slight exaggeration that this was 'almost the only land in Ealing where houses of this class are permitted to be erected'. Although the recently-improved Great Western service was cited as an inducement to build in the area, occupiers of the new houses mostly worked locally.[128]

It was in those parts of outer west London furthest from the existing built-up area that the impact of new railway services could be seen most clearly. Between 1878 and 1881 the District Railway, either directly or indirectly, promoted four Bills for extensions from its system to well beyond the urban area. A locally-backed and abortive project of 1866 for a branch line from the Great Western at Acton to Hounslow was revived in 1878, partly with the same promoters but with the support of the District, which was to work the line. This Bill was rejected, in part because of the failure of the District directors to obtain the prior approval of their shareholders, but not before building on the Beaconsfield estate adjacent to the proposed South Ealing station had begun.[129] Two years later a second Bill for the same line was successful. The other two Bills, both unsuccessful, were submitted in 1880 and 1881 for a nine-mile District extension from Ealing via Hayes to Uxbridge, a town already linked to the Great Western main line by a short branch from West Drayton.

The chairman of the District Railway, J.S. Forbes, gave evidence at the committee stages of all these Bills. Countering objections that the sparse population along the proposed lines would be insufficient to provide adequate traffic, he argued that surburban traffic could be created by the construction of railways in advance of extensive building development. Forbes used as examples the earlier extensions of the District westward from Earls Court to Hammersmith,[130] and from Turnham Green to Ealing. The case of the London, Chatham & Dover line, of which he was also chairman, was cited as further evidence of the relationship between railway facilities and suburban growth – from Brixton and Herne Hill to Penge, Beckenham and Bromley. Forbes pointed out that just as land prices declined from values of £700 or £800 per acre with increasing distance from a suburban railway station, so the generalization could be made that 'probably from 70 to 80 per cent of all houses are built within half a mile of the stations; they thin out at three-quarters of a mile . . .. and at a mile and a half they almost cease except for very luxurious houses inhabited by people who can keep carriages and so forth.'[131]

The main reason given by Forbes for his company's support of the Hounslow &

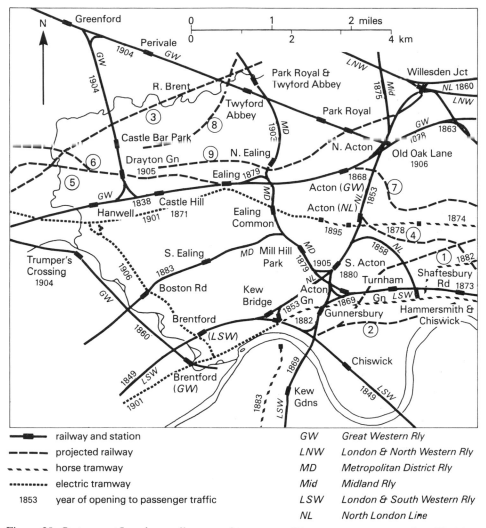

Figure 20. Outer west London: railways and tramways. Horse tramways were electrified in 1901, except for the line south of Kew Bridge. The map shows the development of railway and tramway services to 1906. Stations were opened in the same year as the line, except where otherwise shown. Brentford Road was renamed Gunnersbury in 1871; Acton Green was renamed Chiswick Park and Acton Green in 1887, and Chiswick Park in 1910; Shaftesbury Road was renamed Ravenscourt Park in 1888; Castle Hill was renamed West Ealing in 1899; Mill Hill Park was renamed Acton Town in 1910; Boston Road was renamed Boston Manor in 1911. The railway from Shaftesbury Road to Kew Gardens and Richmond was opened by the London & South Western (and used by the North London) in 1869 and used by the Metropolitan and the District from 1877.

Projected railways mentioned in the text (approximate route shown on map): 1. Kew, Turnham Green & Hammersmith 1864; 2. Metropolitan (extension of Hammersmith & City) 1864; 3. North Metropolitan 1866; 4. Acton & Hammersmith 1874; 5. and 6. Metropolitan District (Uxbridge extension) 1880, 1881; 7. Latimer Road & Acton 1882; 8. Harrow, Ealing & Willesden 1887; 9. North Western & Ealing 1887. (N. Ealing station should be shown just south, not north, of this route).

123

Metropolitan Bill, apart from the possibility of extending the line in the direction of Windsor,[132] was that while most of the existing population might be adequately served by the London & South Western loop line, construction of the branch would open up a new district for building operations and so provide additional traffic for the main District system. A service at 30-minute intervals was to be provided from the outset: 'in order to make . . . traffic you must give facilities at starting; you must not wait for the traffic to go of itself, you must make it go'.[133] In short, 'the theory of all these extensions westward is that they create new traffic . . . [which] serves, or will in time serve, to compensate a company for the enormous cost of the main line'.[134] Whereas the line from South Kensington to the Mansion House had cost £730,000 per mile, little more than £200,000 was spent on the three miles of the Ealing extension. The relative cheapness of these suburban lines was largely due to low land costs. Such expenditure would be considerably reduced by purchase before the areas traversed were considered suitable for immediate building development. The increase by £2,000 to £35,000 per mile in the estimated cost of the 1881 Uxbridge extension as compared with the previous year was attributed solely to rising land costs at Ealing and Castle Hill.[135]

It was also asserted by the District Railway that metropolitan rather than main-line railways were better adapted to suburban traffic. These arguments were applied against both the Great Western and London & South Western. It was contended that the regular-interval services of the District could not be operated over their tracks without delay and unpunctuality. This was in reply to an offer by the London & South Western to give the District access to the Hounslow loop line west of Kew Bridge, in the same way that the Great Western had attempted to prevent the Ealing extension by proposing the admission on to its main line of a District service via the West London Railway. The London & South Western in fact considerably increased the frequency of trains west of Gunnersbury and Kew Bridge in 1878, apparently in recognition of the need to meet criticisms of its loop line service if the Hounslow & Metropolitan was again promoted.[136] The parliamentary committees seem to have rejected the District's Uxbridge extension proposals partly because of the improved service to be provided by the Great Western following the doubling of the Uxbridge branch in 1881.[137] They were also probably influenced by assertions that the districts the line traversed, particularly beyond Hanwell, would not come into the market for suburban development for the next twenty-five years. In the words of one witness, the land between Uxbridge and the Brent was until then likely to remain as 'nothing but a wilderness of grass'.[138]

The distinctiveness of the District's policy of suburban extension was evident to the railway press. At the time the lines were promoted and in the first few years after they were opened comment was generally unfavourable, even though by the later 1870s the value to the company of its first inner suburban extensions was recognized. When the Ealing branch was sanctioned in 1877 the *Railway Times* conceded the success of the District extension across the orchards and market gardens of Fulham and Hammersmith. The risks, however, were greater in more distant suburbs such as Acton or Ealing. And if the prospects for the early profitability of the Ealing line were doubtful, the chances of success for the projected nine-mile continuation to Uxbridge were even less.[139] Yet by the end of the century the suburban lines were contributing a substantial and growing proportion of the District's revenue: 35 per cent in 1889, 42 per cent ten years later.

In 1896 Forbes contrasted the increase in revenue from the branches during the previous five years with the virtually stationary income from the main line, the difference being attributed to increased omnibus competition in the inner urban area.[140] Both the District and Metropolitan Railways, supported by the railway press, had hoped for a considerable increase in revenue on completion of the Inner Circle (partly through the admission on to the line of traffic from a link to the East London Railway).[141] But soon after the opening of its final section in 1884, it became clear that no increase in revenue could be expected to justify the cost of construction, which was at the rate of over £2 million per mile. At the end of the century the *Railway Times* concluded that 'the extension policy — always excepting the Inner Circle – is, without doubt, the best thing the District has done.'[142]

The promotion of the District Railway Uxbridge extension line in 1880 and 1881 aroused hopes of a revival of building in the Castlebar Hill area of north Ealing, where the development of several estates had been largely in abeyance since the 1860s. When the 1881 Bill passed the Commons, 17 acres of the Castlehill Park estate were offered by the British Land Company and sold in plots to a variety of purchasers at £1,200 per acre. The Bill was subsequently rejected in the Lords, and in 1887 it was observed that since then only ten houses had been built, of which five were at the time unlet.[143] Even if the Uxbridge extension had been constructed, however, it is probable that building would have declined with the end of the boom, particularly as the estate would still have been some distance from a railway. The extension of the District Railway service to reach Hounslow, in contrast, secured parliamentary approval and the new branch was opened in May 1883. The frequency of through trains on this branch was always less than on the Ealing extension, and in November 1883 it was decided to withdraw all trains running through from the Hounslow line to stations east of Earls Court.[144] Three years later, at the same time that the interval between up trains from Ealing in the hour after 8.20 a.m. was halved to 15 minutes, the service on the Hounslow branch was still further reduced. All through trains on to the main line beyond Mill Hill Park were withdrawn, and the 30 minute frequency that had initially been provided was halved over most of the day.[145] It seems probable that one reason was that building on the land company property at Ealing Park, begun in 1882, was progressing more slowly than had been anticipated.

Ealing Park, consisting mostly of landscaped grounds sufficiently notable to have been opened to the public,[146] lay midway between Brentford station on the London & South Western loop line and the new District station at South Ealing. Bids of £40,000 and £42,000 made at auctions in 1880 and 1881 for the 77-acre property were below the reserve price,[147] and it was not until a third auction the following year that the estate was sold. Two lots of parkland and market garden then realized £536 and £574 per acre.[148] Ealing Park house itself and several adjacent large villas were not at the time demolished, and a large part of the parkland surrounding them was laid out for building only at the turn of the century.[149] For most of the remainder of the estate plans were submitted in 1882 for a drainage scheme to serve an eventual total of over 900 houses.[150] Rateable values for the houses built by the end of the following decade were in the range £20 to £40, a level comparable to that on the Beaconsfield estate developed from 1877 to the north of South Ealing station, and to that on Arlington and Albany Roads near Castle Hill station in west Ealing. On the latter 20-foot plots with minimum building values of £300 were sold in 1882 at over £1,500 per acre, although no takers were found for adjacent plots on which houses were each to cost at least £700.[151] The Ealing Park district was characterized in 1894 as being chiefly occupied by clerks.[152] For the first time it was now possible, if with considerably more difficulty than from suburbs to the north and north-east of London, for better-paid clerical workers and those in similar occupations to travel to work in inner London from Ealing. These estates were the forerunners of the extensive tracts of lower-middle class housing in south-west Ealing and Hanwell constructed during the renewed upswing in building in the later 1890s and the beginning of the new century.

4 After the second boom, 1885–95

By the time of the 1881 census signs of overbuilding were already apparent. The proportion of houses unoccupied in outer west London was now as high as towards the end of the preceding boom a decade before. Building as a general rule continued in periods of speculative optimism for some time after the number of houses vacant began to increase,[153] but by the mid-1880s the end of the second suburban boom was apparent. For ten or 12 years land sales and building in outer west London remained at a relatively low level. Although on some estates house building continued, only a limited amount of new land was laid out for development. Several attempts were made during the period to sell agricultural or residential estates near the margins of the urban area, but almost invariably without success. Even in Chiswick, which was comparatively well served by railways and was clearly within the suburban frontier, an attempt to develop the remaining open land between Turnham Green and Grove Park was unsuccessful. By the mid-1890s no building had taken place on the Chiswick Park estate except for the erection of half a dozen houses on existing road frontages. Attempts were made in 1886 and 1893 to sell the land as a single lot, [154] and by 1896 its developer, who had extensive interests elsewhere, had become bankrupt.[155] It was not until the middle of the decade that building here began to any significant extent. Similarly on Dukes Avenue and Barrowgate Road land was auctioned without success and subsequently offered to the local council as the site for a recreation ground and museum.[156]

The initial cause of the setback to the progress of building on the Goldsmiths' estate was the injunction secured by the Metropolitan Board of Works in 1882 preventing the drainage into its system of any further houses to be built in Acton. In January 1886 George Wright, the Goldsmiths' principal lessee, observed that as a result no house had been erected on the estate for two years, and there was no prospect of any more being built for the next two or three. The drainage problem together with the end of the building boom, a stagnant brickmaking business and crop damage through trespass from new roads not as yet built on, led to demands for a revision of the building agreements.[157] The acceptance by the Goldsmiths' Company of a postponement of the dates for the fulfilment of the three building agreements, so that all were due for completion by 1892, was only the first of a series of such alterations during the rest of the century. Wright had also requested the sale to him of the ground rents, partly because loans for building on freehold land could be obtained at a lower rate of interest.[158] The Goldsmiths' surveyor recommended acceptance of the proposal, provided the houses were built first; but here the Charity Commission intervened. While accepting the other provisions of the revised agreements, it refused to permit any action that would reduce the reversionary value of the estate.[159]

On the Goldsmiths' other principal building site, Churchfield, no progress was made following the collapse in 1881 of the negotiations over revision of the building scheme. When the Local Board in 1886 proposed to incorporate the land into Acton's first public park, the Company surveyor strongly advocated agreement, and pointed out that adjacent land under different ownership would be taken out of potential competition with building elsewhere on the Goldsmiths' property. Wright saw clearly that the park could beneficially affect the development of his own building sites. As a member of the Local Board he succeeded in having the proposal referred to a special committee. Eventually the land was sold to the Board by the Goldsmiths' Company in 1888 at about £700 per acre, some £550 per acre less than its surveyor's valuation. Adjacent land belonging to the Ecclesiastical Commissioners was sold for the same purpose at about £1,000 per acre, a request by the Local Board for a reduction in price similar to that given by the Goldsmiths' Company being refused.[160] Building operations on the Goldsmiths' estate did not, however, recover during the next four years from the setbacks of the mid-eighties. Despite constant advertisements in the press and at stations on the North London line, only 25 of the 190 houses stipulated by the revised agreements were completed. For the latter the rents obtained were no more than two-thirds those normal for similar houses in Ealing or Hampstead.[161] This was attributed to the general depression in building, to the recent drainage difficulties in Acton, and to the lack of convenient access to the West End.

The importance attached by the Goldsmiths' Company to the provision of adequate rail links with inner London is illustrated by its support for the Latimer Road & Acton line, sanctioned in 1882 to link the Acton Great Western station with the Hammersmith branch of the Metropolitan at Latimer Road.[162] It was hoped thereby to give a more frequent service than could be provided from Acton on the Great Western main line, and that traffic would develop as a result of the stimulus to building on the land north of the Uxbridge Road. Evidence was also given for the line by the surveyor to the Cowper-Essex estate immediately south of the road. Three intermediate stations were proposed, one of them in the centre of the Goldsmiths' estate. Although the railway was presented as an independent line (one of the promoters being George Wright), it was made clear that the ultimate intention was for its operation to be undertaken by the Metropolitan.[163] The absence of a definite working agreement with the Great Western and Metropolitan seems, however, to have hindered the subscription of the share capital: by 1887 less than one-third had been paid up. In 1885 the railway sought the consent of the Goldsmiths' Company to a rent charge instead of requiring acquisition of the freehold. The Goldsmiths' surveyor recommended acceptance, on provision of adequate security, since it was very much in the interest of the estate to facilitate the construction of the line. At the same time he was anxious to prevent the railway obtaining possession of the land unless it was certain that the line would be built. Entry to the first part of the route, extending south-eastwards to the centre of East Acton, was eventually permitted on deposit of the value of the land.[164] By 1886 the Latimer Road & Acton was creating a considerable disturbance to the estate through severance and by leading to uncertainty as to the appropriate layout for building sites.[165] The original Act provided for the construction of the line by 1885; but, with the reluctant consent of the Goldsmiths' Company, the railway obtained extensions of time. Its powers to construct the line finally expired in 1898, when the Goldsmiths' Company was left with an uncompleted embankment across part of the estate. During the entire decade after 1892 only three more houses were built on the East Acton property.[166] In 1904 Wright and his partner Crowle surrendered their building agreements after successive extensions of time for completion had been granted because of the difficulty of securing new lessees. Attempts by the Goldsmiths' Company to secure payment of the arrears of ground rent were unsuccessful.[167]

Difficulties similar to those experienced by the Goldsmiths' Company during the depression following the second boom were encountered on other middle-class estates on the northern margins of Acton. At Springfield Park building virtually halted during the ten years after 1885, while on the adjacent Elms estate it had not even begun, even though a road system to link the proposed development with the Wood property in Ealing to the west was approved in 1879.[168] The 21-acre Friars Place estate immediately south of the Acton Great Western station was unsuccessfully offered for sale in 1886 and was still on the market five years later.[169] On the 11-acre site that had been bought by George Wright in 1883, east of Horn Lane and adjacent to the Goldsmiths' property, little progress was made. The property was sold in 1885 to the National Standard Land Company, which went into liquidation three years later. Even though the land was approximately equidistant from the Great Western and North London stations and the centre of Acton, freehold building plots were being offered on Grafton Road and Baldwin Gardens throughout the later 1880s and early 1890s with a 90 per cent deferment of payment but apparently little success.[170] Further west the available evidence from Ealing again confirms the depression in suburban development on all but the more favoured sites. Building remained at a standstill at Castle Hill except for that part, adjacent to the station, sold at the beginning of the 1880s. An attempt in 1892 to auction the 90 acres comprising Drayton Green Farm met with no adequate response,[171] and the property remained as agricultural land for a decade and more. Nor was any success achieved at several auctions of land at Hanwell Park.[172]

Six years after the abandonment of the District Railway's Uxbridge extension project, two rival Bills were promoted by north Ealing landowners in an attempt to secure the more rapid development of their estates. Both lines were designed to link the area with the North London Railway at Willesden. One scheme, that of the North-Western & Ealing, secured considerable local backing, which included the principal local newspaper, the chairman of the Local Board and the District Surveyor. The main promoter was a local land agent and surveyor, acting for the trustees of 200 acres of partly-developed building land in north Ealing. The second Bill, that of the Harrow, Ealing & Willesden, was for a route slightly further north. This traversed the land of its promoter, who owned 140 acres of building land which formed part of the ill-fated Castlebar Hill estate of Henry de Bruno Austin, on which development had begun twenty-five years before. Although both Bills were rejected, mainly because of the absence of any agreement with the London and North Western for through running, the committee on the North-Western & Ealing Bill accepted the need for a railway across the district as an aid to the resumption of development on estates where building operations had virtually ceased. The projects did have the incidental effect (of little value to their promoters) of inducing the Great Western to institute in 1888 a service from Southall and Ealing to Willesden via a newly-constructed curve linking the Great Western main line with the North & South-Western Junction.[173] The fact that by 1901 services on this route had been considerably reduced possibly indicates that the projected lines of 1887, in competition with the established through services to Moorgate and the Mansion House, could have had little chance of profitability.

In 1894 a successor to the projects of seven years before was promoted, again by local landowners. This was the Ealing & South Harrow, which was to leave the District's Ealing branch near Ealing Common and after traversing north Ealing was to follow the route of the Harrow, Ealing & Willesden to south Harrow. Although the Bill was passed, a working agreement with the District having been obtained, construction did not begin until 1898. Considerable delay followed owing to lack of finance. After the transfer of the line to the District in 1900 (its relationship to the latter company having hitherto been similar to that of the Hounslow & Metropolitan), an extension was opened in 1904 by the Metropolitan from Harrow to Uxbridge. But since significant building operations on the clay lands of west Middlesex did not begin for the next 20 years, the railway remained a classic example of a branch built well in anticipation of eventual suburban development.[174] Until the late 1890s this applied almost equally to the Hounslow branch of the

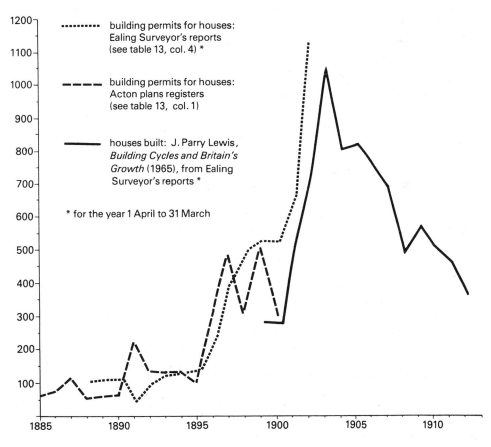

Figure 21. House building in Acton and Ealing, 1885–1912/13.

District Railway. Most of the land sold for building not far from the line at Ealing Park in 1882 was acquired by the British Land Company, and by the following year Whitestile and Murray Roads had been constructed. The sale of land on Whitestile Road was at first relatively successful: at the initial auction in May 1883 two-thirds of the 150 plots offered seem to have been sold. But most of the rest remained vacant for a decade and more. Land fronting Murray Road was also auctioned for the first time in the same year, but in 1898 80 plots were still on offer.[175] Elsewhere at Ealing Park development was little more successful. On Carlyle Road, con-structed by the mid-eighties, less than a dozen houses stood by the middle of the next decade on isolated sites amid over a hundred vacant plots. Similarly the eastern part of Darwin Road had been laid out by 1884, but in 1897 70 plots on the estate were on offer by the National Land Corporation.[176]

Nevertheless on some estates already within the urban area a major decline in building was avoided. At Bedford Park this was partly because its owners secured continued access to the metropolitan drainage system;[177] and unlike others in Acton, the estate had the advantage of national publicity. Bedford Park remained separated by open land from the main part of Acton, and possessed convenient access by the District Railway to the West End and City. Higher-rental villas continued to be built in north Ealing on the Wood and Mount Park estates. On the Wood estate, for instance, 33 leases were granted between 1885 and 1887 on the newly-laid out Mount Park Crescent, close to the Great Western and District stations. The adjacent Mount Park property was developed from 1882, when plots with frontages of 35 feet and upwards to roads already made were offered for sale or lease.[178] Most of these houses were assessed in 1900 at over £50, with many valued at upwards of £70. It was also within the existing urbanized area of Ealing that development began on one of the few new estates to be laid out for building after the second boom. This was the Kerrison Lodge estate, comprising about eight acres to the south of the town centre, surrounded by middle-class housing. First offered in 1889, the land was sold during the next few years with considerable success.[179] In Chiswick the similarly-sized Sutton Court Lodge estate, just south of the Askew property at Turnham Green and not far from Gunnersbury station, was also developed about 1890. Building took place on the leasehold Grange estate immediately east of the station, and on the Stile Hall property close to Kew Bridge station.[180] During this period the Ecclesiastical Commissioners granted the first building agreements for their Prebendal estate, which comprised most of the remaining market garden land between Chiswick and Hammersmith. In 1890 an agreement was made applying to five and a half acres north of the High Road, and the following year development began of 10 acres to the south, immediately east of Chiswick Lane. Here minimum frontages to Homefield Road were to be 25 feet, with houses worth at least £45 *per annum*. By 1893 43 houses had been built on the latter site and others were in progress.[181]

Building of small terraced houses also continued on some sites during the depression. In Ealing this was mostly in Alexandria and Felix Roads, on an estate where operations had begun early in the 1880s, to the north-west of Stevens Town. In south Acton building of low-rental housing continued after the setbacks of the earlier 1880s on those estates where it had already begun. This was despite the liquidation in 1889 of the Berkshire Estates Company, the original developers of the Berrymead Priory site.[182] Less than half the available land on this or the South Acton Station estate had, however, been covered by the early 1890s. In Chiswick the British Land Company began the sale of plots of 17-foot frontage on the Manor House estate in 1893, after paying what was claimed to be the highest price per acre so far realized in the suburb. Three years later some 55 per cent had been sold, mostly for the erection of terraced houses each containing two flats.[183] It seems likely that the evident need for low-rental housing in Old Chiswick at this period was associated with the development of shipbuilding at the local Thornycroft yard, which by the 1890s was at times employing up to 1,800 men.[184]

During the last 15 years of the century serious overcrowding was reported on working-class estates. In 1889 it was claimed that a population of 8,000 at Ealing Dean occupied some 700 to 800 cottages, with cases of 16 to 18 persons per house. Objections had been made earlier in the decade to the further building of mews cottages in Ealing on the grounds that those in existence were overcrowded and inhabited by 'cabmen, "donkey men", laundresses and others not gentlemen's coachmen'.[185] By the later 1890s there were persistent reports of rising rents, attributed at Ealing in part to the refusal of landowners to permit the building of working-class housing on their properties. An investigation in 1896 found rents of 6s. to 8s. per week for four-room cottages in Ealing New Town (immediately south of the Broadway) and Stevens Town in West Ealing.[186] Similar levels obtained at the end of the decade for older houses in Chiswick, for instance in the New Town, an estate of cottages that had gradually been developed during the first half of the century. Improvement of the estate by its owners resulted in the eviction of some existing tenants and their replacement by others able to afford rents of 13s per week for six rooms.[187] Rents of small houses on the adjacent Glebe estate, developed during the 1870s, had risen from 8s. to 9s. per week to between 11s. and 13s.[188] Demand for low-rented accommodation for those working locally appears to have exceeded the supply, even if during the building depression nearby villas for middle-class occupation were standing empty.

The pattern of land sale and building in outer west London during the depression of the later 1880s and early 1890s seems to have been that although activity in some cases continued within the area already urbanized by the mid-1880s, particularly on estates developed during the preceding boom, the sale for building of large tracts of open land virtually ceased. Where such land had already been sold in the early 1880s, development either proceeded slowly, as at Ealing Park, or did not even begin, as at Chiswick Park. No clear evidence emerges that house construction at either end of the rental scale was affected more than building as a whole, but there is some indication that building continued most successfully if it conformed to the existing social character of the neighbourhood, where this was clearly defined. The difficulties confronting the developers of middle-class housing in Acton seem at least in part attributable to the declining social status of the suburb in which their properties were situated.

Such changes in social status seem to have had little direct connection with the development of tramway services in outer west London, except perhaps along the High Road at Turnham Green, until electrification at the end of the century. Horse tramway routes had been promoted almost immediately after the 1870 Tramways Act to run from Shepherds Bush along the Uxbridge Road to Acton, Ealing, and Southall and along the main road from Hammersmith through Turnham Green to Kew Bridge.[189] After considerable delay during the course of construction owing to lack of capital, the first tramway in the area was opened in 1874 from Shepherds Bush to the Acton boundary, and extended along the Uxbridge Road to Acton four years later. This was as far west as the tramway found it possible to proceed: the line was not extended beyond Acton until 1901. In 1881 it was sold by the firm of contractors into whose hands it had fallen during the financial difficulties of the mid-1870s and formed into the West Metropolitan Tramways. During the next two years, after the opposition of the Chiswick Improvement Commissioners had been overcome, extensions were opened from Shepherds Bush to Hammersmith, Turnham Green and Kew Bridge – all within the existing built-up area. J.T. Carr, the developer of Bedford Park, had been among those opposing the tramway extension through Chiswick, suggesting that the Improvement Commissioners should 'see if they could not get a class of houses in the parish not dependent upon a cheaper kind of traffic'.[190]

The new tramway met with little more success than its predecessor, however, and by 1893 was in the hands of a receiver.[191] The relative failure of these tramways, in contrast to many of those serving the inner suburbs, was presumably due mainly to their inability to provide sufficiently rapid and direct transport to inner London. Nor did the West Metropolitan Tramways run early services at cheap fares. In 1893 it was claimed that workmen from Acton wishing to travel to inner London before the trams came on the road at 8 a.m. had to walk the two miles to Shepherds Bush station on the Hammersmith and City line.[192] Through routes to central London were provided by omnibuses, but these were slow and relatively expensive. The journey from Acton to Charing Cross took over one hour in 1895 and the fare was at the rate of 0.9d. per mile. This may be compared with 0.7d. per mile on the tramway between Kew Bridge and Hammersmith and 0.4d. per mile (3rd class return) on the North London between Acton and Broad Street, the journey taking 30 to 40 minutes.[193]

Before the introduction of workmen's tickets the cost of daily travel to and from inner London was beyond the reach of the majority of wage-earners. At the end of the century, when unskilled workers were earning less than 30s. and skilled workers around £2 per week, it was considered that they could afford to spend no more than 1s. to at most 2s. per week on travel, or from 2d. to 4d. per day.[194] In 1879 a third class return from Mill Hill Park on the District to Charing Cross cost 1s. 1d., and a similar ticket 10d. on the North London between Acton and the City.[195] It was not considered that the lowest-paid workers or those in casual employment would be able to take advantage of cheap travel facilities to move to the suburbs: workmen's trains were intended essentially for the relatively better-paid wage-earners. In London the rise in real wages during the later nineteenth century was counterbalanced to some extent by an increase in rents, particularly in the inner districts, a further incentive to migration to the suburbs if sufficiently cheap transport could be provided and if sufficient land could be made available for low-rental housing.[196]

During the last two decades of the century the suburban services of the Great Eastern Railway came to cater on the lines to Tottenham, Edmonton, and Walthamstow predominantly for cheap-fare traffic between inner London and districts that had been transformed into working-class suburbs.[197] This contrasted with the policy of the railways serving outer west London. At the committee stage of the Bill for the Ealing extension it was claimed on behalf of the District Railway that the low-rental housing of South Acton was due to the inadequacy of rail communications with inner London: improved services would lead to a higher standard of building for middle- rather than working-class residents. In 1881 it was stated that building had taken place in Acton 'to suit people who would travel on the District Railway – £30 a year houses, houses for the lower middle class'.[198] At this date the only company to operate workmen's trains in west Middlesex was the London & South Western, which ran two early trains from Hounslow via the Chiswick loop line to Waterloo, but the weekly fare from Hounslow of 5s. (no daily tickets were issued) was little less than that charged for normal third class travel.[199]

In 1882 and 1883 meetings for workmen's trains were held at Hanwell, Acton and Chiswick (but not at Ealing where, it was remarked, the movement was 'not looked upon with any favour'), apparently on the initiative of local traders and property owners. Some fears were expressed that the provision of early trains would lead to the introduction of what was considered an undesirable class of inhabitants; but the general view prevailed that there would be beneficial effects on the prospects for suburban development.[200] The movement eventually secured the support of the Local Boards, and representation were made by these to the railway companies, only to meet in all cases with a negative response.[201]

The effectiveness of the demands for frequent workmen's trains on all lines was considerably strengthened after 1889, when the Metropolitan Board of Works was replaced by the directly-elected London County Council. From then until 1907 the Council was controlled by the radical-liberal Progressive Party, and came to take an active part in the campaign for cheap travel to and from the outer suburbs. A difference in attitude between the London County Council and the Board of Trade was evident over the extent to which the companies should be induced to provide workmen's trains in advance of a substantial working-class population. The Council's Housing of the Working Classes Committee reported in 1898 that despite a recommendation of a Royal Commission in 1885, the 1883 Cheap Trains Act had been 'held to exclude a demand for accommodation for any but workmen [already] needing to travel by railway to their work'.[202] In 1899 a legal judgment relating to an application for workmen's trains on the Great Northern between Edgware and the City confirmed the railways' view that Parliament had not intended the 1883 Act to compel them to open new districts to working-class settlement. The London County Council, in contrast, considered that there should 'from the housing point of view, to induce workmen to live further out, be some minimum provision of workmen's trains on all the Metropolitan Railways irrespective of profit and without waiting for a special demand'.[203]

By the early 1890s the development of workmen's trains in London had attained considerable importance. The extent of the early-morning traffic on the Great Eastern is illustrated by the fact that in the 15-minute periods preceding 7.00, 7.30 and 8.00 a.m., 2,200, 1,400 and 4,900 passengers respectively travelled from Walthamstow to Liverpool Street. Return fares of 2d. were available to 7.00 a.m., 3d. to 7.30 a.m. and 4d. to 8.00 a.m. for a distance from the furthest of the three Walthamstow stations to Liverpool Street of seven miles.[204] In 1892 the Great Western was severely criticized by the London County Council not only for its failure to run any workmen's trains, but also for the fact that only one suburban train of any kind from the main line reached Paddington before 8 a.m. The London County Council suggested the provision of workmen's trains from Southall and intermediate stations to Paddington between 5 and 8 a.m., at intervals of not more than 30 minutes. The report coincided with a request to the London County Council from Hanwell Local Board, established in 1885, for assistance in preparing evidence on the subject for an appeal to the Board of Trade. The Local Board's petition stressed the availability of vacant building land, and the main sponsor was a local auctioneer.[205] The concession finally obtained as a result of the enquiry was scarcely considered adequate by the London County Council: the single train provided was to depart from Southall at 5 a.m. In 1900 three workmen's trains were being run, the last reaching Paddington at 7.30 a.m. The numbers using this service were, as might have been expected, initially very small: on average in the year ending in February 1898 only 51 and 41 passengers per day were departing from Castle Hill and Ealing respectively.[206] In the course of its evidence in 1893 the London County Council provided details of the services to 8 a.m. on all metropolitan railways, indicating that the Great Western mileage rates were on average higher than those of any other company, and that the Great Western, alone with the Great Northern, made no reduction on third class returns. The London County Council stated in conclusion that 'it is the prevailing and apparently well founded opinion throughout the district . . . that the policy of the Company . . . [is] intended to exclude, as far as possible, working men from the locality as a place of residence'.[207]

Although the Great Western was the company considered by the London County Council as the most uncooperative in the provision of workmen's trains, the Council's reports were also critical of the District and the North London. The London & South Western service was viewed more favourably.[208] In 1900 the railway was running from the Hounslow loop four workmen's trains, the last of which arrived at Waterloo after 8 a.m. Criticism by the London County Council was concentrated on the level of fares, which was still considered excessive. The mileage rate of about 0.3d. for workmen's trains on the latter line compared with one of from 0.3d. to 0.15d. on the Walthamstow branch of the Great Eastern.[209] On the North London, after the abandonment of a limited experimental service provided for three months in 1888 and again in 1899, no workmen's trains were run south of Willesden Junction. In 1901 there was still no train from Acton that reached Broad Street before 8.10 a.m., the time of the first train having remained unchanged for the past thirty years. By 1894 three workmen's trains were provided by the District from the Hounslow & Metropolitan line and one early train was operated from Ealing, leaving the latter station at 5.42 a.m.[210] Towards the end of the decade the Ealing Urban District Council tried to induce the District Railway to improve the workmen's services on its Ealing branch. After unsuccessful negotiations with the company, the council applied in 1899 to the Board of Trade for an enquiry under the Cheap Trains Act. The application was subsequently withdrawn in return for an improved provision of workmen's trains. Cheap fares were made available on three early services from Ealing at a level similar to that on the corresponding trains already operated on the Hounslow branch.[211] If the Council was satisfied with these concessions, local labour representatives were not, mainly because no reduction in the level of fares had been achieved. It was considered that the clerks and artisans likely to use the trains would find it difficult to afford a return fare of 6d., which was only 1d. less than the ordinary third class return rate, for so short a journey as that between Ealing and Hammersmith. In 1898 an average of only 25 workmen's tickets per train (giving a total of about 100 per day) had been issued from the three District Railway stations in Ealing.[212] A local comment was that the District Railway had

> offered terms which [were] accepted by the Ealing District Council irrespective of cost, or suitability, so long as something was conceded.

We must hope on for the incoming of the Tramways, when competition will arouse the Railway Companies to the necessity of putting forward an effort to meet the requirements of those who have to travel.[213]

5 The beginning of the third boom, 1895–1900

The major building boom that took place around the turn of the century was experienced throughout suburban London. It was assisted and prolonged in the outer western suburbs by significant transport improvements, first by the advent of electric tramways and subsequently by more frequent services and lower fares on the railways. In 1894 the West Metropolitan Tramways was sold privately after an unsuccessful attempt at auction. The company was acquired by a Bristol-based group with American associates and reorganized as the London United Tramways. Under James Clifton Robinson, appointed as general manager after considerable experience in the tramway industry, the company began to plan a programme of electrification and extension beyond the margins of the urban area. Four years later a Bill was promoted for these purposes. New lines were to run westward from Acton through Ealing along the Uxbridge Road to Hanwell, and from Kew Bridge along the Bath Road to Hounslow. These two routes were to be linked by a line along the Boston Road, through what was still largely undeveloped land, between Hanwell and Brentford.[214] The evidence given at the committee stage of the Bill indicates the hostility with which the proposed tramway extension was regarded by many who considered it likely to lead to an alteration in the social composition of the suburbs it traversed. Hanwell Council, however, supported the tramways in the same way that it had advocated the provision of workmen's trains earlier in the decade.

Opposition to the tramway was particularly strong from Ealing. In contrast to its welcome for the first tramway proposal of 1870, the Local Board had earlier objected to successive proposed extensions of the horse tramway westward from Acton between 1888 and 1891.[215] It was now claimed that 'The tramway brings . . . a different element into the neighbourhood. The old order disappears; the jerry builder appears and the character of the neighbourhood gradually alters.' Such had been the case in Clapham and Streatham. There was much vacant land close to the Uxbridge Road: whether villas or low-rental houses would be built depended on whether the tramway was sanctioned.[216] Against these assertions two arguments were deployed. Firstly it was claimed that tramways did not necessarily lead to a deterioration in property values: thus the Town Clerk of Dublin gave evidence that at the northern suburb of Clontarf expensive houses were being built in anticipation of better transport links with the city. The evidence as to the supposed effect of tramways on the social character of such districts as Clapham was countered, with some truth, by pointing out that change was in any case to be expected in an area built up some forty years before and no longer on the margins of London. The second and somewhat contradictory point in the case for the Bill used the current belief that the provision of cheap transport to the outer suburbs could be a principal means of achieving a significant degree of population dispersal from the inner metropolitan area. Counsel for the Bill observed that 'everybody now recognises how desirable it is [to give] . . . every means you can find of going quickly and cheaply to all parts of the suburbs'.[217] There was much land available locally to

Figure 22a. Part of a panorama of the proposed development by Henry de Bruno Austin on Castle Hill Estate, north Ealing, c. 1860. View to the north with the site of St Stephen's church in the centre foreground (by courtesy of the London Borough of Ealing Library Service).

Figure 22b. 101–111 Argyle Road, Ealing, in 1974 (subsequently demolished). Originally Cleveland Gardens; built by Austin in the early 1860s. Most of these houses were rated at £80 in 1885 (by courtesy of the Greater London Council Photograph Library).

Figure 22c. 5–11 Alfred Road, Acton in 1976. Built between 1862 and 1866 near the North London station; occupied in 1871 by middle-class residents with one or two servants (by courtesy of the Greater London Council Photograph Library).

Figure 22d. 5 Madeley Road, Ealing, in 1976. House dated 1888, on the Wood Estate, near Ealing station (by courtesy of the Greater London Council Photograph Library).

house those able to move from the inner districts – the artisans and the lower middle classes. The remaining market garden land in Ealing south of the Uxbridge Road would 'all be built upon with much the same class of property . . . houses which let at about £26 a year or upwards; not much more than £35.'[218]

The opposition from Ealing was sufficient to induce the committee to strike out of the Bill the proposal for a continuation of the tramway westwards from Acton to Hanwell. This victory was only temporary. The Ealing District Council election of 1898 was fought largely on the tramway question, those candidates supporting a change of policy standing as supporters of Electric Tramways, Incorporation and Progress on a platform that included advocacy of municipal workmen's dwellings. After the election eight anti-tram councillors retained a majority of only one in a council of 16. It was made clear that the policies of the pro-tramway group were not analogous to those of the Progressives on the London County Council: its candidates had included conservatives as well as liberals and socialists.[219] The Council subsequently promoted its own Bill for a municipal tramway system, apparently in an attempt to secure concessions from the London United. As a result, an agreement was reached the following year whereby the Ealing Council's Bill was withdrawn in favour of a second London United Bill which included the extension through Ealing.[220] The electrified tramway was opened in 1901, with extensions from Acton along the Uxbridge Road to Southall and from Kew Bridge to Hounslow. The Shepherds Bush terminus was adjacent to that of the recently-completed Central London underground railway. At a workmen's fare of 2d. return from Southall to Shepherds Bush, and the same rate on the Central London, it was now possible to travel from outer west London to the City and back for 4d. The standard fares between Ealing and the Bank were only twice this amount.[221]

Tramway competition seems to have influenced in turn the evolution of services on railways in the area, all of which reduced their fares during the 1900s. In 1891, for instance, the single third class fare from Ealing to the Mansion House on the District Railway was still 10d. (1s. 3d. return), the same as when the Ealing branch was opened in 1879. By 1901 this had been reduced to 7d. (11d. return) and three years later to 5d. Electrification in 1905 permitted an increase in the number of trains daily from 40 in 1901 to 187 in 1913.[222] In 1901 workmen's fares were issued for the first time from all stations on the District Railway up to 7.30 a.m. At the same time their level was reduced, although it remained high: the return between Ealing and the Mansion House, for instance, was reduced by only 1d. to 8d. Even for those travelling to the inner suburbs, fares were still above the levels it was considered the working class could afford.[223] Of more significance perhaps was the introduction from 1901 of third class season tickets from all stations on the District, and on the London & South Western from 1902. By this means the daily cost of travel between Ealing and the Mansion House could be reduced to $8\frac{1}{2}$d., but it was necessary to be able to afford a month's fare in advance. Similarly in 1901 the Great Western decided to introduce third class seasons to Paddington from stations between the terminus and Southall, and to reduce the cost of third class return tickets to below that of two single fares.[224] The latter concession was introduced long after it had been available on most other railways. The Great Western also now began the construction of new railways across the largely undeveloped claylands of west Middlesex. In 1897 an Act was secured for a new main line that would greatly shorten the route between Paddington and Birmingham, leaving the existing line at Old Oak Common. Within the outer suburban area a link was to be constructed between the new main line at Greenford and the old at West Ealing. A local service began using this line in 1904. The Great Western took steps to promote building in the vicinity of the new line: 'landowners, builders, contractors and others' were circularized. More frequent trains than the initial hourly service were to be provided once building began.[225]

Evidence of a revival of confidence in the prospects for suburban development was already apparent by the mid-1890s.[226] In 1896 The Lawn, an eight-acre residential estate between Hanwell village centre and the station, was put on the market. Building plots were auctioned the same year, when all those offered were sold, mostly for the erection of small terraced houses.[227] The later 1890s saw the sale for building of part of Hanwell Park, which had first been offered for this purpose 15 years before at the time of the proposed Uxbridge extension of the District Railway. From 1896 the southern section of the property was offered in lots as the Drayton Park estate. About £800 per acre was obtained at an auction of 33-foot plots on Shakespeare Road.[228] Although the first houses built here were semi-detached villas for middle-class occupation, later building on the estate was mostly of smaller houses, as foreseen during the local controversy over the probable effect of the London United tramway extension. The largest tract of land subdivided at this period lay south of the already urbanized Uxbridge Road between Ealing Dean and Hanwell. Here the gradual extension of building that during the next 15 years covered most of the remaining market garden land began. Terraces and semi-detached houses for the occupation of clerks and artisans were constructed, sometimes divided into maisonettes. Rents for the latter, comprising three rooms and a scullery, were from 7s. to 8s. 6d. per week. The average rental, exclusive of rates, for houses in the district was about £26, or 13s. to 14s. per week inclusive. The fact that building in Ealing during the third boom reached its peak in 1903, about three years later than in most of outer London, and continued at a relatively high level for the rest of the decade, may largely be attributed to operations in this area.[229] Although an immediate impetus to the building of lower-rental housing in south-west Ealing and in Hanwell was provided by the electric tramways and improved rail services, also of significance were the increasing opportunities for local employment in manufacturing industry at Acton, Southall, and Hanwell during the first decade of the twentieth century.[230] It seems likely that many local residents would have travelled to work within the western suburbs.

In other parts of Ealing and in Chiswick the subdivision of land for middle-class housing was resumed. Building agreements were made in 1898 and 1899 for a further 25 acres of the Prebendal estate in Chiswick. Minimum rental values of houses to be built here were similar to those demanded in the leases granted at the beginning of the decade, ranging on the land between the High Road and Chiswick Mall from £45 to £55.[231] At Chiswick Park building at last began in the later 1890s on land that had been sold for this purpose in 1884. Many plots at a sale in 1899 of land on Barrowgate, Ellesmere, and Park Roads possessed frontages of 40 feet and more, while the lowest minimum building value was £600, the same as on most of the Goldsmiths' estate. The first part of the Rothschild property at Gunnersbury Park to be laid out for building, near Ealing Common station, was offered on a leasehold basis in 1898, with the minimum costs of individual houses to be as high as £1,500.[232] The relative success of these developments in established middle-class areas contrasts with the absence of any resumption of building on similar estates in

Acton. At Mill Hill Park 60 plots of freehold building land were offered for sale in 1900. These comprised about half the estate, on which scarcely any building had taken place since the early 1880s, and which seems to have been left unaffected by the boom of the late nineties. Nor did any building now take place on the Goldsmiths' Company's estate, where amid a changing environment an attempt was still being made to retain its original social character.

In 1900 the Goldsmiths' surveyor was hoping that the West Metropolitan Railway, sanctioned the previous year as a successor to the Latimer Road & Acton, might lead to a revival of building.[233] Four years later, however, this railway too was abandoned after having similarly hampered the planning of roads and building plots on the estate. In 1901 the Goldsmiths' Company entered negotiations with the Town and General Estates Company, whose chairman, Sir Richard Farrant, was managing director of the Artizans', Labourers' and General Dwellings Company and associated with the London United Tramways and Central London Railway. The following year the Town and General leased 111 acres between East Acton Lane and Old Oak Road, including the site of Wright's brickfield. Houses were to be erected to cover the entire site within ten years, and the ultimate ground rent was to be £6,000. The minimum costs were to range from £600 for houses on internal roads to £1,600 for shops and houses on frontages bounding the property. It seems that the minimum values imposed in Wright and Crowle's building agreements were maintained partly because an alteration in the social character of the estate would make letting the existing middle-class villas (some with six and eight bedrooms) in Perryn and Shaa Roads more difficult. Wright himself observed in 1908 that those still in his possession were hard to let partly because they were too large for the district.[234]

One of the principal reasons for the failure of building to resume on the Goldsmiths' estate seems to have been that the stipulated minimum house values were considered by builders too high for the locality. During the 1890s complaints had continued about the continued brick burning in the Vale and the possible threat to health caused by the use of a former brickfield as a municipal refuse tip.[235] By the middle of the next decade the disused brickfields on the south side of the Uxbridge Road were being taken as sites for factories. The views of the estate developers, eventually shared by the Goldsmiths' surveyor, now echoed those of Wright and Eyre 30 years before. By 1905, when the Town and General went into liquidation (three years after Farrant had left the board) only 28 houses had been built, and some of these had cost only £450.[236] Solicitors for the estate company, supporting an offer of finance by the Hampstead estate agent Ernest Owers, on condition that the building agreement was modified, observed that it was 'useless to continue with this class of house'. Owers considered that the nature of adjacent housing and nearby laundries and factories would prevent such property from being let.[237] Others concerned with the estate similarly concluded that if, in contrast, double tenements (i.e. two-storey maisonettes) were to be built, suitable for 'the better class of artizans', there would be little difficulty in letting the land.[238] The Ecclesiastical Commissioners were similarly advised by their surveyors to accept a request from William Willett to substitute the erection of factories for houses on his land at Acton Vale, where the building agreement had hitherto not been enforced because of the changing character of the neighbourhood.[239]

In Acton south of the Uxbridge Road the development of new building estates resumed in the mid-1890s. The first sections of land on two properties hitherto occupied by orchards were auctioned in 1895. At an initial sale on the 10-acre South Acton estate just over half the 65 building plots offered were sold, at an average price as high as £1,700 per acre. At first the plots were advertised as being suited for medium-sized houses, but by 1896 auction sale notices referred to a demand for cottages and laundries.[240] These characterized the property developed earlier by the British Land Company immediately to the north. Between 1896 and 1898 plans were approved for some 200 houses (including those divided into flats), most of which appear to have been built by the early years of the new century. The South Acton estate almost immediately became subject to criticism on the grounds of overcrowding and inadequate building standards.[241] On what became known as the West Bedford Park estate, in contrast, development was slower and took place mostly after 1900. Building here was for middle-class occupation and a wall separated the property from a British Land Company estate to the north. Subsequent attempts to secure through access met with strong resistance from residents.[242]

One of Acton's first local historians, writing in 1912, lamented that it had become 'overstocked with houses, built rather with a view to smallness of cost and the utilisation of the sand and gravel excavated on the sites, than to the attractiveness and convenience of the dwellings'.[243] In 1908 housing in Acton south of the Uxbridge Road, excluding Bedford Park, was characterized as consisting of two main types: six-room houses built twenty to thirty years previously for one family (that is, during the second boom around 1880) and often since subdivided, and more recent constructions designed for two families. The former type, on the land company estates, were usually let to one tenant who in turn sublet the rest of the house. The upper floors of such houses were generally let unfurnished in 1905 for around 6s. 6d. per week. In 1895 the owner of 48 houses on the Priory estate claimed at a successful rating appeal that a plan to let them to single tenants at £32 had been impracticable: each was now let to two families. Even north of the Uxbridge Road, large villas of the 1860s were now being subdivided. Two-room tenements (otherwise unusual in the district) on the upper floors of such three- or four-storey houses were now let for 5s. to 6s. 6d. per week. It was observed that 'these latter were built originally for a superior class of tenant but have since depreciated in character'.[244] In 1911 over 10 per cent of the population of Acton was classified as living in overcrowded conditions, i.e. in tenements with over two occupants per room, compared with an average for Middlesex of seven per cent and for Ealing of under four per cent – although the County of London average was 18 per cent.[245]

The only local authority in the area to undertake a housing scheme before the end of the nineteenth century was Ealing. Following discussion in the local press of overcrowding and rising rents in working-class estates during the 1890s, the question of municipal housing became an issue in the 1898 local election. Sanction was given in 1899 for a loan to the Urban District to cover the cost of 121 cottages on a six and a half-acre site near South Ealing station. The example of a similar local authority scheme already completed at Richmond seems to have been influential. Four-bedroom houses were to be let from 8s. 6d. per week and those with two bedrooms from 6s. 6d., rents which would enable the scheme to be self-financing. Preference was to be given to those employed or for some time resident in Ealing, 'jobbing gardeners, postmen, men engaged locally in the building trade, and so on'. One of the councillors chiefly responsible for the scheme

Figure 23a. Blakeney Lodge, 113 Avenue Road, Acton, in 1976. Built between 1861 and 1866 on the British Land Company's Acton Hill Estate (by courtesy of the Greater London Council Photograph Library).

Figure 23b. 115 Avenue Road, Acton, in 1976. Adjacent to Blakeney Lodge, and built in the same period (by courtesy of the Greater London Council Photograph Library).

Figure 23c. Milton Road, Acton, looking north. On the Acton Station Estate, developed by the British Land Company from 1867. Twenty houses had been built by the 1871 census, with another six under construction (by courtesy of the Greater London Council Photograph Library).

Figure 23d. South side of Vincent Road, Acton, in 1954 (subsequently demolished). Originally 1–8 Junction Terrace, Junction Road. On British Land Company estate in South Acton; plots sold in 1869 and houses built by 1874 (by courtesy of the London Borough of Ealing Library Service).

commented that Ealing was 'not responsible for the housing of London's workmen; we don't want to attract them here', although a certain working-class population was necessary 'for the comfort of villadom'.[246]

Ealing in 1901 was still a predominantly middle-class suburb. The proportion of female domestic servants to the total number of separate occupiers or families was 69 per cent and surpassed in Greater London only by Hampstead, Kensington and Surbiton. The figure for Acton in contrast was 25 per cent and for Hanwell 16; at the other end of the scale in Bermondsey, Bethnal Green and Shoreditch the number of such servants was under seven per cent of the total number of households. The figure fell in nearly all areas of London during the following decade, the Administrative County average declining from 23 to 19. By 1911 Hanwell, at 12 per cent, was no more a middle-class suburb than were Leyton or Deptford. A relatively steeper decline, to 40 per cent, was evident in Ealing than in the other outer west London suburbs,[247] an indication of the nature of the new building in the suburb that continued at a high level during the first decade of the century in contrast to the general metropolitan trend.

6 Summary and conclusions

Until the end of the nineteenth century the railways remained the principal means of travel between the outer western suburbs and inner London. In contrast to the services provided on many lines to the north-eastern suburbs, those of companies in outer west London did not encourage travel by working-class residents. This fact helped determine the social character of much of the area under consideration. The development of railway services falls into three broad phases, covering respectively the first 25 years after 1840, the period from 1865 to 1880, and the remainder of the century. During the earliest of these periods little encouragement was given to surburban traffic. The lines across the area were regarded primarily as routes for through traffic. By the early 1880s an adequate suburban service for middle-class residents had been established on most lines. Attention was increasingly focused on the question of whether, and to what extent, workmen's trains should be provided, at lower fares and earlier times than the existing services. Notable differences in attitude to the development of suburban traffic can be distinguished between the railway companies, in particular between the main-line Great Western on the one hand and the District and (at least during the 1860s and 1870s) the North London on the other. The District Railway by the 1870s saw in the creation of branch lines in advance of substantial building development a partial means of offsetting the cost of its inner urban lines.

Fluctuations in the disposal of land for suburban development in outer west London broadly correspond to the London building cycle. Upswings in building followed not only easier credit and reductions in the number of vacant houses resulting from overbuilding during previous booms, but also improvements to the transport network. Whether the London building booms primarily reflect the aggregate influence of transport improvements at particular periods has been the subject of discussion.[248] There is some indication in outer west London that new railway services influenced the lease and sale of land for building. Examples include transactions following the improvement of the North London service from Acton in 1865, the provision of new stations on the Great Western at Acton in 1868 and

Castle Hill three years later, and the promotion of the District Railway's extensions to Ealing in 1877, to Hounslow in 1878 and 1880, and to Uxbridge in 1880 and 1881.

What proportion of those living in the new houses of outer west London travelled to work in the central metropolitan area is unknown. While many middle-class residents used the improved suburban rail services of the later nineteenth century, inhabitants of houses on working-class estates seem mostly to have been employed in the service industries of the western suburbs. The opportunities for female employment to supplement family income offered by the large number of laundries may have been one inducement to immigration to south Acton. In the second boom from the later 1870s and particularly the third from the later 1890s there was an increase in the construction of housing for the lower middle class and artisans. Parts of Ealing and central and south Acton were laid out for building of this type, with rateable values of from £15 to £35, and from the later 1890s such housing predominated in new building in Hanwell and south Ealing. During the third boom it seems likely that this was associated in the latter area less with the inadequate service of workmen's trains in the 1890s than with the electric tramways and with the improvements to rail services during the following decade, as well as with increasing local employment opportunities.

It is clear that whatever the initial impetus to building on particular estates, development was frequently not maintained after a relatively short period. Operations on large parts of the Goldsmiths' Company's property came to a standstill for periods in some cases of up to 20 years. On only two of eight separate sites was building completed by 1900 even though leases for all had been granted by 1884. On two sites building did not even begin. During depressions, it seems that building in outer west London for middle-class residents was maintained best on sites closest to adequate public transport, as on the Askew estate in Chiswick in the 1870s or the southern part of the Wood estate in Ealing in the later 1880s. But it would be necessary to know more of the financial resources available to builders on specific sites before coming to any definite conclusions.[249] In the building slump from the mid-1880s to the mid-1890s the most successful projects conformed to the established social character of neighbouring estates, whether comprising villas in north Ealing or low-rental housing in south Acton. Local administrative divisions also had some influence on the timing of development. The delay in extending the Ealing Local Board boundary northward in the 1860s may have affected building at Castlebar Hill. By the end of the following decade, with the extension and improvement of the Local Board's drainage system, little further difficulty seems to have been experienced at Ealing, although problems remained over the sanitary condition of the older working-class estates. In Acton, however, the injunction secured by the Metropolitan Board of Works in 1882 undoubtedly contributed to the low level of building in the suburb during the rest of the decade.

The policies of individual landowners and the legal conditions governing the development of their estates were evidently of primary importance in determining the timing of the disposal of land and the nature of building. The latter aspect is well illustrated by the Goldsmiths' estate. Since most of the property was held in trust, the Company had to take into account the likely views of the Charity Commission on projects for building. All proposals made by the Goldsmiths' Company relating to the Perryn Charity land were examined by a surveyor sent down by the Commission.[250] As a corporate landowner, the Company was itself prepared to take a long view of the development of the property, with more concern for its ultimate reversionary value than for immediate profit. This difference of interest between landowner and developers lies behind the continued disagreements between the Goldsmiths' Company and its lessees over the type of building to be permitted. In this respect the position at East Acton parallels that described by Donald Olsen in his study of the Bedford estate in Bloomsbury at a somewhat earlier period.[251]

Yet if the Goldsmiths' Company could demand that its lessees adhered to an attempt to build for middle-class occupation, it could not ensure their success in the absence of sufficient demand for such housing in a district where adjacent properties were developed with different objectives. The operations of the British Land Company in Acton during the 1860s seem to have been crucial in determining that the suburb should not, like Ealing, grow during the later nineteenth century predominantly as a desirable location for middle-class residence. Southern Acton came to contain a substantial working-class population, while nearer the North London station the improved train service after 1865 seems to have encouraged building for lower-middle-class occupation. Ealing, in contrast to Acton, did not come to possess a substantially improved rail service until the end of the following decade. By then development during the first boom and the policy adopted by the Wood settled estate of granting building leases for low-density development had confirmed that at least northern Ealing would retain its existing social character. Here adjacent developers followed the pattern established on the Wood property: the freehold Mount Park estate for instance was developed for similar high-value housing from the 1880s on the southern slopes of Hanger Hill. Even the British Land Company at Castlehill Park recognized that with the abandonment of the projected District Railway Uxbridge extension in 1881 its estate was too far from adequate public transport for any attempt to be made to develop it other than with large villas.

There is little clear evidence of a connection between low-density development and the previous existence of parkland, comparable to that found by Emrys Jones in south Belfast.[252] Examples of landscaped grounds being used for middle-class housing, as with part of the British Land Company's Acton Hill estate from 1860, Springfield Park from 1877, or Castlehill Park in north Ealing, can be contrasted with such properties as Acton Priory, Ealing Park or Hanwell Park. The low-density Devonshire building estate was situated at least in part on what had been market garden or nursery grounds at the edge of the landscaped park. Although in north Ealing topography and, away from the Great Western and District stations, distance from public transport, appear to have influenced the nature of building, this was not the case elsewhere in outer west London. On the level land of Chiswick social distinctions between adjacent estates are primarily attributable to the differing policies of landowners. The Devonshire estate was by far the largest in the parish, and its development for high-value housing (imposed by means of covenants even when the land was sold) helped determine the social character of the suburb. This was reinforced by the policies of adjacent owners such as the Askew family and (when they eventually developed the Prebendal estate) the Ecclesiastical Commissioners.[253] The properties of the British Land Company, developed in a quite different manner, and the older working-class districts, were insufficiently extensive for Chiswick to follow a similar pattern to Acton in its nineteenth-century development.

Both Chiswick and Acton adjoined Hammersmith to the east. The latter grew during the last half of the century essentially as a lower middle class suburb, with some poorer quarters near the village centre and at Starch Green on the margins of Acton. There was no outward-moving frontier of high-value housing similar to that in north-west London.[254] It was therefore only to be expected that parts of Chiswick and south Acton might be developed for lower-rental housing. Yet Bedford Park, Gunnersbury and Grove Park retained their middle-class character at the end of the century. It is in the development policies followed on individual properties that an explanation of the variations in the character of housing within a particular district must be sought.[255] The question of how far estates retained their original characteristics (as shown for instance by the occupations of residents and the extent of subletting) and of whether social segregation within individual suburbs was increasing during the later nineteenth century,[256] must await detailed examination of the census returns as these become available.

The importance of both topography and the social geography of adjacent areas in determining the character of suburban development, whatever the policies of landowners, has recently been emphasized by David Cannadine.[257] These considerations are clearly to some extent significant in explaining the general nature of suburban growth in outer west London. Since the area was in the nineteenth century far from the main concentrations of industry and working-class housing, its development followed a course different from that of most of metropolitan Essex and the Lea valley. The nature of railway services during the period reinforced the incentives to build for middle-class occupation. At a local level, however, variations not merely in the layout of streets but in the nature of housing from one estate to another may largely be attributed to differences in the manner in which land was made available for building. It was the pattern of land ownership and the timing of initial development that ultimately determined the social characteristics of the various districts comprising the nineteenth-century outer west London suburbs.

NOTES

1 This account is based on my 1971 University of London M.Phil. thesis, 'Railways and suburban development: outer west London, 1850–1900', with which a note of any additional information or amendments to the content of the chapter will be placed.
I am grateful to Mr J.W. Scott, the Librarian of University College London, for agreeing to a period of leave so that I could undertake the revision of my thesis. I wish also to acknowledge a grant from the Twenty-Seven Foundation towards travel expenses, and the permission given by the Wardens of the Goldsmiths' Company to quote from their archives. Mr T.F.T. Baker, editor of the Middlesex *VCH*, kindly gave me access to draft chapters from volume 7, to be published shortly. The staff of the libraries and record offices mentioned in the footnotes, as well as officers of the London Borough of Ealing, all readily gave me their assistance. Thanks are due to my former supervisor, Mr H.C. Prince, for helpful comments on a draft of the chapter, and for the same reason to Dr M.J. Daunton, Mr A.D.M. Phillips, and Dr R.V. Steffel.
2 For population see J.T. Coppock and H.C. Prince (eds.), *Greater London* (1964), 34. The two figures cited refer to the Metropolitan Board of Works area and the Metropolitan Police District respectively. The growth of the inner western suburbs is outlined by D.A. Reeder, 'A theatre of suburbs', in *The Study of Urban History*, ed. H.J. Dyos (1968), 253–71.

3 Particularly J.R. Kellett, *The Impact of Railways on Victorian Cities* (1969). See also M. Waugh, 'Suburban growth in north west Kent, 1861–1961' (Ph.D. thesis, University of London, 1968), 73; F.M.L. Thompson, *Hampstead* (1974), 54–62.

4 G.B.G. Bull, 'Thomas Milne's land use map of the London area in 1800', *Geographical J.*, cxxii (1956), 25–30.

5 PRO, IR 29 and 30/21/1, 10, 13, 26: tithe apportionments and maps.

6 T. Faulkner, *The History and Antiquities of Brentford, Ealing and Chiswick* (1845), 163–7.

7 T.C. Barker and M. Robbins, *A History of London Transport*, I (1963), 33, 393–403.

8 E. Jackson, *Annals of Ealing* (1898), 203, 227–35; PRO, IR 18/5474: report on the agreement for the commutation of tithes in the parish of Ealing.

9 See, for example, E.W. Brayley and J.N. Brewer, *The Beauties of England and Wales: London and Westminster, IV, Middlesex*, by J.N. Brewer (?1815), 313–42.

10 *MCT*, 11 and 25 May 1867, 17 Dec. 1892.

11 Bradshaw (July 1850).

12 HLRO, North & South Western Junction Railway Bill, HL SC (1851); M. Robbins, *The North London Railway* (7th edn., 1974), 4.

13 Bradshaw (December 1860).

14 PRO, RAIL 250/16, Great Western Board Minutes, xiii (1859–60), 142; RAIL 1066/2123–6, Metropolitan District Railway [Uxbridge extension] Bill, HLSC (1881), q.1160.

15 Barker and Robbins, *op. cit.*, 122.

16 T.B. Peacock, *Great Western Suburban Services* (2nd edn., 1970), 38, 40.

17 Bradshaw (January 1866); H.V. Borley, 'The early train services of the North & South Western Junction Railway',) *J. Railway and Canal Hist. Soc.*, vii (1961), 21–7.

18 *MCT*, 19 October, 2 November 1867, 1 March 1873, 12 January 1878.

19 PRO, RAIL 250/7, Great Western Board Minutes, iv (1853–4), 237, 249–50; for the initially slow progress of building, *MCT*, 15 February 1868.

20 GLRO, Acc. 224/6: abstract of title . . . Rev. A.W. Wetherall (1870).

21 N. Pevsner, *Middlesex* (1951), 43.

22 MLR (for full references see Jahn, thesis, 36, n. 9); *London Gazette*, auction sale notice [Ibbetson *v.* May], 6 August 1872.

23 PRO, RG 9/777, 1861 Census, Middlesex, Brentford District, Brentford Subdistrict.

24 21–2 Vict. c. lxix.

25 Royal Society archives, 351: Acton estate papers, 37: Report of Special Committee, 30 May 1856; GLRO, Acton enclosure award, 8 Nov. 1859.

26 J. Parry Lewis, *Building Cycles and Britain's Growth* (1965), 129–132; H.J. Dyos, *Victorian Suburb* (1961), 80–2; S.B. Saul, 'House-building in England, 1890–1914', *Econ. Hist. Rev.*, 2nd ser., xv (1962–3), 119–37; *Survey of London, XXXVII: Northern Kensington* (1973), 6; F. Sheppard, V. Belcher and P. Cottrell, 'The Middlesex and Yorkshire deeds registries and the study of building fluctuations', *London J.*, v (1979), 176–217.

27 Royal Commission on Friendly and Benefit Building Societies, Minutes of evidence, PP 1871 [C.452], XXV, QQ. 7264–7449, 7949–8160; 2nd report, PP 1872 [C.514], XXVI, pp. 15–16; Dyos, *op. cit.*, 114–17; S.D. Chapman and J.N. Bartlett, 'The contribution of building clubs and freehold land society to working class housing in Birmingham', in *The History of Working-Class Housing*, ed. S.D. Chapman (1971), 239–46; S.M. Gaskell, 'Yorkshire estate development and the freehold land societies in the nineteenth century', *Yorks. Arch. J.*, xliii for 1971 (1972), 158–65; E. Gauldie, *Cruel Habitations* (1974), 208–13; Thompson, *op. cit.*, 372–6.

28 *Estates Gazette*, 16 March 1868. For the development of railway services see Barker and Robbins, *op. cit.*, 126–65; for the British Land Company properties in Enfield and Barnet see *VCH Middlesex*, V (1976), 218–19, 263.

29 *Freeholder's Circular*, 5 April 1873, 28 March 1874.

30 Hounslow Public Libraries, Layton Collection, 2977: plan of Acton Hill House estate; *Freeholder's Circular*, 10 October 1859; MLR, 1859/16/1146.
31 Hounslow Public Libraries, Layton Collection, 2970: auction particulars (part of Acton Hill estate), 7 March 1860; *Freeholder's Circular*, 20 April 1860.
32 Hounslow Public Libraries, Layton Collection, 2969, 2971: auction particulars (part of Acton Hill estate) 7 March and 23 April 1860; *Estates Gazette*, 1 May; July and August, 1860; MLR (for full references see MLR indexes under British Land Company).
33 *Freeholders' Circular*; MLR.
34 Borley, *loc. cit.*, 21–7.
35 GC, 14.2, East Acton estate: plan and book of reference (1860); *AG*, 17 December 1887.
36 GC, 3.2, sale notice and correspondence, April-May 1862.
37 GC, 4.1, draft building agreement, 1864.
38 GC, 4.1, surveyor's report, 28 March 1864.
39 GC, 12.1, surveyor's report, 17 November 1864; 13.1d, from M.B.W., 8 July 1865.
40 *Survey of London*, XXXVIII: *The Museums Area of South Kensington and Westminster* (1975), 298, 300.
41 GC, 5.1, building agreement, 29 September 1868.
42 GC, 3.4, The Friars, auction particulars; conveyance to GC, 10 December 1868.
43 *MCT*, 29 May 1869; MLR, 1872/7/322, plan: *Post Office London Suburban Directory*, ed. E.R. Kelly (1872); Acton Local Board, register of plans for new buildings, II [1873–84], 872 etc.; PRO, RG 10/322, 1871 Census, Middlesex, Brentford District.
44 GC, 5.1, building agreement, 29 September 1868.
45 Bradshaw (February 1871).
46 GC, 5.1, surveyor's reports, 3 December 1869, 24 March 1870; building agreement, 18 July 1870.
47 GC, 2.26, leases, 9 August 1870, 19 June 1884; 3.13, correspondence and papers (1900–2).
48 Hounslow Public Libraries, Layton Collection, 2972: auction particulars, 5 November 1862; MLR (for full references see MLR indexes under British Land Company).
49 *MCT*, 27 March, 8 May and 14 August 1869.
50 *Post Office London Suburban Directory* (1872); *AG*, 6 May 1898; 1901 Census, *Middlesex*, PP 1902 [Cd.1211], CXX, table 35A. For an example of semi-detached villas in Park Road North offered as suitable for conversion to laundry premises see *West London Observer*, 17 June 1882. The development of the laundry industry in London is described in H. Llewellyn Smith [director], *The New Survey of London Life and Labour*, V (1933), 344–8, 371–82. See also Royal Commission on Labour, *Employment of Women: Reports . . .*, PP 1893–4 [C.6894–xxiii], XXXVII pt 1, p. 22.
51 *MCT*, 7 and 14 November 1874; *AG*, 26 June 1875, 20 August and 17 September 1881, 18 February 1882.
52 PRO, RAIL 1066/2117–20, Metropolitan District Railway [Ealing extension] Bill, HCSC (1877), Q.1666.
53 GC, 3.7, Acton Station estate: abstract of title of British Land Company (1868).
54 *Freeholder's Circular*, 19 December 1868, 18 December 1869, 17 April 1875.
55 PRO, RG 10/322, 1871 Census, Middlesex, Brentford District; for the Birkbeck estate, *MCT*, 18 February, 18 March 1871.
56 S.B. Warner, *Streetcar Suburbs* (Cambridge, Mass., 1962) notes the similarities in the type of housing erected by different builders on freehold land in the nineteenth-century suburbs of Boston, Massachusetts.
57 GC, 5.1, surveyor's report, 6 April 1871; endorsement, 30 December 1872, on 1870 building agreement.
58 GC, 5.3 [copy], from Wm. Cocks, 6 February 1879.
59 GC, 5.1 [copy], Wright to Eyre, 13 January 1871.
60 GC, 5.1, memorandum of revised brickmaking agreement, 1 March 1878; 13.7, surveyor's report, 7 July 1880.

61 MLR (for full references see MLR indexes under Devonshire); see also J. Wisdom, 'The making of a west London suburb: housing in Chiswick, 1861–1914', (M.A. thesis, University of Leicester, 1976). The sales may have been caused in part by the financial requirements of the Devonshire enterprises at Barrow in Furness. See D. Cannadine, 'The landowner as millionaire: the finances of the Dukes of Devonshire, ca. 1800–1926', *Agricultural Hist. Rev.*, xxv (1977), 87; and, for sales of Eastbourne freeholds, D. Cannadine, *Lords and Landlords: The Artistocracy and the Towns, 1774–1967* (1980), 288–96.

62 9–10 Vict. c.6.

63 Barker and Robbins, *op. cit.*, 147–8.

64 *Survey of London,* XXXVII, 303–6; PRO, RAIL 1066/1338–9, Hammersmith and City Junction Railway Bill (1864), HCSC, Q.26.

65 PRO, RAIL 1066/1338–9, Kew, Turnham Green and Hammersmith Railway Bill, HCSC (1864), Q.239ff. (George Burchett, Surveyor to Askew and Tubb estates); Q.475.

66 *Freeholder's Circular,* 21 March 1870, 5 April 1873; *West London Observer,* 22 September 1877; GLRO, Acc. 1327.

67 MLR (for full references see MLR indexes under Askew); GLRO, Acc. 1395/13, building agreement, 30 December 1872.

68 MLR, 1856/15/435; 1863/22/324–6; 1864/20/819; 1865/16/198, 17/91, 23/787–8; 1866/9/805–6.

69 Ordnance Survey plans; *Estates Gazette*, 8 July 1862.

70 *MCT*, 19 September 1868; *Estates Gazette*, 23 July 1867.

71 MLR, 1869/18/9; Law Reports: ex parte Austin, in re Austin (1876), IV Ch.D. 13.

72 *MCT*, 27 May 1882; *ibid.*, auction sale notices, 8 April, 20 May, and 30 September 1882; 17 February 1883, 23 February, 7 June, and 23 August 1884.

73 For example, *MCT*, 7 April 1877, 5 May 1883.

74 MLR (see Jahn, thesis, 63, n. 14); Ealing Reference Library, British Land Company, abstract of title (Castlehill Park, Ealing) (1880); MLR, 1870/14/462–6, 680; building agreement, 16 July 1870, cited in K. Hodson, 'A housing development in 1870', *Local Historian* (Ealing Local Hist. Soc., 1963), 22–4.

75 British Land Company, abstract of title; MLR, 1880/32/735.

76 PRO, MH 13/67, Local Government Act Office correspondence: Ealing, 1862–71; 36–7 Vict. c. cxl; *AG*, 11 November 1876.

77 *MCT*, 10 July 1875, 19 October 1878.

78 *MCT*, advertisement for property on estate, 20 November 1869.

79 GLRO, Acc.1429/41, Conveyance Monins Trustees to John Galloway, 14 May 1868; *Post Office London Suburban Directory* (1876).

80 MLR, 1870/13/769–70; *MCT*, 20 March 1869.

81 GLRO, Acc. 842.

82 *MCT*, 1 May 1886.

83 1871 Census; for comment on the depression, *MCT*, 25 March 1871; for the effect of the slump on the inner west London suburbs, see D.A. Reeder, 'Capital investment in the western suburbs of Victorian London' (Ph.D. thesis, University of Leicester, 1965), 321.

84 HLRO, Acton and Hammersmith Railway Bill, HCSC (1874), 173.

85 Hounslow Public Libraries, Layton Collection, 2975; auction particulars, 20 May 1869, 16 May 1873; MLR, 1877/35/905; Thompson, *op. cit.*

86 *MCT*, 14 February 1891.

87 PRO, RAIL 267/6, Great Western General Manager's report: Suburban passenger traffic, 4 February 1869. Some of the deficiencies in the General Manager's analysis have been indicated in Kellett, *op. cit.*, 62–4.

88 Barker and Robbins, *op. cit.*, 53; G.F.A. Wilmot, *The Railway in Finchley* (1962), 19–30; J.N. Young, *Great Northern Suburban* (1977),73–81.

89 PRO, Metropolitan District Railway [Ealing extension] Bill, HCSC (1877), QQ2466–8, 2475; E.R. MacDermot, *History of the Great Western Railway*, II (1931), 322–4.
90 *MCT*, 27 January, 1 June 1872.
91 PRO, RAIL 267/22, General Manager's report: Proposed Shepherd's Bush & Brentford Railway, 7 October 1874.
92 PRO, RAIL 1066/1338–9, London & South Western Railway (Kensington & Richmond) Bill, HCSC (1864), Q.1262.
93 *MCT*, 25 May and 3 August 1878; 27 May 1876.
94 *AG*, 21 July 1877.
95 PRO, RAIL 1066/80–1, 1364–5, Hounslow & Metropolitan Railway Bill, HCSC (1880), QQ1036, 1053.
96 MLR, 1875/24/356.
97 T.A. Greeves, 'London's first garden suburb', *Country Life*, cxlii (1967), 1524–9, 1600–2; *Building News*, xxxii (1877), 253.
98 *AG*, 8 May, 30 October 1880, 1 March 1884; G.W. Bacon, *New Large Scale Ordnance Atlas of London and Suburbs* [1885]; S.E. Rasmussen, *London: The Unique City* (1960 edn.), 198–9; W.L. Creese, *The Search for Environment: The Garden City Before and After* (1966), 87–107; M.J. Bolsterli, *The Early Community at Bedford Park* (1977).
99 MLR, 1882/10/374; *AG*, 30 April 1881, 23 June 1883.
100 Acton Local Board, Register of plans for new buildings, II (1873–84).
101 *AG*, 30 October 1880, 12 November 1887; *AG*, advertisements, 23 April, 6 and 13 August 1881.
102 GC, 10.1, tenders for St Dunstan's Church, March 1878; *City Press*, 23 July 1879.
103 GC, 5.2, surveyor's report, 21 February 1878; *AG*, 18 February 1927, obituary of Sir George Wright.
104 GC, 5.3, surveyor's report, 3 October 1878.
105 GC, 13.7 [copy], from Eyre, 6 January 1880.
106 *Ibid*., from Eyre, 6 October 1880.
107 GC, 4.3, surveyor's report, 20 February 1879; building agreement, 13 June 1879.
108 GC, 4.5, surveyor's report, 20 February 1879; building agreement, 26 November 1879.
109 GC, 4.6, building agreement, 26 June 1880; correspondence (1882); building agreement, 12 June 1883.
110 GC, 4.8, surveyor's report, 30 May 1883; building agreement, 29 January 1884.
111 GC, 4.9, surveyor's report, 26 May 1886.
112 Royal Society archives, Domestic, vol. 7; and 467 (Cmb. 41), Acton Estate Committee minutes; MLR, 1882/10/56.
113 Bacon, *New Large Scale Ordnance Atlas*; *AG*, auction sale notices, 8 April, 6 and 27 May 1882, 28 May 1887; *Builder*, xlii (1882), 567.
114 *AG*, auction sale notices, 25 March, 29 April, 3 June, 18 November 1882.
115 *AG*, 22 July 1882, 12 November 1887; for the history of the house, see W.K. Baker, *Acton* (1912), 116–31.
116 *AG*, 2 June 1883; *Builder*, xlvi (1884), 403.
117 *AG*, 30 June, 21 July 1883, and subsequent issues; 1 May 1886 and subsequent issues; 12 November 1887.
118 *AG*, 22 August 1885, 16 October 1886; *Builder*, lii (1887), 534.
119 Acton Local Board, Register of plans for new buildings, ii (1873–74), 1311.
120 PRO, RAIL 1066/1493–4, Latimer Road & Acton Railway Bill, HCSC (1882), Q. 257, notes of building agreements; *AG*, 1 March, 5 and 26 July 1884.
121 *AG*, 28 April 1883; Church Commissioners, File 61105, from Willett, 4 September 1885.
122 MLR, 1879/11/767, 30/12, 35/29; 1880/9/424, 28/448; 1881/7/895, 20/327, 30/191, 33/719, 35/208.
123 *Builder*, xlii (1882), 207; MLR, 1885/2/642; *AG*, 1 May 1896; *Chiswick Times*, 18 April 1902.
124 *MCT*, 28 August 1880.

125 *Ibid.*, 28 June 1879.
126 MLR, 1880/24/201, 1881/29/876, 1888/6/784; Bacon, *New Large-Scale Ordnance Atlas.*
127 *MCT*, 10 February 1877.
128 *Ibid.*, auction sale notices, 4 March, 27 May, 8 July 1882, 2 June 1883, 9 May 1885; comment, 7 November 1891.
129 GLRO, Acc. 1369/1, conveyance, 27 September 1880, with schedule of leases; *MCT*, 27 December 1879.
130 PRO, RAIL 1066/1361–3, Hounslow & Metropolitan Railway Bill, HCSC (1878), Q.1140.
131 PRO, RAIL 1066/2122, Metropolitan District Railway [Uxbridge extension] Bill, HCSC (1880), Q.1084; *ibid.*, RAIL 1066/2123–6 (1881), Q.1080.
132 PRO, Hounslow & Metropolitan Railway Bill, HCSC (1878), Q.1027.
133 *Ibid.*, HLSC (1878), Q.225.
134 PRO, Metropolitan District Railway [Uxbridge extension] Bill, HLSC (1881), Q.593.
135 *Ibid.*, QQ.553, 773–5; HCSC (1881), QQ.740, 759.
136 PRO, Hounslow & Metropolitan Railway Bill, HLSC (1878), Q.112–14, 197.
137 PRO, Metropolitan District Railway [Uxbridge extension] Bill HLSC (1881), Q.1162.
138 *Ibid.*, Q.982.
139 *Railway Times*, XL (1877), 777; *Railway Times*, XLIV (1881), 729; *Herapath's Railway and Commercial J.*, quarto ser., XLIII (1881), 196.
140 *Railway Times*, LXIX (1896), 249.
141 Barker and Robbins, *op. cit.* (1963), 238–9; *Railway Times*, XL (1877), 683–4.
142 *Railway Times*, LXXVII (1900), 209.
143 PRO, RAIL 1066/1343–4, North Western and Ealing Railway Bill, HCSC (1887), Q.790–4; *Builder*, XL (1881), 743.
144 *MCT*, 19 May and 3 November 1883.
145 *Ibid.*, 17 April, 1 and 8 May 1886.
146 J. Weale (ed.), *London Exhibited in 1851* [n.d.], 518–20.
147 *MCT*, 5 June 1880, 21 May 1881.
148 *Ibid.*, 10 June and 8 July 1882; MLR, 1882/35/143, 203–4, 325, 912; 1882/36/966; 1882/37/101.
149 *MCT*, auction sale notice, 8 July 1899.
150 *MCT*, 15 and 29 July, 12 and 19 August 1882.
151 *Builder*, XLII (1882), 567.
152 GLRO, Middlesex County Council, Reports of local inquiries (1889–97), 99, Application for the division of the Ealing Local Board district into wards (1894).
153 Parry Lewis, *op. cit.*, 130–1; Dyos, *op. cit.*, 81–2; Reeder, *op. cit.*, 302, 309. For comment on the depression in building, *MCT*, 7 November 1891.
154 *AG*, auction sale notices, 23 October 1886, 17 June 1893.
155 *AG*, 31 January and 1 May 1896.
156 *Ibid.*, 7, 14 May, 4 June 1892, 4 November 1893.
157 GC, 4.9, from G. Wright, 13 January and 8 April 1886.
158 HCSC on Town Holdings, *Minutes of evidence*, QQ.7094, 7237, PP 1887 (260), XIII.
159 GC, 4.9, surveyor's report, 26 May 1886; from Charity Commissioners, 25 June 1886.
160 *AG*, reports and correspondence; GC, 3.5, from G. Wright, 17 February 1887; 3.10, correspondence, conveyance to Acton Local Board, 8 August 1888; Church Commissioners, File 67780. The transaction between the Goldsmiths' Company and the Acton Local Board has been simplified here.
161 GC, 4.9, from G. Wright, 1 January 1893; surveyor's report, 22 February 1893.
162 45–6 Vict. c. ccxlvii.
163 PRO, Latimer Road & Acton Railway Bill, HCSC (1882); A.A. Jackson, *London's Local Railways* (1978), 370–2.
164 GC, 7.1, surveyor's report, 22 January 1885; agreement, GC and Latimer Road & Acton Railway, 3 September 1885.

165 GC, 4.9, surveyor's report, 26 May 1886.
166 *Ibid.*, 22 February 1893, 7 July 1896; *ibid.*, 5.4, surveyor's report, 22 March 1899; *ibid.*, 5.6, surveyor's report, 21 October 1902.
167 GC, 5.6, correspondence and papers relating to East Acton Brickworks and Estate Company (1902–6).
168 Acton Local Board, Register of plans for new buildings, II [1873–84], 1327–8, 1474; Bacon, *New Large-Scale Ordnance Atlas.*
169 *AG*, 12 November 1887; auction sale notices, 29 May 1886, 16 May 1891.
170 *Ibid.*, auction sale notices, 7 October 1882, 2 March, 22 June and 19 October 1889, 8 February and 3 May 1890, 11 March 1893; GC, 4.8, from Freeman & Bothamley, solicitors, 28 September 1888, surveyor's report, 14 November 1888.
171 *MCT*, auction sale notices, 28 May and 18 June 1892.
172 *Ibid.*, 8 September 1883, 10 May 1884, 23 May 1885; *VCH Middlesex*, III (1962), 225.
173 Peacock, *op. cit.*, 17.
174 A.A. Jackson, 'North-west from Ealing', *Railway Magazine*, cv (1959), 602–12, 711–19; *idem, op cit.*, 214–36.
175 *MCT*, auction sale notices, 12 May, 2 June, 7 July, 8 September 1883; 7 April 1894, 23 April 1898.
176 Bacon, *New Large-Scale Ordnance Atlas*; Ordnance Survey plans; *MCT*, auction sale notices, 29 March and 12 April 1884, 6 March and 29 May 1897.
177 *Builder*, XLVI (1884), 403.
178 MLR, 1888/6/784 (gives ground rents and dates of leases of houses on Wood estate, 31 January 1888); *MCT*, 22 July 1882, 28 July 1883, 29 March 1884, 24 January 1885; Bacon, *New Large-Scale Ordnance Atlas.*
179 *MCT*, auction sale notices, 9 March 1889, 11 April, 29 August, 3 October 1891, 17 June 1893, 30 June 1894.
180 Sutton Court Lodge: *AG*, auction sale notices, 15 August 1888, 23 March 1889, 14 May 1892, Ordnance Survey plans; Grange: GLRO, Acc. 1395/36–44; Stile Hall: *AG*, 25 June 1892.
181 Church Commissioners, Files, 71014, 71468.
182 *AG*, auction sale notices and result, 18 May and 29 June 1889.
183 *AG*, 1 April 1893; auction sale notice, 8 July 1893; GLRO, Acc. 891/2/9/11–12, auction particulars (Manor House estate), 18 May 1896; Wisdom, *op. cit.*
184 *AG*, 6 August and 29 October 1897.
185 *MCT*, 23 November 1889, 3 November 1883.
186 *Ibid.*, 4, 18, 25 January 1896, 1, 8 February 1896, 26 June 1897.
187 *AG*, 13 and 20 September 1884; 3 and 10 March 1899.
188 *Ibid.*, 17 February 1899. For the Glebe estate, MLR, 1868/24/376 (999-year leases from 1868); 1880/28/426; *West London Observer*, 2 April 1870.
189 Board of Trade, *Proceedings under the Tramways Act, 1870*, PP 1871 (211), LX; Metropolitan Tramways Orders Confirmation Act, 1873, no.2, 36–7 Vict. c. lxxxv.
190 *West London Observer*, 19 February 1881, 7 January 1882.
191 B. Connelly, *The London United Tramways* (1964), 5; G. Wilson, *London United Tramways* (1971), 17–28.
192 HLRO, West Metropolitan Tramways Bill (1893), HCSC, pp. 42–3, 109–17, 122.
193 Barker and Robbins, *op. cit.*, 196, 221; LCC, Statistical Department, *Locomotive Service: Return of Services and Routes . . .* Pt 1, *Tramways, Omnibuses and Steamboats* (1895).
194 HCSC on Workmen's Trains, *Minutes of Evidence*, QQ.42–8 (E. Harper, Statistical Officer, LCC), PP 1904 (305), VII; Board of Trade, *Report on Standard Time Rates of Wages . . . 1900*, PP 1900 [Cd.317], LXXXII.
195 *MCT*, 27 September 1879.
196 G. Stedman Jones, *Outcast London* (1971), 207–9; E.H. Hunt, *Regional Wage Variations in Britain, 1850–1914* (1973); Gauldie, *op. cit.*, 157–8; A.S. Wohl, *The*

Eternal Slum (1977), 285–316; J. Burnett, *A Social History of Housing, 1815–1970* (1978), 145–52.

197   R. Wall, 'A history of the development of Walthamstow, 1851–1901' (M. Phil. thesis, University of London, 1968), ch. 3ii.

198   PRO, Metropolitan District Railway [Ealing extension] Bill, HCSC (1877), Q.25; *ibid.*, HLSC (1877), Q.2293; Metropolitan District Railway [Uxbridge extension] Bill, HLSC (1881), Q.936.

199   Board of Trade, *Railways (Workmen's Trains on the Metropolitan Lines): Report . . . by Major Marindin*, PP 1883 [C.3535], LXI.

200   *AG*, 23 December 1882, 14 and 21 April 1883; *MCT*, 11 and 18 November 1882.

201   *AG*, 21 April, 12 May and 7 July 1883; 13 November 1886; 18 June 1887; *MCT*, 5 May 1888.

202   LCC, *Workmen's Trains: Extract from Reports of the Housing of the Working Classes Committee Adopted by the Council* (1898).

203   Kellett, *op. cit.*, 375; GLRO, LCC, Housing of the Working Classes Committee papers, 38, from Statistical Officer, 1 May 1901.

204   HCSC on Workmen's Trains, *Minutes of evidence*, Q.1112, PP 1904 (305), VII.

205   LCC, *Workmen's Trains: Further Report of the Public Health and Housing Committee . . . on Workmen's Trains North of the Thames* (1892); GLRO, LCC, Public Health and Housing Committee papers [E.16], from Hanwell Local Board, 11 May 1892.

206   PRO, RAIL 1968/160, London United Tramways Bill, HCSC (1898), Q.2246.

207   GLRO, LCC, Public Health and Housing Committee papers (E.16), LCC Inspector to Clerk of Council, 13 April 1893.

208   LCC, *Workmen's Trains: Analysis of Reports* (1892); LCC, *Workmen's Trains: Report of Statistical Officer . . . South London Railways* (1897).

209   Board of Trade, *Workmen's Trains: Return . . .*, PP 1900 (187), LXXVI. pt.i.

210   Barker and Robbins, *op. cit.*, 220; *AG*, 7 July and 29 September 1888, 24 March and 10 November 1899; Board of Trade, *Railways (Workmen's Trains on the Metropolitan Lines)*, PP 1894 [C.7541], LXXV.

211   Ealing Municipal Archives, Borough Treasurer and Town Clerk's Department, File 35, Box 187, Clerk of Ealing Urban District Council to District Railway, 31 July 1897, 9 November 1898; from District Railway, 1 March 1900.

212   PRO, London United Tramways Bill, HCSC (1898), Q.3172–3.

213   Ealing Municipal Archives, File 35, Box 187, from E.J. Thomas, 28 March 1900.

214   Connelly, *op. cit.*; Wilson, *op. cit.*

215   *MCT*, 1 December 1888; 3 and 21 January 1891.

216   PRO, London United Tramways Bill, HCSC (1898), counsel against Bill (15 June); Q.2233 (Dr. F.E. Fenton).

217   *Ibid.*, Q.684; *ibid.*, p. 78, counsel for Bill, 20 June 1898.

218   *Ibid.*, Q. 1242.

219   *MCT*, 19 March, 2, 9 and 16 April, 3 December 1898; 17 and 24 February 1900.

220   Ealing Municipal Archives, Notice of application by Ealing Urban District Council for Bill, 15 November 1899; agreement London United Tramways and Ealing Urban District Council, 2 February 1900.

221   LCC, *Housing Development and Workmen's Fares: Report by the Valuer to the Housing of the Working Classes Committee* (1913), 9; Royal Commission on London Traffic, *Minutes of Evidence*, Q.24779, PP 1906 [Cd.2751], XL; Barker and Robbins, *op. cit.*, II, 21–2, 31–4, 115.

222   M. Rees, 'The economic and social development of extra-metropolitan Middlesex during the nineteenth century, 1800–1914' (M.Sc.Econ. thesis, University of London, 1955), 84; LCC, *Third Class Season Tickets: Report by the Statistical Officer* (1902); *To Uxbridge from the City . . . by Train, Tube and Car* (published by W.T. Pike, Brighton, c.1904).

223   GLRO, LCC, Housing of the Working Classes Committee papers, 38, from Local

Government and Statistical Department, 19 June 1901.

224 LCC, *Third Class Season Tickets* . . . (1902); PRO, RAIL 250/45, Great Western Board Minutes, XLII (1899–1901), 423.

225 Peacock, *op. cit.* 50–63; A.W. Arthurton, 'The G.W.R. suburban motor car service', *Railway Magazine*, XIV (1904), 487–93.

226 See comment in *AG*, 7 August 1896; for Chiswick, comment in *Chiswick Times*, 7 January and 11 November 1898.

227 *MCT*, auction sale notices and result, 23 May, 17 October and 7 November 1896.

228 *Ibid.*, 2 and 23 May, 6 and 27 June, 5 September 1896.

229 *Ibid.*, 28 July 1900, and advertisements during year; Saul, *loc. cit.*, 125.

230 M. Robbins, *Middlesex* (1953), 56; *VCH Middlesex*, III (1962), 228; B.A. Baton, 'Some aspects of the recent industrial development of west London' (M.Sc.Econ. thesis, University of London, 1954), 77.

231 Church Commissioners, Files 77301, 77832, from Cluttons, report on proposed building agreement with M.N. Rhodes, 20 December 1898.

232 Hounslow Public Libraries, Chiswick Reference Library, MP 3221, auction particulars (Chiswick Park estate), 18 October 1899; *MCT*, 29 January 1898; PRO, London United Tramways Bill, HCSC (1898), Q.2726.

233 GC, 5.4, surveyor's report, 10 July 1900.

234 GC, 6.2, building agreement, 18 July 1902, and related correspondence; 13.17, auction sale notices for two houses in Shaa Road, 21 October 1910; from G. Wright, 17 January 1908.

235 *AG*, 7 May 1897; 14 October 1898.

236 GC, 6.11, Town & General [Liquidation]: Summary of the statement of affairs, 29 May 1905; draft reply on behalf of GC to Town & General (in liquidation), 23 November 1905.

237 GC, 6.9, from Freshfields, 10 January 1905; surveyor's notes, 17 January 1905, on proposals by E. Owers.

238 GC, 6.2, surveyor's report, 4 January 1904, i.e. 1905; 6.9, from Clerk of Town & General's Acton Park estate, 19 April 1905.

239 Church Commissioners, File 69885, from Cluttons, 23 May 1905; 61105, from Cluttons, 24 July 1905.

240 *AG*, 18 May 1895; auction sale notices, 8 and 15 June, etc. 1895.

241 *AG*, 9 June 1899; 9 March 1900.

242 *AG*, 29 June 1895; Acton Urban District Council, building plans register; Ealing municipal archives, Acton, Misc. file 6; *AG*, 9 June 1911.

243 Baker, *op. cit.*, 312.

244 Board of Trade, *Cost of Living of the Working Classes: Report of an Enquiry* . . ., 48–50, PP 1908 [Cd.3864], CVII; *AG*, 21 September 1895.

245 1911 Census, England and Wales, vol. 8, Tenements, table 8, PP 1913 [Cd.6910], LXXVII.

246 *MCT*, 30 September 1899.

247 LCC, *London Statistics*, XXIV 1913–14 (1915), 76–7, 86–7. Chiswick: 33.5 in 1901.

248 Saul, *loc. cit.*, 132; Parry Lewis, *op. cit.*, 129–39.

249 For examples see Dyos, *op. cit.*, 132–7; Reeder, *op. cit.*, 326.

250 *AG*, 17 December 1887.

251 D.J. Olsen, *Town Planning in London: The Eighteenth and Nineteenth Centuries* (1964), 20, 35.

252 E. Jones, *A Social Geography of Belfast* (1960).

253 See comment in *Chiswick Times*, 28 December 1900.

254 Reeder, *loc. cit.*, 266–71; H.C. Prince, 'North-west London, 1814–1863'; '1864–1914', in J.T. Coppock and H.C. Prince (eds.), *Greater London* (1964), 103–7, 121; Thompson, *op. cit.*, 65–6.

255 For a recent illustration from a provincial city see Mark Shaw, 'Reconciling physical and

social space: Wolverhampton, 1871', *Trans. Inst. British Geographers,* N.S. IV, no.2 (1979), 211. The importance of land ownership is stressed in M.J. Daunton, *Coal Metropolis: Cardiff, 1870–1914* (1977), 73–88.

256 For social change in sample areas of Leicester in the later nineteenth century see R.M. Pritchard, *Housing and the Spatial Structure of the City* (1976), 90–100.

257 Cannadine, *op. cit.,* 394–401.

The process of
suburban development
in north Leeds,
1870–1914

C. TREEN

The process of suburban development in north Leeds, 1870–1914

C. TREEN

1 Context

The thesis which forms the basis of this paper examined the process of building and estate development in three out-townships of the former borough, earlier still the parish, of Leeds between 1781 and 1914.[1] Headingley cum Burley, Potternewton, and Chapel Allerton out-townships lay to the north of Leeds in-township, the three comprising an area of approximately 12 square miles (see fig. 24). Work which began with the aim of discovering the historical explanation for the particular suburban *genius loci* evolved into an exploration and identification of the process of suburban residential development.

The evidence was found amongst property deeds, estates' sales particulars and plans, and the records of large landed estates. Other sources had local disadvantages. There is a paucity of surviving Poor Rate Books for the northern out-townships of Leeds. Before the 1820s Leeds newspapers and directories showed little awareness of the existence of the outlying parts of the parish. Not until the late 1880s did directory compilers attempt comprehensive coverage of the rapidly increasing suburban areas, and even then the lower strata of the population were omitted. Property sale advertisements in the local press provided an indication of what was for sale and where, but not of what was sold. Property deeds provided a prosaic antidote to the hyperbole of vendors' claims in sale particulars.

Large-scale maps and census enumerators' returns enabled assessments to be made of the physical extent and social composition of the suburbs, but only at the dates for which they were available. It will be 2001 before the census enumerators' returns for the period of most rapid suburbanization in north Leeds, 1881–1901, are fully accessible. Complete township surveys and accompanying maps produced in the carrying out of Acts of Inclosure and of Tithe Commutation Awards were especially valuable as starting points from which to work both forwards and backwards in time. Unfortunately the development detail provided by the material is static, the occasional building ground artificially frozen into inactivity. Another

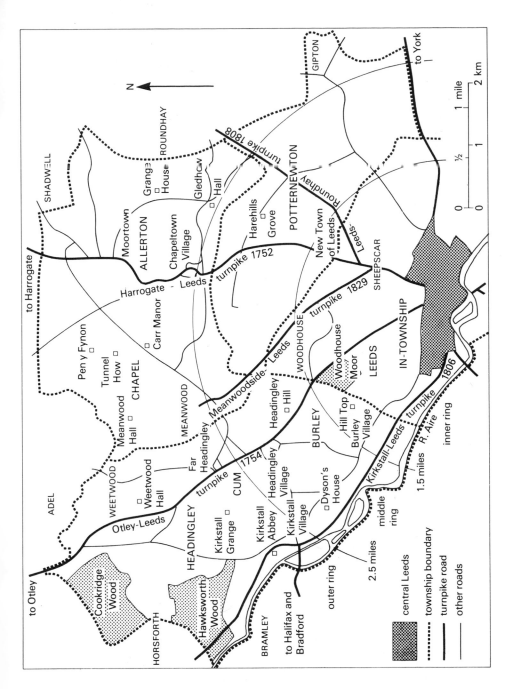

Figure 24. The northern out-townships of Leeds, c. 1830.

major disadvantage of a wholly map-based approach arose from the resulting tendency to examine suburbanization as a two-level process, equating the land-owner of the survey period with the future developer of the estate and ignoring for want of evidence the role of the speculator.

The re-creation of the making of suburbs from the evidence of thousands of title deeds recording land and building transfers leads almost inevitably to a system based on identification of the roles played by those involved. The establishment of a role-playing model is an essential prerequisite for the reconstruction of the development process from the vast amount of data generated and preserved by the legal profession. It also more readily facilitates comparisons between different times and places. Chalklin's work on the provincial towns of Georgian England is the most notable example of this type of approach.[2]

Table 14 Roles in the suburban residential development process

category	sub-category
A pre-development landowner	A1 agricultural estate landowner
	A2 land speculator
B developer	B1 agricultural estate landowner
	B2 builders
	B3 associated professions (lawyer, surveyor, estate agent)
	B4 entrepreneur
C builder	C1 speculative builder
	C2 contractor
D building owner	D1 landlord
	D2 owner occupier
E resident	E1 tenant
	E2 owner occupier

Attention to each role in the process in turn enables an assessment to be made of the relative importance of each role, of significant subcategories within each role, of the extent to which roles were combined by individuals, and of changes in the form of the process through time and place. Each role (see table 14) embraces a distinct sphere of activity with the exception of the owner occupier who would be identified both as a building owner (sub-category D2) and resident (sub-category E2). Of the sub-categories of role D, building owner, that of landlord (D1) was the more significant reflecting the use of house and cottage property as an investment medium. In 1886 Edward Ryde, a past president of the Surveyor's Institute, described the letting of houses and cottages to working-class tenants as almost a distinct trade carried out by small capitalists.[3] The landlord-tenant relationship was a feature of the villa and respectable terrace neighbourhoods as well as the cottage property districts populated by artisan and labourer. For Headingley cum Burley and Potternewton the Poor Rate books of 1834 and 1837 respectively show that two-thirds of house property was let rather than owner-occupied. The balance was unchanged in Headingley cum Burley in 1861 when two-thirds of even the best class of houses, annual value above £25, were let.[4] In 1861 there was no overlap between the landlords of the lower density neighbourhoods of detached and semi-detached villas and the landlords of the higher density cottage neighbourhoods.

The sub-category of speculative builder (C1) may be further subdivided to distinguish between the builder as landlord, erecting property as a speculative investment, and the builder erecting property speculatively for sale as rapidly as market conditions would allow. It is also possible to refine the definition of role A, pre-development landowner, to distinguish between land purchase without subsequent development by the owner, land resale without development or subdivision, and land speculation with subdivision and resales.[5]

What was the impact of variations of tenure upon the development process? During the nineteenth century, building land development in Leeds was carried out overwhelmingly upon a basis of freehold tenure. In 1886 material collected by Charles Harrison, a London lawyer, for the Select Committee on Town Holdings demonstrated that Leeds was similar in this respect to Liverpool and Bradford. It was reportedly unlike Manchester, developed on a system of perpetual chief rents, and unlike Sheffield, Birmingham and London, areas primarily, though not entirely, of leasehold development.[6]

The emphasis upon freehold tenure in Leeds was not readily explicable by contemporaries. Martin and Fenwick, Leeds surveyors, land agents, and civil engineers of repute nationally and considerably involved in north Leeds development between 1860 and 1914, were unable to explain this emphasis when quizzed upon it by a London-based trustee of a Potternewton estate in the 1890s. As four of the five forms of tenure identified by the Select Committee on Town Holdings – freehold, 99-year leasehold, long leasehold, chief rents – had been attempted in the northern out-townships of Leeds, the emphasis upon freehold appears to have been a matter of demand control rather than supply. In Sheffield the Duke of Norfolk controlled sufficient land to ensure that builders would accept the leasehold tenure which he favoured. In Headingley cum Burley, although owning half of the township, the Earl of Cardigan's estate was unable to dispose of 99-year building leases around the mid-nineteenth century. During the 1860s a Cardigan estate attempt to dispose of land on a system of chief rents achieved little success: 17 only were obtained, of which no more than four were in excess of £30 per year.[7] The one success of the long leasehold system was between 1823 and 1852 in the development of the industrial village of Kirkstall on 299-year building leases by Sir James and Sandford Graham. They had to adopt the system because the title to their estate derived from a 500-year lease granted in 1652, commencing 21 years after the longest of three lives. The ample supply, indeed over-supply, of potential building land in north Leeds during the nineteenth century ensured that purchasers were able to indulge their proclivity for the independence which freehold tenure provided.

In 1889 the conclusion of the Select Committee on Town Holdings was that leasehold produced quicker development of building estates, but freehold towns could not be held to have suffered in consequence of freehold tenure.[8] This balanced conclusion was not necessarily echoed by specialist witnesses who tended to be confirmed adherents of one or other of the forms of tenure. The evidence of E. Yates, a south London developer and builder whose Camberwell career was investigated by Professor Dyos, suggested from his own experience that there were significant differences. Yates's experience of both freehold and leasehold enabled him to demonstrate that houses built by him on freehold land could be let for ten per cent less than identical houses build on leasehold.[9] It cost less to borrow money on freehold than leasehold property, and trust funds were more readily forthcoming for building on freeholds.[10]

The Select Committee thought that builders would be more active on leaseholds because only a ground rent needed to be paid rather than the purchase price of a freehold. However, this advantage was negated when developers in freehold areas were willing to accept a deposit on the purchase price of the land whilst building went ahead. Alternatively, in Leeds at least, a purchaser might borrow two-thirds of his capital outlay on building land on security of the title deed to the freehold.[11]

Except for the evidence of Yates one might conclude that there was no significant variation in the profitability of the development process caused by variations of tenure. The five roles of the development process were present both in freehold and leasehold developments, although in the latter case the roles of pre-development landowner and developer might be expected more frequently to be combined. Irrespective of the form of tenure the greatest profitability lay in real estate subdivision and disposal of building plots to those who would build, rather than in the building operation itself.

2 Precursors

The search for a beginning of the movement of the wealthier inhabitants of Leeds to residences in the surrounding countryside was taken back to the dissolution of the monasteries by Whitaker, the early nineteenth-century antiquarian historian of Leeds. His claim, made in 1816, that 'a new race of gentry, raised by trade, planted themselves principally on the parcelled demesnes of Kirkstall Abbey' was misleading.[12] Even in 1816 the most significant feature both in Headingley cum Burley township, where the ruins of Kirkstall Abbey still stand, and in Potter-newton township, where monastic influence had been slight, was the large acreage held by members of the aristocracy. The Earl of Cardigan had owned over half of Headingley cum Burley since obtaining it by inheritance in 1671. The estates of Earls Cowper and Mexborough comprised more than half of Potternewton. Of the three earls, only Mexborough had the major part of his estates and his principal residence in Yorkshire.

The first large modification of the eighteenth-century pattern of landownership produced by Leeds town dwellers occurred during the 1760s in the third northern out-township, Chapel Allerton. Jeremiah Dixon, a major Leeds woollen cloth export merchant, created a 1,000-acre estate by a series of land purchases in 1764, 1766, and 1771; he also had a new mansion, Gledhow Hall, built in 1770 after fire damage to the earlier house on the site. An investment on the scale of Dixon's was essentially a halfway stage towards the life of the county gentry; it was completed in the 1820s by his son, Henry, who withdrew from trade and purchased the Chester estates of Lord Delamere.[13] A contemporary of Jeremiah Dixon was his Chapel Allerton neighbour, Sir Thomas Denison. Member of another wealthy Leeds merchant family, Denison had entered the legal profession and had risen to become a judge on the Court of King's Bench. When he died in 1765 he had but recently completed the erection of a new house and park, Meanwood Hall.

The improvement of road access to Leeds from the north and west for business traffic by the turnpiking of the roads between Leeds and Halifax in 1740, Leeds and Harrogate in 1752, and Leeds and Otley in 1754, had a secondary affect of increasing the residential potential of parts of the northern out-townships for those able to commute on horseback or by horse and carriage. New turnpike routes, to

Kirkstall in 1806, through Potternewton to Roundhay in 1808, and to Meanwood-side in Chapel Allerton in 1829, completed the basic road network for later nineteenth-century north Leeds commuters.

It was possible to obtain a rural retreat from Leeds less expensively than Denison or Dixon by leasing accommodation. The availability of country houses on short leases with all or a portion of their grounds became an increasingly common feature of the advertisement columns of the Leeds press during the final quarter of the eighteenth century. Merchants, bankers, and the new industrialists of Leeds, who withdrew to the northern out-townships between 1775 and 1820, mostly did so by taking leases either of property within the villages of Headingley and Chapeltown or of farmhouses with potential for improvement. An example of the latter was the residence of Joseph Oates, of another Leeds merchant family, on the estate of Earl Cowper in Potternewton. In 1808 the Cowper surveyor described it as 'a substantial brick and stone messuage of an old construction, sash fronted and slated, with barn, stable and farm buildings'. In spite of the addition of a separate stable and coach house and a 'cottage lodge' at the entrance, it was noted that the roof and front of the house 'in point of modern improvement . . . stands in need of a great deal being done'.[14] The following year Oates was claiming rent reductions in respect of his expenditure on a new kitchen and other improvements.

Earl Cowper was the first large landowner to consider capitalizing upon this demand for accommodation by the sale of building plots. Claridge, his London-based surveyor, also reported on this aspect of the Potternewton estate in 1808.

> This estate will always be a very valuable one from its contiguity to the great
> Manufacturing Town of Leeds; and the Rent it produces from time to time will
> always depend upon the prosperity of the Trade therein. Yet notwithstanding
> the high price the Land may produce for occupation it will bear no proportion to
> its value in fee; and there is no doubt but if this Estate were to be sold in small
> parcels it would provide an increasing sum of Money.[15]

A further review of the prospects of a sale was made at the next rent review, in 1819. An appraisal by the local agents, Tottie, Richardson, and Gaunt, suggested that an immediate sale of six acres nearest to the town of Leeds would produce £1,900, even at a time of depressed trading conditions and of social and political unrest. However, a gradual sale was expected to boost the sum to between £3,890 and £4,670.[16] The higher prices had the disadvantages of a need to divide the land into small plots, to find more purchasers, and of an expected development period of six years.

A third review was made in 1825 by a surveyor, Jonathan Taylor, who summed up the case for undertaking estate development, but with a proviso which most north Leeds developers in the nineteenth century learnt by experience to be a major disadvantage. 'As a general rule . . . the less the quantity in each lot the better price it will fetch; a smaller quantity being within reach of a greater number of persons, and consequently commanding greater competition: the more the subdivision, the greater will be the profit to be realized; but this increases trouble, and the profit is longer in realizing.'[17] Cowper rejected the idea of the estate carrying out its own subdivision and sold 55 acres close to the boundary with Leeds in-township for £29,860. The unlikely purchasers were London booksellers and publishers, T. and J. Hurst and J.O. Robinson; their development was to be a New

Town of Leeds. The editor of the *Leeds Intelligencer*, Griffith Wright, also a neighbouring landowner, expressed great enthusiasm for this scheme in his newspaper. 'We fully anticipate the success of this project, and the result will be, that in a few years, land adjoining Lord Cowper's estate, which at present might be purchased for a few shillings per square yard will be sold at highly advanced prices.'[18] Wright and others were to be disappointed, within three years the promoters of the New Town of Leeds were bankrupt. An ignominious anti-climax occurred in April 1829 when the fifth Earl Cowper repurchased the land from the mortgagees for just under £20,000, the amount of the outstanding mortgage debt. Griffith Wright was amongst the neighbours who refused offers of the land adjoining their estates.

Reluctantly the Cowper estate was drawn into the minutiae of building land sales. In 1845 'New Leeds' consisted of a mere 20 dwellings surrounded by unsold plots which were let as cow pastures. Plots were still being sold by the estate in 1871; some remained unbuilt upon until the 1930s. The built form of the new town failed to reflect the aspirations of its promoters. Hopes of grandiose terraces around a central square rivalling Edinburgh or Bloomsbury were destroyed by the sporadic and piecemeal nature of the development. For the sixth and seventh Earls the whole New Leeds experience seems to have confirmed the wisdom of the family's initial unwillingness to become involved in building estate development. They did not enter the process again at the developer level.

The Cowper experience was the common lot of would-be developers in north Leeds between 1825 and 1850: the dream of profit, the wait for purchasers, a search for purchasers, enticements of lowered standards for building development in order to finally dispose of the land.

Developers in Headingley cum Burley not only had to face competition amongst themselves for purchasers, but also had to face competition from the auction sale of allotments of former common land held to defray the expenses of the Inclosure Act for the township. Twenty-six small and medium sized lots, mostly of less than half an acre, the largest 2¼ acres, of the former Headingley Moor were offered for sale in 1831. Prices obtained were as low as 3d. per square yard; only 11 lots sold for more than 9d. per square yard; the highest price, 2s. 3d. was achieved for the smallest lot, just 300 square yards. By 1850 a community known as Far Headingley had arisen on the former common land, 2½ miles from central Leeds.

A rival development along the Leeds–Otley turnpike, one mile nearer to Leeds on Headingley Hill, had commenced in 1829 with the offer of single-acre plots by a Leeds merchant, George Bischoff. Having purchased 25 acres in 1827 at 10d. per square yard, Bischoff subdivided and resold acre plots at 1s. 8d. per square yard in 1829 and 1s. 5d. per square yard in 1830. No sales were made during the period 1832–4, but a single sale in 1835 obtained 2s. 6d. per square yard. Competition from the Far Headingley development in the early 1830s was succeeded in the second half of the decade by the availability of plots on two adjoining Headingley Hill estates, those of J.H. Fawcett and of Mrs Barbara Marshall. These made available an additional 120 acres of building land at a time when Bischoff had managed to sell only seven acres in eight years. In 1845 a fourth Headingley Hill estate, that of R.W.D. Thorp, was put on the market, adding a further 20 acres to the total available. All four estates were intended to be sold for the erection of mansions and villas.

The acreage available was far in excess of the demand for building land intended

164

for that class of development. Sales made by the Bischoff and Fawcett estates for which price data is available show that during 1840–3 the prices received per square yard dropped to between 9d. and 1s. 0d. Bischoff withdrew from his developer role between 1841 and 1843 by selling the remaining half of his 1827 purchase to one person, the Leeds druggist Samuel Glover, who had taken a residence on the estate in 1836. Mrs Barbara Marshall succeeded in selling 20 acres, over half of her estate, to the Leeds cornfactor, Thomas England. He moved out of Park Square in the formerly fashionable west end of Leeds and established a large mansion called Headingley Castle in its own parkland setting. Most of the remainder of the Marshall estate remained unsold until the 1860s. J.H. Fawcett died in 1850; his heir held on in hope for ten years before selling the remaining nine acres at 6d. per square yard. The profits foregone by the Fawcetts after 23 years of piecemeal development were reaped by a new generation of land speculators and developers during the 1860s and 1870s; in the latter decade prices rose to 4s. 0d. and 5s. 0d. per square yard.

On Headingley Hill sites for 'numerous mansions and villas of superior class' of the 1830s became sites 'suitable for commodious and respectable dwelling houses' by 1850 (see fig. 25). The Thorp estate in 1852 was 'for the first time divided for sale in small lots'; nevertheless, adherence to requirements for detached or semi-detached villas of £30 annual value, or good terrace houses with large gardens meant that part of the estate remained unsold seven years later. Under such circumstances the social seclusion of the neighbourhood was at risk, dependent upon the patience of the developer and the legal force of restrictive covenants.

Limited success from the developers' point of view between 1825 and 1850 should not be taken as an indication that all was well amongst the residences of central Leeds. The evidence of Leeds people to parliamentary enquiries into the state of urban centres and manufacturing districts during the 1830s and 1840s was explicit on this point. In 1845 Darnton Lupton, then mayor of Leeds, told the Select Committee on Smoke Prevention of a fall in house values in the inner areas, 'almost 25 per cent to 30 per cent with good houses; because everyone does as I did a few years ago; I went out, I could not bear it any longer; and everyone who can is going out of town'.[19] The Inspector of Nuisances for the borough, T.C. Rusher, confirmed that 'a great number of parties have left Leeds, no doubt on account of the smoke affecting the houses, making them dirty and unpleasant to live in'.[20] At mid-century the exodus was still largely restricted to the upper echelons of Leeds society. William Beckett, Leeds banker and member of parliament, who had been safely ensconced on a 450-acre Headingley estate called Kirkstall Grange since 1830, made this clear in a letter to the editor of the *Leeds Mercury* in 1849. 'Whilst our opulent merchants and bankers resort to their country residences, the clergy, the medical profession, the shopkeepers, the artisan and the operative, are compelled to live with their families in an impurity of atmosphere that destroys every comfort of life.'[21]

Between 1850 and 1870 many of the groups that Beckett had noted as being confined to the urban core succeeded in moving out. The quickening of the pace of growth in the northern out-townships was first experienced in Headingley cum Burley during the 1850s, and then in Potternewton during the 1860s. These two decades comprised the latter half of the horse drawn bus era in north Leeds. The first successful bus services had been introduced in 1838 along the Leeds–Otley turnpike between Far Headingley, Headingley village, Headingley Hill and Leeds.

This was followed in 1840 by the introduction of a service along the Leeds–Harrogate turnpike between Chapeltown, the New Town of Leeds and Leeds by one of the proprietors on the Headingley route. Both routes appear to have been started at the instigation of existing out-township residents who had presumably been dependent on their own transport resources. When J. and W. Atkinson opened their Potternewton route they announced that this was at 'the earnest solicitation of a number of highly respectable inhabitants of Chapeltown and Potternewton'. The horse bus services of the 1830s and 1840s were operated at times and fares beyond the reach of the mass of the Leeds population. No omnibus mania gripped Leeds to match the enthusiasms of the early railway promoters.

Between 1840 and 1860 the bus services in north Leeds altered little in their fares, frequency, and starting times. There were occasional changes of proprietors, and new routes were attempted, often unsuccessfully. From 1847 to 1853 a bus ran from Kirkstall, via Burley, to Leeds, five times daily in each direction on weekdays in 1847, four times on weekdays in 1853.[22] It appears to have been withdrawn sometime in 1853, and no service was provided until 1861. In the latter year the *Leeds Mercury* published a plea from a correspondent for the inhabitants of Burley and the surrounding district to help 'establish for ourselves a comfortable and easy passage from the town home by supporting the omnibus which has just commenced and not allowing it to fall through, as all previous attempts have done, for want of support. We have now every comfort provided and the fare is such that all can embrace the opportunity'.[23] By July 1862 it appeared that the new venture had proved successful, another correspondent complaining of 'excessive and shameful overcrowding'.[24] Once again the period of success was short-lived. A service in operation between Burley and Leeds in 1866 was discontinued after a few months; it was not only unprofitable, the buses were not waterproof, 'the time was as the proprietor thought fit', and street urchins appear to have been employed as conductors. Under such conditions, another letter writer concluded, 'is it surprising that ladies refused to ride, or that business men could not put up with such unpunctuality'.[25]

Even on the profitable routes all was not well; a *Leeds Mercury* correspondent in 1861 claimed that Leeds was less well served than Manchester by its public transport.

> The present omnibus accommodation in Leeds very inadequately supplies the wants of the public and is dearer than in other large towns . . . Mr. Stork of Chapeltown has . . . commenced a new 'bus between Leeds and Moortown, charging only 2d. and 3d. for the shorter distances of New Leeds and Chapeltown. This is a movement in the right direction, and ought to be encouraged, for as the town population are gradually extending their dwellings in the out-townships, a cheaper and more ample transit accommodation becomes not only important but necessary.
>
> In Manchester and other large towns people can travel twice the distance for the same fares as are charged here, in some places 3 or 4 miles for 3d. or 4d. But in Leeds, until Mr. Stork's bus started, you could not ride to New Leeds for less than 6d., and even now if you go from Leeds to Woodhouse Moor, a little more than a mile, the 'buses will set you down for 4d. if only half full of passengers, but if any are left for want of room, you must pay the full fare of 6d. . .
>
> It is said that the great obstacle to improvement in 'bus accommodation are

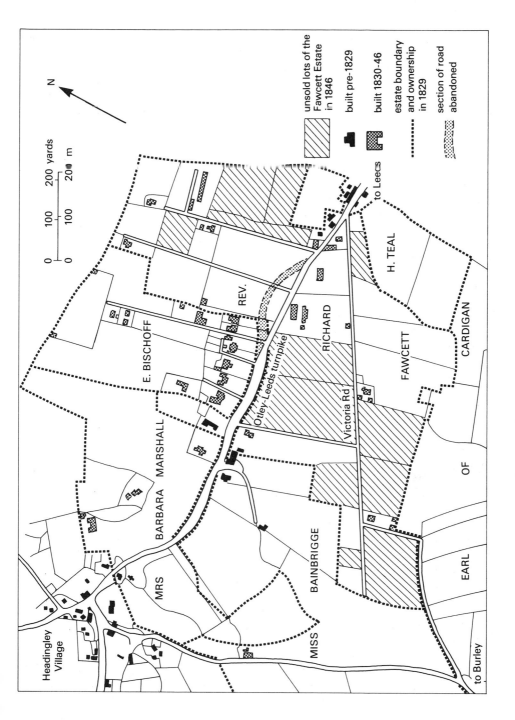

Figure 25. The development of Headingley Hill, 1829–46.

the toll bars, involving as they do the daily payment of 10s. 0d. for each 'bus – at least so it is said. In the neighbourhood of Manchester, the same difficulties presented itself. How was it met and overcome? By some of the 'bus proprietors taking the tolls themselves, making a profit out of them, and allowing their own vehicles to pass on the road free . . .

Unless some of our own townsmen undertake the task of introducing a better system in Leeds, the public will not regret if the rumour, which is current, proves true, that Mr. Greenwood, of Manchester, is about to put some of his 'buses upon our thoroughfares to compete, at lower fares, upon an improved plan, for the growing traffic of this rapidly increasing borough.[26]

The opportunity to experience Greenwood's Manchester buses had been provided for Leeds people on the occasion of the Royal Agricultural Show of 1861. Over five days 145,000 had visited the showground in Burley, and Greenwood's buses had been brought in to cope with the demands for additional transport. Clearly there is a sense in which the development of north Leeds neighbourhoods between 1850 and 1870 took place in spite of, rather than because of, the introduction of horse drawn bus services. New development of those 20 years took place within three miles of the centre of Leeds, a reasonable walking distance for those with the working hours of middle class occupations.

The new arrivals of the 1850s and 1860s are associated with the erection of 'respectable' terraces of houses, intended to face open spaces rather than another terrace across a street. The building type allowed for the accommodation of one or two servants, but rarely was provision made for stable or carriage house. Developers found the same problems of a slow pace of sales and piecemeal building up of sites that had been characteristic of mansion and villa developments. In the period before physical planning control these problems often resulted in a variety of built forms. Kensington Terrace on the former estate of Henry Teal, surveyor, at Hyde Park, Headingley cum Burley was a prime Leeds example. Two storey bay-windowed houses and plain fronted three storey houses reminiscent of central Leeds building of the 1830s appeared to have been distributed at random along the terrace between 1851 and 1867. The terrace was completed by the erection of two pairs of three storey back-to-back houses at the western end.

It was this type of development problem which was instrumental in producing press questioning of the ability or willingness of those involved in building and estate development to produce a satisfactory environment for future residents.

It is by no means uncommon to see a row of good small houses with gardens faced by one consisting partly of pretentious looking back-to-back dwellings, and partly by a couple of semi-detached houses which turn their back on the first named row, and present to the dwellers therein a fine view of their ashpits and other conveniences . . . Those who have land to sell inform us that it sells best when it is subject to no restrictions as to the style of house to be built, and when it can be disposed of in small lots . . . Thus good, bad, and indifferent houses are seen cheek to jowl with one another, and there is an utter want of uniformity even in mediocrity . . . It seems extraordinary that the owners of land should be allowed to erect rows of houses in a town without making any provision whatever for roads, excepting by leaving a vacant space of ground between them. . . . Specimens of which may be found . . . [in] the district on the other side of Woodhouse Moor, known as Hyde Park.[27]

Who were the new neighbours? One of them explained in 1862: 'we are mostly tradesmen who have our place of business in Leeds, and pay from £20 to £40 per year for our dwelling houses in Hyde Park, or professional men, who transact business at our offices in Leeds during the day, and hope to return home at night to quietness – peace'.[28] Unfortunately the new residents of Hyde Park found themselves at the centre of a quarrel in the township affairs of Headingley cum Burley which was not of their making. It commenced with a debate on the incidence of illness at the foot of Headingley Hill and amongst the Hyde Park terraces. The basic problem was that Headingley Hill residences of the 1830s and 1840s on the former Bischoff and Fawcett estates had been provided with sewage pits which had never been emptied. As a result percolation of the effluent downhill towards the River Aire had taken place via the wells, cellars, and basement of less elevated neighbours. This fact was challenged vociferously, and the Leeds piped water supply from Eccup which passed through the vicinity was amongst the alternative culprits suggested. Another view, held by local medical practitioners amongst others, was that debate was irrelevant because statistics proved that Headingley mortality rates were lower than those of any other part of the borough.

Before decisions were taken to remedy the situation the scope of the debate widened to include not only the real cause of the disease, but also the right of Leeds Corporation to interfere in out-township affairs, economy in local government expenditure, and the unreasonableness of other neighbourhoods in the township having to become embroiled in the shortcomings of a new neighbourhood. The township's preferred scheme for improvement entailed simply channelling its sewage, untreated, into the River Aire immediately upstream of central Leeds. In-township objections to this were at one stage derided as self-interest, and a call was made to all nine out-townships of the borough to unite against compulsory sewerage imposed by the Corporation. Until 1867 the opposition to services which caused additional impositions upon local rates was triumphant, as had been the case in 1831 when the township had refused to establish a board of health in the face of an approaching cholera epidemic.

At the height of the quarrel Headingley's image of an area of unified respectability cracked under the considerable pressure. Letters to the press carried references to 'sordid owners of property', the self-interest of those whose living depended upon the township's 'high reputation for salubrity', and a description of Headingley Hill as 'a little aristocratic neighbourhood where ladies and gentlemen have a good deal of leisure time'. Lost amongst the general outcry was a more sober note from an inhabitant of Hyde Park. 'The road between Woodhouse Moor and Hyde Park . . . is a sea of mud, . . . in asking that this neighbourhood may have decent roads and good drains we do not demand any fanciful improvement.'[29]

When in April 1862 Leeds Corporation agreed to share the cost of making a road to replace the sea of mud, opposition was voiced on the grounds of providing free aid to developers of building land. However, the scheme was halted a month later because property owners, not necessarily residents, at Hyde Park Terrace had changed their mind and refused to co-operate. Although the exodus to the developing suburbs had its attractions, the benefits of the promised land were largely promised to the developer and the land speculator.

It may have been possible for vendors of building land to differentiate with equanimity between developments of varying quality, but such distinctions were frequently not only apparent but objectionable to residents in the superior areas.

New developments were liable to be regarded as harbingers of future social and physical deterioration of the quality of a neighbourhood. For the out-township resident who had already rejected the central Leeds environment the question of whether to move once again arose during the 1850s and 1860s. Farther out, between three and four miles from central Leeds, were the more rural aspects of Chapel Allerton township and the outer fringes of Headingley cum Burley. It was even possible to contemplate removal beyond the borough boundary into the townships of Adel and Roundhay. These areas became the new location for the establishment of country houses and parkland on a larger scale than those built nearer to Leeds in the 1830s and 1840s. The estates were founded by a small number of wealthy Leeds entrepreneurs whose fortunes were based on textile manufacture, engineering, banking, and brewing.[30]

The over supply of building land between 1825 and 1850 worsened considerably after 1845. During the 20 years down to 1865 a further 750 acres were made available in addition to the residue of unsold land on estates first offered for sale before 1845. Developers who insisted on villa-type residences being built suffered from a resulting dearth of purchasers. The most impressive failure was that of the Mexborough estate, 335 acres offered for sale by auction in October 1845, divided into only 35 lots. The market for 10 acre villa estates in Potternewton was proved non-existent in 1845. Smaller lots adjoining Earl Cowper's New Leeds development or the existing village nucleus at Chapeltown also failed to attract purchasers. The one success was the sale of 68 acres to the Beckett family of bankers; they incorporated the land with their holdings in Chapel Allerton and founded a model farm in the late 1840s.

For development of a building estate to be successful within a reasonable time it was known from experience during the first half of the nineteenth century that restraints on the type of property to be erected had to be removed so that the widest possible market could be attained. The result of the unrestricted approach reached the columns of the *Builder* in 1862. 'The increase in population has led to a brick-and-mortar crusade which is defiling every green spot near the town. Some of the sites are magnificent; and are being spoilt by the erection of houses fit only for grooms and railway porters.'[31] An outstanding example of this crusade in the northern out-townships was the building of Lower Burley. This low lying area between the Burley Road old (1752) turnpike and the new (1806) Kirkstall Road turnpike had been the subject of several development attempts since the Upton family of lawyers had gained full possession of land there in 1814. Successive attempts to sell $8\frac{1}{2}$ acres were made by T.E. Upton in 1814, 1816, and 1818. When Upton died in 1838 his Lower Burley land remained unsold. Elsewhere in Leeds he had achieved considerable development; at his death he was the owner of six building estates, including a mill, warehouse, foundry, five houses, 74 cottages, other uncompleted cottages, and undeveloped building land.

An adjoining Lower Burley estate between Kirkstall Road and the River Aire owned by the Beckett family was developed during the early 1840s. Of five acres sold little more than one-quarter of an acre went to house and cottage builders. The principal developments were the ironworks of S. and J. Whitham and a worsted manufactory established by R.F. Green. Between 1838 and 1846 the Upton estate trustees succeeded in selling only three-quarters of an acre; developments included a public house, and a gasometer for the Leeds New Gaslight Company. The Leeds–Thirsk Railway Company purchased a route along the western side of the

Upton estate and between 1846 and 1848 contractors were busy erecting a large viaduct to carry the railway across the Leeds–Liverpool Canal, River Aire, and the Aire valley floodplain.

In 1851 the remaining area between the Upton estate and the in-township boundary was also made available for building upon; this was part of the estate of T.W. Lloyd of Cowestry Hall near Thirsk. An earlier generation of Lloyd, Upton, and Beckett landowners had in their Lower Burley purchases anticipated the expansion of a wealthy and salubrious west end of Leeds apparent in the Park Row, Park Square area of the in-township at the close of the eighteenth century. The new neighbourhood which was produced by development after 1850 was mostly the result of investment by in-township residents in the expansion of a working-class west end of Leeds. It included public houses, a brewery, and workshops; all types of development which were banned by restrictive covenants on estates on the higher ground to the north along the Leeds–Otley turnpike in Headingley, and in New Leeds in Potternewton township. The proximity to potential workplaces outweighed the environmental disadvantages of railway and gasometer in the eyes of purchasers of building plots. In 1851 the Whithams' iron foundry employed 270 men and the textile mill employed 240 women and 120 men. Other factories lined the banks of the river within the in-township. In 1862 the vendors of the textile mill announced that 'the surrounding population will at any time supply sufficient hands'. In 1870 a vendor of cottages in Lower Burley described them as 'letting well, being near several large manufactories in Kirkstall Road'.

The form in which the Lower Burley estates were laid out influenced subsequent building. On the Upton estate plots were narrower than on the Lloyd estate. A result was that back-to-back property on the former Upton estate was built in long rows, doors opening directly onto the street, with privies at intervals punctuating the row. The frequency with which privy blocks occurred in a row tended to reflect the number of separate building developments in the row; the larger the scale of building development, the longer the walk. On the Lloyd estate the blocks of land for building were wider, allowing the retention of unbuilt on areas in the centre of the block. These spaces were subdivided, each building development having its own yard and privies. The yards often had impressive names such as Bell's Square and Inkermann Court. The privacy of the yards, approached by tunnels from the street, was considered important; in 1864 three owners of cottage and yard property between Greystone Street and Wordsworth Street agreed that existing inner boundary walls between yards should be raised an additional three feet 'to prevent the public trespassing across the yards'.[32] The Upton estate also permitted yard development where irregular estate boundary lines precluded rectangular plot layouts.

Where no restraint on building type or function was exercised by the developer the possibilities were considerable. On a portion of the Upton estate purchased and subdivided by the Becketts between 1869 and 1873 there was a sequence of machine workshop with steam engine, joiner's shop and house, cowshed, dairy, and cottages. Restrictive covenants on the Upton and Lloyd estates were very similar and were confined to roads and sewerage. In 1851 James Thornton, a stone mason, was required in his purchase from the Upton estate to make his half of adjoining streets 'with good and substantial tooled flags', to kerb the causeways, and 'to pave and keep in good repair with the materials aforesaid the said streets'. In addition he was to pay on demand half the cost of making, cleansing, and repairing the common sewers to be laid down the middle of the two streets alongside his building plot. The only additional covenant on the Lloyd estate was permissive, allowing cellars to be built as long as they had brick arches and were at least 7 ft from the sewers.[33] However impressive restrictive covenants appeared on paper, the extent to which they were enforced was always questionable, even in wealthier neighbourhoods. In Lower Burley, in spite of the covenants entered into by both sides during the 1850s, it was not until Leeds Corporation enforced paving, flagging, and levelling orders in the mid 1870s that anything was done.[34]

Surprisingly, in view of their other similarities, sales on the Upton and Lloyd estates began at considerably different price levels. From 1846 to 1855 the prevailing Upton price was 3s. 6d. per square yard; during the first half of the 1860s this dropped to as low as 2s. 0d. per square yard. Most of the Lower Burley portion of the Lloyd estate was sold at 2s. 6d. per square yard, with additional premiums of 8d. or 1s. 0d. per square yard for the turnpike road frontage. A reduction in activity in 1854 and 1855 lowered the Lloyd price to 2s. 0d. per square yard, but it was restored to its previous level in 1856. The more traditional yard-type layout of the Lloyd estate and the early price differential between the two estates must have been instrumental in enabling the disposal of all its Lower Burley land between 1851 and 1858. The Upton estate's development period extended into the 1870s. On the Becketts' subdivision of the Upton estate a *laissez-faire* attitude may have been the factor which enabled them to obtain prices ranging from 2s. 11d. to 4s. 10d. per square yard on eight of nine lots sold between 1869 and 1878.

The purchasers of building land in Lower Burley were mostly speculators in cottage property, either for sale or for investment in rents. Very few built solely for their own occupancy, although many built several cottages, lived in one and let the remainder. Half of all cottage property in the area of Lower Burley and Burley village was held in this way in 1861. Only in 13 of 86 traceable building developments in Lower Burley were the cottages built and sold within two years of erection. Although members of the building trades comprised a similarly low proportion, 17 of 75, of Lower Burley building ground purchasers, there was no simple correlation between members of the building trades and cottages built speculatively for sale rather than investment.

The overall picture of building development in Lower Burley is one of small scale complexity and diversity in the creation of a working-class neighbourhood on freeholds in the period before building and planning regulations (see fig. 26). Those operating on the larger scale were more likely to be people investing business profits rather than members of the building trades. George Noble, the only builder to erect as many as 40 back-to-back cottages at one time, was a retired bookseller who turned builder in 1872. James Gray, a joiner, and James Hargreaves, bricklayer turned builder, erected the most dwellings in Lower Burley, but in five and six stages respectively; neither built more than 14 at one time. Gray succeeded in building 57 cottages between 1855 and 1858, but went bankrupt in 1861 under the weight of his mortgage commitments.[35] Any assessment of the scale of building operations should take into account contract work for the 77 per cent of building plot purchasers who were neither builders nor building craftsmen. Contracts may have been let out to members of the several building crafts or the whole contract may have been given to a builder. No firm evidence is available on which to base analysis of this aspect of the building operations in Lower Burley.

Although permanent building societies were growing in Leeds during the second

Figure 26. The development of Lower Burley, 1846–74.

half of the nineteenth century they were negligible as a source of building finance in north Leeds between 1850 and 1875. Private mortgages or personal capital were the principal sources of building finance. The Leeds Permanent, founded in 1848, largest and most lauded of the local societies, remained strongly antipathetic to the speculative builder until the late 1880s. Of 650 dwellings in Lower Burley for which title deed information is available only 53 were erected with the aid of building society finance, slightly more than eight per cent.

The experience of Henry Hodgson, stone mason and builder, who built on 843 square yards in Lower Burley in 1856 may have been typical of the financial arrangements between small scale speculative builders and their mortgagees in the nineteenth century. Hodgson borrowed £700 at 5 per cent yearly interest rate from a solicitor, John W. Cudworth. The transaction commenced well before the date on the legal conveyances of the land. Cash was handed over gradually, in amounts sufficient to maintain progress during the building season. Of 26 payments between 1 April and 19 September 1856 six were for less than £10, six for between £11 and £20, six between £21 and £30, three between £31 and £40, three between £41 and £50, and one of £97 16s. 0d. The latter represented the payment for part of the land. In December 1856 Hodgson sold 13 houses and a shop built with Cudworth's money. They sold for £780, of which £700 went to the solicitor, all interest having been paid previously. The interest on an eight month mortgage would have been £22, leaving Hodgson with a maximum possible profit of 12.5 per cent.[36]

By the early 1860s the progress of building, though incomplete, had given the neighbourhood a distinct identity because of the 'densely populated part of Lloyd's field'.[37] It had also contributed to the higher mortality rate for the Burley area, 23.5 per 1,000 compared to 15.5 per 1,000 for that part of Headingley along the Leeds–Otley turnpike axis. In 1861 Lower Burley together with the agricultural village of Burley consisted of nearly 700 dwellings, 80 per cent of them back-to-back cottages valued for Poor Rate purposes at between £4 and £7 per year.

Typical of the better cottage property of Lower Burley were six cottages built for William Asquith, a fuller, on ex-Lloyd estate land in the 1850s. In 1870 they were let for £7 each, the accommodation 'a cellar, kitchen, sitting room, and two bedrooms'.[38] Only one piece of evidence survives for the separate letting of cellars; in 1862 Samuel Fleming, an engineer, sold four back-to-backs 'and cellar dwellings'. For £10 10s. 0d. in 1861 it was possible to rent the through house of W. Willows, an ironfounder, in Willow Road, consisting of 'scullery, pantry and passage on the basement floor; sitting room, kitchen, passage and staircase on the ground floor; three lodging rooms on the chamber floor'.[39]

Only 23 of 623 dwellings of less than £10 annual value in Burley and Lower Burley in 1861 were owner occupied; 36 per cent were let by absentee landlords; 47 per cent were let by local landlords; the remaining 13 per cent were let by agricultural estate owners. The back-to-back cottages were provided as a means of earning 8 per cent gross yearly on invested capital for their owners. This property was sold between investors at prices which reflected an agreed annual rate of return. Thus the critical factor in a sale advertisement was the size of the rental income from the property. Calculation of net income is more difficult. The only details for yearly outgoings on insurance, repairs, and taxes are for Bell's Square, built in 1860. The evidence is for 1889, by when outgoings accounted for one-third of the gross rental, a proportion also stated by E. Ryde to the Select Committee on Town Holdings in 1886.[40] If this level of deduction is related to the 8 per cent gross returns advertised in the 1860s then net returns of between 5 and $5\frac{1}{2}$ per cent would have been achieved. Although this net figure is close to the more easily earned 5 per cent interest on mortgage money in the 1860s, it was possible to boost the figure in several ways: by delaying property repairs, by owning property worth so little as to be exempt from the Poor Rate; by compounding the Poor Rate payment at up to 50 per cent discount and omitting to share the saving with the tenant. James Hole, the Leeds housing reformer of the 1860s noted that the smallest houses produced the largest percentage profits.[41] It has been estimated that a pair of back-to-back cottages produced 20 per cent more rental per ground surface occupied than a through house.[42]

By 1870 there were several distinct foci of new settlement in the north Leeds out-townships: the expanded village nuclei of Headingley and Chapeltown, the still incomplete New Leeds terraces in Potternewton, the proto-garden suburb of Headingley Hill, the respectable terraced housing at Hyde Park, the back-to-back cottages of Lower Burley. The coalescence of these neighbourhoods into a contiguous suburban extension of Leeds commenced after 1870. Although individual owners of small parkland estates might attempt to stand firm against the increasing amount of building after 1870, it did not prove possible to overturn the basic sequence of the previous century. The search for seclusion of the mansion dwellers had been spoiled by the arrival of the respectable terraces. In turn the search of the new neighbours for peace and quiet was to be foiled by the myriad inhabitants of streets of small through houses and back-to-backs. Whilst middle-class out-township residents may have been able to rely upon the pace of development in their neighbourhoods being slow and piecemeal before 1870, there can have been little complacency as to the rate of development of higher density more plebeian property. Even during 1874–7, the boom years of the Leeds building industry in the 1870s, it was suggested that the population growth of the borough was such as to readily outstrip the rate of building of cottage property.[43] Years of recession in the local economy during the 1880s appear to have had little impact on cottage property development whereas the building of better class property had been drastically cut back.[44]

The introduction of horse-drawn tramways, Leeds–Headingley in 1871, Leeds–Kirkstall in 1872, and Leeds–Chapeltown in 1875, must have given developers increased hope of an increase in the suburban expansion of the northern out-townships. Leeds Corporation, newly responsible for the upkeep of former turnpike roads within the borough in 1871, had granted a 21-year lease to W. and D. Busby, omnibus proprietors, for the introduction of a tramway between Far Headingley and Leeds. Tramway development in Leeds nearly came to a premature halt during its first year. The additional traffic on the former Leeds–Otley turnpike road produced rapid deterioration of the road surface; this led to a legal dispute with the Corporation over maintenance of the road. Other road users complained of inconvenience and damage to carriages from the protruding rails. The Corporation threatened to stop the tramway from operating if the space between the rails was not paved at the proprietors' expense, a move which produced the earliest Leeds defence of the tram.

> Since the tramway was laid down, . . . the omnibuses have almost entirely fallen into disuse. . . . And whilst this has taken place, there has been at the same time a very large increase of the passenger traffic on the road, so that for one person

who used the omnibus it may safely be said that at least six use the tramway car. . . . To suspend the whole of the traffic between Leeds and Headingley would be to dislocate the arrangements of numberless households and businessmen, and to put all who reside in that district to an amount of inconvenience which it would be difficult to exaggerate.[45]

Fortunately for Headingley residents the *Leeds Mercury* proprietor was one of them. By 1877 bus operators had adjusted to a new reduced role on the tramway routes, providing connector services between the out-township termini of the tramways and more distant settlements. Ten services daily ran from Chapeltown village out to Moortown in Chapel Allerton, and five from Headingley to Adel. Tram services were more frequent, earlier starting, and later finishing than the horse drawn buses had been; fares were cheaper too. However, the earliest morning tram service on the north Leeds routes in 1877 was the 7.57 a.m. from Kirkstall to Leeds, too late for a Leeds factory operative to become a tramway commuter. In spite of the support for the trams when first introduced, expansion of the system under private ownership was very limited. After a quarter of a century of operation only 22 miles of tramway were in existence. Leeds Corporation took over the system in 1894, introducing electric traction in 1897, withdrawing the last horse drawn tram in 1901, and increasing the system to 70 miles of tramways by 1926.

3 Developers

Ironically, after being the principal sufferers of the slow pace of development during the previous half-century, agricultural estate owners mostly opted out of building estate development after 1870 at the time when the pace of growth was quickening. Between 1870 and 1914 three of the largest north Leeds estates, Cardigan in Headingley cum Burley, Cowper in Potternewton, and Simpson (ex-Dixon) in Chapel Allerton placed land on the market in large quantities and found purchasers amongst the ranks of land speculators and developers rather than builders (see fig. 27). All three estates were controlled from a distance, Cardigan from Deene, Northamptonshire, Cowper from Panshanger, Kent, and Simpson from Regent's Park, London. Simpson sold 618 acres in 1870 to a three man Leeds syndicate of Riley Briggs, flaxspinner, Richard Robinson, linen manufacturer, and William North, solicitor for £36,783, equivalent to £143 per acre. This appears to have been the common agricultural value of land in the northern out-townships between the 1840s and the 1870s.

However, land with short or medium term development prospects was much more valuable, even when sold in large lots. Between 1873 and 1875 Earl Cowper obtained £445 per acre for 12 acres; further sales between 1885 and 1891 produced £588 per acre. In Headingley cum Burley Cardigan estate sales between 1885 and 1893 produced average prices of £420 per acre. Cardigan land on the outer fringe of Headingley cum Burley with only agricultural potential could only be sold for between £70 and £80 per acre in 1890. Clearly the temptation to sell at a time of falling agricultural land values and achieve returns at least five times the agricultural value was enough for some large estate owners to give up even higher profits which involved taking part in building and estate development. In the context of

176

the building booms in Leeds during the early 1890s and 1900s the potential profits were much higher. Heppers, Leeds auctioneers, advised clients in their annual report for 1889 that 'those who can afford to let their capital wait, with little or no interest for the rise in values, should purchase land on the margin of the town, as for some years to come, builders are likely to be busy in providing for future requirements'.[46] A similar view was expressed in 1904 by R. Ernest, author of *How to Become a Successful Estate Agent*. 'If your clients want to speculate and have a chance of making enormous profits, they can safely do so by investing in the right kind of real estate – such operations, for instance, as are afforded by the real estate operations in the suburbs of the large cities'.[47] A copy of Ernest's book was on the shelf of at least one advisor to Leeds developers, the architect Frederick Mitchell, in 1905.[48]

Who were the developers, willing to pay so much for unimproved agricultural land in anticipation of a future rush of builders? Although the interposition of a new set of developers was a major factor in the growth of the north Leeds suburbs on freehold tenure between 1870 and 1914, the developers themselves largely remain as background figures whose records have seldom descended into public view. By piecing together their appearances amongst the thousands of title deeds in the possession of Leeds Corporation it has been possible to identify them and estimate the scale of their operations. From the 1870s onwards individuals and partnerships of two or three people were responsible for the majority of building estates which were developed. Three principal groups were involved, builders, entrepreneurs, and members of professions having peripheral connections with the development process (see table 15). Builders were the most significant category of purchasers of more than one acre of land for development purposes, both in terms of number of separate purchases and total quantity of land purchased. However, the prominence of the builders as a whole was established by the activities of one retired builder, Charles Stott, and two builders each in partnership with a source of capital. Manufacturers, land/estate agents, and active builders without capital-supplying partners were of equal significance as purchasers from pre-development landowners of the nine estates from which table 15 is drawn. Although the average size of each purchase was 10 acres and the average purchased in total by a developer was 17 acres, there were a small number of individuals operating on a much larger scale. The four leading developers purchased 40 per cent of the 578 acres (see table 16).

Mortgage support for developers was the exception rather than the rule; building societies were not involved. Other forms of financial support for developers from pre-development landowners were unusual. If the purchase price was to be paid from the developer's sale of building plots then the pre-development landowner was as dependent on the vagaries of the development process through time as if the developer role had been retained with its prospect of even higher profits. One example illustrating such pitfalls for the pre-development landowner was the disposal of the Newton Lodge estate in Potternewton by the trustees of the late Charles Naylor, solicitor. Their agreement of April 1891 with the Leeds builder, Joseph Boothman, also provides a reminder of the extent to which the process operated on a time schedule at variance with the dates enshrined in title deeds.

It was thereby provided that the said Joseph Boothman might have the said premises conveyed to him or sub-purchasers from time to time by separate deeds

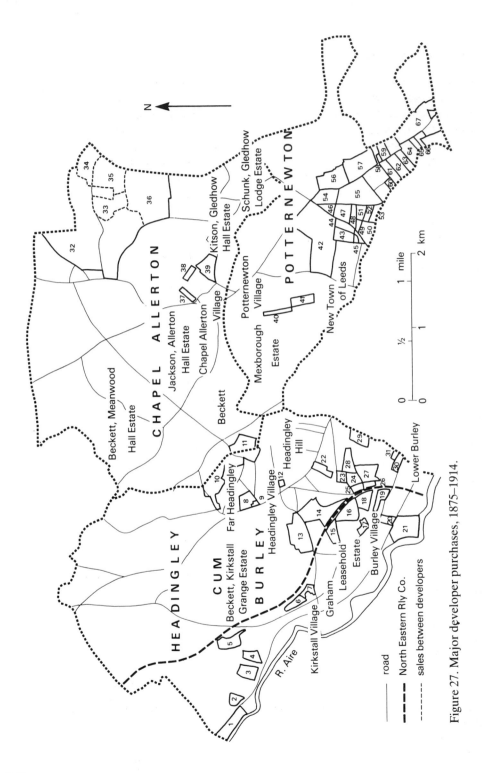

Figure 27. Major developer purchases, 1875–1914.

The process of suburban development in north Leeds, 1870–1914
C. TREEN

Developer and date of purchase:

1 G. Watson 1888
2 W. Wade Milnes 1888
3 P. Denton and W. Plews 1888
4 W. and G. Irwin 1888
5 W. Robshaw 1890
6 G.E. Isles 1895
7 J. Bowling and J. Richardson c.1888
8 T. Simpson 1874
9 R. Wood 1884
10 T. Ambler 1874; 'Oates' 1874;
   R. Wood 1883; W. and J. Rayner 1874
11 C. Stott 1897
12 M. Marcan 1888
13 C. Stott 1900
14 G. Bray 1888
15 C. Stott 1888
16 C. Stott 1888
17 R. Wood 1888
18 B. and W. Walmsley 1889
19 B. and W. Walmsley 1889
20 W. Child 1888
21 C. Stott 1888
22 C. Stott 1898
23 F. Postill 1880
24 B. and W. Walmsley c.1888
25 B. and W. Walmsley c.1888
26 C. Stott 1888
27 B. and W. Walmsley 1889
28 B. and W. Walmsley 1890
29 J.R. Ford 1885
30 E. and W. Strickland 1886
31 E. and W. Strickland 1884
32 R. Briggs, W. North, R. Robinson 1870
33 M.H. Carter and G.M. Atkinson 1900
34 E. Wray 1894
35 E. Wray 1894 to H.M. Carter and
   E.O. Wooler 1894

36 J.W. Archer 1887
37 *T. Ward's Estate Trustees 1876-*
38 H.H. Hodgson 1901
39 *W.J. Cousins 1902-*
40 J. Newton Sharp 1896
41 J. Boothman 1891 and 1896
42 *Brown Trustees' Harehills Estate 1890-*
43 E. Wray 1876
44 T. Pape and J. Maude 1875
45 T. Pape and J. Maude 1874
46 C. Morgan 1887
47 J. Newton Sharp 1887
48 J.W. Archer 1889
49 W. and J. Rayner pre-1889
50 W. and J. Rayner 1885
51 J.W. Archer 1888
52 J.W. Archer 1888
53 J.W. Archer 1888
54 H. Lax and J. Boyle 1906
55 J.W. Archer 1889
56 J.B. Mays 1902
57 H. Lax and J. Boyle 1903
58 C. Higgins 1896
59 W.S. Arnold 1898
60 E.O. Wooler 1894
61 J.W. Watson 1897
62 J.W. Watson 1898
63 J.W. Watson 1898
64 J.W. Watson pre-1901
65 J.W. Watson 1901
66 J.W. Watson 1902
67 H.H. Hodgson and W.S. Arnold 1899

(those cases where the developer role was undertaken by the pre-development landowner from the date given are shown in italics)

179

Table 15 Developer purchases from nine Headingley cum Burley and Potternewton estates, 1873–1903

developer category	purchases no.	%	purchasers no.	%	area acres	%
1 builders	22	39	10	29	243.6	42
a. singly	13		7		117.4	20
b. in partnership[a]	3		2		37.1	6.5
c. retired	6		1		89.1	15.5
2 entrepreneurs	10	18	6	18	109	19
a. manufacturers	8		4		107.2	18.5
b. merchants	2		2		1.8	0.5
3 professions	16	29	10	29	144.5	25
a. land/estate agents	9		5		109	19
b. architects/surveyors	4		2		13.2	2
c. lawyers/solicitors	3		3		22.2	4
4 others	4	7	4	12	43.6	7.5
5 insufficient data	4	7	4	12	37.6	6.5
total	56		34		578.3	

a With non-builder source of capital.
Sources: Title deeds; Headingley cum Burley estates: Cardigan, Headingley Glebe, Headingley House, Leeds Horticultural Gardens, Ludolf's trustees; Victoria Road Estate, Manor House. Potternewton estates: Cowper, Griffith Wright's trustees; Harehills estate, Newton Lodge.

but that the said Joseph Boothman should have vacant possession of part of the said premises immediately after the signing of the now reciting Agreement and of the remainder on the 31st day of December 1891. And the said Joseph Boothman should commence to lay out and use the said premises for building purposes. . . . And whereas . . . he has laid out the said lands for building purposes and . . . has set out streets . . . and has divided the residue . . . into portions and . . . prepared a plan upon which the said streets and the position of the buildings intended to be erected and the building lines or frontages thereof and other particulars are delineated . . . and he has obtained the sanction of the Municipal Corporation of Leeds to such plan in accordance with the bye-laws of the said Corporation. . . . The said lands now set out in streets and so laid out for building purposes . . . are now collectively known by the name of 'The Hall Lane Estate'.
     . . . The said Joseph Boothman has already contracted for the sale of certain lots . . . and it is his intention to sell the residue.[49]

Although Boothman had to finance the laying out of the building estate he did not have to pay for his nine acres at that stage. Between December 1891 and September 1896 he was able to dispose of six acres of his Hall Lane estate. The income from sales of land was shared between the trustees and Boothman; a sale in

Table 16   Largest developers' land purchases, Headingley cum Burley and Potternewton, 1871–1914

developer	period[a]	land area (acres)	purchases price (£)	average price per square yard[b]
C. Stott, retired builder, Armley	Y, Z	89.1	60,575[c]	3s. 4d.
J.W. Archer, woollen manufacturer, Potternewton	Y	51.3	19,008[c]	2s. 2½d.
B. & W. Walmsley, builders, Leeds	Y	46.3	21,994	1s. 11¼d.
H.H. Hodgson, estate agent, Leeds, and W.S. Arnold, contractor, Doncaster	Z	45.2	12,500[c]	1s. 2d.
E. Wray, builder and brickmaker, Leeds	X	33.3	5,233	8d.
J.W. Watson, estate agent, Leeds	Z	32.6	8,700[c]	1s. 5d.
H. Lax, builder, Leeds, and J. Boyle, brickmaker, Leeds	Z	29.4	25,017	3s. 6d.
W. & J. Rayner, boot and shoe manufacturers, Leeds	X, Y	27.9	3,499[c]	1s. 1½d.
J.B. Mays, retired publisher's agent, Roundhay	Z	25.5	15,526[c]	4s. 0d.
J.N. Sharp, builder, Leeds	Y	16.6	8,654	2s. 2d.

[a] Period: X 1873–82; Y 1883–92; Z 1893–1902.
[b] Of land for which financial data available.
[c] Incomplete purchase price data.
Sources: Title deeds.

1895 of 1,766 square yards to a builder, Joseph Richardson of Chapel Allerton, produced £486. This sum was divided equally between Boothman and the trustees. Another 1895 sale fetched £967, of which £713 went to the trustees. In spite of achieving prices of 5s. 6d. per square yard for building plots sold in conjunction with Boothman, Naylor's trustees opted to dispose of the remaining three acres to Boothman in 1896 for a single payment of £1,098, equivalent to 1s. 6½d. per square yard. Boothman continued to sell plots to other builders at 5s. 6d. per square yard, and also built on his own account.

In February 1896 Naylor's trustees attempted another method of dealing with a developer. The northern part of Naylor's Newton Lodge estate was sold to the builder-developer, John Newton Sharp, for £4,000: 1s. 10d. per square yard for nine acres and the mansion upon it. Instead of accepting payment as sales were made, the trustees provided Sharp with a £7,000 mortgage. Unlike the other north Leeds builder-developers Sharp appears to have undertaken all building on the estate himself as a long term project, raising a second mortgage of £4,000 in 1912.[50] In 1896, when he purchased the Newton Lodge land, Sharp also obtained a mortgage of £8,100 at 3¼ per cent from W. and C.L. Brooke, the latter a cotton thread manufacturer. Sharp's security was land, part of an 1887 purchase from the Cowper estate in Potternewton; 36 back-to-back houses and two shops in Banstead Grove and Harehills Terrace; and 10 cottages and 19 houses in Leeds in-township built on land purchased in 1886.

The biggest operator amongst the developers was Charles Stott, a retired builder of Armley, another out-township of Leeds. His purchases were on a sufficiently large scale to enable him to subdivide land and still provide subsequent purchasers with opportunities of further subdivision and development. Stott's emergence as a north Leeds developer followed the decline of the Cardigan family's fortunes during the 1870s and 1880s. He spent £27,500 on 40 acres of potential building land after the Cardigan estate in Headingley cum Burley was put up for auction in 1888. During the 1890s he was able to sell 20 acres, purchased at 10½d. per square yard, in two lots for 2s. 0d. and 1s. 7d. per square yard. The first sale was of 10.5 acres to Henry Marvell and Benjamin Paver, Leeds contractors. Stott's contribution to the rise in value of this land was to lay out a basic street pattern before reselling.[51] Little building had taken place by 1899 when nine acres were resold at 3s. 0d. per square yard. Significant building activities did not take place until the third set of Leeds developers, R.G. Emsley and J.B. Smith, solicitors, and A.G. Binner, a builder, laid out blocks for building upon and a complete network of streets. The predominantly back-to-back terraces of the Grahams were erected on part of this land between 1901 and 1905. Even then their development was disturbed by an agreement with the North Eastern Railway Company for an exchange and sale of land to facilitate widening of the permanent way. This necessitated the demolition of several newly erected end-terrace houses. The adjoining part of the land had a much longer development period. It commenced in the early 1890s with Marvell and Paver, but completion of the through houses of Beechwood View was delayed until 1914.

The other half of Stott's 20 acres was sold by him in 1892 to Leeds Corporation as a site for allotment gardens. His price of 1s. 7d. per square yard was low for potential building ground, but he obtained a profit of 8½d. per square yard without incurring costs of preparation for building purposes, and gained an amenity for future residents on his adjoining land.

Between 1898 and his death in 1902 Stott purchased and began subdivision of three other north Leeds estates: the Bentley House estate in Chapel Allerton; the Headingley House and Manor House estates in Headingley. The Headingley House estate founded by the flax-spinning Marshalls of Leeds was Stott's most expensive purchase. He paid £33,000 for it to J. Hepworth, Leeds clothing manufacturer, who had bought it from the Marshalls 12 years earlier for £17,000. Although Stott had paid the equivalent of 4s. 4½d. per square yard for the estate his trustees were able to subdivide and resell to builders at 6s. 6d. per square yard in 1904, 7s. 0d. per square yard in 1910, but only 3s. 9d. per square yard in 1912.

Only two other builder-developers were able to operate at Stott's scale in purchasing more than 20 acres of land in a lot. They were Edward Wray during the 1870s and Henry Lax in partnership with Joseph Boyle in 1903. Both had their principal base of operations in Potternewton, and both were also involved in the manufacture of building materials. Wray and Boyle were both brickmakers, Lax was a patent stone manufacturer.

The size of Wray's purchase was not a result of his having more capital available than his contemporaries in the north Leeds developer world of the 1870s. In 1876 the Cowper estate had had left in its hands for three years land designated for sale as building ground. It was unattractive to builders because of its elongated triangular shape, its hillside nature, and its proximity to a local stream, the Gipton Beck. Wray had first bought land in this vicinity as a sub-developer in 1874, paying

2s. 9d. per square yard for 15,510 square yards. This had been followed in 1875 by purchase direct from the Cowper estate, 6,620 square yards at 2s. 0d. per square yard. His success on these plots during a period of boom conditions in the Leeds building industry must have been instrumental in persuading him to buy the more awkward site of 32 acres. Another factor was Cowper estate willingness to accept 7d. per square yard, a total of £4,571.[52] This was the lowest price per square yard paid by a developer in nineteenth-century Potternewton. Between 1873 and 1876 Wray had spent £7,366 on land without requiring mortgage assistance.

His development of the 32 acre site had to contend with a depression in building activity between 1878 and 1882; not until 1888 did activity return to the level prevailing in 1876. Nevertheless Wray was rapidly able to realize a higher value on part of his new land. In February 1876, 11,608 square yards were sold to earlier sub-developer purchasers from Wray, the colliery proprietors J. and C.E. Charlesworth, for 3s. 0d. per square yard. An additional 4,284 square yards were sold to J. Robinson, a Leeds builder, in 1878 for 3s. 6d. per square yard; and 10,011 square yards were sold in 1879 to T.R. Clarke, a Leeds woollen cloth manufacturer, for 2s. 8½d. per square yard. This is unlikely to represent the full extent of Wray's resales, but sufficient evidence is available to demonstrate the profitability of his actions. The four sales described disposed of 23 per cent of Wray's land, but recouped 77 per cent of his purchase price. In addition Wray obtained a considerable supply of land, albeit unfortunately situated, for his own building activities. These began promptly; in December 1876 Wray obtained a mortgage on four houses, including his own. He was still building on this land during the 1890s. Wray also built on other developers' land. When he died in 1899 his estate included nine houses in Leam Terrace, Potternewton, an area developed by the Leeds boot and shoe manufacturers, W. and J. Rayner. The possibility of purchasing more Cowper land was actively pursued during the 1880s, but an agreement to buy five acres at 2s. 6d. per square yard was transferred to J. Newton Sharp in 1887 for a consideration of £80. When Wray did buy more land for development he repeated his search for cheap land. In 1894 he purchased 94 acres farther away from central Leeds, in Chapel Allerton. He paid £8,000, only 4d. per square yeard. Wray immediately resold half of the land to two Leeds solicitors, E.O. Wooler and H.M. Carter, for £5,394, or 6d. per square yard. Wray's descendants were still trying to sell plots of this land in 1905 when a block of 5,377 square yards sold for 1s. 8d. per square yard, less than one-quarter of the price commanded by building sites on the fringe of the advancing urban frontier of central Leeds.

The other brickmaker, Joseph Boyle, had first been involved in Potternewton development in 1869 when he had purchased 1,562 square yards on the then 40 years old Cowper New Town of Leeds. Having purchased at 1s. 9½d. per square yard, he resold in 1874 at 3s. 2½d. per square yard. Boyle's largest contribution to north Leeds building estate development began in 1903 when, with Henry Lax, he paid £25,000 for 29 acres of the former Griffith Wright Harehills estate. The price of 3s. 6d. per square yard was much higher than any developer had paid for northern out-township land during the 1870s, but the demand for building land in the rapidly growing northern suburbs of the early 1900s was sufficient to support prices of 6s. 0d. and 7s. 0d. per square yard for building plots. The estate was laid out for Lax and Boyle by a Leeds architect, Frederick Mitchell. He laid out 34 blocks for building, 21 for through houses and 13 for back-to-backs, also leaving space of a 50 ft wide road through the estate as the line for a prospective tramway route. Griffith Wright's mansion was sold to The Wallpaper Manufacturers Limited. Within four months nine full blocks and parts of another six blocks had been sold.

In 1906 Lax and Boyle turned their attention to 12.5 acres purchased from the Brown estate in Potternewton. On this land Boyle introduced a restrictive covenant which bound purchasers to use the products of his brickworks. The covenant was to remain in force in 1907 as long as Boyle could provide good quality common bricks at £1 5s. 0d. per 1,000 and pressed bricks at £1 17s. 0d. per 1,000, including free delivery. In 1912 the covenant still applied, but was subject to a decrease in prices, commons were down to £1 0s. 1d. per 1,000, pressed bricks to £1 15s. 0d. per 1,000.

Few Leeds entrepreneurs became significant purchasers of real estate. Those who did so were mostly manufacturers and tended to invest in building land only once. The main northern out-township attraction proved to be the Cardigan estate auction of 1888. William Plews, a linen manufacturer, purchased 15 acres of very unripe building land on the boundary of the borough in partnership with a publican, Philemon Denton; they paid only 4d. per square yard. A woollen merchant, Maurice Marcan, paid 5s. 2½d. for 5,780 square yards adjoining his house on the fringe of Headingley village. George Bray, a gas lighting engineer, spent £14,750 on 12.75 acres, equivalent to 4s. 2½d. per square yard. Part of this prime building land to the south of Headingley village was purchased to provide a site for the Leeds Cricket, Football, and Athletic Company, better known today as the home of the Yorkshire County Cricket Club and the Leeds Rugby League team. Had Bray and his fellow sporting enthusiasts been prepared to purchase an earlier sporting venue, the Cardigan Cricket Fields, they could have bought more cheaply, as it was sold to developers for only 2s. 2½d. per square yard. However, Bray conveyed the sports ground site to the Company for 1s. 1½d. per square yard.[53]

Only three entrepreneurs, all manufacturers, were primarily concerned with building estate development rather than land speculation alone. They were J.W. Archer, a woollen manufacturer, and W. and J. Rayner, boot and shoe manufacturers. At first the Rayners had been involved in land speculation. In February 1873 they had purchased 3 acres of Cowper land in Potternewton, reselling the whole in 1874 at a gross profit of £732. In June 1874 they had purchased 9.75 acres of the Headingley Glebe estate in partnership with G. Hancock, a Leeds surgeon; this was resold almost immediately at a gross profit of £687. The first resale represented a gross profit of 67 per cent, the second a gross profit of 28 per cent, on their purchase prices. The Rayners did not resume a developer role in the northern out-townships until the second half of the 1880s when between 1885 and 1889 they bought 15 acres of Cowper land in three lots. Building activity on this land included the work by Edward Wray in Leam Terrace, miserably sited back-to-backs at the rear of the boundary wall of Leeds Workhouse by J.W. and H. Charles, Leeds architects, and back-to-backs built for John Rayner himself.[54] One possible indication of the small size of the north Leeds suburbs' developer world was that John Rayner was sufficiently well acquainted with Benjamin Walmsley, a Headingley builder-developer, to appoint him as one of the trustees of his will.

The other manufacturer, J.W. Archer, appears to have commenced his developer operations in the opposite way to most developers by starting with unripe building land in Chapel Allerton and subsequently purchasing land with immediate development potential in Potternewton. In 1887 Archer purchased a 93 acre farm in Chapel Allerton for £6,700, less than 4d. per square yard. In 1888 and 1889

Archer purchased 51.25 acres of Cowper land, the latter purchase costing £19,008, equal to 2s. 2½d. per square yard. The former Cowper land in Potternewton was resold in blocks to builders during the 1890s, prices of 6s. 0d. per square yard being attained in 1890, 1891, and 1894. Progress on the Chapel Allerton land was slower and less profitable. In 1898 only 2s. 6d. per square yard could be obtained, and in 1900 Archer sold 13 acres of this land to a fellow developer, J.B. Mays, at 1s. 8d. per square yard. When this land was conveyed to Mays, a retired publisher's agent, in 1901 he had already agreed to resell to a Nottinghamshire bleacher, A. Bexon, for £6,811, a gross profit to Mays of £1,572. Bexon in turn made a gross profit of £1,018 on his own resale to A.S. Musgrave of Settle.[55] Archer's willingness to forego potential future profits was in anticipation of his going to live at Bournemouth from 1902 onwards.

The third category of developers – land and estate agents, surveyors and architects, lawyers and solicitors, were members of professions which provided services to the development process. To their nineteenth-century contemporaries it is doubtful if any but the lawyers would have been recognized as belonging to a profession. Although the Royal Institute of British Architects had been founded in 1835, only 11 per cent of those calling themselves architects in 1881 were members, and the number had only increased to 27 per cent in 1911.[56] A separate Surveyor's Institute had been founded in 1868,[57] but throughout the nineteenth century there continued to be a considerable overlap between some of the activities of those calling themselves architects, surveyors, land and estate agents. The estate agents' role of bringing together buyers and sellers of property grew rapidly in importance in Leeds during the second half of the nineteenth century. Headingley property was first advertised by estate agents in the local press in 1855; the first were Hobson and Hindle who had offices in Park Row, Leeds. By 1857 W.B. Hindle handled cottage property for sale in Lower Burley and houses to let in Headingley. Not until 1864, however, did the compilers of Leeds directories recognize estate agency as a separate occupational category.[58]

Throughout the nineteenth century estate agency included men without training who were agents for the sale of their own building land. B.H. Richardson, an insurance agent in 1871, had become an estate agent by 1874 and was developing land on the former Headingley Glebe estate. Richardson and his partner, T.H. Watson, announced in May 1874 that they were forming 'a Club for the Erection of Terrace Houses, with eight rooms each and large gardens . . . to be called Oakfield Terrace'.[59] The scheme was to enlist 16, later 18, members in a building club for the erection of £500 houses. Richardson and Watson were members of the club and its secretaries. Having purchased 2.5 acres at 1s. 11½d. per square yard, the pair promptly resold it to the building club at 3s. 5d. per square yard, a gross profit of £900. Notwithstanding the financial transactions of its founders, the club was successful and had completed its programme by the agreed terminating date of June 1877.[60] Enthusiasm for their first venture encouraged Richardson and Watson to form another building club in August 1874 for the building of a row of £300 houses to be called Spring Hill Terrace. This club was also successful, and was reported to have encouraged the founding of others elsewhere in Leeds during the later 1870s. However, the firm of Richardson and Watson had disappeared by the end of the decade, and the building club as a mechanism for the creation of a demand for building land fell into abeyance.

Charles Higgins, an estate agent-developer on former Cowper land in 1896, had a more varied career than Richardson. After Higgin's death he was described as 'formerly a cabinet maker, afterwards a grocer and general dealer and subsequently for a period of nearly twelve months prior to his decease an estate agent and mortgage broker.'[61] Two other land/estate agent developers bought land with long-term development potential. As such their purchases were highly speculative but inexpensive. William Robshaw, land agent, purchased 27 acres of the Cardigan estate on the outer fringe of Headingley cum Burley township at 3½d. per square yard. Its development potential was not realized until it was purchased by Leeds Corporation in 1935. Robshaw's immediate return in 1890 was a yearly rental income of £33 8s. 0d. from 24.5 acres of arable land, plus the proceeds of any sales of timber from the 2.5 acres of woodland.[62]

Earl Cowper's successful disposal of the last of his Potternewton estate after 1890 was almost entirely the result of sales to estate agents. The land with the longest-term development prospects was purchased by H.H. Hodgson, in partnership with a Doncaster contractor, W.S. Arnold. They had purchased jointly from Cowper in 1891 and 1892; this was followed in 1899 by the purchase of 44 acres for £12,500, at 1s. 2d. per square yard. Hodgson and Arnold also purchased 76 acres of adjoining land outside the borough boundary from the Meynell–Ingram estate for £15,000. Within twelve months £20,000 was recouped by the sale of 45 acres to Leeds Corporation for use as a cemetery.[63] In 1913 they also sold land to the Corporation at 2s. 0d. per square yard as the site for a school. The prices reflected the lack of immediate demand from builders for land. However, Hodgson and Arnold had anticipated a continued high demand for building land during the first decade of the twentieth century and had proceeded to lay out their land accordingly. In 1902 they sold 8,850 square yards at 2s. 0d. per square yard to the owners of a neighbouring Potternewton estate, the trustees of James Brown, as part of a co-operative effort to improve road access to both estates. The Hodgson and Arnold land was laid out in 15 building blocks, all for back-to-back houses; the only exception was the land adjoining the cemetery, this being intended for factories. The regimented layout of the estate aptly commemorated the events and personages of the Boer War. There were streets for Buller, Kitchener, Kimberley, and Ladysmith. Like the Boer War, results were not entirely satisfactory; only four blocks were ever built upon, the rest was sold to Leeds Corporation in 1921 and 1925, still only at 2s. 5d. and 2s. 0d. per square yard respectively.

Most successful of the estate agent-developers was John Wainwright Watson. His earliest involvement was in Potternewton as agent for the Low Moor Iron and Steel Company's land. In 1902 whilst selling the Company's land at 3s. 7d. per square yard he was purchasing adjoining Cowper land on his own behalf for less than 1s. 0d. per square yard. His first purchase had been from other developers, E.O. and E.P. Wooler, in 1895, when he bought 16,485 square yards at 2s. 2d. per square yard. Within 12 months he had been able to subdivide and sell to builders at 6s. 0d. per square yard. Between 1897 and 1902 J.W. Watson bought 32.5 acres of Cowper land adjoining the in-township boundary; each of his successive purchases cost less, from 1s. 9d. per square yard in 1897 to 11d. per square yard in 1902. Between 1898 and 1902 he resold building blocks on this land at 5s. 0d. and 5s. 6d. per square yard. These prices charged by Watson were between 1s. 0d. and 2s. 0d. per square yard lower than those prevailing on adjoining Potternewton estates. This represented a saving of £80 on the purchase of an 800 square yard block suitable for the erection of eight back-to-backs. Consequently development of Watson's land was rapid, although even he was not totally immune to the downturn in building activity in Leeds after 1902. Watson countered this by undertaking some building on his own behalf.

Lawyers had been involved in land transactions for centuries; through mortgage arrangements and conveyancing the lawyer was in a good position to know the current state of the market in building land. Where many chose to become mortgagees, few became developers. Two Leeds legal practices became involved in the development of building estates for small through houses and back-to-backs after 1870. These were Lupton and Fawcett, and Ford and Warren. John Rawlinson Ford had been drawn into development as mortgagee of the Leeds Horticultural Gardens Company which had set out in 1875 to combine the functions of plant nursery and recreation centre with the aid of an £11,000 mortgage from J.R. Ford's father.[64] The mortgage had been continued by J.R. Ford after his father's death in 1878. It was apparent by 1885 that the venture had failed, no-one would buy it at auction, so J.R. Ford took over in December 1885, extinguishing the mortgage and paying £1,300 for the fixtures. Ford, having taken the land for the equivalent of 4s. 5d. per square yard, resold six acres to his legal partner W. Warren and J. Franks, a surveyor, at 7s. 0d. per square yard in June 1888. This price limited the opportunities for profit; resales to builders at 8s. 6d. per square yard in 1888 were reduced to between 6s. 6d. and 6s. 9d. per square yard in 1892. Ford was also selling at 6s. 9d. per square yard in 1892.[65] Part of the problem for Ford and Warren must have been the decision to sell the Cardigan estate in 1888.

At the first attempt to sell the land for building purposes Ford had announced that 'facilities may be offered to investors or speculative builders which will give them advantages they do not usually obtain in the development of building estates'.[66] Lawyers and solicitors were excellently placed to be able to find sources of financial support for builders, a factor demonstrated by W.A. Lupton and W. Fawcett, sub-developers in Potternewton. In 1903 they joined with J. Hobson, a Holbeck joiner and builder, to develop 7.25 acres purchased from the developer J.B. Mays at 6s. 0d. per square yard. Between 1903 and 1905 they succeeded in reselling to builders at prices ranging from 7s. 6d. to 10s. 9½d. per square yard, a much higher price than Mays was able to obtain from his own sales to builders. Lupton, Fawcett, and Hobson offered their builder-purchasers mortgages at 5 per cent yearly interest rate. A. Maude, another Holbeck joiner and builder, probably introduced by Hobson, paid 11s. 0d. per square yard for 1,885 square yards, but was also provided with a £2,700 mortgage at the same time. He received an additional £1,116 while building was in progress. Once building was completed all but £566 of the mortgage debt was transferred to other mortgagees, 12 houses and a shop built by Maude standing as security. The disadvantage of this policy was the possible need to foreclose on a mortgage, but even this could be a source of profit. In 1904 W.A.C. Walters, a builder, was provided with £3,050 as a mortgage for the erection of 13 houses. He defaulted in 1907 but the property was successfully sold by the mortgagees for £3,800.

Architect-developers were to be found at both ends of the spectrum of suburban building types. George Corson, a notable Leeds architect, was purchaser of land on the northern fringe of Headingley village in the late 1860s. He proceeded in 1885 to lay out a new street, Shire Oak Road, with the object of selling half-acre lots to purchasers willing to build houses from designs by him. This had been attempted at Far Headingley during the 1870s by another architect, Thomas Ambler. Both

Corson and Ambler had difficulty in finding sufficient clients, and their ventures did not encourage others. Architects such as Charles Fowler in 1870 and John Hall in 1875 were willing to act as developers in the more usual pattern, subdividing and reselling to builders.

Another architect, Robert Wood, a purchaser of land at the Cardigan estate auction of 1888, had elevated himself from the ranks of builders and contractors where he had been in 1884. It was at this level that the boundaries between the titles of architect, surveyor, and builder were most blurred. However, it was also here that the greatest awareness was displayed of the needs of the small builder. 'Land for scullery houses, nineteen feet frontage, with gardens fifteen feet long, including sewering, kerbing, free conveyance and plans, drawing and passing by the Corporation, only £22 per house; for through houses fifteen feet frontage £29. To a purchaser of land for eight cottages, upon paying 10 per cent deposit, money would be advanced until ready for occupation'.[67] Wood's offer emphasized the problems facing small builders during the last quarter of the nineteenth century. Since 1866 in Leeds they had been increasingly subject to the constraints of building regulations. Not only did it mean having to conform to standards of construction but also having to make and submit plans for approval. For builders of the older generation in the 1860s and 1870s the changes represented a challenge to their traditional modes of practice. Heppers, the Leeds auctioneers, considered that more stringent building regulations applied in 1875 had caused a check in building operations in some quarters. They also lamented the lack of training, technical knowledge, and acquaintance with the first principles of geometry in the trade.[68]

The introduction of bye-law regulation of building also extended to the development of estates for building. The new conditions gave rise to two sets of experts: the Borough Surveyor and his staff for Leeds Corporation; and individuals amongst the professions with peripheral involvement in building and estate development for the developers. Even Lax and Boyle, with many years experience of the Leeds building trades had the support of the architect Frederick Mitchell. He in turn drew upon the portfolios of designs for houses and cottages sold by the Birmingham architect J.J. Raggett, an echo of the eighteenth-century metropolitan builder's pattern book dependence. For developers who were not members of the building world, support was even more necessary. J.W. Archer, the woollen manufacturer, had the support of the architect John Hall and the solicitor R.S. Wigin. Not all members of these professions developed a special interest and expertise in building and estate development, but some did and provided invaluable service. To them there seemed to be considerable contemporary ignorance of their role. This still held true in 1910 when Thomas Bright, surveyor, valuer, and member of the Auctioneer's Institute published his handbook on the development of building estates.

> To the ordinary observer . . . building land may seem to acquire its potentialities *per se*, and entirely apart from any external assistance or management on the part of the owner. . . . In the case of larger properties, however, their early maturity under normal conditions, as well as their ultimate success from a financial point of view, depend in no small measure on the skill and foresight bestowed on their management during the period of transition from agricultural to building value.[69]

The most satisfactory evidence for the role played by specialist advisers in the development of building estates is provided by the experience of the trustees and devisees of the Brown estate, Potternewton, between 1882 and 1907.

4 Specialist Advisers

The trustees of the estate of James Brown II, who died a bachelor in 1877, were his three sisters. They were also the surviving devisees of the adjoining estate of their father, James Brown I, who had died in 1845. As trustees and devisees (hereafter referred to simply as trustees) the sisters, and later their children, were the possessors of a 770 acre estate in Potternewton, created by purchases of James Brown I during the 1830s. The trustees were widely dispersed geographically and placed considerable reliance on their agent, Gervase Markham, who was based at Malton, 45 miles from Leeds. Markham and the trustees utilized the services of a Leeds firm of civil engineers, surveyors, and land agents, Martin and Fenwick. The partnership of S.D. Martin (1803–1877), surveyor, and Thomas Fenwick (1824–1905), civil engineer, was formed in 1861. After Martin's death, the firm had continued in business under the name of Martin and Fenwick. By the time Markham and the Brown estate trustees approached Fenwick in 1882 he had had 20 years experience of Leeds development, including work in the northern suburbs for the Cardigan and H.C. Marshall estates. As Fenwick had also been Borough Surveyor of Tynemouth in Northumberland from 1851 to 1861 he was well suited to the responsibilities of developing the Brown estate during a period of local authority regulation of the development process.

The Brown estate trustees relied upon Martin and Fenwick to devise a strategy for the sale of the estate as building land, to produce an optimum layout, and to handle negotiations with builders and local authority planning officials. Martin and Fenwick's advice and information was conveyed to the trustees by Gervase Markham. Markham, at Malton, relied upon a clerk, O.W. Stone, who ran the Harehills estate office, to carry out instructions from Martin and Fenwick on matters relevant to the development of building land.

Once preparations were underway and negotiations commenced with builders another party became involved, the Leeds law firm Ford and Warren. The Ford was John Rawlinson Ford, active during the late 1880s with his partner in the development of the Leeds Horticultural Gardens estate in Headingley for building purposes. Apart from the normal legal duties involved in the conveyancing of property Ford also carried out investigations into the probity of those who applied for building land on the trustees' estate and generally interested himself in the progress of the development. From the surviving correspondence between the parties involved it is apparent that there was a sense in which Martin and Fenwick and J.R. Ford felt they were the *de facto* rulers of the estate, irritated both when the trustees failed to follow their advice and when the Leeds Borough Surveyor and his staff insisted upon modifications to their plans which upset their strategy for the development. It was not necessarily that they rejected the need for planning, rather that they rejected the quality of some of the decision making.

Thus in 1894 Martin and Fenwick wrote to Markham:

The Streets Committee have imposed conditions upon our deposited Sections, making very objectionable Cuttings and Embankments in order to get one continuous gradient for each Street. We saw the City Engineer upon the subject and remonstrated with him, and these plans and sections have been again before the Committee and we are glad to say they have given up their requirements and agreed to our gradients which will make a considerable difference in the cost of forming these streets.[70]

In 1898 the relationship had become rather more strained.

The Building Inspector now refuses to pass the Chapel Plans unless the sewer and kerb are put down in Avenue Crescent as well. . . . There is no limit to this arrant stupidity.[71]

There is to be no connection with the Chapel, yet he insists in the most unreasonable and stubborn manner that the sewers and kerbs are to be laid for about a quarter of a mile beyond the buildings to be erected. Such is the deplorable excess to which this Autocrat is allowed to domineer.[72]

Nevertheless, Martin and Fenwick succeeded in having this requirement abandoned. They were not always successful, however. 'We have made several attempts to obtain approval for a plan of the Pond Site, but have not yet satisfied the unknown and unwritten laws by which we are governed in these matters'.[73]

Their disapproval of the bye-law regulations was at times a reflection of the rigidity with which they were applied in cases where experience suggested a need to allow site conditions to dictate the most satisfactory response.

We consider this [four acres adjoining Roundhay Road] will be an exceedingly awkward piece of ground to lay out, and to sell for dwellinghouses, there is a sharp rise in the ground; just over the wall at one point the surface is about twelve feet above road level, it rises quickly beyond – access for dwellings would be difficult. The by-laws [sic] require a cross street, regardless of the fact that it will be positively dangerous and impracticable with a gradient of 1 in 6 or thereabouts.[74]

Most annoying too were the occasions when the Leeds Corporation officials attempted to use the granting of a planning permission as a lever to obtain action on other matters. This was a problem Ford and Warren met in 1901: 'We have been to the City Engineer's Office to try and expedite the passing of the plans of the land between Harehills Lane and Avenue Crescent. We think we have made some progress, but the Authorities are very tiresome people to deal with, as they refuse to pass the plans until the question of the widening of Harehills Lane is settled.'[75]

The original enquiry from the trustees in 1882 had been about the possibility of a sale of building land by auction. It was followed up in 1883 by an auction sale of 112 acres of the estate to the north of the Cowper New Town development; this land had been purchased from the sixth Earl Cowper during the 1840s. Martin and Fenwick divided the land into 13 lots, valued it, and set reserve prices for the sale. Only four of the lots were sold in 1883, and only one of those reached its valuation price of 2s. 6d. per square yard.

Disposal of the remaining nine lots was not achieved until 1890. The final success of the sale was primarily determined not by developers and builders, but by the three people who between them purchased over 100 acres of the land; Sir James Kitson of Kitson and Company, locomotive and general engineers, E. Schunk of Schunk and Company, stuff and woollen merchants, and Robert Benson Jowitt, woollen merchant. All three entrepreneurs moved into residential estates carved out of the break-up of James Brown's Harehills Grove, park, and surrounding agricultural land. Jowitt expanded his estate with additional purchases in 1887, 1890, and 1891; his 35 acre estate and the former Brown mansion were purchased by Leeds Corporation in 1900 for £35,000 at 4s. 7d. per square yard, to form Potternewton Park.[76]

During the intervening time the rapid growth of population in the vicinity decreased the attraction of these residences and their illusion of country life, replacing views of fields with rows of roofs of terrace houses all the way down to the centre of Leeds. By the mid-1890s this change was being firmly established, but the purchasers of the 1880s made an attempt to stand fast against it. Unfortunately for Kitson, Schunk, and Jowitt, the Brown estate was in the hands of Martin and Fenwick, who were aware of the exact situation. In 1892 Mrs Schunk considered the purchase of 2.5 acres at 2s. 7d. per square yard, but when her agent called upon Martin and Fenwick to say she had changed her mind they reported: 'We told him a Builder had been in treaty for it and would probably build a small class of house, which might be objectionable to the residents in the House near the old quarry'.[77] However, this appears to have been a tactical manoeuvre because after Mrs Schunk refused to be persuaded they revealed to Markham that they had no immediate purchaser, 'the land will probably be no worse for being in hand a few months.'[78]

By 1896 such subterfuge was unnecessary; when Jowitt offered to purchase seven acres adjoining his park at 1s. 5½d. per square yard he was informed that its sale in small lots with frontage to a new street would produce prices of 3s. 9d. per square yard. In 1897 Sir James Kitson offered £5,250 for nine acres and Harehills House, 2s. 4d. per square yard, but he wanted in return a restrictive covenant imposed upon all other nearby purchasers of land not to build houses costing less than £400. His offer was a counter to an offer of £5,000 from Messrs Charles, 'builders and architects . . . their intention being to cut it up and build a small class of terrace houses or cottages.'[79] Messrs Charles raised their offer to £5,500 but the Brown estate trustees rejected it. They were not entirely antipathetic to Kitson's offer; in 1897 Martin and Fenwick informed Markham that they had been unable to persuade Sir James to raise it 'but that having regard to the amenities of the neighbourhood he should perhaps preserve them better than a Speculative Builder.'[80] In 1898, when the house and land were put up for auction it was decided by the auctioneer, Hepper, and Martin and Fenwick that it should be offered in one lot because in that way it might still entice bids from both Sir James Kitson and Mr Schunk.[81] At auction it was sold for £10,500 to Seth Joy Stott, a builder; neither Kitson nor Schunk thought it worthwhile to safeguard their environs from despoliation when the cost had risen to a building land price of 4s. 8d. per square yard.

The failure of the 1883 auction to dispose of all the land quickly at its estimated value must have been instrumental in producing a decision to sell building land directly to builders. The exclusion of developers of building land as purchasers had made it unlikely that the land would be disposed of at the estimated value; the alternative of selling in smaller lots to builders at higher prices over the same length of time had considerable appeal. When a large lot was sold to a developer in 1887 the trustees could only admire the purchaser's ability to convert 21,000 square yards at 3s. 0d. per square yard into building sites at 6s. 0d. per square yard within 12 months.[82]

By August 1886 Martin and Fenwick had drawn up a layout plan for part of the Brown estate and obtained the approval of the Leeds Corporation. In spite of the gradual recovery of building activity between 1886 and 1889 nothing was done to implement the proposals. It was necessary in March 1889 for Martin and Fenwick to remind Markham and the trustees that if nothing was done soon then the planning permission would lapse.[83]

The year 1890 was one of considerable activity in the preparation of the estate. Builders were interested in purchasing, but in January Martin and Fenwick had to re-emphasize that streets needed to be made as soon as possible if houses were to be built during the summer.[84] In March the lifting of 4,800 square yards of turves along the line of the intended Harehills Avenue was put out to tender. Even at this stage it was possible to contemplate profit; Martin and Fenwick had considered a tender of three-farthings per square yard excessive but Oswald Stone, the Harehills estate clerk, had discovered that the cut sods could be sold for 3d. per square yard.[85] Earth-moving to achieve the required gradient for a road was more expensive, but by judicious planning it was possible to coordinate activities so that surplus soil from the making of one street could be used to raise the level of another.[86] At that stage it was also necessary to decide whether trees along the line of intended new streets should be felled or left standing.[87] Markham, the trustees' agent, was aware that suitably located trees enhanced the value of a street, and was prepared to pay to have them planted along Harehills Avenue, a street reserved for the most expensive houses.[88]

Road making activities were not without attendant problems. J.R. Ford had to find out whether the formal bye-law requirement that streets be paved and flagged meant that tarmacadam could not be used. The excavation of a road provided the neighbourhood with an opportunity for dumping which, if not stopped, could become a nuisance. At one stage the Harehills Avenue excavation was being used as a tip for ashpit refuse; Martin and Fenwick suspected the culprits to be Corporation contractors. In addition, the requirements of local authority officials had to be considered. In October 1890 the foundations for a road on the estate were declared to have been unsatisfactorily levelled; this was briefly dealt with by instructions from Martin and Fenwick that their contractor 'level the edges of the tipping a little.'[89] However, once Martin and Fenwick had staked out a new street on the ground and Markham's clerk, Stone, had superintended the work it was possible for negotiations with builders to be concluded.

The earliest offer received in 1889 came from Charles Morgan, gentleman, and land speculator. In July he offered £900 per acre, 3s. 8½d. per square yard, for 9.5 acres with frontages to the Leeds–Harrogate road and the estate's intended new road, Harehills Avenue. He was willing to build houses of £45 annual rental value on the latter, but only houses of £25 annual value on the former. The backland would have been covered with £16 minimum rental houses, 'all to be through houses and none of the kind known as back-to-back houses, provided also that shops may be built at the gable ends of houses if he "thinks fit".'[90] Martin and Fenwick described him as 'a speculator' who would rival the estate's own attempts to sell building land. He was willing to pay £3,000 or £4,000 on receiving vacant possession, but had a definite idea of the price which would enable a satisfactory profit to be made from subsequent subdivision and resales. Martin and Fenwick, attempted to persuade Morgan to increase his offer to £1,200 per acre, 'which he flatly refused, but we think he may be induced to advance to £1,000 an acre but not more.'[91] In addition they wanted a contribution of £300 towards the estate's much earlier costs of making one-half of Cowper Street in the New Town of Leeds. The trustees proved willing to accept £1,000 per acre but their rival developer, Morgan, refused.

At first the trustees attempted to obtain building land prices from builders who were wanting large blocks of land suitable for subdivision and resales. In 1891 Martin and Fenwick received an enquiry for the price of between eight and ten acres in large blocks, anywhere on the estate. Martin and Fenwick set an asking price of £600 per acre, 2s. 6d. per square yard, but advised acceptance of £500 per acre, 2s. 0½d. per square yard, for any quantity above three acres. On the Harehills part of the estate Martin and Fenwick suggested only semi-detached villas and terrace houses of £25 annual value should be built.[92] However, Markham passed on the trustees' instructions that only £600 per acre would be acceptable for between eight and ten acres with a stipulation that only semi-detached villas would be satisfactory.[93] Martin and Fenwick acknowledged their instructions, but commented 'we shall probably have to be satisfied with terrace houses.'[94]

Builders had their own set of opinions, based on experience, as to what was and was not profitable. In May 1889 Martin and Fenwick informed Markham of their negotiations with the Leeds builders, Isaac and Wilson.

> We have had some builders this morning wanting the Corner block of Chapeltown Road and Cowper Street, but we wished them to treat for a Plot nearer to the proposed Harehills Avenue. They finally asked to have prices named for each of the three blocks . . . assuming that we do not require houses of a high class, which are not wanted so near the town. They built most of the houses in Reginald Terrace and Scholebrook [sic] Avenue for which the rents had to be lowered, and yet were not well let. . . . They required an early answer, as they are ready to commence work, and say they cannot remain idle. They were going to look at a 20 acre lot in Hunslet.[95]

However, the sympathy for local experience Martin and Fenwick were liable to display at times did not always find a reciprocal chord in the mind of the trustees. Isaac and Wilson never came back to Potternewton.

Both trustees and professional advisers were agreed on the need to deal with only the best of the builders. They were apparently identifiable in two ways; through their financial situation and from the demand for their end product. However, these people tended to be developers too, and also to demand special conditions before they would undertake to build themselves. In 1891 Martin and Fenwick were negotiating with one of the good builders who wanted the width of the building blocks to be decreased and a new back road introduced. 'We should not have entertained this proposal from a common builder, but Mr. Franks has got a name for building very tasteful detached and semi-detached Villas and we feel sure the houses he will put up on this land would be exceedingly nice and would probably induce other builders to adopt the same style in the neighbourhood.'[96] Franks was willing to build only semi-detached houses and to have the elevations of his houses approved by the trustees, but was not prepared to countenance paying

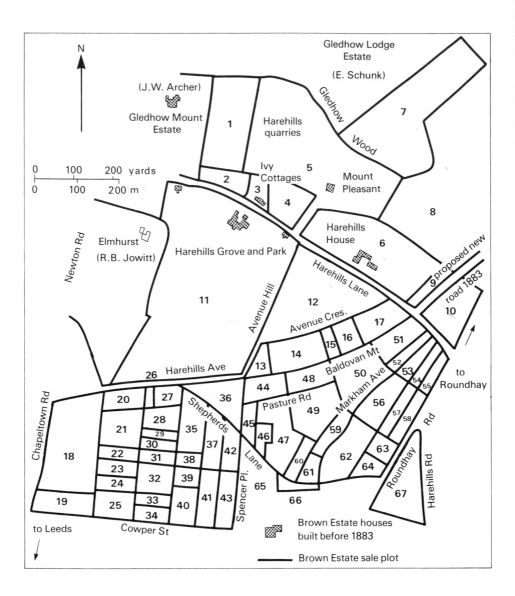

Figure 28. Brown Estate layout and development, Potternewton, 1883–1904.

The process of suburban development in north Leeds, 1870–1914

C. TREEN

Name of purchaser, date of sale, size of plot (sq.yds) and price paid per sq.yd, as known:

1 Sir James Kitson 1885: 28,895 @ 1s.
2 Sir James Kitson 1885: 7,804 @ 2s. 6d.
3 W. Myers 1883: 3,993 @ 2s. 7d.
4 E. Schunk 1887: 9,468 @ 2s. 6d.
5 E. Schunk 1887: 89,927 @ 8d.
6 S.J. Stott 1898: 45,064 @ 4s. 8d.
7 E. Schunk 1883: 65,776 @ 7½d.
8 Sir James Kitson 1889: 69,406 @ 1s.
9 J. Eastwood 1883: 6,352 @ 1s. 8d.
10 R. Addyman 1883: 20,207 @ 1s. 5½d.
11 R.B. Jowitt purchases: 1887, 38,139 @ 1s. 10½d.;
     1889, 85,668 @ 2s. 6½d.; 1890, 9,982 @ 6d.;
     1891, 39,597 @ 2d.
12 1901 auction of 40,139 sq.yds purchased by
     six builders: H. Lax, W. Lolley, J. McKay,
     S.J. Stott, A. & J. Shaw and C. Wilson.
     Average price paid was 7s. 5½d.
13 Presbyterian Church 1897: 3,500 @ 4s.
14 W.J. & H. Lax 1901: 12,000 @ 6s.
15 Primitive Methodist Church 1897: 2,650 @ 4s.
16 G. Lax 1894: 2s. 8¼d.
17 W.H. Lax 1894: 2s. 8¼d.
18 G. & J. Hutton 1891: 36,614 @ 5s. 6d.
19 G. Hutton 1890: 3,731 @ 6s. 6d., 5,636 @ 7s. 6d.
20 G. Hutton 1897: 5,900 @ 7s.
21 G. Hutton 1902: 7,090 @ 6s. 4d.
22 J.C. Spivey 1898: 4,256 @ 5s.
23 S.W. Milner 1897: 4,459 @ 5s.
24 Beale Bros. 1898: 4,430 @ 6s.
25 G. Hutton 1896: 8,536 @ 5s.
26 J. Speight 1898: 1,530 @ 8s.
27 G. Ball 1898: 3,300 @ 8s.
28 S.W. Milner 1904: 5,905 @ 6s. 6d.
29 no information
30 vacant 1911
31 1899: 3,235 @ 6s. 6d.
32 Mr Milner 1899: 7,256 @ 6s.
33 J. Routh 1897: 3,546 @ 5s.
34 J.C. Spivey 1896: 3,422 @ 5s. 6d.
35 C.E. Smith 1899: 12,000 @ 6s. 6d.

36 W. Holmes 1890
37 C.E. Smith 1897: 8,350 @ 4s. 6d.
38 C.E. Smith
39 vacant 1911
40 Board schools
41 T.E. Heavyside 1896: 8,586 @ 4s. 7¾d.
42 and 43 T.E. Heavyside 1894:
     10,600 @ 3s. 6d.
44 A. & J. Shaw Bros. 1898
45 C.E. Smith 1900: 3,464 @ 6s. 6d.
46 no information
47 vacant 1911
48 no information
49 R. Steven 1898: 15,000 @ 4s. 6d.
50 R. Steven 1896: 18,656 @ 3s. 9d.
51 R. Steven pre-1896: 8,705 @ 2s. 9d.
52 R. Steven 1896: 3,610 @ 1s.
53 no information
54 no information
55 no information
56 R. Steven 1900: 10,090 @ 7s. 6d.
57 T. Gelsthorpe 1900: 5,300 @ 8s. 6d.
58 S.J. Stott 1903: 5,240 @ 15s.
59 R. Steven 1898: 3,480 @ 4s. 6d.
60 Leeds Industrial Co-operative Soc.
     1897: 3,980 @ 5s.
61 no information
62 C.E. Smith 1899: 14,523 @ 6s.
63 no information
64 New Leeds Constitutional Club 1896:
     3,920 @ 7s. 6d.
65 R. Steven 1892: 10,890 @ 3s. 6d.
66 R. Steven 1896: 9,170 @ 2s. 3¼d.
67 Boothman & Morgan 1887: 21,000 @ 3s.

additional road costs caused by the trustees' decision that the width of one road should be increased from 18 feet to 36 feet.[97] By September 1891 terms had been agreed; Franks was to take 6.5 acres, build £30 annual value houses on the major street frontage and £25 houses on the backland. However, he also wanted purchasers of lots on the opposite frontage also to be bound by a £25 minimum annual value restrictive covenant.[98] Bargaining continued into December, when Franks refused to continue with the matter unless allowed to purchase the opposite frontage.[99] Eventually negotiations were dropped, and in February 1892 Martin and Fenwick reassured Markham that they had other applicants for the land besides Franks.[100] However, Franks tried briefly in March to obtain the frontage to Harehills Avenue without any backland for 2s. 6d. per square yard, providing he also had an undertaking that no back-to-back houses should be built on the opposite frontage. Martin and Fenwick rejected his offer immediately.

The earliest successful negotiations with builders took just as long. In October 1889 an offer by Messrs Huttons, Leeds builders, to buy 4.75 acres with frontages to the Leeds–Harrogate Road and Cowper Street had been rejected by the Brown estate trustees. George Hutton's response was to offer 6s. 0d. per square yard for a portion of the land, 10,070 square yards. However, the offer was subject to his being allowed to pay for it in four instalments, paying £100 deposit on signing the contract, and interest at 4 per cent per annum on the balance.[101] Martin and Fenwick were not prepared to accept the proposal without a larger deposit 'and a more satisfactory arrangement as to Completion of the purchase.' By November Hutton was prepared to buy 9,367 square yards at 6s. 0d. per square yard, paying £300 deposit, and the balance on 5,636 square yards of the total area immediately upon obtaining possession in February 1890.[102] Martin and Fenwick found this offer more acceptable and reported enthusiastically upon it. 'He will build three villas fronting Chapeltown Road and a respectable row of terrace houses in Cowper Street of not less value than those opposite. They will have front gardens 24 feet wide whereas those opposite are only 6 feet . . . Mr. Hutton wants to have a decision as he has the offer of other plots at Woodsley House and Hillary Street where he has already built some good houses.'[103] This offer was refused by the trustees and Hutton raised his offer to 7s. 6d. per square yard for the Cowper Street frontage and to 6s. 6d. per square yard for the remainder. In addition to the financial arrangements agreed in November 1889 he wanted until November 1890 to pay off the balance. Restrictive covenants were to be imposed for small villas of £35 minimum annual rental on the Chapeltown Road frontage, £30 houses on the Cowper Street frontage, and £25 houses on the remainder. In return Hutton had the length of the gardens of houses on the backland reduced from 15 ft to 12 ft.[104]

In 1891 the Huttons, father and son, offered to purchase 36,614 square yards to the north of George Hutton's 1890 purchase at 4s. 6d. per square yard. This was declined by Martin and Fenwick, who wanted 5s. 6d. per square yard. George Hutton then offered 5s. 0d. per square yard, subject to being allowed to make three separate purchases with three different deposits and conveyancing in six lots. He was only willing to offer £900 deposit, not £1,500 as Martin and Fenwick and J.R. Ford wanted.[105] By March the Huttons were prepared to pay the asking price for the land, 5s. 6d. per square yard. A compromise of £1,000 deposit was agreed, the balance to be paid by instalments as determined by J.R. Ford. The Huttons were to bear the cost of making the roads, but they were to receive the land in three conveyances.[106] This arrangement was accepted by the trustees, and a contract drawn up in May 1891. However, George Hutton requested that they should have the land in five separate conveyances; Martin and Fenwick agreed to three, but Ford and Warren proposed acceptance of Hutton's request as he was willing to pay the cost of the two additional conveyances.[107] The trustees were anxious about the possibility of the builder going bankrupt before the conveyances were completed, but Ford and Warren assured them of their legal title to the unconveyed land, and their right to retain the deposit as most of it was to be deducted from the first conveyance, leaving only £300 of £1,125 to be reclaimed from the bankrupt's estate, if the situation should arise,[108] Final adjustments were made to the transaction in June 1891; five payments were to be made between then and March 1892 in addition to the deposit, making a total purchase price of £10,125; interest at 4 per cent per annum was to be paid on all but the deposit until final completion. One final modification divided the land and the deposit between George Hutton and his father, John Hutton, a retired builder.[109] George Hutton subsequently transferred his business from Enfield Terrace in the adjoining Sheepscar part of the in-township to a house which he built on the Cowper Street frontage of his land.

One of the trustees' problems was that acceptable builders were apt to reveal unsuspected speculative tendencies once they obtained the title to sufficient land enabling subdivision and resale at higher prices. In 1890 Martin and Fenwick had been negotiating with Messrs Lax, Leeds builders, whom J.R. Ford had investigated and found to be 'respectable men'.[110] These negotiations had been set aside when the Huttons made a better offer for the land. However, in 1894 George Lax purchased an acre in Harehills Avenue at 2s. 8d. per square yard, and W.H. Lax purchased the adjoining two acres at the same price.

George Lax had been active in the northern out-townships since the late 1860s when he had built on part of the former T.W. Lloyd Hill Top estate in Headingley. From 1878 onwards he had been working on the former Potternewton Hall estate. In the late 1860s he had been a joiner, by the late 1870s he was a builder, proprietor of a brickworks, and also purchaser of land from developers for further subdivision and resale. In 1878 he had paid £5,945 for five acres of the Potternewton Hall estate at 5s. 0d. per square yard. It was part of a larger plot purchased by Thomas Whiteley, a Leeds contractor and builder, at 2s. 4d. per square yard in 1869. Whiteley had resold at 3s. 9½d. per square yard, and the purchasers, an estate agent and a surveyor, had resold to Lax.[111] Although Lax had paid twice the original cost of the land he had still been able to subdivide and resell at a profit. His own building activities had been temporarily in financial difficulties during a slump in demand for property which lasted from 1878 until 1883 when demand, especially for cottage property, improved. However, Lax had been building semi-detached villas worth at least £30 annually, a class of property for which the recovery in demand was much slower. In 1882 Lax had abandoned his mortgage on part of his property and it was sold by the mortgagee for £2,163.[112] Between 1890 and 1892 he was active on J.W. Archer's former Cowper land, building small through houses and back-to-backs. He had been paying Archer 6s. 0d. per square yard for land supplied in a series of conveyances, reselling in one case at 8s. 0d. per square yard.[113]

However, by 1896 Lax had not built upon his acre on the Brown estate, causing Martin and Fenwick to doubt his intentions; they suspected that he wished to obtain building land cheaply for the erection of low value houses, and for subdivision and resales.[114] Lax put his case in a letter to Martin and Fenwick.

Being in need of a plot of land as a Store yard, I telephoned to ask you to sell me the land bounded by Markham Avenue–the Beck–Ellars [sic] Road and Beck Road. You replied that you would not sell any land except that abutting into Harehills Avenue. I felt rather surprised on hearing this seeing that the whole of the estate was understood to be for sale, and that for my present purpose the land in Harehills Avenue was to me of no use, I afterwards thought that perhaps the making of the roads, kerbing etc might have something to do with it. But seeing that for probably 5 or 6 years I should not need either kerb or Road making as it would not be used for building purposes before that time. I have as you know an acre of land already in the Avenue but I do not wish to use that even *temporarily as a yard – as a wood fence* and *piles of timber* might be considered objectionable, in fact would be objectionable in so prominent a place as Harehills Avenue. But alongside the beck there could be no objection taken by anyone as the only use at present it can be put to so far as I can see is for accommodation land.

As for buying any more land on the top side of Harehills Avenue there is not much encouragement so far seeing that for a £800 house only £30 rent can be obtained and that only with difficulty. So my little acre will have to bide a wee. As regards the land on the low side of Harehills Avenue towards the beck, I see by the plan that the main Streets are fixed. The space between apparently been left to set out as the purchaser and the corporation can agree except so far as the frontage to Harehills Avenue is concerned which have to be Terrace houses of a rental of £25. That is all right. The land remaining from the back of those houses down to the beck being unrestricted as to rental value. That being so – and if you are determined to get of [sic] the land in Harehills Avenue before you proceed to deal with any other portion of the estate, I dont wish to be awkward. So you will please put in price to me the portion bounded by Harehills Avenue–the Beck. Ellars [sic] Road and Beck Road upon which I propose building similar Houses to those we have built in Roundhay Road and letting from 5s. 3d. to 7s. 0d. per week – but seeing that is in a position not so good I should have to give them more accomodion [sic] and considerably larger gardens and more space – with perhaps a few Small Through houses if I saw there were any demand for them, which is rather problematical as so far as I can see they are a kind of house much disliked by the tenants. I should have been glad to have negotiated for a much larger piece only interest at 4 per cent on unproductive land and the much larger expences [sic] of Road making, kerbing, Sewering etc etc kills it. If you could see your way to *lower the rate of interest* for a stated time it would be a great inducement to make a larger purchase.[115]

Although J.R. Ford was in favour of some form of agreement with Lax, Martin and Fenwick added their own comment to Lax's letter, 'it would be absurd to place a large block at the disposal of a speculator.'[116] Lax's point that meeting a £30 annual value restrictive covenant meant an outlay of £800 during a period of apparently depressed rents and low demand for such property, whilst a considerable demand existed for lower value back-to-back houses, failed to convince Martin and Fenwick. However, 1895 and 1896 were the two worst years for house building in Leeds during the 1890s. George Lax was unable to buy any additional land on the Brown estate but other members of the family did so after 1900.

The most active builder on the estate was Robert Steven who purchased 17.25

acres for £16,250 between 1892 and 1900. He appears to have made the transition from model machine maker to builder in 1891, when he purchased Cowper land at third hand for 3s. 0d. per square yard. He proceeded to subdivide and resell at between 4s. 2½d. and 5s. 0d. per square yard.[117] In the development of this land Steven purchased right of access to the extension of Spencer Place from the New Town of Leeds onto the Brown estate. In 1892 Steven offered to buy two acres of the Brown estate which adjoined his 1891 land. Although informed it was not for sale he raised his offer from 2s. 6d. to 3s. 1d. per square yard. Martin and Fenwick advised acceptance of the revised offer because it would transfer half the costs of making two roads for a considerable length from the estate onto a purchaser.[118] In August 1892 Steven requested an additional six months to pay the balance of his purchase money, £856, paying 4 per cent *per annum* interest in the meantime; J.R. Ford was willing to advise this.[119]

In June 1894 Steven was reported to be in difficulties; what his problems were is not known but they were short-lived because in September he was negotiating for more land.[120] This was a less attractive plot of nearly two acres, dissected both by the tail goit of a corn mill and a public sewer, for which he was only willing to pay 2s. 6d. per square yard.[121] In July 1895 a revised offer of 2s. 8½d. per square yard was accepted. Martin and Fenwick erred in this sale by not preventing Steven from making cross streets, but a compromise was reached by which he was to be allowed a diagonal street, over the line of the public sewer.[122] Ford's opinion had been that as an exchange for layout alterations Stevens might be permitted to build a shop in a back street. Martin and Fenwick were also in favour, 'in the course of time the necessities of the community will make it expedient to have shops on this or some other portion of the estate.'[123]

From this stage of the development onwards J.R. Ford took a greater part in providing advice, which at times tended to be critical not only of the trustees' attitudes, but also of Martin and Fenwick.

> As I told you we are in difficulty in regards to the land already sold to Steven because Mr. Fenwick did not bind him to build a continuous row of houses to Harehills Avenue and he can therefore lay out cross streets if he likes. And I look upon such a plan as most injurious to the Avenue and the land fronting at and lying to the westward. It removes all line of demarcation between the better houses and the cheaper ones which is most necessary if we are to sell our best land to advantage. Some sacrifice will have to be made now and the question is what is the least we shall have to make.[124]

By the time Steven purchased 18,900 square yards in 1896 at 3s. 9d. per square yard the trustees had accepted that houses on the estate could no longer be of the standard they had hoped for originally; Steven was required to build houses of £25, £18, and £16 annual value on his land. Further negotiations in 1897 were upset by the discovery that he was re-selling land bought from the trustees at 2s. 8d. per square yard for 5s. 6d. per square yard. Both Martin and Fenwick and J.R. Ford attempted to reassure the trustees that Steven's profits from subdivision were not as high as at first appeared. 'Steven asserts that his actual profit on the land is not more than a shilling a yard, there having been much expense incurred in various ways. That I can quite believe, as I was from my own experience in the case of an estate I bought and laid out and then retailed to purchasers. . . . You must remember he makes it his business to hunt up purchasers, and that is by no means easy work.'[125] However, it was difficult to explain why other developers were more successful at obtaining higher prices than the trustees' professional advisers. Subsequent sales were at higher prices and for smaller lots. In May 1897 Martin and Fenwick rejected a possible sale of 15 acres at 3s. 0d. per square yard as being 'too large a plot to pass . . . in one lot to speculative builders, who would only expect to make a considerable profit out of the transaction.'[126] When Steven purchased additional land in 1898 and 1900 he had to pay considerably higher prices, 4s. 6d. and 7s. 6d. per square yard. The search for higher prices was rewarded because of a high demand for building land during the building boom at the turn of the century in Leeds.

Steven still attempted to obtain favourable terms. The sales to him had only been recommended 'subject to a plan limiting him to a certain number of houses with proper open spaces.'[127] He requested that he might be allowed two shops and a reduction in the annual value of the houses to be built to £14.[128] He was allowed one shop in January 1898, but requested a second in April. Martin and Fenwick considered Steven had received enough concessions and demanded an additional payment 'representing the additional value of the land as a site for a shop.' This was refused by Steven who replied that 'considering the result of the sale . . . it would be a gracious act.'[129] In 1900 he made a final purchase on the estate, 10,090 square yards, for which he paid the prevailing cost of land for builders, not developers, 7s. 6d. per square yard.

During the boom in building activity at the turn of the century most of the remaining Brown estate building land north of the New Town of Leeds was sold. Twelve acres were sold at auction in 1901; divided into lots of up to one acre it was purchased by builders at prices ranging from 5s. 7d. to 11s. 0d. per square yard. Not only the current demand for building land at a time of considerable prosperity in the trade, but also the spread of the built up core of Leeds to the borders of the estate contributed to receipts £1,224 above the reserve price, a much more satisfactory outcome than that of the 1883 auction.

Brown estate land to the east of the built up area now began to be considered for future disposal as building land. At this stage the failure to negotiate successfully with the Low Moor Iron and Steel Company for the return of mineral rights under the land became a disadvantage. In addition the topography of some of the land made it less suitable for building sites, some of the flatter land was badly roaded, and there was a danger that developments on adjoining estates might prove detrimental to the prospects of the Brown land. J.R. Ford was the driving force behind long term planning for this land.

> As the land is very hilly and rises a good deal above the level of Roundhay Road it will be difficult to lay out, the price is probably very nearly as much as it is worth as it now stands. The alternative to accepting the offer is to lay the land out ourselves for building purposes, and retail it in smaller pieces. This will not be easy to do, on account of the nature of the land, but if a purchaser can do it, there is no reason why we should not. It will of course involve outlay on roads, and kerbs, and sewers.
>
> Before doing this we should consult Mr. Childe [Civil and Mining Engineer, Wakefield] as to whether the subsequent working of the coal would let down the houses. If so we must arrange with Fittons to leave sufficient pillars and pay

them for doing so. If we do not do so, the small purchaser will shy, as he cannot go to the Fittons and arrange for coal being left under a small portion except at relatively disadvantageous terms.[130]

In 1898 Fittons, sub-lessees of the mineral rights under the Brown estate, offered £12,000 for 16.25 acres. Martin and Fenwick persuaded them to raise it to £14,790, but this was short of the required price of £16,000. The alternative of selling in small lots was examined by Thomas Fenwick in 1898. He considered that a sale period of 16 years would be insufficient to dispose of all the land. Possible sales were estimated at 3 acres at 4s. 7d. per square yard, 1900–4; 4 acres at 6s. 0d. per square yard, 1905–10; and a further 4 acres at 7s. 0d. per square yard, 1911–16, leaving nearly 5.5 acres in hand in 1916.[131] The difficulty of the mineral rights was brought out in 1903 when an offer of 4s. 7d. per square yard was received for 20 acres. The prospective purchaser was John Wainwright Watson, the estate agent and developer active on adjoining former Cowper land since the 1890s. Although Watson's offer was raised by 5d. per square yard he had difficulties in negotiating with the Low Moor Iron and Steel Company for the release of the land from their mineral rights; they refused an offer of 2s. 1d. per square yard from Watson although he had been agent for their property interests.

Once a policy of small sales had been established, consequent upon the failure of negotiations for large sales, the possibility of improving the land's desirability for building purposes became more important. In 1899 agreement was reached with H.H. Hodgson, an estate agent, for the improvement of road access to both the Brown estate and Hodgson's adjoining estate from the Leeds–York Road.[132] This agreement was contingent upon withdrawal of Brown estate opposition to the establishment of a cemetery on Hodgson's land. For Hodgson the sale of this land to Leeds Corporation was crucial if he was to regain a major portion of his outlay on unripe building land. Fenwick was against the cemetery; J.R. Ford was not so certain but expected little consideration from the Corporation to opposition based on the protection of building land.

> I suppose if we refuse our consent we shall have to give some good reason, though the real reason might be that the proximity of the cemetery might possibly prejudice our subsequent sale of land for building purposes. I don't know that it would prejudice the sale and the presence of a large piece of open ground might be an advantage. The houses to be erected on this land in the future will be small, and I dare say we might be able to sell some of the land for manufacturing purposes, but whatever reasons we may have in our own minds we could only object to the cemetery on grounds affecting the existing farmhouse.[133]

The road was more important than the cemetery because, as Ford pointed out in 1899, building operations were approaching rapidly, and the southern part of the estate would only sell cheaply as backland if access was not improved.

There still remained the drawback of a mineral lease to the Low Moor Iron and Steel Company which was not due to expire until 1914. Ford was totally committed to a policy of negotiating the prior termination of the lease. This led to disagreement with the devisees who shared this part of the estate, who were reluctant to give up assured mineral lease income for the uncertain profits of building land sales. In 1904 Ford was the more adventurous, looking forward to future gains.

> When the next building boom comes, which will be, I hope, in two or three years' time, the estate of the Devisees will be the only land available at this end of the City, and ought to command good prices, and meantime some of it might be sold even now. But if the Low Moor lease be not put an end to as regards land for sale, we cannot hope to sell, or if we do, we must submit to low prices on account of the risk of subsidence. Until June 1914 we should have to go on as we are . . .

> If Lady Graham does not on reflection see her way to join in the proposed scheme, it must fall through, for which I shall be sorry. I have had the development of this estate very much at heart, and have hitherto lost no opportunity of securing such improvements as would improve its value when the time for sales has arrived. The town of Leeds has travelled towards it quicker than I expected, and I can see that before long we shall have many applications to buy, and if we are not able to sell, there is danger that the applicants will go in a different direction for what they want and for a time leave this property in a backwater. There are fashions in building as in everything else.[134]

However, in 1905 Ford was more cautious because of factors external to the estate. 'Disappointment might afterwards ensue by reason of the land not coming onto the market as quickly as we hope . . . Leeds is at present suffering from a depression in trade . . . it might be two or three years before the sale of land for building purposes revives.'[135] Had Ford known that building activity in Leeds was not to pick up with the general improvement in trade in 1907, but to decline steadily down to 1914 his advice would undoubtedly have been more cautious. As it happened the more sceptical judgment of his clients, derived from 25 years' disillusion at the failure of building estate development to produce instant wealth, proved to be accurate, although in 1905 they did not know of the factors which were to make it so.

5 Profitability

> Theoretically, this estimate of profit should be based on the amount of the purchase price, plus expenditure on development.[136]

Preparation costs were of two types, professional services and physical preparation. In 1910 Bright listed the costs of the first type. The vendor's solicitors received conveyancing fees of 1 per cent on sales under £3,000 for negotiating the sale plus 1.5 per cent on the first £1,000 for deducing title and drawing up the conveyance. The percentage was reduced on values above those amounts.[137] Surveyor's charges also varied with the type of work. Preliminary analysis of a prospective building estate with guidelines for management cost between £1 1s. 0d. and £3 3s. 0d. per acre. Detailed plans, levels, and cross-sections in accordance with local bye-laws cost between £1 10s. 0d. and £2 10s. 0d. per acre. Detailed plans and working drawings of roads and sewers for local authority approval, tender, and contract amounted to between 5 and 6 per cent of the cost of the work. A bill of quantities for the work added another 2 to 2.5 per cent of the cost of the work; acting as Clerk of the Works was another 1 to 1.5 per cent of the cost of the work. Setting out building plots and plans for building agreements cost £1 1s. 0d. to £3 3s. 0d.; examining the purchaser's plans cost £2 2s. 0d. per set. The incidental expenses of letter writing and travelling costs were also added to the developer's bill.[138] Bright's generalized analysis assumed these costs to be 11.5 per cent of the value of an undeveloped building estate, 5.5 per cent of the developed estate value. His estimate of speculative profit was equivalent to 16.7 per cent of the sale price; 25 per cent of the outlay.[139]

Evidence for the costs of physical preparation were provided in the Brown estate correspondence. Deturfing before work began was tendered for at ¾d. per square yard in 1890. It was possible to make a profit on this, however, by selling the cut sods at 3d. per square yard.[140] In 1890 cut and fill operations cost 11d. per cubic yard;[141] in 1891 levelling ground cost 9d. per square yard;[142] in 1896 filling hollows cost 3d. per cubic yard.[143] However, developers usually needed only to pay these costs on small portions of a building estate, principally along the line of roads.

Until the 1870s it was always possible to shorten the period during which preparation costs were borne by the developer by delaying the making of streets and sewers until sufficient purchasers had settled on the estate to pay the bulk of the expense. In areas of low quality housing streets might remain unmade and sewers unlaid for many years; the Lower Burley development under way by 1850 was subject to local authority enforcement notices for kerbing, sewering, and paving during the 1870s. After the introduction of building regulations in 1866 it became more difficult to defer such expenses. Building plans were not passed until roads had been sewered and kerbed. By 1898 controls had been further tightened, and it was necessary for the complete length of a street to be kerbed and sewered, not merely the part adjoining a plot which had been sold.[144]

After seven years of development as building land the Brown estate's trustees' outlay for road making on their Leeds estates amounted to £3,275, of which only £821 had been recouped from purchasers.[145] One consequence was that lower prices were accepted for plots which transferred a considerable proportion of road making costs from developer to builder.[146] An attempt by the Chapel Allerton developers Carter and Wooler to shift the responsibility for road making costs directly to the builders in 1906 failed when the Leeds Town Clerk, R.E. Fox, ruled that it was the developers' duty to have the expense of collecting the money from their purchasers.[147] Nevertheless the eventual transfer of road making costs onto the purchasers, and the fact that purchasers also paid for the land on which the streets were laid out, suggests that only half of the outlay costs need to be deducted from the gross income from sales in order to establish the net profit.

The Brown estate also provides evidence of the comparative profitability of selling in plots directly to builders rather than in larger quantities to lesser developers. In 1894 Martin and Fenwick valued 45.3 acres of the estate at £27,712, equal to £611 per acre; the valuation included preparation costs of £1,550 or 5.6 per cent of gross value. The calculations were for large plots expected to be sold in from two to eight years. A further more tentative valuation of £55,000 to £60,000 was made on a basis of sale in smaller lots over a longer period. Although the gross value might be doubled thereby it was pointed out that much would depend on the uncertain course of building speculation over the following years.[148] The highest valuation represented a selling price of £1,325 per acre, 5s. 6d. per square yard. During the peak period of building activity 1898–1901 Martin and Fenwick's estimates were surpassed. Their best achievement was the sale of 12 acres in lots to builders at auction in 1901 for an average price of 7s. 5½d. per square yard, £1,815 per acre.[149]

The profitability of the developer role was considerably increased by the willingness to become involved in the minutiae of building estate management, albeit with professional guidance. The comparative gross income of the Brown, Cardigan, and Cowper estates during the last 20 years of the nineteenth century reflects this (table 17). Although Martin and Fenwick were also agents for the sale

Table 17   Building land sales and gross income, 1883–1902

development period	estate	acreage sold	no. of sales	gross income (£)	average per acre (£)	price per square yard
1883–1902	Brown	209	66	207,077	992	4s. 6d.
1884–1893	Cardigan	211	22	92,429	438	1s. 10d.
1885–1902	Cowper	161	15		402[a]	1s. 8d.

[a] Based on price data from 10 of 15 known sales. Gross income from the sale of 121.5 acres was £48,847.
Sources: Brown; B.E.P. Schedules of Land Sold.
Cardigan; title deeds.
Cowper; title deeds.

of the Cardigan estate their instructions in that instance were to divide it into lots for auction in 1888, not to manage it as a building estate. The Cowper estate policy during this period was for sales by private contract in large lots to developers. In order to maximize profits it was necessary to prepare building sites and negotiate directly with builders.

Study of the residential development process in the nineteenth century leads one to doubt whether the suburbs were created for the benefit of their residents. The editor of the *Builder* approached a similar viewpoint in 1881.

> There are many ways of regarding the house, and most of them, it must be confessed, are prosaic. There is the picturesque architect's point of view, which is the least prosaic. . . . There is the contractor's point of view of it, as a piece of construction out of which to make money. There is the sanitarian, who regards it as a place liable to develop smells and gases; and the investor of money, who regards the house as property worth so many years' purchase.

> It may be that, if we could only recognize it, there is after all, a suitability to the circumstances, an occult fitness of things, even in the speculating builder's street house. It may be the true expression of the circumstances of the life that is lived in it, – most dwellings are so in one way or another; but then how very unfit the fitness of things must be in that case.[150]

The freedom to control one's residential destiny, and the criteria employed, varied according to rank in society. Although the nineteenth-century suburbs undoubtedly exhibited myriad social distinctions to their residents it is possible to distinguish three principal groupings, each corresponding to a distinct suburban form. Firstly, the mansion and villa dwellers, equipped at least with stable and shrubbery, and at best with carriage house and landscaped estate. Secondly, the respectable terrace house dweller, usually without horse or carriage but employing one or two servants; the employment of a general servant, sometimes graphically described as a 'maid of all work' by census enumerators, was the minimum distinction between these residents and the remainder; without a servant a family lacked a fundamental item in the trappings of respectability and middle class status. Thirdly, the mass of artisans' and labourers' families, recognizing distinctions amongst themselves based on occupational groupings, religious denomination, temperance, and thrift. To the majority of the higher echelons of society such distinctions were blurred and their habitations unexplored. The working class streets of cottage property, with their corner shops and public houses constituted a totally different milieu from the servant-supported society.

The tram may have produced a measure of egalitarian rubbing of shoulders by 1914. The disparity between the hours of manual labour and those of professional and commercial workers may have been reduced. However, the social distance between entrepreneur and artisan had widened since the beginning of the industrial revolution, and during the second half of the nineteenth century the gap was filled by the insertion of the burgeoning ranks of white collar workers-managers, clerks, commercial travellers. Churches largely failed to provide a social leavening of these disparate groups. The new, more socially homogeneous neighbourhoods were each provided with their own places of worship.

The improvement of living conditions in new cottage property neighbourhoods during the last quarter of the nineteenth century was imposed by local bye-law control of developers and builders. After the 1872 Leeds Improvement Act the minimum standard cottage was more spacious internally, with minimum 8 ft ceiling height for living and sleeping rooms and 6 ft average height for attic rooms. All rooms were required to have a specified amount of window space; a requirement for an attic room window to be not less than 6 ft above the floor level made the dormer window or skylight of cottage property as ubiquitous as the bay windows of terraces which proclaimed their respectability. Through terraces had to have private open space – a back yard and/or a pocket size front garden of at least 150 ft square.[151] In 1885 Dr Goldie, Medical Officer of Health, confirmed that the housing in the suburbs was very much better than the earlier built houses of inner Leeds.[152] The best back-to-back dwellings could now hardly be described as cottages, having two principal stories, plus attic and basement, garden and bay window to front, individual water closet at basement level.

For those who regretted the laying out of new streets in Headingley and Potternewton, whether for back-to-back, through house or semi-detached, there remained available the traditional response. Developers and builders beckoned, not only in Chapel Allerton, but beyond the Leeds City boundary. In 1908 J.R. Ford, the lawyer, noted that an estate called Fearneville had been purchased by a syndicate who were 'establishing what they are pleased to call a Garden City, which means apparently that they are cutting the estate up into a number of plots for sale on each of which only one house is to be built thus leaving a considerable area of land for garden purposes. This estate is in Roundhay.'[153] The Cowper estate steward of the 1800s, J. Richardson, and G. Bischoff, merchant and developer of a Headingley Hill estate in the 1830s would have recognized the process.

6   Epilogue: The rise and fall of the suburb

'Joshua XXI. 42: These cities were everyone with their suburbs round about them; thus were all these cities.'[154]

The truth is that the history of Button Hill, like the history of everything else, consists of a succession of infinitesimal changes – some for better, some for worse. At first every tiny change that came to Button Hill had been hailed as a change for the better, as indeed it seemed at the time. Then a sort of slack-water period had ensued when the value of such changes were counter-balanced by other tiny changes, the value of which was more open to question. Eventually at some quite implaceable date little changes for the worse tipped the scale.[155]

Where wealth and fashion led, money followed. The years 1912, 1913, and 1914 saw a steady secession from the terraces of Button Hill to the newer suburbs.[156]

Possibly high-class residential suburbs, like almost everything else, carry within them inevitably the seeds of their own destruction.[157]

Thus concluded Gordon Stowell who disguised his experience of living through the growth of Potternewton in a novel, *The History of Button Hill*. In the 1970s the development process continued, but in Headingley and Potternewton it took a different form, with choices between urban renewal, rehabilitation, and conservation. The Cowper New Town of Leeds is gradually being eroded and the area given a new name. Pre-1870 middle-class neighbourhoods in Headingley have stood the test of time rather more successfully, albeit with much changed functions. Headingley Hill, Cardigan moor land developments of the 1850s and 1860s, and Far Headingley have been given Conservation Area status which constitutes some measure of control upon the developers. The pre-1870 working-class neighbourhoods, about which the least documentation survives, have already gone. In Chapel Allerton the pre-1914 developments are but islands in a sea of semi-detachedness.

NOTES

1 C. Treen, 'Building and estate development in the northern out-townships of Leeds, 1781–1914' (Ph.D. thesis, University of Leeds, 1977).
2 C.W. Chalklin, *The Provincial Towns of Georgian England: a Study of the Building Process, 1740–1820* (1974).
3 *Select Committee on Town Holdings*, PP 1889, XV, QQ. 7905–6.
4 Leeds City Archives, PL/17/6, LO/HE1,2.
5 Treen, *op. cit.*, glossary and tables 11, 12, 23, 24, 28, 29 and 30.
6 *SC on Town Holdings* (1889), 6–8, summary of types of tenure.
7 LCD, 2925, second schedule of the Chief Clerk's Certificate, 5 August 1873.
8 *SC on Town Holdings* (1889), 15.
9 *Ibid.*, 14.
10 *SC on Town Holdings* , PP 1887, XIII, Q. 7094.
11 *Ibid.*, Q. 3265.
12 Rev T.D. Whitaker, *Loidis and Elmete* (1816), 121.
13 LCD, 12336.

14 Herts CRO, Cowper MS, D/EPT 4949, J. Claridge, Survey and Valuation, 1808, 4–6.
15 *Ibid.*, 5–8.
16 Herts CRO, Cowper MS, C4951, J. Richardson, Report respecting the Estate of Earl Cowper, situated at Leeds, 1819.
17 *Ibid.*, C4952, J. Taylor, Report on Earl Cowper's Estates Leeds, 1825, 8–9.
18 *Leeds Intelligencer*, 28 July 1825.
19 *Select Committee on Smoke Prevention*, PP 1845, XIII, A. 443.
20 *Ibid.*, A. 410.
21 *LM*, 22 December 1849.
22 W. White, *Directory of Leeds* (1847), 229; *Ibid.*, *New Directory of Leeds* (1853), 290.
23 *LM*, 11 December 1861.
24 *Ibid.*, 16 July 1862.
25 *Ibid.*, 24 August 1866.
26 *Ibid.*, 20 July 1861.
27 *Ibid.*, 30 December 1862.
28 *Ibid.*, 22 March 1862.
29 *Ibid.*, 16 December 1861.
30 Treen, *op. cit.*, 254–7.
31 *Builder*, xx (1862), 623.
32 LCD, 14011.
33 *Ibid.*, 13951.
34 *Ibid.*, 13950.
35 *Ibid.*, 13929.
36 *Ibid.*, 13983.
37 *LM*, 11 June 1862.
38 *Ibid.*, 23 July 1870.
39 *Ibid.*, 8 June 1861.
40 LCD, 13910; *SC on Town Holdings*, PP 1886, xii, A. 7883.
41 J. Hole, *The Homes of the Working Classes* (1866), 8.
42 M.W. Beresford, 'The back-to-back house in Leeds, 1787–1837', in *The History of Working-Class Housing*, ed. S.D. Chapman (1971), 115.
43 *LM*, 31 December 1876, editorial.
44 *Ibid.*, 29 December 1888, annual trade review.
45 *Ibid.*, 10 January 1872.
46 *Ibid.*, 28 December 1889.
47 R. Ernest, *How to Become a Successful Estate Agent* (1904), 237–8.
48 Mitchell's copy in the author's possession.
49 LCD, 21477.
50 *Ibid.*, 6098.
51 *Ibid.*, 577; 21145.
52 *Ibid.*, 12529; 12919.
53 University of Leeds, Bursary Deeds, 356.
54 LCD, 12240; 12502; 12599.
55 *Ibid.*, 3783.
56 B. Kaye, *The Development of the Architectural Profession in Britain* (1960), 175.
57 *Ibid.*, 13.
58 Charlton and Anderson, *Directory of Leeds* (1864).
59 *LM*, 19 May 1874.
60 C. Treen, *A Short History of the Oakfield Terrace Building Club* (1975).
61 LCD, 6521, declaration of M.J. Prentis, clerk.
62 *Ibid.*, 4495.
63 *Ibid.*, 2800.
64 *Ibid.*, 12456.
65 *Ibid.*, 15896.

66 *LM*, 5 June 1886.
67 *Ibid.*, 23 October 1886.
68 *Ibid.*, 1 January 1876.
69 T. Bright, *The Development of Building Estates. A Practical Handbook for the Use of Surveyors, Agents, Landowners, and Others Interested in the Development, Management, Equipment, Administration, or Realization of Building Estates* (1910), 4.
70 Leeds City Archives, Accession 1415, BEP, letter, Martin and Fenwick to G. Markham, 20 September 1894.
71 *Ibid.*, 14 June 1898.
72 *Ibid.*, 13 June 1898.
73 *Ibid.*, 13 December 1899.
74 *Ibid.*, 14 April 1905.
75 BEP, Ford and Warren to G. Markham, 13 August 1901.
76 LCD, 1254.
77 BEP, Martin and Fenwick to G. Markham, 9 February 1892.
78 *Ibid.*
79 *Ibid.*, 13 September 1897; 16 September 1897.
80 *Ibid.*, 17 September 1897.
81 BEP, J.R. Ford to G. Markham, 8 February 1898.
82 LCD, 15624; 15614; 18167; 21998; 18147.
83 BEP, Martin and Fenwick to G. Markham, 7 March 1889.
84 *Ibid.*, 27 January 1890.
85 BEP, Martin and Fenwick to O.W. Stone, 5 March 1890.
86 BEP, Martin and Fenwick to G. Markham, 9 September 1890.
87 BEP, Martin and Fenwick to O.W. Stone, 13 September 1890.
88 BEP, G. Markham to O.W. Stone, 22 January 1896; Martin and Fenwick to G. Markham, 12 June 1895.
89 BEP, Martin and Fenwick to G. Markham, 29 October 1890.
90 *Ibid.*, 22 July 1889.
91 *Ibid.*
92 *Ibid.*, 27 April 1891.
93 BEP, G. Markham to Martin and Fenwick, 30 April 1891.
94 BEP, Martin and Fenwick to G. Markham, 2 May 1891.
95 *Ibid.*, 14 May 1889; Hunslet, a southern Leeds out-township.
96 *Ibid.*, 28 July 1891.
97 *Ibid.*, 8 August 1891.
98 *Ibid.*, 17 September 1891.
99 BEP, Ford and Warren to G. Markham, 11 December 1891.
100 BEP, Martin and Fenwick to G. Markham, 26 February 1892.
101 *Ibid.*, 19 October 1889.
102 *Ibid.*, 1 November 1889.
103 *Ibid.* The alternatives were Leeds in-township sites.
104 BEP, T. Fenwick to G. Markham, 11 November 1889.
105 BEP, Martin and Fenwick to G. Markham, 20 February 1891.
106 *Ibid.*, 9 March 1891.
107 BEP, Martin and Fenwick to G. Markham, 25 March 1891; Ford and Warren to G. Markham, 11 May 1891.
108 BEP, Ford and Warren to G. Markham, 20 May 1891.
109 BEP, J.R. Ford to G. Markham, 25 June 1891.
110 BEP, Martin and Fenwick to G. Markham, 27 January 1890.
111 LCD, 10977.
112 *Ibid.*
113 LCD, 18857; 18205; 12140.
114 BEP, Martin and Fenwick to G. Markham, 30 April 1896.

115 BEP, G. Lax to Martin and Fenwick, received 30 April 1896. Underlining by Martin and Fenwick.
116 *Ibid.*
117 LCD, 12699; 12566.
118 BEP, Martin and Fenwick to G. Markham, 28 January 1892.
119 BEP, J.R. Ford to G. Markham, 15 August 1892.
120 BEP, Martin and Fenwick to G. Markham, 27 June 1894.
121 *Ibid.*, 15 September 1894.
122 BEP, J.R. Ford to G. Markham, 21 December 1895.
123 BEP, Martin and Fenwick to G. Markham, 13 December 1895.
124 BEP, J.R. Ford to G. Markham, 3 January 1896.
125 *Ibid.*, 7 May 1897.
126 BEP, Martin and Fenwick to G. Markham, 13 May 1897.
127 *Ibid.*
128 *Ibid.*, 18 January 1898.
129 *Ibid.*, 4 April 1898.
130 BEP, J.R. Ford to G. Markham, 7 May 1897.
131 BEP, T. Fenwick to Ford and Warren, 17 August 1898.
132 BEP, J.R. Ford to G. Markham, 30 October 1899.
133 *Ibid.*, 11 October 1899.
134 *Ibid.*, 22 November 1904. Lady Graham was one of the devisees.
135 *Ibid.*, 12 January 1905.
136 T. Bright, *The Development of Building Estates* (1910), 234.
137 *Ibid.*, 328.
138 *Ibid.*, 331–3.
139 *Ibid.*, 233–4.
140 BEP, Martin and Fenwick to O. Stone, 5 March 1890.
141 BEP, Martin and Fenwick to G. Markham, 9 September 1890.
142 BEP, Martin and Fenwick to O. Stone, 9 September 1891.
143 BEP, Martin and Fenwick to G. Markham, 21 January 1896.
144 *Ibid.*, 28 May 1898.
145 BEP, Memorandum, Leeds Outlay on New Roads, 28 April 1896.
146 BEP, Martin and Fenwick to G. Markham, 28 January 1892.
147 LCD, 7516, letter, R.E. Fox to E.O. Wooler, Burrows and Burton, 12 October 1906.
148 BEP, Martin and Fenwick to G. Markham, 16 January 1894. Additional pencil notation, 20 January 1894.
149 BEP, results of sale by auction, J. Brown 1877 estate, 8 October 1901.
150 *Builder*, XL. i (1881), 1.
151 35 and 36 Vict. c. 97: *Leeds Improvement Act*, (1872), 23, 1; 23, 2; 23, 3.
152 SC on Town Holdings, PP 1884–5, xxx, Q.9788–9.
153 BEP, J.R. Ford to G. Markham, 14 February 1908.
154 G. Stowell, *The History of Button Hill* (1929), 23. The text taken by the Reverend A.S. Knight.
155 *Ibid.*, 203.
156 *Ibid.*, 204.
157 *Ibid.*, 202.

The development and character of a metropolitan suburb: Bexley, Kent

M.C. CARR

The development and character, of a metropolitan suburb: Bexley, Kent[1]

M.C. CARR

1 Introduction

Location and analytical framework

Old Bexley borough now incorporated since 1963 into the Greater London Borough of Bexley and an outer metropolitan suburb in north-west Kent, is transitional in its position (fig. 30). At some 15 to 20 miles from the centre of London it lies between the older inner suburbs and the Green Belt as designated in Abercrombie's Greater London Plan. But it is also adjacent to a heavily industrialized part of Thameside forming a buffer zone between this and the true commuting country further south such as Sidcup-Chislehurst-Orpington and Bromley-Beckenham-Penge. The borough incorporated features giving it an affinity with each of these different parts of Greater London.

From its earlier phases of dormitory growth it had strong links with nearby Woolwich and Erith, receiving the families of many of the workers drawn to these rapidly industrializing Thameside areas. Improvements in the rail link with London in the 1930s led to Bexley Borough being the fastest growing outer London suburb. This acquired suburban character gave it a feature in common with earlier established suburbs, such as Bromley to the south of it. But in Bexley further suburban expansion was generally halted when part of the borough in the south-east was incorporated from 1938 into London's Green Belt.

In seeking an appropriate analytical context within which to consider the development of this suburb, Kirk provides a useful starting point in seeing the purpose of geography as the study of the geographical environment and the problems it creates.[2] As human communities are perpetually confronted by the problems concerning their particular environment they are obliged to take decisions which have spatial and other environmental consequences for it at any one time, as well as for any future decision-taking in respect of it. The suburb is one particular type of cultural-spatial diversification with its own set of problems and can be looked at within the framework of a decision taking model along the lines suggested by Kirk.

It follows then, that if we are to understand the nature of the suburb and the processes contributing to its growth, we must examine in so far as we can, those individual decisions and series of decision making situations which at various times have helped to determine the character of the suburb as we see it today. Such an examination is basic to this study of Bexley Borough.

To do this, two scales need to be considered – those of time and space. This study takes some recognition of development prior to 1880, but it is essentially concerned with the period after 1880. The choice of 1880 is not an arbitrary one; it is the date at which Bexley began to manage its own local affairs and therefore has special significance in the transformation of the local landscape. But scale in time implies not only a span of time but also units of time; in the case of the suburb these mark phases of growth which are distinguished from one another not only by the character of growth at any one period but also by a change in the circumstances underlying it. The dates at which changes in the decision making circumstance occurred divide one phase of growth from another.

A review of the main influences
Though it is usual to equate population change with the spread of the metropolis, this should more specifically be equated with the movement of households or families. Changes in the number of families have been the long run determinants of the amount of residential building at any one period.[3] Movement of people, however, is not so much the cause of metropolitan expansion as like housing a visible expression of it; the two go together.

Much emphasis, too, has been placed on the influence of transportation links but there is, as Course points out, no automatic connection between railways and settlement.[4] The relationship may be tenuous and much complicated by other factors. It has made possible, but in no sense produced, the vast London dormitories. For example, whilst the establishment of a rail link between London and Bromley in 1857 was followed by a rapid spread of suburbs in the northern part of the district, this was not the case for the Bexley district either when the Dartford Loop line through Bexley was opened in 1866 or the Bexleyheath line in 1895. Dormitory growth related to employment in Central London did not come on a large scale until late into the 1920s. Prior to this growth was largely related to the spread of industry at Woolwich and Erith on Thameside.

The cause of suburban development is more complex. Significant as population and transportation are, there is need to enquire into underlying circumstances, origins of which lie as much at a national level as at the metropolitan and local level. As has been frequently emphasized, housing demand and population pressure in Greater London have been generated to an important extent by the inequalities in economic and social opportunities between one part of the country and another.[5] These in turn arose largely out of the country's changed position within the general world economy. A shift already evident by the 1880s was accelerated by two world wars and an intervening economic depression.

The regional effect of this can be briefly illustrated from the interwar period. At the time of the depression, unemployment ran at a high level in the older industrial areas such as the North East and South Wales, with any house building being done limited to that completed with national and local government financial support. On the other hand where there was much less unemployment, as in Greater London and parts of the Midlands, residential building was largely financed and completed

Figure 29. Aerial view of the area of Bexley under study (reproduced with the permission of the Controller of Her Majesty's Stationery Office, Crown Copyright reserved).

by private enterprise. In Bexley district for example, building went on at an increasing pace into the mid-1930s as employment opportunities in nearby Thameside and particularly in Central London expanded.

Again both the overall national level of building and its regional components have been affected by a further complex set of economic forces studied by Robinson.[6] Others also have related the building cycle to the trade cycle and the cycle of general business activity.[7] Upswings in the building cycle appear to be related to downward swings in the trade cycle, investment being diverted from manufacturing and commercial activities into the building industry. Robinson points out that particularly for the periods between 1873 to 1937, fluctuations in the level of residential building were closely related to the interplay between such things as the levels of real income, rates of interest, building costs, and the level of rents. House building is stimulated on the one hand by increases in rents or business activity and on the other by decreases in building costs and lower interest rates.

Social habits and the aspirations of individual households have also been influential. Ruth Glass for example notes the frequent association of the idea of suburbia with respectability;[8] Mumford also develops this theme.[9] In the course of many interviews with residents it became clear too in the Bexley district that movements into the area were motivated by social aspirations and the desire for change.

Beyond the interplay of economic and social forces operating in the market of supply and demand for housing, there is also the effect of central government measures for the country as a whole as well as those in particular for the Greater London area. Directly and indirectly these have been of great importance. For example, a large number of families coming for the first time into the owner-occupier group in the Bexley district from the turn of the century right on into the 1920s did so with the aid of a mortgage granted under the Small Dwellings Act 1899.

Again under the 1919 Addison Act, and subsequent planning legislation local authorities were made responsible for supplying houses to meet the needs in their particular area. This was the beginning of the public housing sector which along with the owner-occupied one increasingly dominated the housing scene, whilst the private rented sector so prominent at the turn of the century dwindled away.

All these influences have collectively determined the rate at which suburbs have developed, but within any given suburb it is the constraints and influences within the established landscape at any given time, together with local circumstances and decision taking, which have determined the scale and pattern of development from one part of that suburb to another. These are the two themes running through the detailed study of each phase of growth of the Bexley suburb which follow.

The established landscape
Underlying geological conditions, and the relief and drainage of the area, have had an important influence on the pattern of residential development. The northern part across Welling and Bexleyheath is an undulating plateau, averaging 125 to 150 feet in height. Disturbed Blackheath and Woolwich beds, mainly sands and coarse gravels, sometimes overlain with patches of heavier London clay, cover most of it. The sand and gravel beds, firm and well-drained, have provided a large expanse of suitable building land lying either side of the old Dover Road running west to east across the plateau.

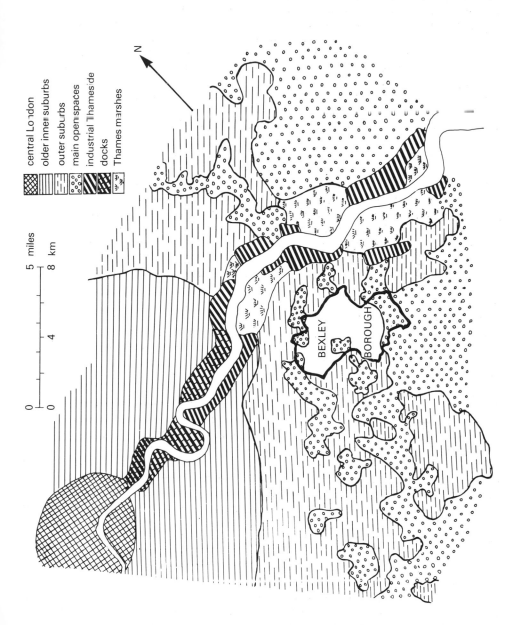

Figure 30. The transitional position of Bexley district (drawing by Elaine Butt).

It forms a low watershed between streams flowing north across the marshes into the Thames, and the Shuttle flowing south-east into the lower reaches of the Cray, before it joins the Darent and enters the Thames. Most of the drainage is in this direction, but in the north-west the plateau edge at East Wickham is sharply dissected by a system of minor valleys trending northward towards Woolwich. This dissection and the difficulty of sewering the area due to the inconvenient direction of gravity fall limited the spread of settlement in this north-western part of the district.

To the south of the plateau the land falls sharply to the Cray valley and its tributary system of the Shuttle. However, a spur capped by London clay rising to 100 feet intervenes between the Cray and the Shuttle. Until the inter-war years much of this dissected southern area and particularly the valley floors, was considered unsuitable for building land. Since then Green Belt restrictions have prevented any comprehensive residential development.

Terrain and drainage influences have thus acted as some constraint to residential development in the north-west and south-east of the district, whilst particularly favouring settlement across the plateau which dominates the northern part of the area. But historically the centre of settlement lay at Bexley in the south east. Here the flood plain of the Cray narrows and terrace remnants of the Flood Plain and Higher Taplow series approach close to the river and provided a dry site for the linear spread of the settlement above the flood-plain. Further south above Bexley, the land rises steeply eastward from the Cray valley up to Dartford Heath. Wider exposure of Thanet sand and chalk are here capped by fairly extensive spreads of Boyn Hill gravels. Here, however, dene holes penetrating into the chalk have hindered settlement development; but further across the settlement at the aptly named Coldblow occupies one of the gravel spreads, and comes within the district boundary.

Since the historical centre of settlement lay at Bexley, the economic and social life of the area focused along the Cray and away from the northern plateau. In earlier times settlement avoided the busy main highway running across it and connecting London to the cross-channel ports. Much of the plateau was wild heathland, 'a wilderness traversed by the Old Dover Road'. Another writer commented that as late as the early nineteenth century 'Welling and Bexleyheath scarcely existed, their future sites marked only by a few hovels',[10] together with the occasional coaching inn, such as the Red Lion on the borders of Bexleyheath, a welcome sight to travellers surmounting the notorious Shooters Hill on their way out of London.

But even at this time the first of the sequential patterns in the development of the metropolitan fringe discussed by Whitehand,[11] and Wissink,[12] could be discerned. True, it was very much in the nature of Wissink's chaotic and widely scattered area, not part of the 'compact hem'.[13] But it included more than the occasional coaching inn, serving travellers to and from the metropolis. By the end of the eighteenth century apart from open land on the heath and an expanse of woodland on the heavier clays, there were town estates such as Bellegrove Park in Welling and the older established Blendon Place at Blendon, separated by larger landed estates such as Danson. The landed gentry renting out most of their land were very much men of the city. Lord Bexley, for example, occupied a prominent position in the government. The district was also economically tied to London for much of the agricultural produce from these estates supplied the London markets.

Small hamlets were attached to the larger landed estates, being socially as well as economically dependent on them. The big house required its domestic servants, gardeners, grooms and handymen, whilst the main parkland and home farm, together with tenanted farms, needed agricultural labour.

In the nineteenth century additional features appeared, so that the period to the 1870s can be regarded as the second of the sequential stages leading up to the full incorporation of Bexley into the metropolitan fringe.

The dominance of Bexley as the main focus of economic and social life began to be overshadowed by developments on the heath to the north. The increasing number of squatters threatened the rights of Bexley freeholders to pasture and gravel extraction on the heath.[14] Thus they sought to secure these rights in the Enclosure Act of 1819.[15] Unappropriated land was apportioned amongst the freeholders and a new planned township established on the heath. Roads and footpaths were laid out from a triangular green, the site of which marks the commercial centre of Bexleyheath as we see it today. These provided the framework within which later residential development occurred and the arteries along which the main streams of traffic still flow.

Once the Enclosure Act was effective and the new township planted, incorporating at its centre those unplanned plots established by squatters' rights, new Bexley or Bexleyheath as it later became known developed rapidly. In 1847 it was described as 'a thriving district, situated one mile north of Bexley Church. On the high road from London to Dover, the township of Bexleyheath stretches over a mile in length and is now a populous hamlet on a fine elevation with many good houses and respectable shops'. In 1857 it was connected by horse-drawn omnibus to Abbeywood station on the recently opened North Kent railway line into London and this provided an important stimulus to further development. An increasing number of town houses appeared, and among others were occupied by business people from the city and nearby Woolwich.[16] Thus the younger township began to rival the old village.

Closer links with London also greatly altered the character of agriculture in the district. Though the agricultural returns for this period are incomplete, the general rapid trend towards market gardening and fruit growing is clearly evident. Bexleyheath area began to be described as an area surrounded by orchards in full blossom, strawberry and raspberry fields, their produce like that from the more extensive area of market gardens largely destined for Covent Garden.

Elsewhere in the district, apart from some limited development at Welling, largely connected with the demand for housing by workers in the expanding industries at Woolwich, the character of smaller hamlets did not essentially change in this period before the 1870s.

However, in 1866 the opening of the Dartford loop line established a direct link between Bexley and London. This encouraged some expansion of the village and some development at Coldblow on the Dartford heath above it. Apart from a small estate directly adjoining the railway station, the development in the village was largely of better class housing – detached villas standing in their own variously sized grounds. These included in some cases a grazing paddock, since journeying to and from the station and locally was commonly done by pony and trap. The owners of these villas were the forerunners of those suburbanites who were so active later in preventing the invasion of the village by the masses moving out to the suburbs in the 1930s. Until 1929 growth was by a process of accretion from the established settlement centres of Bexley and Bexleyheath, together with that around the smaller settlement of Welling. But during the 1930s, whilst some accretionary growth continued, much greater development occurred in areas distinct from existing settlements and depending upon the availability of large tracts of land rather than on being adjacent to existing built up areas.

After 1945 development was more sporadic, occurring wherever land was still available. Most of it was of a piecemeal nature and included not only infilling on backland, but also redevelopment of older housing sites. Thus the pattern of the suburb had already been largely completed by the late 1930s (fig. 31).

As growth went on from the 1880s the town plan or cadaster as it then existed proved to be the most conservative element in the total morphological scene, persisting in its influence through to the present. Borrowing words of Emrys Jones's discussion of Northern Belfast,[17] the Bexley district was a distinctive human landscape before it became a city suburb and that landscape had an effect both on the nature of subsequent development and on the details of the urban landscape which replaced it.

Besides the locational influences exercised by existing nodes of settlement there were others such as the established communication network. The influence of earlier track ways and footpaths as well as the road network, and later the railway lines crossing the district, is there in the present morphology of the suburb. Ownership and tenurial boundaries, together with field plots, were also apparent in the pattern of building estates (fig. 32).

The essential contrast between large building estates developed on the larger land-ownership units dating back to at least the time of the original tithe apportionments of 1839 and 1844, and of smaller scale development in areas where land ownership had become fragmented, is the main feature in the pattern of spatial variation over the district. Fragmentation had become particularly notice-able round the older settlement nuclei but occurred elsewhere for example in association with the speculative sale of land around the railway stations.

However, whilst building estate boundaries to an important degree reflect the pattern of the pre-urban cadaster, the density and character of development which occurred within these lines at first sight appear to reflect bye-law and planning controls. But these in turn reflected what was already there, and the perceptions of those responsible for local planning were influenced in no small way by the established social values placed on particular parts of the district. For example, the northern part of the district already had some high density housing at the turn of the century and was regarded as of lower status than areas such as Bexley village to the south. Thus a zoning of 12 to the acre for future building in the interwar years was to be expected. In the south zoning was in contrast at eight to the acre or less. In highly valued residential areas such as on the edge of Bexley Wood and at Coldblow it dropped to as little as four and six to the acre.

Open spaces appearing in the first Town Plan of 1926 had also already been preserved from building, either by difficulties of terrain or by earlier private and rather belated public efforts, as was the case for Danson Park. The only major alterations made by planning towards the preservation of open spaces was the reservation of more sites for schools and other public amenities, and the reserva-tion of much of the southern district as part of the Green Belt under the Greater London Planning Acts, and even here it was the low lying nature of much of the land, and private efforts, which had preserved this part as open space long enough for it to be ultimately incorporated into the Green Belt under planning legislation.

Thus developed the established landscape and the localized decision taking situations upon and through which the general influences outlined in the previous section were modified before making their contribution to the development of Bexley from a rural village into a metropolitan suburb. Before considering in turn each of the main phases of suburban development, it is also important to note that except for a short period from 1863 to 1880 when Bexley parish was included in the district coming under the Dartford Highway Board, most of the area had been under one local body from Saxon times onwards.[18] This sense of continuity and oneness in the directing of local affairs must also be particularly emphasized as a contributory factor to both the nature and process of suburban growth in the ensuing periods under discussion.

2 Dormitory growth begins, 1880–1920

The average annual increment of houses over this period was only 40, but in total 1,500 houses were added, doubling the housing stock. Thus the increase which was small by metropolitan standards was nevertheless very important to the district (fig. 32). The greatest amount of growth occurred in the northern part and was mainly for working and lower middle class families. A small amount occurred in the south round Bexley village before 1900, but did little to alter its character.

Bexleyheath in the north was by 1881 already a prosperous and thriving community with a diversified economic base including local commerce and an expanding market garden industry. Whilst it retained and expanded these functions, after 1900 it became an important dormitory area for Thameside workers and their families, as did the area around the small hamlet of East Wickham further west.

The effect here was to transform the area into a bustling and noisy Thameside dormitory area linked to Woolwich by the rattling tram. The small hamlet of East Wickham was soon eclipsed by the shopping area along Welling High Street serving the families who had come to live in the small cul-de-sac estates extending off it, or who lived in the 627 wartime hutments built in 1916 to house some of the influx of munition workers coming to work in the Woolwich Arsenal.[19]

Over the period then the broad contrast already evident between the village and the new settlement on the heath was heightened and altered. It was no longer just the established rural village contrasted with the young radical township but now also the more select residential neighbourhood to the south, as opposed to the spreading and largely working class dormitory area to the north.

Considering the character of residential development in more detail, for Bexley village recently linked to London by the Dartford Loop line, most development occurred on its northern and western edges, extending out towards Bexleyheath. Next to the railway station a small estate of leasehold terraced houses was developed, but on the whole most of the development was of middle class housing including large detached villas along the North Cray Road and above the village at Coldblow. The prime development occurred out along Hurst Road in the form of a number of fine houses set in their own grounds backing on to Bexley Woods, and fronted by a fine commanding view across the village to the North Downs. Those were the homes of wealthy businessmen and professional men working in the city

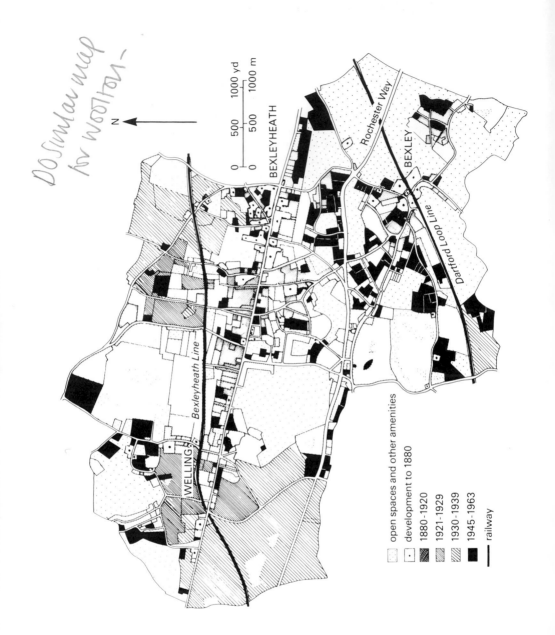

Figure 31. The development of Bexley (drawing by Elaine Butt).

The following labels appear on the map:

BEXLEYHEATH

BEXLEY

WELLING

Rochester Way

Dartford Loop Line

Bexleyheath Line

N

1000 yd
1000 m
500
500
0
0

Legend:
- open spaces and other amenities
- development to 1880
- 1880-1920
- 1921-1929
- 1930-1939
- 1945-1963
- railway

Do similar map for Wootton - (handwritten annotation)

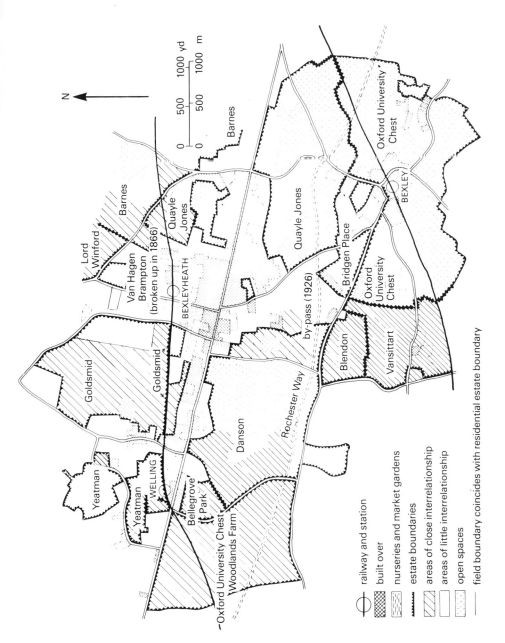

Figure 32. The interrelationship of residential estates with earlier land holdings, estates and field boundaries as at 1910 (drawing by Elaine Butt).

who included the chairman of the Chatham and South Eastern Railway Company which had built the Dartford Loop line.

However, the largest estate development was the Parkhurst–Knoll Road estate on the western edge of Bexley village. Intermediate in character, it was set well back from the centre of the village but curved round to join terraced housing of lower quality built earlier along Victoria and Albert Road. A sales catalogue relating to part of the Parkhurst-Knoll Road estate makes it quite clear that this development was intended for the city commuter.[20] The detached and semi-detached two storey houses built in grey brick and bay fronted, had an air of the city about them. What is more, estate development here warranted its own imposing Anglican and Congregational places of worship. It may have been somewhat distinctive in character but it was socially acceptable to a village community intent on preserving and perpetuating its rural peace.

In contrast to the accretionary pattern of growth round Bexley, the development at Bexleyheath was linear in character spreading as the map shows westward either side of the tram route and reaching towards a similar development extending out from neighbouring Welling. Most of this building consisted of lower middle and working class estates of bay fronted terraced houses, typical of much of the outer suburbs developing at this time. Oaklands and Sandford estates built either side of Broadway were the largest. Like most, these were developed by the local landowner with the assistance of a local builder. The landowner retained a lease on the housing plot site if not always ownership of the property.[21]   The two attempts to build better-class housing estates in this part of the district and away from existing settlements failed.[22] One was the speculative development around Bexley-heath station intended for the city commuter, and the other an attempt by a local landowner, Alers Hankey, to develop the Mount Pleasant Garden Suburb estate. Despite the presence of the railway station giving a direct link to the City, demand from prospective commuters was not strong enough to support estate development near to the station.

Elsewhere, at East Wickham, building was on a smaller scale and almost exclusively working class in character. The wartime hutments remained until the 1950s as a legacy of this early period, whilst the district itself became known as Welling as the original hamlet at East Wickham became a relic feature eclipsed by this later nineteenth-century development.

A pattern of accretion around existing settlement centres was a general one. Development near an established settlement had numerous advantages over a location midst open fields. For one thing there was easier and cheaper connection to existing services such as sewers, piped water, and lighting. Frontages were available on already made up roads within easy walking distance of shops and other amenities. Besides these advantages most people prefer to live within the social ties of an established community. This was particularly so for lower income groups who had to be within easy reach of an established community in order to be part of it, whereas those on higher incomes could live at some distance away and yet still remain in contact with the general social life of the community. Further, their social network was wider, making them less dependent on local community life.

Development of outlying estates, including those around the stations then at some distance from the centres of settlement, generally followed later. Those who financed the railway, including owners of land in the vicinity, expected and accepted this lag in building development. Land, not building speculation was one of the short term aims.[23] Building followed when the increase in passenger traffic warranted it.[24]

We have already seen that one of the most important stimuli to the district's development at this time was the need for housing associated with the increasing number of workers drawn to the expanding industries at Woolwich, Erith, and Crayford on Thameside.[25] By the late nineteenth century much of Woolwich and Plumstead had already been taken up with high density housing, and as needs continued to rise the pressure was most felt in the adjacent districts of Lewisham and Bexley. Though the opening of the tram route from Bexleyheath and Welling to both Woolwich and Erith in 1903 was significant, the main cause for the increased rate of building undoubtedly lay in the greatly expanded employment opportunities on Thameside coupled with the shortage of housing there.

However, housing need had to be translated into an effective demand. Not all workers could afford, or even desired, housing in less congested districts away from factories. The demand was a selective one coming from those who desired better living conditions, were not tied by large families or other domestic commitments, and who had the initiative and money to move. Myers for example writes of nearby Lewisham as 'the Elysium of South East London, to be moved to when you had made or saved enough money to move from Bermondsey and Deptford'.[26]

Towards the end of the nineteenth century and for a few years after 1900 the worker was increasingly in a better position to afford a house. Whilst monetary wages rose by 15 to 20 per cent, retail prices also fell by 15 per cent.[27] In addition, an increasing number of workers were being classified as in the better paid skilled job category, particularly for the types of industries found on Thameside, and for these wages rose by another 12 per cent on top of the basic increase.

Also the reduction of the working week to an average of 52 hours gave the worker more leisure to educate himself, more time to travel to and from work, and to visit and compare housing conditions in less congested neighbouring districts with those in the densely built up areas around the factory. Many more thus aspired to better themselves; the desire for better living conditions was as important to the working man's aspirations then as it is today.

The central government and local authorities helped the better paid of the working class and clerical workers to realize this desire. The various Health Acts ensured better sanitary conditions and housing in the new residential districts, whereas improvement of older housing areas was still difficult and costly. Under the Small Dwellings Acquisition Act of 1899 the government made it possible for Bexley Urban District Council and other local authorities to make numerous mortgage advances. In the Bexleyheath area, for example, many houseowners obtained advances in this way.[28] In Welling letting of houses was more characteristic.

The increased accessibility afforded by the tramway was also important. Whereas it had been difficult to obtain financial backing for the proposed Bexleyheath railway line, the construction of which was consequently delayed for 15 years, this was not the case for the tram service. Its potential profitability indicated from the amount of housing for Thameside workers already being provided in the district, resulted in a number of promoters wanting permission to undertake a service from Bexleyheath and Welling to Woolwich and Erith. Before 1900 two private companies had been refused permission,[29] but then the local council itself investigated the prospects. Its consultants, Dawbarn and Mordey, reported that 'in the case of Woolwich and Erith the lines would be highly remunerative from the start apart from the immense influence they would have on further developments in the district.'[30] This quickly proved to be the case: between 1903 when the tramway was opened and the slump of 1906/7 the rate of house building appreciably accelerated. The tram service was cheap and efficient. The daily service began in time for the first work shift due on at 6 a.m. at Erith and 8 a.m. at Woolwich Arsenal, with trams running at five-minute intervals at change of shift times. Through the rest of the day they ran every 20 minutes. A weekly book of coupons for tickets for the Bexleyhealth to Woolwich journey, for example, was 1s. 6d. From 1908 the service was electrified and the Reports of the Tramway and Lighting Committees indicated that the service was increasingly being used by office workers and shoppers as well as by factory workers.

Before 1900 conditions were generally favourable for the building industry and this no doubt influenced the rate of building in the Bexley district. But after 1900 at a time when the rate of house building quickened in Welling and Bexleyheath, conditions were generally moving against the building industry. Interest rates were rising and the cost of building materials increasing.[31] Also with new taxation measures small firms making up the major part of the building trade faced a somewhat uncertain future. By 1906 both national and local conditions had become so unfavourable that up to the outbreak of the 1914 war new housing was insufficient even to replace the number of houses being demolished as unfit for habitation.[32]

Paradoxically at this same time the depression in agriculture, and various financial pressures, including heavier taxation, were beginning to bring substantial tracts of suitable building land on to the market.[33] Had money been available to the intending house purchaser and the builder, the rate of housing construction would most likely have continued to increase after 1906, for the demand was there.

If these national and regional influences controlled the rate of dormitory development and the general location of building estates, local circumstances dictated the precise location and configuration of them.

In Welling and Bexleyheath estates were built where small units of land were available close to the tram route. Local business men such as Dale and Alers Hankey secured some of this land and were ready to sell or develop plots at the financially opportune moment.[34] Alers Hankey, for example, developed part of Oaklands estate himself and also sold individual plots to prospective houseowners. At Welling small units of land were already available on the margins of the Danson and Goldsmid estates. Bean of Danson, Chairman of the Bexleyheath Railway Company, discouraged a proposal to take the line through the main part of his estate, but consequent upon the opening of the railway and later the tram route and as land values rose, sold off marginal units along the Welling main road frontage. Meanwhile Avigdor Goldsmid undertook development on the margins of his estate at Elsa Road and on sites along Upper Wickham Lane. Marginal building also occurred on the Oxford University Chest estate at Bexley. In this way a large estate owner could realize a useful profit without cutting into the main part of the estate.

The actual size and layout of a building estate tended to reflect those of the original land-unit. At Bexley, for example, the Salisbury Road estate of leasehold houses close to the station coincides with the shape of a field separated from the rest of College farm by the construction of the Dartford Loop Line Railway. The landway on the western edge of the field became Manor Way, the road bordering the estate. Again at Bexley, Parkhurst Knoll Road estate fits the configuration of the field over which it was built as does the earlier Bradbourne field/Albert estate next to it. At Bexleyheath, Oakland estate south of the main Broadway is appreciably largely than the nearby Sandford estate simply because the sizes of the initial land holdings were different.

The influence of terrain conditions at this time was more apparent round Bexley than on the northern plateau where most of the land was suitable for building. At Bexley gravel terrace sites above the floodplain of the River Cray were more extensive north of the river, and this was one of the main reasons why the main expansion of the village occurred on this northern side.

Overall, this period from 1880 marked the beginning of a suburban cycle. For the first time specific estate building took place to serve the needs of an immigrant population, commuting out of the area to earn its living on Thameside and to a lesser extent in the city. Previously metropolitan influences had been largely restricted to the intensification of market gardening and the needs of the occasional city man for a house or estate in the country. These had added a touch of the metropolis without radically altering the character of the settlement pattern. Now at the turn of the century, accretionary growth round existing centres was drawing the northern settlements into the orbit of Thameside, whilst Bexley village slowly but inextricably increased its links with the city.

The layout of settlement in the north, both at Welling and Bexleyheath, took on a familar linear pattern, the tram route providing the central artery of movement. At Bexley growth remained nucleated, partly due to the location of the station near the centre of the village. As the contrast between the village and its younger northern counterparts increased processes of social segregation and sectorization became more clearly evident. But the resultant zonation was essentially aligned to the Thameside industrial area and not the city.

Thus Bexley district, like other areas similarly placed, was progressing as part of the metropolitan fringe from the situation of being part of Wissink's 'highly dynamic chaotic fringe extending over a wide area' to 'incorporation as part of the compact hem'.[35]

There were also signs of Whitehand's 'fringe within a fringe' developing.[36] Both around Bexley and Bexleyheath such fringe characteristics as playing fields, market gardens, nurseries, cemeteries, country houses, and certain institutional buildings were evident. For example, around Bexley beginning from Coldblow there were country houses, the Trewint Industrial Home for Girls, a mental hospital, whilst near the station and on the Cray floodplain there was the cricket ground and allotments. North of the river there was the nursery close to St John's Church, tennis courts off Parkhurst Road, more allotments, and the Memorial Hall together with St Mary's Recreation ground off Bourne Road.

Whilst settlements were growing as dormitory areas, this impetus also set in motion forces which ensured the district retained some capacity for self expansion. Provision of services was encouraged; existing shopping areas were expanded and new ones arose on the outer edges of the main settlements. Transport facilities were improved and local employment opportunities increased in the construction industries, in horticulture, and in domestic service as well as in various tertiary activities. Thus whilst the district was becoming a dormitory, its own importance and size were enlarged, increasing its chances of retaining a recognizable and distinctive identity.

The forces producing these changes were those operating collectively from national to regional and ultimately to local level. Moreover, social influences such as the growing aspirations of the working class were as potent as economic ones in generating an effective housing demand, as were political decisions in ensuring their satisfaction or otherwise.

3 The transitional phase: from Thameside dormitory towards metropolitan suburb, 1921–9

This period has tended to be overshadowed by the much greater suburban expansion of the 1930s and has consequently received very limited attention. Yet, as will be shown, it is an important one. Johnson in discussing this decade following the First World War emphasizes the role of the private developer in the further growth of the suburban ring and felt the influence of central government and local authorities a minor one.[37] But this is not the case for the Bexley district, and events here can be paralleled by similar developments across the river in parts of suburban Essex.

The metropolitan fringe at this time was in fact characterized by two broadly different types of residential development. On the one hand, there was that referred to by Johnson, private building for the better-off purchaser such as occurred in neighbouring Chislehurst and Sidcup, and on the other hand, such development as occurred in the Bexley district adjacent to industrial districts and the lower class inner suburbs. In this latter type, both the central government and local government played a direct and active part in supplying houses to meet the needs of the lower middle and working classes. Any generalization about the outer suburbs at this time needs to take account of both these types of development.

In Bexley district itself housing expansion to the mid 1920s was largely undertaken to meet the intense shortage created by the war years and by stagnation in the building industry in the years immediately preceding it. Then, from about 1926, the housing needs of Thameside workers lessened, and were increasingly replaced by the demands of white-collar city workers, stimulated both by the general easing of economic conditions and the electrification of the suburban railway lines passing through the district. The phase, therefore, can be seen as a transitional one during which the district was ceasing to be predominantly a Thameside dormitory suburb and was becoming instead a metropolitan suburb.

It was during this time that the national government and local authorities began to play a direct part in the supply of housing. Before 1914 local authority building accounted for only five per cent of all housing construction. 'The prevailing political philosophy regarded the operation of the free economy as an adequate incentive to ensure that supply would meet demand'.[38] But after the war the whole attitude of both the national government and the local administration changed as private enterprise failed to meet the situation created by wartime arrears. These revised attitudes were evident in a number of ways, ranging from direct local authority building, subsidy assistance to private builders, and mortgage advances to private builders, through to increasing town planning controls,[39] and continued public works such as sewering and by-pass construction.[40]

However, whilst national and other external circumstances dictated the rate of housing expansion and its general location, local influences remained powerful.

National and regional decisions had to be interpreted at the local level. Planning measures were frequently based on suggestions from the local authority, and local circumstances remained paramount in decisions related to the detailed location and configuration of housing estates.

A study of what happened in the Bexley district over this period lends further support to these points. For example whilst the population and number of families had increased by 25 per cent and 38 per cent respectively between 1911 and 1921, only 31 houses had been built apart from the wartime East Wickham hutments. Even without the replacement of these the local Medical Officer of Health estimated a need for approximately a thousand more houses. Also further demand arose from the continued immigration into the district from the heavily congested areas of Woolwich, Plumstead, and Erith. Until 1926 these remained the dominant pressures, but after this date the effects of slum clearance from the older inner suburbs, and local increases, became important.

Grave difficulties besetting the building industry here as elsewhere were largely responsible for the limited building to 1921. Labour was costly,[41] and materials dear and in short supply. It was also extremely difficult to obtain building capital, as most capital was still tied up either in war loans or enterprises offering higher returns than the building industry. Without government assistance the much needed building programme could not get under way.

Two types of need had to be met. On the one hand, there were those of the large groups of unskilled workers and others on relatively low incomes who, even with assistance, could not afford to buy houses on the open market. On the other, there were those of the better paid such as the skilled artisans, foremen and supervisors who, given economic house prices and mortgage facilities, could afford their own houses. Private enterprise if aided could meet the needs of the prospective purchaser, but since private builders and landlords could not afford to build houses for letting at a rent which could be afforded by prospective tenants, the housing needs of families on lower incomes had to be met by the local authority.

Various housing acts and associated legislation, including some wartime measures, provided some sort of framework for an assisted building programme but it was the major Housing Acts of 1923 and 1924, together with the measures leading up to and immediately succeeding them, which turned the tide. Without these it is difficult to envisage expansion on the scale which actually occurred. Support and pressure for these much needed acts came from enlightened individuals, associations, and local authorities as well as from within the central government.

For example, the Clerk to the Bexley Urban District Council pressed for direct council building, stating 'The Council should devote attention to the provision of houses to be built of brick or concrete blocks for sale or letting to persons less favourably placed, at prices or rents they can afford. I believe this to be possible at little or no loss.'[42]

The Welling Housing Scheme arose largely from the Clerk's promptings, and illustrates some of the circumstances surrounding the expansion of local authority building at this time. As early as 1909 a housing inspection under the Housing and Town Planning Act of the same year had indicated Welling as being the one area in the district most in need of more housing. But because of the war guaranteed government aid under a Housing Act of 1914 could not be utilized to initiate a Council building programme. Action was again contemplated in 1919 but the local authority despite pressure from the majority of ratepayers, was reluctant to act until it was satisfied that the promised materials and money would be forthcoming from the government.[43] However, it did point out that given assistance it could not only alleviate pressing needs within the district but had sufficient building land to also help relieve neighbouring and congested housing areas in inner London.[44]

After further assurances and increasing local pressure, the authority borrowed £400,000 to undertake the large Welling Housing Scheme.[45] The schedule given below indicates how the sum was apportioned and emphasizes some of those cost factors which are often overlooked in assessing economic aspects of residential development.

Table 18   Cost schedule for Welling Council Housing Scheme, (submitted to a General Meeting of the Bexley Urban District Council, 18 August 1920)

	£
Thomas Edge & Son for cost of constructing 426 houses	407,850
cost of land and compensation: Warwick 670	
Yeatman 6,150	10,620
Goldsmid 3,800	
clearing the site	550
road construction	23,370
foul and surface water drainage	7,861
staff expenditure on roads and sewers	1,000
architects' fees	5,000
salaries of Clerk of the Works, Quantity Surveyor, Clerk and help	2,557
street lighting	665
open spaces	195
footpath diversion	50
Total cost (approx.)	460,000

426 houses were planned over 50 acres between Wickham Street and Upper Wickham Lane which was the most convenient site for the tram route and Welling shops.

Acquisition of the land involved the Council in dealings with three landowners, one of whom was unwilling to sell. Yeatman Estate Trustees parted readily with 40 acres and Colonel Warwick with five acres of nursery land, but the Goldsmid Estate Trustees refused to sell the vital frontage land along Upper Wickham Lane necessary to gain access to backland. The Acquisition of Lands Act 1920, however, enabled the Council to purchase this frontage compulsorily. The estate was begun in March 1920 and by July 1922, 337 houses had been built but the estate was not finished until 1926. Once access roads had been made the rest of the valuable Upper Wickham Lane frontage was sold for private shop development.

Since applicants had to have a five year residence qualification the estate was largely occupied by people living in the district at the end of the war. As others qualified so the council completed the smaller schemes indicated on the map. The greatly decreased rate of building after 1926 was not so much due to fewer applications for housing as to the limited amount of financial help available through the London Housing Board.[46] Following slum clearances, and with the increasing need to lessen congestion in older inner housing districts of Greater London, less money was made available to districts like Bexley. In nearby Lewisham, for example, a vast sum was required for the London County Council's Great Downham Estate covering 522 acres, built between 1924–1930. But fortunately in the late 1920s falling house prices enabled an increasing number of even the lower paid workers to purchase their own houses privately.

If we turn now to look at the rate of private building, subsidies and local authority mortgage facilities were two of the most important factors. Only one development in the district did not qualify for the building subsidy, but even for this a number of occupiers relied on mortages from the Council.

To qualify for aid under the 1923 Housing Act, the Minister had to be satisfied that there was a need for houses in the district and that the demand could not be met without financial assistance. Aid took three forms: a subsidy payment of £70 to £75 could be made to the builder for each house or bungalow completed; local authorities were empowered to obtain money at low rates of interest so that they could extend loans to builders for house construction; and mortgages, up to 90 per cent of house valuation and repayable up to 30 years, were made available to purchasers. The Wheatley Housing Act of 1924 modified but did not essentially alter these provisions.

Apart from their effect on the rate of building these provisions had also important effects on the density and character of residential development. The subsidy was limited to houses not exceeding 880 super feet and to bungalows not exceeding 950 super feet.[47] Since the subsidy was progressively reduced on dwellings falling below this maximum limit it encouraged building to a standardized size. A density limit of 12 to the acre also led to further standardization, because to maximize land-use every builder tended to build to this maximum density. Each dwelling had to have a bathroom and mains drainage. This meant in effect that estates could only be built where access to existing sewers was available.

Though standardized in some respects, subsidized housing was far more attractive to purchasers than the older high density terrace housing. The lower density encouraged a more open layout. The introduction of bungalows added further attractions and some variety in dwelling type. Purchasers were also drawn from Woolwich and Erith by the provision of bathrooms and a hot water supply.[48]

Mortgages could be advanced by the local authority on houses up to £1,500 in value, so they covered all types of residential building in the district. That this was the major source of mortgages for prospective purchases is clearly indicated when the record of council mortgage advances is compared with the housing total for a particular period. Between 1923 and 1931 the Bexley Council advanced 1,512 mortgages totalling £765,952, which covered approximately three quarters of the dwellings built.[49] On the terms offered, it made it possible for better paid workers to buy houses. For example, on an average house costing £650, a purchaser had to put down £65 deposit and could repay the mortgage at £1 a week over 30 years. This compared favourably with renting a new Council house at 12s. 0d. to 14s. 0d. a week or an older terrace house in Woolwich or locally for 8s. 0d. to 10s. 0d. a week. A skilled manual worker on a basic wage of about £4 a week could afford to buy on these terms, but the unskilled worker earning about £3 usually still had to rent.[50]

Up to 1925 the builder still found it difficult to build to the limit of £600 set to qualify for the subsidy and building loan grants. The Council Surveyor himself estimated the cost of building a house in 1925 at £750 – £120 for the land, £15 for the fencing and £615 for the building. In 1925 the subsidy qualification limit was raised to £650, and this does seem to have had a favourable effect on the rate of building.[51] It is difficult to estimate how much, because other factors were also more favourable after 1926. For instance the cost of labour and materials was lower, interest rates were beginning to fall, and falling house prices increased the market demand.[52] By 1927 the subsidy could be limited to houses selling for £550.[53] Then in 1929 it abruptly ceased. In spite of this 229 houses, begun under the guarantee of a subsidy, were still completed. Clearly by 1929 economic conditions had become favourable enough to provide adequate incentives to ensure that the supply of housing would meet the demand. It represented a return to the dominance of private enterprise in the supply of suburban housing.

Council building and government aid to builder and purchaser had played a very large part in transforming the housing situation, in spite of the increasing numbers of families coming into the district. Whilst between 1921 and 1931 the number of families increased by 63 per cent the number of dwellings increased by 83 per cent.[54] In 1931 very few families were short of housing accommodation.

The advent of Town Planning legislation was also very important at this time. Measures were for the first time available, under which the local authority could exercise some powers of control on the location and density of specific housing estate layouts. There was also an increasing awareness of the need for some overall measure of control. To begin with, however, powers were more permissive than obligatory. Thus the influence of town planning measures in any particular district depended very much on the attitude of the local council, a group of individuals thinking about and discussing at a local level the needs of their own particular area.

Fortunately the Bexley Council was generally progressive in outlook.[55] But its planning decisions were also very much influenced by the prevailing character of residential development in the district, as expressed not only through its visible spatial variants, but also by the social values attached to them. As Levett puts it 'There has always been much self zoning in the development of an existing town, far more subtle, sensitive and powerful than any scheme can be. This phenomenon is a strong and undeniable part of a town organism arising from the qualities given to certain streets and sites by the existing layout and derived from social custom and need.'[56] This can be clearly illustrated from particular instances related to the general interim Town Plan for the Bexley district.

There were, for example, two cases of direct local authority intervention to protect select residential neighbourhoods, thus ensuring their maintenance as part of the fabric of later residential patterns. In 1922 Ellingham, a builder wanting to develop some prime building land facing Danson Park, was refused planning permission on the grounds that the 98 houses he proposed were of too low a quality and not in keeping with the area.[57] A little later Norman was similarly refused permission for proposed housing facing high quality detached property on Broomfield Road.[58] It is significant that these two areas are today regarded as amongst the best residential areas in the district.

Intervention was not limited to better housing areas. For instance north of Bexleyheath station the local authority considerably modified the suggested Cooper's Woodland estate layout of 114 houses in blocks of five to 18 houses. Under powers granted by the Interim Development Order of 1922 the authority suggested a revised layout of semi-detached houses at a lower density.

An overall measure of control as suggested by the council was embodied in the 1929 Town Development Plan. Zoning densities and other features it incorporated laid the foundation for the later suburban development to 1939. As planning proposals were generally in keeping with the then prevailing character of the district, the zoning of the northern part with its largely working class housing was at 12 to the acre, whilst the more attractive areas round Bexley were zoned at only six to eight to the acre. In addition certain localities here were subject to private restrictions which, in the event of a sale of the land, meant densities as low as three to the acre, as for example bordering Bexley woods, Thus zoning densities for housing confirmed the broad social zoning already apparent before the First World War.

Turning to consider the physical constraints and other influences exercised by the existing settlement cadaster and other local conditions, at Welling the most clear-cut influence of site layout is seen in the relationship of Bellegrove Park Building Estate to the configuration of Bellegrove Park, the small country seat purchased by the building speculator. Opposite, if a little more complex, the Welling Council Estate and small adjacent private estates offer more interesting detail. The Council estate, whilst cutting across landownership boundaries, does show the restraining influence of the line of the railway on its southern margin and the line of roads bounding it on other sides. The layout is an enlightened one following Unwin's suggestions and making very good use of the shape of the site; an outer crescentic ring road follows the perimeter line of railway and road, with a central development along two intersecting diagonal routes (fig. 33). Inside the resulting quadrants, cul-de-sacs completed the layout, though Dovedale House and grounds were left untouched in the northern quadrant. Nearby Little Danson Estate on the south side of Welling High Street has a somewhat similar layout and fits snugly into the pre-building plot lines.

To the west of the Council estate, private estate building could only occur because access to main water pipes and sewers was made possible by council extension of these to serve their own Welling estate. Hitherto development had been prevented on the west side of Welling station.[59] The Stevens development closely mirrors field boundaries on the land units bought on option by him from the Yeatman estate. Next door Norman's estate was similar and next to this Norman also developed a small estate in the grounds of Westwood House. Barnes and Bridges then built an estate on the orchard behind the house.[60] Adjacent to this Oxley could then sell his Hefty Pig Farm, hitherto poorly drained and too far away from existing settlement to attract the builders' attention, at a good price as building land.[61] Such was the sequence of development.

The break up of Danson estate and the consequent building development are particularly interesting for they illustrate the complex interaction of circumstances underlying much of the suburban development, one which can only be fully understood if detailed case studies are undertaken. Danson was the most imposing landed estate in the district and its successive owners consequently the most influential. Danson mansion, its surrounding gardens and lake laid out by 'Capability Brown', lay at the centre of the park (fig. 34). Around it were the farms, small-holdings, orchards, smithy and cottages belonging to the estate. The untimely death of the landowner brought the estate on the market in 1920, initially as one lot, but it had to be withdrawn since the highest offer, £35,000, was unacceptable. Though demand for building land was increasing, this period was characterized by small scale developments. No one developer could afford or risk a large outlay, particularly in a case such as this where much of the land was backland without essential services.

Against the wishes of the Trustees the estate was divided into lots at the second auction, though the great central parkland was on their insistence retained as one large unit of 222 acres.[62] This insistence and the forethought of the Clerk to the Council in purchasing it as a park for the district,[63] are the basic reasons why this remains as public open space today, one of the largest and most gracious in Greater London. Later suburban development in the 1930s surrounded it on all sides, giving it a central position and therefore making it easily accessible from most parts of the suburb. Here we have a good case of a central part of the suburban pattern being largely determined by the character of the pre-urban land use and the decisions made by a few thoughtful individuals.

Of the other sale lots, few were sold at auction, most went privately later. But the lot plot lines, decided by the trustees and auctioneers, became the building lines within which housing development occurred. The lots were in many cases fields, but on the west of the park the farm and small holdings were sold as the lot units. The relationship of building development patterns and estate lot patterns is clearly evident on the map showing details of the Danson estate sale and subsequent building. The by-pass road cut across the southern edge of the estate but did not eradicate the influence of field boundaries. Thus no less than in the pre-1914 period, suburban growth continued to be influenced by local decisions and the pre-urban cadaster.

The phase generalized

Though the first part of this phase was largely concerned with meeting the backlog of housing demands made by Thameside workers, it became increasingly clear that the future of the district would be largely that of a metropolitan suburb. Links to the Thameside industrial areas would remain but would be overshadowed by those tying the district to the heart of the metropolis.

These closer ties were already being expressed on the ground through the expansion of housing around Bexleyheath and Welling railway stations. The stations appeared as important secondary growth areas; it would, however, perhaps be more correct to see the stations, at least initially, not as the hubs around which settlement grew, but rather as the locations to which housing expansion was drawn as growth extended outwards from the established main settlement centres. Given that future housing would have to be located at an increasing distance from these established nuclei and that each successive estate extended essential services, such as mains drainage, lighting, and water supply, station locations had a distinct advantage. They provided the links between residence and workplace for the increasing numbers of City workers coming to live in the district. To follow Firey's concept concerning the use of marginal land, areas around the station had become in effect places of greater accessibility and therefore now had greater social utility when used for residential purposes than if left under cultivation.[64]

As residential development went on around the stations, secondary service centres were also established to provide the everyday goods and services. Whilst the suburban settlement continued to fill out with the continued process of accretion around the main settlement centres and with secondary growth around the stations, the location of the most select residential development continued to be influenced more by the quality of site and status of neighbourhood than by physical distance to a station or to central shopping, for in fact the advent of the motor car effectively brought these within easier reach. Hence, for example, select housing

Figure 33. Welling Council Estate, looking north (centre) (Aerofilms Ltd).

began to be found in the Danson Park vicinity and in the wooded area of Broomfield Road, both prime quality sites at some distance from service amenities.

Morphologically, in this phase greater variety was introduced into the residential scene. Council estates added a new facet to working class housing and within the intermediate range bungalows, as well as semi-detached housing, were available. More varied building materials were being used, for instance cement rendering and pebble dashing over brick, and various coloured roofing tiles. There were also significant changes in estate layout.

Some private and council estates continued to be laid out on the established grid-iron principle, but under the influence of the Tudor Walters Report and of enlightened individuals such as Howard, Parker, and Unwin, freer layouts were being adopted such as those for the Welling Council and Little Danson estates. Crescents and closes helped to make an aesthetically more pleasing layout. These also made for economic use of land as well as enabling architect and builder to produce an estate plan which fitted more happily into the particular shape the site offered.[65] The introduction of planning controls added another determinant into the residential scene. As Lederman states, zoning control might have been negative but it curtailed and modified the pattern of residential development.[66] A fixed classification was imposed over what was in fact an ever changing scene.

Within the social zones already established, sub-units as a secondary level of zonation, were beginning to occur as the number and variety of estates increased, enlarging the built up area. For instance, Welling within the general zoning remained the lowest ranked part of the district, but it could now itself be subdivided into its constituent building estates, and these ranked in order of social preference. At the lower end lay the East Wickham hutments and the Council estate, at the upper end Bellegrove Park estate, and in between estates such as those built by Normans and Stevens west of the station.

On the theme of metropolitan fringe development we see generally at this time the turning point between Wissink's 'scattered fringe' phase, and the development of Bexley district as part of the 'compact hem'. Whereas in 1921 Westergaarde could number Bexley among those outer districts of the conurbation still largely beyond the 'daily sphere of influence of the centre of London',[67] by 1931 it fell firmly within it. The changing occupation structure for the working population of Bexley district indicated in the occupation tables for the 1921 and 1931 census reports, the character of residential development and the views of local people concerned with the period, all point to this change.

In terms of local fringe development there was little further addition either at Bexley or Bexleyheath and Welling. As Whitehand points out, this was not a period conducive to fringe development but one of making better use of existing fringe plots.[68] Recreation grounds and other public open spaces offered greater facilities and were more fully used. Moreover, sites for various amenities such as schools, cemeteries, and recreation grounds, were increasingly becoming incorporated into residential development as part and parcel of it. The 1920s mark a transitional stage towards the concept of the neighbourhood unit emerging as increasingly important during and after the 1930s, though it may be worth emphasizing that neighbourhoods can, and have in fact emerged of their own volition, and been a part of the pattern of living ever since cities have existed.

236

Figure 34. A view looking east across Danson Park, land preserved as a municipal park when the Danson Estate was sold in 1922–4. The remainder was developed in the two inter-war phases of building. Little Danson Estate built in 1926–7 is in the foreground, left, and better-class housing along Danson Road borders the other side of the Park. Beyond lies Upton and far right Bexley Wood (Aerofilms Ltd).

4 The emergence of the mature metropolitan suburb, 1930–9

This was the period of greatest growth: housing increased from 6.704 to 24,760 and the population from 28,120 to 80,110, increases of 269 per cent and 189 per cent respectively.[69] Multiple family occupation and a housing shortage were things of the past. By the close of this period little remained of the orchards, market gardens, and farmland so characteristic of the district at the turn of the century.[70] The transformation was in fact largely completed by 1936, building having reached a peak in 1934–5 when just over 4,000 houses were completed.[71] After this time it became increasingly difficult to find good building land at a reasonable price and so the rate of building slackened. Rapid and radical changes reflect equally radical changes in the nature and balance of circumstances underlying them. But a number of these have been obscured by an over-emphasis in the literature on population movement and transport developments. There were equally important changes in the structure of the building industry, and the emergence of a new class of purchaser made possible by easier finance and arising from the growing aspirations of lower paid workers for their own homes in semi-rural surroundings. There were also changes in the mechanism by which builder and purchaser were effectively brought together. Recognition of these is fundamental to any real understanding of this outer suburban spread of the 1930s which forms such a major part of the present total metropolitan scene. However, for those still unable to afford their own homes, it continued to be the local authority which with government support provided houses for rent. Private investment in new working class houses to let, except for a small revival in the later 1930s, had disappeared and has never since been of any great importance. A process begun in the 1920s which had increasingly shifted the responsibility for lower income housing onto the public authorities was firmly established by the 1930s.

Speculative private enterprise, priced out of the rented sector of the housing market and faced with a progressively saturated market for more expensive housing, was driven to find ways of enabling families with very limited capital to become owner occupiers. As a consequence of this and other factors a new and mass housing market appeared, the needs of which had in turn marked repercussions on the scale of operation and organisation within the building industry itself. Bowley has aptly summarized the conditions which enabled these changes to take place.[72]

A fall in the rates of interest after 1932 coincided with a steep fall in the cost of building and a rapid increase in real incomes for important sections of the population. Following on the gradual growth of real incomes since the First World War, this made possible a significant transfer of families from the group who normally had to rent houses to those who could just afford to move into the social class of small houseowners. Although definite statistical evidence is lacking there is really no doubt that the movement brought into the category of owner occupiers families from further down the economic and social scale than had previously been in this class.[73]

Carver goes further, calling it a social revolution – 'the social revolution gave the family a house in the suburb and all it contains'.[74] It in effect created that broad and ill defined group which has become known as the lower middle class and which dominated the suburban housing scene of the 1930s. This, not population or transport changes, is the most fundamental feature underlying this outer suburban growth. Population movement into the suburbs was a visible result of its effects; transport developments, apart from the initial stimulus given to these population movements, were largely a consequence of it – a response to the proven demand arising from the needs of those very large numbers of families who had already made up their minds to move out to the suburbs.

While more favourable economic circumstances made the move to the suburbs possible, this should not lead us to overlook the element of choice. As House reminds us, 'migration is one of the most complex human phenomena, a summation of countless individual decisions and pressures, from an imperfect knowledge or understanding of prospects, often with a strong reluctance to leave kith and kin.'[75] Increasing educational opportunities, greater mobility as well as the growing mass communication media were very influential in encouraging the rise of a working class movement, and giving more freedom of expression to the wishes and aspirations of the womenfolk in the family. These developments in turn encouraged large numbers of families to seek an improvement of social status. A house of one's own in the suburb, to such a family enmeshed in the inner areas of large cities, was both the greatest material possession and the most obvious visible expression of the improved status to which it aspired.

One would agree with Waugh and others that the decreases in house-hold size and the break up of the composite household were contributory factors to the rate of suburban expansion,[76] but these were consequences of social aspirations, part of the visible evidence of the changing way in which a larger number of the better paid working classes regarded the family and its place in society. We need to know more about these circumstances underlying the decision to move, more about the ways in which this new lower middle class regarded itself, and about social interaction at family, kinship, and neighbourhood level. For though large numbers of young families did move to the suburbs it is equally evident that many, though financially as well off, preferred to stay in the older housing areas of London. What was the decisive difference between the young family which chose to move and those who chose to remain behind, becomes a central question.

Choice of housing location is related to location of workplace, but in the expanding economic opportunities of the Greater London region the head of a family had greater opportunity to choose his workplace. Further, there were usually a number of possible housing locations within varying but reasonable access of any particular workplace. Unsatisfied by accessibility: distance/cost friction arguments, one must return to the point that the family chose to live at a particular location within a particular suburb, and the question of the bases on which the choice was made remains. Mayer suggests the right approach to this question when he states, 'In spite of the wide range of attributes among suburbs it is generally evident that the suburban areas are largely populated by (those) people who seek a better environment than that offered within the boundaries of the central city.'[77] This is the decisive difference between the suburban dweller and his counterpart in the central city. Some see the city as the preferred environment – others the country-side on the fringe of the city.

Aspiration and economic opportunity lay on the one hand at the root of a new housing demand, and on the other the reorganization of the building industry enabling it to satisfy this demand, but the two had to be brought together. Here also important changes occurred to make this possible. Mumford, reflecting on the nature of suburbs, points to the influence of a new trinity dominating the metropolitan scene, 'Finance, insurance and advertising . . . extending the metropolis rule over subordinate regions.'[78] New methods of finance for the building industry and the house purchaser were closely linked with the increasing importance of building societies.[79] Better insurance facilities also helped to give confidence and security to the large scale builder and more adequate protection to the intending house purchaser. Together, finance and insurance helped to initiate and support the building boom of the thirties.

But as the housing market expanded and the scale of operations escalated it also became increasingly necessary to have more efficient means of disseminating information between builder and purchaser. That dissemination of information still went on through that social network of inter-personal communications emphasized by Hagestrand in his discussions on population migration,[80] but the most important contact was no longer one between relative, neighbours, regular and chance acquaintances, but one consequent upon an initial impact made through the new impersonal mass communication media – housing advertisements in the popular national press, particularly the Sunday papers, on cinema screens, and bus and railway station hoardings. Following on from this, the essential personal contacts were those between the estate agent or the builder's own selling agent and the prospective house purchaser. A highly organized and personal sales pressure was exerted – the car waiting at the station to whisk each intending buyer personally out to look at the houses, and the offer of every possible incentive to purchase. As estate agents multiplied and estate development expanded, competitive efficiency on the selling side became increasingly vital, and equally the opportunities greater for young families to compare various houses and suburban areas before coming to a decision.

The pace and character of suburbanization in the Bexley district in the light of these and other external influences can now be reviewed. Mary Waugh in her very useful analysis of suburban growth in north-west Kent has dealt adequately with the comparative advantages which the London region had over other regions in the national economic climate of the 1930s.[81] Bexley as part of the north-west Kent suburbs shared in these advantages.

Though detailed statistical evidence is not available and there was no census for 1941, it is clear that the main demand for housing in the outer suburbs came from households migrating out of the older inner suburbs. The birthplace table for Bexley Borough in the 1951 Census offers some supporting evidence; 35,975 people, over half of the 1951 population, were born in London, as against 10,500 born elsewhere outside the borough (table 19).

Interviews and conversations with many local inhabitants who came in at this time, and with builders, estate agents, as well as local officials intimately concerned with developments, also leave no doubt that most of the migration was from South East London, and in particular the nearby areas of Woolwich and Plumstead on Thameside. The move appears to have been by a series of short-distance migrations, a migration pattern already noted as common in outward growth of a metropolitan region.[82]

The rapid rise in the birth rate for Bexley district from 16.0/1,000 in 1929 to 18.2/1,000 in 1935 during the time of the main influx of population and the equally marked fall in the death rate from 12.0/1,000 to 8.4/1,000 over the same period indicate that it was mainly a migration of young households. Although immigration declined after 1936, these changes in the birth and death rates ensured a continued

Table 19   Birthplaces of Bexley borough residents, 1951

area of birth	male	female
London	17,369	18,606
Kent	13,153	13,568
Rest of the South East	3,184	4,471
Essex	1,965	2,176
Middlesex	990	1,044
Surrey	823	849
Sussex	365	469
Herts.	41	33
Eastern	1,253	1,508
The South	951	1,118
South West	733	846
N. Midlands	434	523
Midlands	418	495
East and West Riding of Yorkshire	455	512
The North	642	690

Source: Decennial Census 1951, table 19.

rise in the population, the increased rate of natural increase offsetting the decrease in the number of immigrants.

The type of house built in the 1930s is clear evidence that most of the immigrant families belonged to the lower middle class. By 1951 some 60.1 per cent of the male population over 15 years of age, belonged to Social Class III as given in the Census,[83] a class largely composed of skilled manual and non-manual workers. Only 4.1 per cent belong to class I, the professional groups, and 17.5 per cent to class II, the intermediate groups. Moreover within class III it is also clear that for Bexley borough the proportion of manual workers to non-manual was higher than for other north-west Kent suburbs to the south of Bexley. Census occupation tables show a high proportion of male workers in the distributive, building, contracting, and manufacturing occupations.[84] This to a large degree, then, reflects Bexley's greater affinities with the Thameside manufacturing belt.

By 1951 Bexley borough was a commuter suburb of London, with just over 17 per cent of its male workers and 25 per cent of its female workers commuting daily to the city (table 20). This level of commuting brings the borough well within the accepted definition of a metropolitan suburb.[85] However, the district also continued to be an important dormitory area for Thameside, giving it thus a dual affinity and distinctive suburban character not found in other outer suburbs of Kent.

Efficient and economic transport to these workplaces continued to be important requirements. Plans to electrify the two railway lines into central London made before the First World War were realized in 1926. This undoubtedly helped to stimulate the further expansion of housing. On both the Dartford loop line and the Bexleyheath line by 1930 trains were running at a six minute interval during peak times and every 20 minutes at other times. A quarterly season ticket, costing between £3 15s. and £3 19s. depending on which local station was used, was within the reach of the skilled manual or clerical worker earning about £250 a year.

Table 20   Relative proportions of resident occupied population working inside the borough and working in areas outside the borough, 1951

	male	female
total occupied resident population (over 15 years of age)	29,325	12,002
numbers working inside the borough	5,088	3,495
numbers working outside the borough	24,237	8,506

PRINCIPAL WORKPLACES OUTSIDE THE BOROUGH

workplace area	male numbers and percentages of total working population resident in the borough		female numbers and percentages of total working population resident in the borough	
Central London	5,197	17.7	3,037	25.3
City	2,436	10.0	1,345	15.8
Westminster	2,194	9.0	1,427	16.8
Holborn	567	2.4	265	3.1
Woolwich	5,331	21.9	1,827	21,5
Thameside (Kent area) mainly Erith but + Crayford and Dartford	3,124	12.8	744	9.4
other areas of Inner London excluding Thameside borders i.e. Bermondsey, Camberwell, Lambeth, Finsbury	1,884	7.9	(insignificant)	
other London areas bordering Thameside (south)	2,326	9.6		
Greenwich	1,676	6.9	263	3.1
Deptford	650	2.7		
other areas of London bordering Thameside (north)	1,144	4.7	70	0.9
other areas of metropolitan Kent, i.e. Chislehurst, Sidcup and Bromley, Beckenham, Penge	1,044	4.4	990	11.7

Sources: Decennial Census 1951, table 20: Occupations, and table 6: Residence and Workplace.

Whereas in 1930, 135,000 ordinary tickets were issued at Bexleyheath Station, by 1939 it had risen to 718,000 in addition to 550,000 season ticket issues.[86] But as Course and Ashworth both emphasize it is dangerous to use this sort of passenger traffic increase as evidence of a direct cause-effect relationship between railway facilities and housing expansion.[87]

There is considerable evidence to show instead that once on the upswing, housing expansion in the 1930s ran in advance of both the provision of adequate railway services and adequate means of access to a railway station. There were frequent references to overcrowding on the trains and of no station being built by the railway company to serve a large housing area alongside a line. Also, for most of the period there were no bus services to the stations.[88] Yet it did not deter families from settling in these inconvenient areas. Commuters from the new Hurst housing estates for example were prepared to walk one to two miles to Sidcup or Bexley stations.

As they so often do today, builders embarked on estate development, and families bought houses in the belief that reasonable transport facilities would ultimately come in response to agitation and a proven demand. In the borough, Ideal Homestead Limited was a sufficiently wealthy and powerful organization to persuade the railway authority to allow it to build Albany Park and Falconwood Stations in order to serve the needs of residents on large housing estates already practically completed.[89] Improved transport facilities here as in some other areas followed a proven demand. But in certain areas, notably north western London, the reverse was the case. Here as Johnson indicates the opening of new lines and the effective linking of them with areas around resulting from the extension of motor bus services, together with extensive advertising, were needed before suburban building increased.[90]

The Thameside tram route continued to provide an efficient and economic link between home and workplace.[91] It encouraged a further expansion of lower middle class housing in Welling and Bexleyheath, for tram stops were within easy walking distance from most parts of the new housing estates. The service was also increasingly used by women on shopping visits to Woolwich, its largest shopping centre and street market being within easy reach. In 1935 trams were replaced by a more efficient trolley-bus service, and a four minute service operated. Expansion of transport services seems to have kept pace with demand.

The quality of bus services within a district is also held to have some influence on housing expansion. Travelling time to local service centres is, for example, particularly important to the housewife. But in the Bexley district expansion went on during the 1930s, in spite of rather than because of the condition of internal bus services. Beyond the tram route, and the Eltham to Old Bexley bus service, running along Blendon and Bridgen Roads, the district was badly served. Continuous references to this are found in Council Minutes and local press reports. In May 1931, Bexley Chamber of Commerce, Bexleyheath Ratepayers Association, and the National Citizen's Union combined in a deputation to the authorities, demanding improvements,[92] and in 1936 the inadequacy of bus services in the Bexley district was the subject of a parliamentary question.[93]

The London Passenger Transport Board was aware of the district's needs. But as in other rapidly growing outer suburban areas certain services could not start until some roads along the intended route were widened and obstructions, such as overhanging trees, removed.[94] For example, the Board wished to extend its number 132 service from Eltham, terminating at the Woodman, Blackfen, to Bexleyheath Market Place, but could not until Danson Road was improved. In the northern part of the district extension of bus services was held up by the railway company's refusal to strengthen and widen railway bridges on Pickford Road and Woolwich Road.[95] Complex and protracted negotiations caused long delays, during which time residents might well vigorously protest, but still had to put up with the unconveniences these caused. A reasonable bus service network was not created until 1936, by which time most of the housing development had already been completed.

For the house purchaser the two outstanding benefits of the 1930s were a fall in house prices compared to those of the 1920s, and easier facilities for raising the money to buy a house. Until 1936 the cheapest houses in the district sold for £350 to £395 compared to £525 to £550 in the late 1920s. The intermediate range lay between about £570 and £700, and the highest price range from £975 upwards.[96]

The most important fall in house prices was that for the cheapest houses. As wages also rose and employment opportunities expanded after 1932, the effective fall in house prices was even more than the difference between the advertised prices indicates. Families with an income of £3 to £4 a week generally bought this cheaper type of house. The somewhat better houses, as for example those on the Davis Estate near Bexleyheath Station, went to families with an income of £4 to £8; sometimes the wife and family of a factory foreman or supervisor, but more commonly of a lower grade civil servant or local small businessman.

In contrast to the 1920s, the local authority played little part in financing house purchase.[97] Most of this was done through the local offices of building societies, working in conjunction with an estate agent or directly with the builder.[98] Building society advances were normally limited to 75 per cent of the purchase price, leaving a deposit of 25 per cent to be found by the purchaser, an amount usually beyond the resources of the lower middle class family. This raised a serious problem, which was solved by the cooperative efforts of the building society and the builder. The deposit required from the purchaser was reduced to a nominal amount because the building society advanced almost all the 25 per cent by arrangement with the builder against cash and/or other collateral deposited by him. The house purchaser then repaid the total advance by instalments in the usual way, including interest, so that in the course of time the builder's collateral was automatically redeemed.[99] As a result of this system, keys to the cheapest houses could be had for a deposit of £5. If the purchaser had not the £5 readily available it was common practice for him to be lent it by the estate agent or builder. Repayments on the mortgage advance could be made at 11s. weekly over 20 or 21 years, a weekly outlay which compared very favourably with 10s. 3d. rent on a council house or 8s. rent on an old terrace house lacking in any modern conveniences and in particular a bathroom and hot water supply.[100]

This easy and revolutionary means of house purchase was a major factor in the spread of cheaper housing in this and other similar outer suburbs. Never before or since has house purchase been made so easy. It was also a method used to finance the purchase of better quality housing. For example, Ideal Homestead offered houses on the Falconwood Estate at Welling, costing £675, for an initial deposit of only £10, and a further £25 on possession. Weekly mortgage repayments were a modest 22s. and rates 4s. 5d.[101]

Competition within the local building industry, as elsewhere, was intense in the cheaper housing market. The largest developers, Stevens and Ideal Homesteads, operated their own selling agencies, but smaller ones, such as Alabaster, used the local estate agents. However, despite the high rate of building expansion there is little evidence of cheaper houses remaining unsold for any length of time. On a smaller scale competition was also intense in the better priced housing market, but the tempo of selling was very much slower. The smaller builder, unable to compete with large building speculators in the cheaper housing market because he could not take advantage of economies of scale, chose to concentrate on the better type of housing.[102] Faced with limited financial resources and a limited demand he bought up small units of land or individual plots on a medium sized development site, such as Blendon Hall or Bellegrove Park Estate, completing and selling a house or a pair of houses before beginning the next. Within this sort of market the prudent and industrious small developer was successful. He had certain advantages over the larger organization. He could personally supervise the work of his men as he commonly worked alongside them. He also had the organizational flexibility to undertake the specialized fittings or construction details which the individual purchaser frequently required. But these small estates of better and more varied housing took a long time to complete. In a number of cases, including that of Bowyer's Blendon estate started in 1929, development was still not completed by the outbreak of war.

Bowley and Robinson both also note the national conditions favouring investment in the building industry during the first half of the 1930s,[103] as an important factor in the national building boom. Depressed conditions in agriculture and the older staple industries, together with reduced investment opportunities abroad, encouraged the financier to invest in building development. Once again it was evident that the building cycle operated inversely to the trade cycle. As Robinson puts it, 'In a depression residential building becomes more and more profitable, as costs of building and the rate of interest fall until finally it leads out of the depression and through the operation of cumulative processes induces recovery.'[104] Building costs fell to 1934 and then began to rise. There was a general set-back in the building industry in 1935, followed by a recovery from 1936 but at a much slower rate of building, since costs were higher and the demand more limited. Building rates in the Bexley district corresponded fairly closely to this national pattern.

Some local firms acquired capital in the open market whilst others relied on loans from such sources as the major building societies. The main initial capital outlay was for purchase of suitable building land. Some firms bought the land outright, whilst others bought some of what they required taking out an option to purchase on the remainder, as was the case, for example, with two builders concerned with developing Goldsmid estate land.

Up to 1936 there was no shortage of building land and this contributed both to the speed and scale of housing expansion. Depressed conditions in agriculture and market gardening hastened the sale of land to the waiting developer.[105] Much of the available land was still in large units, an advantage to the large building organization, and one of the reasons why large estates of cheaper standardized housing are characteristic of this suburban phase. After 1936 all larger lots of suitable building land had been sold. This slowed down the rate of housing expansion and forced the developer on to land considered physically marginal during the 1930s. It also hastened a process of infilling which continued after the war.

As Denman indicates, it is extremely difficult to assess the general price of building land for any given time and therefore its influence on building costs and the price of housing.[106] The actual price varied, depending on such attributes as length of road frontage, relative depth of plot, access to essential services, size and convenience of shape, together with location. Generally, however, it is safe to say that in the Bexley district prices were higher than they had been in the 1920s and continued to rise as good building land became progressively scarcer.

Table 21   *Some building land prices, 1920–9*
             (based on estate sales detail and Estate Exchange Year Books)

land sold by acreage				land sold by foot frontage		
year	acreage	price (£)	price per acre (£)	footage	price (£)	price per foot
1921	2.1	600	240			
1922	36.2	3,000	83			
	1.4	800	571			
	29.9	3.000	100			
	11.0	750	70			
1923						
1924				365	730	2.0
1925	2.6	250	96	252	819	3.3
				3,361	6,049	1.8
average price per acre 1921–5		£213		average price per foot 1921–5		£2.5
1926				48.5	450	9.3
				350	1.000	3.0
				112	280	2.5
1927	22	4,000	182	66	120	2.0
1928						
1929	8	2,500	313			
	88	21,250	241			
average price per acre 1926–9		£208		average price per foot 1926–9		£3.4
1930	18	5,230	279	170	285	1.7
1931				30	125	4.2
1932	73	23,097	327	114	513	4.5
				350	1,008	3.0
1933	9.0	4,500	500	91	375	4.0
	6.0	2,520	420	79.5	400	5.0
	17.5	16,250	300	30	200	6.9
	76.0	15,200	200	321	725	2.2
	2.5	1,200	485			
	7.5	3,00	400			
1934	2.5	1,560	625			
	3.5	3,350	950			
	1.2	796	663			
1935	4.0	3,000	750	47	4,725	100[a]
	62.0	25,000	400			
average price per acre 1930–5		£426		average price per foot 1930–5		£4.1
1936				68	11,028	162[a]
				577	2,452	4.3
1937		not known	700			
1938		not known	800			
	21	9,845	475			
average price per acre 1935–8		£658		average price per foot 1935–8		£4.3

[a] Reported price of prime land on Broadway bought for Townley Road access. The average excludes these.

Where, for example, zoning regulations limited the density to 12 to the acre, the approximate average price, so far as one can work out, rose from between £250 and £300 per acre in 1933 to between £400 and £450 in 1935–1936 and then to between £450 and £500 in 1937 (table 21). Small units of prime building land could by this time cost up to as much as £1,000 an acre.[107]

The cost of building land was however a comparatively small proportion of total building costs.[108] Ideal Homestead, for example, estimate the cost of a plot on their Hurst Road Estate begun in 1932, as £20 for a house selling at between £395 and £580.[109] The increase in land prices during the first half of the 1930s had therefore little influence on housing costs and it was more than offset by economies in the costs of construction and services. Later, however, the rise in the price of land did have some noticeable effect on house prices since it was not offset by a fall in other building costs. On the contrary, building costs were also rising, especially those of labour and raw materials which formed a substantial proportion of the total. These were rises felt nationally but also, additional pressure was felt locally. Building firms had to complete for labour with Thameside factories, particularly with Woolwich Arsenal where wage rates were rising and employment opportunities expanding.[110] There is little doubt that increased housing prices before the war were more a consequence of increased labour and raw material costs than of changing land prices.

When due regard has been given to the financial resources of the private sector of the building industry, and to land, labour, and raw material costs, one is still left with an inadequate explanation of the industry's remarkable success. Much of the rest of the answer lies in the flexible and efficient response of the industry to the opportunities presented by a new and expanding market. Bowley points out that this arose, not out of access to better information on organization and building techniques, but partly from a 'number of accepted rules of thumb, as well as the practical experience developers gained in the course of time'.[111] In the intensely competitive conditions of the time, success depended on the discovery of what sort of house with what sort of fittings was wanted within each price range.[112]

Some of the requisites necessary for success can be illustrated from the work and methods of Stevens and Ideal Homestead Ltd. Each of these was completing cheaper houses at the rate of one hundred a week in the early 1930s (fig. 35).[113] Designs were strictly standardized and no requests for additional fittings were entertained. This allowed the sub-contracting of much of the work, and the usual economies of scale, such as savings on bulk purchase of building materials and fittings. Both firms imported Belgian bricks and large quantities of doors and window frames from Czechoslovakia, cheaper sources than their British counterparts, particularly since building sites were only a short road haul from the docks at Erith. Cement works lay close by at Stone, Swanscombe, and Greenhithe. Each firm had its own local sand and gravel pits. For a time Stevens also operated its own brick pits. Fittings such as baths and kitchen fitments were regularly delivered, usually by road direct from the factory.

The very speed of construction cut down labour costs. A house was commonly built within three weeks and sometimes in less.[114] Sub-contractors who were offered large firm contracts, with the prospects of more to come, moved systematically across an estate from one road to the next. Their workers were encouraged by piece rates and as much overtime as they could manage. Never before or since has housing development gone on so quickly. A rural landscape could be transformed in a month.

In contrast to the preceding phase of development, local authority building, whilst important in certain nearby areas, contributed little.[115] Further, the national government and local authority exercised only a limited influence through town planning measures. The framework for these remained the ones already laid down in the Draft Plan of 1928. Widened powers granted under the Town Planning Act of 1932 and exercised under a General Interim Order to 1938, failed to give that adequate measure of overall control which such large scale and rapid changes made particularly desirable.[116] One feature discouraging stronger control was that where a planning decision deprived the developer of the opportunity of using his land, substantial compensation might have to be made.[117] The local authority was in the strongest position when it could be shown that too much public money would have to be spent in providing necessary sewerage, drainage and other services, for in such cases the builder was not entitled to compensation. On these grounds development was effectively delayed in the area of East Wickham for example. Frequently, however, a private party appealed successfully to the Minister of Health against a particular planning decision.

It was a situation which produced the reverse of orderly planning. Somewhat haphazard, and in some areas piecemeal, development resulted. Moreover the local authority further accentuated these features. South of Bexleyheath, under the Town Development Plan, Townley and Latham Roads were laid out across Quayle Jones estate land and school sites reserved, thus preventing its development as one unit. Further the authority's readiness to accept backland left by a developer adopting the 'clustering' principle outlined by Tankel,[118] unwittingly increased fragmentation as well as, in effect, increasing the density of building on the rest of the land beyond the zoning limits shown in the Town Plan. The Council therefore found itself with open spaces arbitrarily scattered through residential areas, without any due regard to the actual needs of residents. These spaces were frequently inconveniently located, costly to maintain and not of the most useful size or shape.

Public policy was, however, more enlightened in one direction. In conjunction with the Greater London Regional Planning Committee the council was able to obtain a grant with which to acquire a large area, part of Hall Place estate, as part of the 'Green Belt Girdle', for Greater London.[119] Even so it is worth emphasizing that most of the land in the southern part of the district which later became incorporated in Abercrombie's Green Belt owes its preservation not to any planning measure, but partly to the physical unsuitability of the River Cray flood plain for building purposes before the war, and partly to successful private efforts preventing the encroachment of cheaper housing development on Bexley Village and its immediate environs.

While critical of public measures one must also recognize that no matter how aesthetically undesirable much of this monotonous suburban sprawl of cheap private housing appears today, its development did enable a large section of the community at the lower end of the wage scale to escape out of older areas of inner London into the healthier more open outlying areas. It also helped it to fulfil another aspiration: ownership of a modern house with amenities, hitherto denied them. In these ways the large speculative private builder performed a very real and necessary service to the community at large.

Within the pattern of suburban expansion in the Bexley district, three aspects of that pattern are apparent – the large lower middle class housing estate, areas

Figure 35. Building development across Welling in the mid-1930s on the site of Westwood Farm looking south-east. Welling Way and the railway in the centre bisect the northern part of the farm (Aerofilms Ltd).

of piecemeal development usually of higher quality housing, and land left undeveloped mainly to the South.

In respect of the larger developments it is clear that their locations depended very much on prevailing land-ownership conditions, since each is located where a large unit of suitable land was still held under one ownership. The large scale developer did not want the inconvenience or the additional cost and difficulty of acquiring and combining a number of neighbouring smaller units in order to make up a site. In any case it was seldom that adjacent sites were available for sale at the same time.

In cases where road and rail lines crossed land held under one title, each division affected the configuration of any successive estate development. The history of Westwood Farm illustrates this and the sort of stages by which an area was changed in part of the suburbs.[120]

Westwood Farm originated in 1875, when Oxford University cleared and reclaimed an area of woodland. One of the largest farms in the district, it covered 398 acres.[121] With the construction of the Bexleyheath Railway line in 1896 it was divided into two parts; the northern part was thus cut off from the main farm buildings and therefore made into a separate farm. Both parts were again divided when Welling Way by-pass and Rochester Way Trunk Road were opened in 1926. Had Westwood Farm remained in one unit it is likely, as for other large areas, that it would have been developed as one housing estate, but in fact development was more complex.

Between 1930 and 1931 the University disposed of both the two northern-most areas and the southern area to developers active at the time in the adjacent Eltham district. The decision to sell was to some extent made on the grounds that it was increasingly difficult to manage the land separated from the main central part, but it was principally because of the increased value of the land accruing from a lengthened road frontage and better access to basic services (fig. 35).

The very size of the central area raised problems at the beginning of the 1930s, for few building companies were than able to make the necessary capital outlay.[122] However, as the building boom began to gather momentum so certain local firms expanded. Ideal Homestead, later to become one of the largest developers in the London region, had already built the Pelham Road Estate in Bexleyheath on Oxford University land, and by 1933 felt in a position to develop this central area of Westwood Farm. The firm bought the land on a series of options, and the shape and location of each option is still evident in the detailed layout of its Falconwood estate. The central green of the estate marks the site of the Westwood farm buildings, and until recently some were still standing as a visible reminder of an earlier land-use. Thus the phases in the division of Westwood Farm are clearly imprinted on the present suburban scene even down to the site of the farm itself.

This development together with that by Stevens, another large local firm, and some smaller developments, entirely altered the character of the urban landscape in the Welling area. Between them these two firms built 5,000 houses from 1930 to 1936, adding 18,000 to the population of Welling. Shopping development in the vicinity of Welling Corner at the junction of Upper Wickham Lane and the High Street, together with smaller shopping parades on the large estates, schools, churches, and open spaces completed the transformation. Suburbia had come to Welling and with it a new community pattern – the estate neighbourhood. Most of the newcomers came from similar backgrounds and the very speed of development brought common problems – the need to ensure adequate provisions of school, transport services and other community requirements. These and other features were conducive to the development of a neighbourhood feeling amongst residents, expressed for example in the formation of Resident and Ratepayers Associations which have remained active to date.

Extensive development of considerable interest occurred also in Blendon and Hurst (fig. 36). Despite somewhat similar physical conditions and in theory the same zoning density of 8 to the acre the Blendon Hall estate is different from the Hurst–Albany Park Ideal Homestead estate to the south of it. Blendon Hall estate is one of good class housing of varied design attractively laid out at a density of 7.5 to the acre, whereas Albany Park estate is of uniform and poorer housing, much of it in terraces of four and six, one road looking very much like the next. It was built on a larger scale and far more quickly than the Blendon estate, which was begun earlier, in 1929, and not finished until after the Second World War.

The two estates clearly catered for different market demands, the one at Hurst for the lower middle class mass market, the other, smaller one, at Blendon for the families of professional and businessmen. The physical contrasts between the two housing estates is therefore paralleled by marked social differences between the two types of residents. It is worthwhile looking at the reasons for these differences.

Blendon Hall,[123] was an old established small country seat standing in 88 acres of parkland. Like Danson estate it came on to the market with the death of the owner; his widow was faced with heavy death duties and wished to move away from the district. But knowing the likelihood of the area being developed for building purposes, limitations were laid down at the time of sale to preserve what was best and to ensure a good standard of residential development. The suggested layout of the estate for housing, approved and backed by the Urban District Council, was given in the sales catalogues. The area had to be developed as a whole, even if lots went to different owners. The Hall with grounds immediately around it was to be left standing. No building was to be within 50 feet of a main road and all private dwellings were to be of stone or brick with a tiled or slated roof. Stipulations were made as to the density of buildings and the minimum value of houses to be erected on particular lots. Lots 7 and 16 for example were to be developed at six to the acre and houses erected had to be of a minimum value of £1,000. Lots 9 to 13, and lots 14 and 15 were to be at 8 to the acre and houses erected of a minimum value of £800 and £700 respectively. Except on Blendon Road frontage no shops were to be built on the estate and even on Blendon Road the minimum value of each shop building had to be £1,000. These limitations guaranteed that this was to be an area of select residential development. The sales brochures also emphasized this intention by its reference to the close proximity of well-known 'County Seats' and of Bexley and Lamorbey Park golf links.

With considerable foresight Bowyer, a local builder noted for the quality of his work and at this time half way through completing his Brampton Park bungalow estate development, bought the whole estate for £21,250. He believed it a good future investment and an estate which he could get great satisfaction out of developing. It would also provide steady work for the firm over a number of years. He aimed to develop part of it himself, and to sell frontages at a reasonable profit either to other builders or directly to intending houseowners, and he also hoped to retain the Hall and its grounds, including two small lakes, by selling it for development as a private school. He thought it a particularly suitable site for this purpose and was encouraged by the number of private schools being established in nearby areas in response to the growing needs of middle income families.

The record of plot sales kept by the firm indicates that building development went on steadily from 1929, the dates of purchase reflecting a limited market for better type of housing.[124] Unable to sell the Hall and grounds, Bowyer had to obtain exemption from the building clause limitation and develop the site. This later development is reflected in the divergence of layout of this part from the rest of the estate. Until 1964 the larger lake remained, but it has now been drained and a development of high density town housing has been started. The estate thus reflects three phases of development, that of the major part of the estate, followed by development of the Hall and its grounds, and then ultimately of the lake site.

Hurst and Tanyard farms represented a different type of pre-urban landscape to that of the country seat, Blendon Hall. The owners were willing to sell at the right price without building restrictions.[125] Ideal Homestead, already with the experience of the large scale development at Welling as well as at nearby Lamorbey and Blackfen, were urgently in need of large sites, and as one of the directors emphasised, Hurst and Tanyard farms were the only suitable ones left in the district.[126]

Catering for a mass housing market, Ideal Homestead aimed to build at the highest permitted density and the lowest competitive price. Whilst similar layouts in the northern part of the district had raised no objections, the original layout plan for Hurst and Tanyard farms brought strong protests from Bexley Ratepayers Association, Bexley's representatives on the Council, and also influential individuals resident in Bexley, since they considered this development would lower the social status of the Bexley area.[127] A Council member for Bexley succinctly summarized local feeling – 'The thing was a disgrace in an area such as old Bexley'.[128]

At a permitted density of eight to the acre the first estate layout could accommodate 874 houses on the 109 acres. But although Ideal Homestead proposed to build less than this, the 780 houses scheduled on the layout plan took up only 61 acres, giving a net density of nearly 15 to the acre. Though the Town Plan did not include any open spaces 48 acres were to be left undeveloped. Ideal Homestead hoped for a later relaxation of planning regulations enabling them to fill in some of this backland with additional housing. However, even without this the proposed layout was more economic than one using up all the acreage available giving an effective density of eight to the acre, because the intention was to build houses in terraced blocks of four, six, and eight. This way housing construction was cheaper, and there was also a reduction in the amount of road frontage required and in the length of basic service connections. Some modifications were made in the layout to meet the protests from Bexley residents but most of the ultimate development was still with terrace housing, giving an effective density of 12 to the acre.[129] The Council bought up one area of backland for a much needed primary school, but most of the rest remains largely wasted.

Pahl's discussions about the conflict of power groups in society as a major determinant of urban patterns finds some support from the circumstances just considered. The built environment is the result of conflicts, in the past and the present, between those with different degree of power in society – landowners, planners, developers, local authorities, pressure groups of all kinds, insurance companies, and others.[130] Ideal Homestead was a sufficiently large and influential

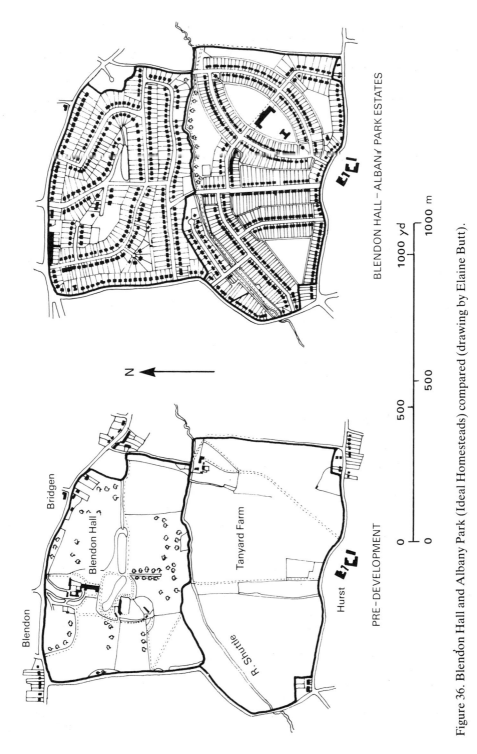

Figure 36. Blendon Hall and Albany Park (Ideal Homesteads) compared (drawing by Elaine Butt).

organization to moderate Council pressure and achieve on the whole the type of development it wanted in the Hurst area. Further it persuaded the Southern Railway to allow a station to be constructed to serve this estate.[131]

Whilst development did occur at Hurst, in and around Bexley village itself the combined vested interests of influential residents and Oxford University Chest policy prevented what was considered to be potentially undesirable development. In Welling and Bexleyheath, in contrast, the absence of such vested interests, and favourable commercial interests, enabled outside social and economic forces to operate freely within lines laid down by the pre-urban cadaster and the terrain.

But the nature of the terrain and drainage problems in the southern-most areas were also important deterrents to building on the Cray valley flood plain. It was thus preserved as an open space until it could be protected under a green belt policy. Physical difficulties were equally important in preventing development in the north-west corner of the district at East Wickham and on Quayle Jones estate land south of the Broadway until after the Second World War.

By 1939 the Bexley district had become a mature suburb; practically the whole area whether built over or not was primarily devoted to the needs of a surburban population. True, the influence of the earlier pre-urban landscape had left its mark but the last vestiges of the earlier land use pattern were fast disappearing.

The change had been brought about by a social revolution, the bringing of house ownership within reach of a whole new group of lower paid workers. Their aspirations and initiative, allied to information obtained via the growing mass communication media, together with a new situation in the building industry and favourable economic conditions, essentially created the interwar metropolitan suburb.

Morphologically, the phase made the suburban landscape more complex than urban theorists concerned with internal land use patterns would have us recognize. Summarizing the main contributory factors it must be emphasized that for the 1930s the location and type of housing development were primarily dependent on size of sites, not upon their accessibility as defined in concepts linking accessibility and land-values.[132] The size of sites available depended upon the prevailing pattern of land-ownership and field boundary lines, together with the willingness of any particular landowner to sell. The large uniform lower middle class housing estate was developed wherever the large scale speculative private builder could find the size of site which gave him the most efficient use of the scale advantage he had over the smaller builder. Smaller plots were developed by the small builder with better housing, because whereas he could not compete with the larger builder in the mass housing market, he could in many cases operate at an economic advantage in the limited market for better quality housing. Consequently available large sites physically suited to building, whatever their location, were normally developed in the 1930s with lower middle class housing. Exceptions to this occurred where land was, like Blendon Hall estate, endowed with status characteristics and its sale contained building restrictions, in which case better class housing resulted.

A further contributory factor was, paradoxically, planning legislation and the local authorities' interpretation of it. Local authorities had insufficient powers to exercise that measure of overall control which at this critical time in suburban development was necessary for a well-ordered urban pattern to emerge. Moreover, by allowing 'clustering' and accepting open spaces left over by speculative builders and scattered haphazardly over the district, local authorities introduced a further element of fragmentation. Post-war infilling has, where possible, occurred on some of this backland, adding to the complexity.

Lastly there were the areas of interrupted development, areas where physical conditions had delayed development to the later 1930s when demand had slackened. This, with the outbreak of war, brought a premature cessation of building. Then under the building restrictions of the immediate post-war years, not only was piecemeal development inevitable but also a mixture of housing types, council housing being built alongside the better class of private housing.

Together these factors produced the complex morphological pattern which is characteristic of the outer suburban ring. Nevertheless one can still see beneath the complexity a broad socio-economic zoning. The higher status area in the south around Bexley was largely preserved due to the efforts of local residents, whilst the lower class housing areas geared to the housing needs of Thameside workers remained predominantly in the northern part of the district, particularly in Welling. On the western side of the borough, between the two, lay a zone of lower middle class housing serving the needs of the commuter to Central London, and to the east an area reserved for better class housing.

Though more varied layouts characterize this period, the basic structure and appearance of houses within each particular price range was fairly uniform. In the lowest range supplying the mass market were blocks of terraced or semi-detached two- to three-bedroomed housing, with garage space frequently reached by means of a back lane. In the intermediate price range semi-detached houses or bungalows with garage and short front drive beyond a double-gate, were the basic types. In the higher price range typical houses were three to four bedroomed and detached, sometimes in mock Tudor style with leaded windows. As Bowley puts it, 'Builders discovered that particular designs were both cheap and popular and this led to constant repetition, although other designs might have been equally satisfactory or better from these points of view and aesthetically preferable'.[133] She goes on to point out that though non-traditional houses were not popular, people who bought a house still wanted it to be clear that they were independent of local authorities. 'The most popular houses were those with minor superficial alterations to a popular type and among the intermediate income group a cut down version of a more expensive design. However, relatively elaborate fittings and domestic amenities were, it was generally considered, more important to practically minded housewives than the external appearance of houses.'

The urban fringe now lay beyond Bexley and also beyond the green belt which was beginning to materialize in a fragmentary way by the late 1930s. The Bexley area was a compact suburb now, in places, joined up by building to other parts of the metropolitan suburb (fig. 29). Within the suburb the fringe within a fringe feature as indicated in the preceding section, had already disappeared; amenities were being more fully utilized and incorporated within residential neighbourhoods. Playing fields, school sites, community centres were developed at the heart of the larger estates and served surrounding smaller developments as well.

Overall, though Bexley in terms of commuting and transport was firmly incorporated into the metropolis, it had retained an identity. The tremendous population growth of the 1930s had brought by 1939 the full development of internal services and a particular character to the suburb. The granting of borough status in 1937 – the development of a range of local societies serving the whole borough – the establishment of a hierarchy of service centres from the main service centres at Welling and Bexleyheath down to the parade of shops on the larger estate – the balance of structure between local employment and out-commuting – and the establishment of a transport network which has basically altered little since, all point to a community with an existence of its own. This loose community framework and the local neighbourhood provided a social context enjoyed by the suburbanite not only because of the conveniences it offered, but because its demands did not interfere with his strongest allegiances, those to the family and the house and garden which it owned.[134]

5 Postscript

Over the inter-war period, the sheer scale and pace of their expansion, focused attention on the outer suburbs; in them the dynamics of metropolitan growth were clearly evident. But over the post-war years the spotlight has been switched away from them and is now divided between the newly developing more widespread metropolitan fringe and the pressing problems of urban renewal in Inner London. Outer interwar suburbs, such as Bexley Borough represent the end of an era. They mark the end of continuous accretion on the periphery of the metropolis. The more stringent and comprehensive planning of post-war years has been responsible for the creation of a Green Belt, a break physically separating this earlier continuous growth of London, culminating in the interwar suburb, from the new metropolitan forms beyond it – the urbanized villages and expanded towns. In one sense therefore the interwar suburb is the last metropolitan suburb, the last outlying district of a city. The new post-war growth points, unlike those earlier ones out on the former metropolitan fringe, are not likely to coalesce and stretch back to join the main mass of suburbia. More positive planning is aimed at keeping them physically separate. They represent the move towards a new kind of open-work metropolis linked to the built up area of Greater London by corridors of rapid public transit. The use of the terms Inner and Outer Country Rings for this openwork part of the London metropolis is indicative of the changed conceptions behind metropolitan expansion. The incorporation of the interwar suburbs into the new Greater London County, and the recent submission of a Greater London Development Plan covering this built up area up to and into the margins of the green belt, will further serve to emphasize the break between the new and old metropolitan forms – the one an open network, the other a compact one broken only by the breathing spaces of public parks and protected vestiges of woodland.

If the Bexley suburb has ceased to grow it continues to change. As Blumenfeld reminds us 'If any pattern can be discerned, it can only be the pattern of flux'.[135] As one suburban cycle is drawing to a close, another is beginning. Although substantial areas of open land remain and the demand for housing is a pressing one, planning control has effectively prevented, for the time being at any rate, further development on virgin land. Any new residential development must increasingly take up land already under some form of urban use; so redevelopment – suburban renewal – is beginning to occur in response to new social and economic requirements. There has been a change in the composition of the housing market. The lower middle class so dominant in the 1930s is no longer significant. Instead the market is composed of higher income groups whose demands have been met by the private sector of the building industry, and also by the lowest paid and deprived groups for whom housing has been provided by the public sector. The framework within which suburban renewal occurs is exclusively an urban one, the constraints of the earlier rural pattern such as landownership and field boundaries, are only indirect, being expressed through the plot patterns and backland shapes of those earlier suburban forms over which it had direct influence.

The very fragmentary nature and small scale of post-war development has added complexity to the suburban morphology. Small post-war developments are inter-mixed with earlier suburban forms. But powers of compulsory purchase, and dominance in the period of restricted building to 1953, have also made the local authority a significant contributor to this complexity, for now council estates are also to be found among better class residential areas. At Hurst and Halcot, however, the scale of local authority development has been sufficiently large to create clear morphological subdivisions, distinct physically and socially from neighbouring residential areas.

But the overall broad zoning remains, despite the greater complexity in the morphological detail. Post-war redevelopment in the Bexley area has served to further emphasize this as the better class residential area, whilst the concentration of much of the council building in the 1960s at East Wickham has accentuated this as a lower class housing area. From north to south across the borough the graduation towards better class housing is still evident.

The fringe theme is no longer present except in the fossilized remnants of its earlier forms. The metropolitan fringe continues to advance, but well beyond Bexley Borough. There are however, signs pointing to renewed local fringe development. As restrictions on 'white areas' of the Green Belt are relaxed one can expect to see certain fringe elements such as sites for schools, other public institutions, and utilities being favoured above residential development.

6 Conclusion

Using an evolutionary approach to highlight the suburban process in as much detail as possible, and weighing the evidence of it against what others have written about it, either from other detailed case studies or from a broad but personal and comprehensive look at the total metropolitan scene, it has become increasingly clear that beneath its dynamic complexity it is possible to discern some order. There is a progressive change in the spatial order of the suburban environment – a sequence of development in response to a set of inter-related formative factors. Despite variation in detail from one metropolis to another, or from one part of the suburbs to another in any one metropolis, these in essence have been similar for most of those metropolitan areas in the Western world belonging to that same cultural system, the advanced industrial society.

Warner, working within a limited time and spatial scale, like Wissink on a higher level of generalization, and others such as Blumenfeld and Mumford on a wider canvas still, have sought a key to the phenomena of suburbia. The most fundamental feature that emerges to me as to them is that the suburbs owe their origin and growth to the search by families for better living conditions. 'The development and shaping of London for instance clearly reveals a passion on the part of the "average" Englishman for a single family home and a plot of garden. He seems to like feeling a private land-holder on his own private "estate". This feeling

257

has now been canalised into a kind of suburban vision, a limited dream'.[136] Further, since the beginning of the 'city and suburban' era towards the end of the nineteenth century, this dream could be realized with each successive stage in the suburban cycle progressively down the social scale, until 'the dominant impression is that of a middle and lower middle class environment.'[137] Slum clearance and planned decentralization have even taken those lowest on the social scale into some parts of suburbia as well as further afield. Technological developments and the filtering down of effective economic and political power from the few to the mass of society have enabled the suburban movement to develop from the selective migration of the privileged into a mass exodus from the city, reaching its culmination in the large scale developments of the 1930s. Today this exodus still goes on, but not to the suburbs. Here then is the basic motivation and the main trend in the suburban process.

Considering the interplay of factors surrounding this motivation and trend, it is useful to consider them as operating on four decreasing spatial scales; at the national and even international level down to the metropolitan scale, through to the suburban level, and finally to the level of the specific local area. In other words, one is approaching these factors in a concentric way, accepting that influences generated on the wider scale will operate through, be affected by, and be added to, by those influences found at each point in the scale below it, until all cumulatively come into effective play at that location in the suburb where the residential development is actually taking place.

At every point in time during the suburban process the specific residential development taking place is the cumulative result of thousands of individual and group decisions taken on these various spatial scales in response to given problem-producing situations and conditioned by the nature of the existing framework within which they have to be taken.[138] Where in time the balance of circumstances radically alters, producing a different emphasis or emphases in the response to them, so we can mark the division between one suburban phase and the next. On the basis of these reflections a decision taking filter model is thus suggested. It is also possible to produce a series of map-models tracing the cumulative spatial consequences or the spatial dynamics for the suburb following from the operation of this filter. As has been repeatedly emphasized, the pace and scale of suburban growth are determined mainly by the larger scale influences, the general and metropolitan ones, whilst the spatial pattern, the suburban mosaic, is decided by the more localized influences, and conditioned in particular by the existing morphological framework into which further suburban development has to be fitted.

Elements of tomorrow's changes in the suburb and its society are already evident. The fullness of its actual course cannot be predicted, but one can ascertain that in the near future piecemeal redevelopment is likely, increasing the weave detail of suburban patterns. It will also continue to be conditioned by what has gone on before, and to represent the composite results of human actions borne from human desires.

NOTES

1 Based on M.C. Carr, 'The growth and characteristics, of a metropolitan suburb: Bexley, N.W. Kent, 1880–1963' (Ph.D. thesis, University of London, 1970).
2 W. Kirk, 'Problems of geography', *Geography*, XLVIII, pt4 (1963) 361ff.
3 H.W. Robinson, *Economics of Building* (1939), 153.
4 A.E. Course, 'The evolution of the railway network of south eastern England', (Ph.D. thesis, University of London, 1958), 662.
5 M.J. Wise, 'The role of London in the industrial geography of Great Britain', *Geography*, XLI, pt4 (1956), 219–32; A.A.L. Caesar, 'Planning and the geography of Great Britain', *Advancement of Science*, XXI (1964).
6 Robinson, *op. cit.*, 104.
7 C. Ward, 'The building cycle and the growth of the built up area of Leeds', *The Northern Universities' Geog. J.*, I (1960), 54.
8 R. Glass, *London – Aspects of Change* (1964), xxxi and xl, n.15.
9 L. Mumford, Chapter on 'Suburbia and beyond', in his *The City in History* (New York, 1961), 482ff.
10 *Bexley R.* no. 110 (1938).
11 J.W.R. Whitehand, 'Fringe-belts – A neglected aspect in Urban Geography', *Trans. Inst. Brit. Geog.*, XLI (1967).
12 G.A. Wissink, *American Cities in Perspective – with Special Reference to the Development of Their Fringe Areas* (Assen, Netherlands, 1962). Wissink, in his study of the social geography of the rural-urban fringe distinguishes between the compact hem and the other fringe – 'highly dynamic, chaotic and extending over a wide area.'
13 R.E. Pahl, *Urbs in Rure* (1964), 75.
14 *Bexley R.*, no. 110 1938. A report stated that the number of squatters increased from 8 to 96 in the four years 1810–14.
15 F.deP. Castells, *Bexley and Welling* (1910). This is largely an ecclesiastical history of the district but it does contain a good account of the Enclosure Award.
16 14 May 1863, Marsh's of Charlotte Road, London E.C., offered for sale Oak Villa in Bexleyheath. The sales details comment on it as being a '$\frac{1}{4}$ mile from the proposed loop-line, now under construction, 2 miles from Erith Station and 12 miles from London – overlooking woodland scenery and picturesque country. The dwelling has two ornamental ponds, shrubbery and paddocks extending over 6 acres'. See also photostat details in *Our Own Magazine* (Bexley, 1857), (Dartford Reference Library).
17 E. Jones, *A Social Geography of Belfast* (1960), 248.
18 F.R.H. Du Boulay, *Medieval Bexley* (1961), 11, 13.
19 *Annual Report of Medical Officer of Health for 1916* presented to the BUDC General Meeting, Vol. 29, Record of Minutes. The population increase of 2,000 at East Wickham was almost entirely attributed to the construction of 627 hutments by the Government for munition workers.
20 Dann & Lucas, Land agents, Dartford, Kent, Catalogue and record of sale of part of Parkhurst Estate held at the Auction Mart, London, 3 July 1876; '16 plots of very valuable freehold building land situated within 5 minutes walk of Bexley Station on the Loop Line to Dartford – each lot with 50 foot road frontage and extending some 200 ft. in depth'. Dann & Lucas, 20 April 1892, Sale of Lot 1 Parkhurst and two large meadows – 8a 1 rood 35 perch: 'A large portion could be laid out as a building estate without detriment to house and grounds.'
21 BUDC General Purposes Committee Meeting, 15 February 1897. The Surveyor was requested to make up Lion Lane, Royal Oak Lane, and Upton Road in view of J.H. Hankey's building estate fronting them. Most of the planning for housing was submitted piecemeal and it seems that J.H. Hankey had contracted with a number of builders, e.g. Oaklands Road – 2 houses submitted by Albert Clarke, a local builder, April 1906 – 15

houses by J.C. Butler, 11 May 1905 – 4 houses by E. Box 10 March 1902: reports to General Purposes Committee of the BUDC.

22 Woodlands Estate, plan submitted by A.H. Kersey, 21 Finsbury Pavement, London E.C. 18 June 1898. By 1914 only ten houses had been built.

   Mount Park Garden Estate Suburb. This was not developed until the 1920s though submitted by James Alers Hankey to BUDC in November 1910 and again on 25 January 1911. It was conveniently planned next to the Bexleyheath Golf Course.

23 Mr James Rolph, an estate agent, giving evidence before the Lords Committee considering an application for the building of the Bexleyheath Railway Line, compared Blackheath land values £1,000–2,000 an acre with those of Bexleyheath £600–500 an acre, and ascribed the difference almost entirely to lack of railway facilities in Course, op. cit., 308n.

24 J.H. Johnson, 'The suburban expansion of housing in London, 1918–1939', in Greater London, ed. J.T. Coppock, H.C. Prince (1964), 144.

25 Reports in the BUDC Minutes, e.g. 10 October 1917: General Purposes Committee – reply to the Local Government Board's Enquiry regarding the housing of the working classes in the post-war years: 'The needs of the district itself are not great. It is high and healthy and not densely built over. Large numbers of the workmen employed in factories around it like to live in it, the same being well provided with tram services.'

   See also evidence from the Medical Officer of Health's Annual Reports covering the period, footnotes in the Decennial Censuses relating to the district as well as e.g. Residence and Workplace tables for the 1921 Decennial Census.

26 Quoted in R.W. Pepper, 'Urban development of Lewisham' (M.A. thesis, University of London, 1965).

27 The attitudes and financial position of workers is summarized by W. Ashworth, An Economic History of England, 1870–1939 (1960), 196–204. See also Glass, op. cit., iv–ix.

28 BUDC, Minutes of the Finance Committee: E.g. the Committee approved a mortgage advance of £275 on no. 20 Royal Oak Road, 6 November 1899. During the difficult time after 1906/7 there are very few records of advances.

29 Report by the Clerk to the Council to a BUDC General Meeting, 15 December 1880, on the tramway proposals of Mr S.C. Nicholls. There was a similar report, 8 November 1899, on a proposed tramway from Plumstead to Dartford, linking up with the LCC line already extending out to Plumstead from Woolwich.

30 Report given to the BUDC, 5 November 1900, by Dawbarn and Mordey, Consultants of 82 Victoria Street, Grosvenor Mansions, Westminster.

31 H.J. Dyos, 'Suburban development of Greater London south of the Thames', (Ph.D. thesis, University of London, 1952), 329–3. Dyos, for example, indicates that in 1906–13 on the basis of the Builder, weekly returns, raw material prices rose considerably in London. Brick prices increased by 25 per cent, wood by 5 to 9 per cent, iron by 12 per cent, lead by 12 per cent and cement by 38 per cent.

32 Report to the BUDC meeting, 10 October 1917, extract: 'In the period (1906–13) preceding the war building activity by private enterprise had practically ceased because of the new taxes introduced by the Central Government, the uncertainty felt as to their scope and the further likelihood of more taxes, coupled with the withdrawal of capital from building financiers.'

33 H.J. Gayler, 'Land speculation and urban development contrasts in south east Essex, 1880–1940', Urban Studies, LXXI (1970), 23ff. and BUDC General Meeting, 22 May 1912. Quayle Jones Estate: Mrs Quayle Jones proposed to sell the whole of her Bexley Estate (and Gravel Hill improvements might be affected by it). Records of Dann & Lucas, the land-agents, indicate that very little was sold. But as payment of death duties on Mrs P.M. Dashwood (Quayle-Jones) Estate the Inland Revenue were offered Long Lane Farm, Bexleyheath, covering 44 acres.

34 O.O. Dale, for example, held land in the Albion-Warren Road area, and Alers Hankey

most of the land between Lion Road and Upton Road, north of Upton. Examples are also available from other sources: (a) The records of sales of the Danson Estate at Porter, Putt, Fletcher, Surveyors and Estate Agents, Dartford, who took over Dann & Lucas the land-agents for the Danson Estate. (To give an example of marginal disposal of land, seven outlying units of the Danson estate fronting Parkview Road, Welling, were offered for sale on 13 June 1895.) (b) The Avigdor Goldsmith estate, details made available by the Goldsmith family, at Waterhouse & Co. Solicitors, Lincoln's Inn Field, London. (c) Records made available at the Oxford University Chest Estates Office, Oxford.

35 G.A. Wissink, 'Part II "The Fringe" – "American Cities in Perspective" ', *Social Geografische Studies*, v (Assen, Netherlands, 1962), 63.

36 Whitehand, *op. cit.*

37 Johnson, *op. cit.*

38 Housing: *Encyclopaedia Brittanica,* II (1962), 178.

39 The need for some measure of control over development was being advocated even before the First World War, not only in publications but also at local level, e.g. on 9 January 1908, BUDC General Purposes Committee, it was reported that a letter had been received from the Incorporated Association of Municipal and County Engineers calling for the attention of local authorities to the necessity of legislation on the subject of Town Planning and enclosing a memorandum which the BUDC decided to fully support.

40 There are many references to public works to help unemployment, e.g.
   (a) 27 June 1922: a list of schemes was presented to the General Purposes Committee e.g. including making up of Westwood Lane to help link areas south of Woolwich with the Thames.
   (b) 17 June 1922: £1,900 passed for a sewer down Danson Road, to help building.
   (c) 18 June 1923: a sewer was suggested between Cross Lane and Gad's Bridge, Bexley, to help unemployment and building to take place.
   (d) 25 February 1920: Welling Way and Shooter's Hill by-passes required but not approved without funds being available. (They were in fact completed in 1926.)

41 J.H. Clapham, 'An epilogue, 1914–1929', in his *An Economic History of Modern Britain*, III (1938), 545. Since 1914, 'The building operatives . . . had secured, like most of the labourers, an 80 per cent rise at least, some of them upwards of 100 per cent.'

42 BUDC Housing Committee Report, 21 June 1919.

43 BUDC Housing Committee Minutes, 24 July 1919, and 30 October 1919.

44 Letter, 25 August 1919, to the Chairman of the London Housing Board from T.G. Baynes, the Clerk to the Council: '850 acres of level land with gravelly soils was available as building land'. He was convinced that 'houses could be built to let at prevailing rents in the district'. Further 'with improved communications to London via the railways and the tramways the development of housing in the area might alleviate housing problems within the City of London'.

45 The original suggestion was for 400 houses at East Wickham/Welling, 300 in Danson Park and 400 between Bexleyheath and Bexley. Had these latter two schemes been implemented like the former one, the spatial organization of residential areas in the district would have been very different from that which we can see today.

46 21 June 1921, letter to the BUDC from the London Housing Board, stated even then that there were so many schemes in the London area it could not include another 126 houses in the Hartford Road development at Bexley.

47 Circular 388 of the Ministry of Health, 27 April 1923, Subsidy clause, Clause 2 of the Act.

48 Interview with R.W. Norman of Norman's Housing (Bexleyheath) Ltd, 7 February 1963.

49 Examples from BUDC Financial Committee Records: 13 May 1924 – £1,035 to W.B. Hitchcock for a house on Danson Road; 21 January 1925 – £790 for a house on

Bellegrove Road, and £495 for a house on Izane Road; 26 March 1929 – £525 for a house on Sidney Road; 22 January 1930 – £820 for a bungalow on Basildon Road.

50 BUDC General Purposes Committee Minutes, 10 October 1928, indicate that a labourer and driver in the Council's employment got 59s. and 63s. respectively a week, a joiner got 76s., and a costing clerk £4 a week. Local builders also indicated that these were fairly average wage rates for the time.

51 Between July 1925 and September 1928, 454 subsidies were granted, compared with 241 between October 1923 and May 1925.

52 Robinson, *op. cit.*, 131.

53 19 January 1927, Circular 755 Ministry of Health – Housing Acts – Revision of Contribution Order.

54 Calculated from Decennial Census Tables 1921 and 1931.

55 As early as 1908 Bexley UDC had supported a letter from the Incorporated Association of Assistant Engineers to the Local Government Board calling for the necessity of legislation on the subject of Town Planning: BUDC Minutes, 9 January 1908. The North-West Kent area was among the first to set up a Joint Advisory Planning Committee in 1924 under the Housing and Town Planning Acts 1909 and 1919, together with the Interim Development Order of 1922.

56 'Planning in relation to land values'. A Report on the Annual Conference of the Town and Country Planning School (1938), 57.

57 General Purposes Committee of the BUDC, 11 October 1922. The actual density was comparatively low, approximately 3.8 to the acre.

58 Meeting of the BUDC General Purposes Committee, 12 December 1928.

59 Norman, a local builder, indicated that access to the council's new sewer was the deciding factor since subsidy aided housing had to have mains drainage.

60 Records of sales of units of Yeatman Estate and other properties: Dann & Lucas, Land Agents, Dartford (now Porter, Putt & Fletcher of Dartford).

61 22 May 1929 – 23 February 1930: BUDC General Purposes Committee Minutes indicate considerable correspondence between Oxley and the Clerk to the Council concerning drainage, and the need for access through Stevens building estate since Oxley wanted to develop this land for building.

62 Details of sales are contained in Danson Estate papers and sales catalogues (19 July 1922) – Daniel Smith, Oakley & Garrard in conjunction with Dann & Lucas – Auction Mart, Queen Street, London; Dann & Lucas files contain records of later private sales of lots, including the purchase of the park by G. Baynes who immediately passed it on to the Council.

63 At a special BUDC Meeting, 24 Marh 1924, it was suggested that if the park was required then the cost should come out of Christchurch and Welling Ward rates since the residents there were the ones most likely to use the park. An amendment was carried to purchase only 50 acres and the house, but the Trustees refused to subdivide the land. G. Baynes, the Clerk, so incensed with the Council's lack of forethought, with the guaranteed backing of friends went ahead and bought the park area and was subsequently able to persuade the Council to take it over.

64 W. Firey, 'Ecological considerations in planning for urban fringes', in *Cities and Society*, ed. P.K. Hatt and A.J. Reiss (1975), 791ff.

65 Examples such as those at Welling could well be used to illustrate the points made by Raymond Unwin or Barry Parker about more enlightened residential building, as indicated in W.L. Creese, *Town Planning in Practice: The Legacy of Raymond Unwin* (Massachusetts, 1967), 68–108; and B. Parker 'Economy in estate development', *J. Town Planning Inst.*, XIV (1928).

66 R.C. Lederman, 'The city as a place to live in', in *Metropolis on the Move*, ed. J. Gottman (1967), 90.

67 J.H. Westergaarde, in *London – Aspects of Change*, 99.

68 Whitehand, *op. cit.*, 230.

69 Annual Reports of the Medical Officer of Health for Bexley 1929–39, and Housing Statistics supplied by the BUDC Housing and Planning Departments. It would have been more useful to have compared the rate of housing increase with that of the number of families, but statistics for the latter are not available.

70 Even in 1928, 3,135 acres were still under crops and grass but by 1937 it was only 727 acres. (Annual Returns of Bexley and East Wickham Parishes; Agricultural Census and Sampling Branch of the Ministry of Agriculture, Fisheries and Food.)

71 Planning applications covering 1,500 houses were passed at one single Council Meeting alone: BUDC Minutes, 20 September 1930.

72 M. Bowley, *The British Building Industry*, (1966), 362–95.

73 *Ibid.*, 364. Bowley cites supporting evidence from tables in Appendix D: Valuation for Rates 1939, (HMSO, 1945). Her calculations based on these indicate the percentage of houses built between the wars which were owner-occupied, in various classes of houses as defined by rateable values. She points out, for example, that if houses built by local authorities are excluded from the calculation for houses of not more than £20 10s. rateable value, 54 per cent of those built between 1919 and 1939 were owner-occupied.

74 H. Carver, *Cities in the Suburbs* (Toronto, 1962), 12.

75 J.W. House, *The Frontiers of Geography* (1965), 18.

76 M. Waugh, 'Suburban growth in north-west Kent' (Ph.D. thesis, University of London, 1968), 203.

77 H. Mayer, 'The pull of land and space', in *Metropolis on the Move,* ed. J. Gottman (1967), 28. H.J. Gans also makes this point in his *Anatomy of Suburbia* (1967), 288.

78 Mumford, *op. cit.*, 535.

79 H. Bellman, 'Building societies. Some economic aspects', *Economic J.*, XLIII (1933), and *idem, Bricks and Mortar* (1949).

80 From J. Hagestrand's *Migration Monograph* referred to by A. Pred in *Behaviour and Location,* pt1, ser. B, Human Geography: No. 27, *Lund Studies in Geography* (1967), 13.

81 Waugh, *op. cit.*, 146.

82 Interview with Mr J. Norman, Director of Normans Ltd, Orpington, a local building firm, 7 July 1963. Operating mainly in Welling during the interwar period and dealing directly with house purchasers, he indicates that a large number moved first out of the older area of Woolwich to large Victorian houses in Upper Woolwich and Plumstead and then out to the 'country' at Welling.

83 Table 27, 'Social class of males over 15', Decennial Census 1951.

84 Classification of occupations, Table A, Decennial Census 1951. Also note, for example, that at the BUDC Meeting on 27 September 1933, concern was expressed at the unsatisfactory features of the private Ridgeway Estate, Welling, built largely for serving the needs of the Thameside workers: 'The Council view with grave concern the large number of houses of an unsatisfactory character, especially those of a small superficial area.' Although it recognized the 'need to serve the working classes', it resolved to send a deputation to the Prime Minister, the Minister of Health and the Urban District Council's Organisation.

85 The percentage of resident occupied population working in the Central City was well above the qualifying level either basing it on the lower limit of 10 per cent commuting to Central London or 15 per cent commuting into London County as the definition of the Metropolitan suburb. (Waugh, *op. cit.*, 20).

86 *Bexley R.*, no. 120 (1939).

87 Course, *op. cit.*, 662; W. Ashworth, in *London – Aspects of Change,* 70.

88 For example, *Bexley R.*, June 1931, reports on a deputation to the Council indicating that though the train service was good, most people had too long a walk to stations. 20 March 1934, BUDC Minutes record the concern of the Council for overcrowding on the Dartford Loop Line trains.

89 Interview with the Director of Ideal Homesteads Limited, Carlton House, Epsom,

12 January 1963. In addition to discussing the details and circumstances underlying their developments in the Bexley area, he emphasized that by the mid 1930s the firm was building in a number of outer suburban areas and was therefore able to exert greater influence on the railway company than a local firm could have done. Hurst Estate with 1,200 houses was largely completed in 1932–3 and Albany Park Station opened in 1934. Falconwood Estates nos. 1 and 2 with 2,325 houses were completed by 1933, but Falconwood Station was not opened until 1935.

90 Johnson, *op. cit.*, 151.
91 *Bexley R.* no. 81 (December 1935).
92 *Bexley R.*, May 1931.
93 *Bexley R.*, July 1936.
94 BUDC Minutes, 8 September 1936. The London Passenger Transport Board indicated to the Council that obstructions were still holding up the development of routes. *Bexley R.*, April 1934. The London Passenger Transport Board was willing to introduce services covering estates north of Broadway; the Council, however, indicated that it would cost £15,000 to put roads into a fit condition for bus traffic and it was not prepared to provide the finance for it.
95 *Bexley R.*, July 1936. BUDC had improved Avenue Road for buses but the Southern Railway would not improve their portion of Pickford Road which lay along the route.
96 This average is obtained from figures provided by the builders, local press reports and Estate Exchange Yearbooks. In view of the large numbers built by Stevens and Ideal Homestead for between £350 and £395, more expensive housing would not sell. (Interviews A. Watson Ltd, Bexleyheath, 3 March 1963, and J. Normans Housing Ltd, 7 July 1963.)
    The intermediate house price range is well illustrated from the Davis Estate built to the south of Bexleyheath station. The estate covered 14 acres at 12 houses per acre giving 171 houses, together with shopping sites each side of Pickford Lane. (Details attached to plan submitted 30 September 1935 to the BUDC)

type of house	freehold price £	leasehold price £
terrace	600	480
terrace with garage space	620	500
semi-detached	660	530
detached with separate garage	835	675
semi-detached with garage	860	690
semi-detached with garage	870	700
semi-detached with garage	975	865

A letter received from Davis Estate Ltd, 346–350 Kilburn High Road, London NW6, dated 10 February 1963, for example, indicates this as the general income range of purchasers of their Pickford Road Estate.

97 Advances under the Small Dwellings Acquisition Acts were suspended from 1931 to 1936. Records of the Defaulters & Small Dwellings Committee of the BUDC show that only 133 mortgages were advanced from 25 March 1936 to 1 September 1939.
98 For information on the local work of building societies I am indebted to Mr J. Hawkins of Hummerstone & Hawkins, Welling, long established land and estate agents, intimately connected with housing development in the district in the interwar period. The societies most active locally were the Halifax, Lambeth, Abbey National, Bradford Third (later renamed the Provincial), and the Woolwich Equitable Building Society.
99 Bowley, *op. cit.*, 374.
100 Sales brochures of Ideal Homestead Ltd, Stevens Ltd, and Absalom (Little Danson Farm Estate) together with the BUDC Housing Committee Minutes, 2 November 1932. Records of D.C. Bowyer & Sons Ltd. The Lodge Blendon Road, Bexley, and interviews with other smaller builders.

101 Ideal Homestead's Falconwood Estate Brochure. *The Purchasing Scheme explained and the New Ideal Homesteads organisation.*
102 Bowley, *op. cit.*, 380.
103 Ribonson, *op cit.*, 129–31.
104 *Ibid.*, 156.
105 Interviews with farmers and landowners connected with farming in the area at this time, in particular T. Chapplin, Shooters Hill Road, Welling, (26 October 1963); Weekes & Sons Ltd, Wickham Street, Welling, (6 January 1963); G. Gibson, Lumbersland Farm, Wilmington, (24 September 1963); and H.J.W. Vinson, Kingshill Farm, Borough Green, Kent, (16 October 1963).
106 D.R. Denman, *Land in the market*, *Hobart Paper* 30 (Institute of Economic Affairs, 1964), 11–12.
107 Sources: Estate Exchange Yearbook Returns, deeds in estate and land agents' offices notably Waterhouse & Co., Lincolns Inn Fields (Goldsmid Estate); Oxford University Chest Estate Offices, Oxford – Baynes & Sons, Solicitors, Welling; Dann & Lucas, land agents, Dartford, and Prall & Prall, estate agents, Dartford.
108 BUDC Housing Committee Minutes, 2 November 1932. The surveyor estimated the cost apportionment of a house on a Council estate had the Council been required to build, as: land £16, road frontage £30, sewers £9 per house plot and the cost of the house itself as £320. There is no reason to believe that the cost apportionment would be much different for the cheaper type of private house. The profit margin would be small and success therefore depended on selling a very large number of houses.
109 Records of Ideal Homestead Ltd, Carlton, Epsom, Surrey and an interview with a director of the firm, 12 January 1963.
110 A letter from the Senior Superintendent, Woolwich Arsenal, of 7 January 1965, gives the total strength of the labour force on 1 January of each year as: 1931 – 7,222; 1932 – 7,066; 1933 – 6,736; 1934 – 7,482; 1935 – 7,992; 1936 – 11,250; 1937 – 15,770; 1938 – 19,240; 1939 – 19,883.
111 Bowley, *op. cit.*, 377.
112 *Ibid.*, 380.
113 Information largely supplied by the two building firms but confirmed by other evidence. Some idea of the rate and scale of building in the Bexley area is also indicated by the following figures in plans passed for the firm concerned by the BUDC

Ideal Homestead
1931 92 houses on the Pelham Road Estate;
1932 2,325 houses on the Falconwood Sections 1 & 2 Welling;
1932/3 1,200 houses on the Hurst Estate – Hurst/Albany Park;
1934 263 houses on the Broadwood Estate, Welling;
1936 600 houses on the Royal Park Estate, South of Albany Park Station

Stevens–Goldsmid Estates only
1930 214 houses on the no. 4 estate south of the railway, Welling;
1932 880 houses on the no. 5 estate north of the railway, Welling;
1934 1,910 houses on the no. 6 estate north of the railway, Welling

Bexley R., April 1934: Ideal Homestead sold 983 houses in one month and in April 1933 the concern directly employed 3,000 people in the Bexley district alone.
114 A Report of the Surveyor to BUDC General Purposes and Planning Committee, 28 March 1934, gives a case on Ideal Homestead's Albany Park Estate. Excavations for foundations of the house were commenced on 26 March, the foundations were laid by noon, 27 March, and the brickwork completed ready for roofing by noon, 28 March.
115 BUDC Housing Department Records and Housing Committee Minutes, e.g. 4 June 1936. 166 houses were completed in 1931: 130 on the Pickford Council Estate, north of Bexleyheath Station, and 36 houses on Victoria Road, Bexley. Only 24 were built under

the Housing Acts of 1935; these were on the Glenmore Estate, East Wickham. But in 1939 as part of the scheme to rehouse the East Wickham hutment tenants, 92 houses were built on more land at East Wickham.

116 BUDC meeting, 29 November 1932, The BUDC Chairman outlined these powers to the rest of the Council. But local authorities were very aware of these limitations, for example the minutes of the BUDC Special Meeting, 10 December 1931.

117 *Bexley R.*, January 1934 and BUDC Finance Committee Report, 21 November 1934. The owner of land fronting Broadway which was required as the access to Broadway for the planned road, Townley Road, appealed against loss of land. The appeal was dismissed by the Minister of Health but he recommended that the owner, Mr Winston, should receive the full value of the land as a building site. Winston received £4,725 for the lost 47 feet 3 inches frontage.

118 'Clustering, as you know, consists merely in taking the number of dwelling units permitted by the zoned minimum lot size and distributing on smaller lots, so that while the overall density is unchanged, some larger more natural chunks of land are left open for common use.' Tankel thus states theoretically how clustering could be beneficial to the community. In practice it worked largely in the interests of the builder. S.B. Tankel, 'The Importance of Open Space', *Cities and Space*, ed. L. Wingo Jr (Baltimore, 1963), 64–5. This was common practice on the part of Ideal Homestead and Stevens Ltd. For example a letter from Hargreaves, acting for Stevens Ltd attached to a plan dated 17 February 1932, in the BUDC Planning Department files relates to the Stevens no. 4 Estate, Westbrook Road in which open space adjacent to the railway was offered 'in consideration of plan approvals'.

119 A letter, 7 November 1934, to the BUDC Chairman from the Technical Adviser to the Greater Regional Planning Committee concerned with the 'green-belt' to be put round London, indicated that grants were available for acquiring land the Committee considered desirable to include in the 'green-belt'. On this basis 62 acres of Hall Place Estate were acquired for £25,000 (*Bexley R.* October 1935) and 40 acres of Halcot Estate for £20,410. (*Bexley R.*, March 1938). *Bexley R.*, August 1935, indicates that W.E. Molins, the seller, had originally bought the whole of Halcot Estate (82 acres), for £21,500, in 1935.

120 *Westwood farm – phases of development*

Northern Area	Falconwood I			
	(Land sold to Headstone Manors – 16 June 1931, 100 acres 2 roods for £25,000)			
	Later sold to Ideal Homestead			
Middle Area	Falconwood II			
	(Sold in parts, options 1–6 direct to Ideal Homestead 1933/34)			
	1. 8 Nov. 1933	22 acres	£12,000	
	2. 27 Nov. 1933	18 acres	£10,000	
	3. 7 Dec. 1933	12 acres	£6,446	
	4. 22 March 1934	11.3 acres	£6,220	
	5. 28 March 1934	9.5 acres	£5,225	
	6. 1934	116 acres	£35,809	
Southern Area	(Sold to W. Childs – 28 Jan. 1930, 70 acres 2 roods, £13,600)			
	Later disposed of by him in the two parts, A and B,			
	A to J. Leech			
	B to Wates Limited			

121 Details of the farm, its division and subsequent sale have been provided by Major H. Mills, land agent to Oxford University Chest, who gave access to the relevant records, 2 May 1963. T. Chaplin of Woodside, Shooters Hill, who farmed the area north of the railway, also provided other useful detail.

122 W. Norman (Ltd) was offered it, but had to refuse because of the scale of development required.

123 The text concerning Blendon Hall is mainly based on the following sources: Sales Catalogue and Conditions of Sale for Blendon Hall Estate: 1 July 1929, Estate Room, 20 Hanover Square, London WC1. Auctioneers Dann & Lucas, together with Knight, Frank and Rutley. A letter of 19 June 1929 from Knight, Frank and Rutley sent together with two plans for the layout of Blendon Hall Estate and the 'Building Restrictions and Stipulations', to the BUDC General Purposes and Planning Committee. Records of D.C. Bowyer Ltd, 'The Lodge', Blendon Road, Bexley.

124 From 1929 to 1939 there is frequent submission of small lots of houses by various builders to the DUDC General Purposes & Planning Committee, e.g. 3 November 1930: six bungalows (Sykes & Pomfret); 18 December 1931: a pair of houses (C. Buck); 30 September 1931: one bungalow (C. Buck); 27 July 1932: 44 semi-detached houses (D.C. Bowyer); 28 March 1934: four houses, at 53–9 The Drive (Brian Construction Co.); 25 March 1935: three pairs of houses, at 10–20 Bladindon Drive (Brian Construction Co.); 31 October 1938: 11 pairs of houses, at Bladindon Drive (Brian Construction Co.).

125 I am indebted to Mr H.W. Vinson, Kingshill, Borough Green, Kent, who tenanted Hurst Farm, for information about the Vansittart estates and the conditions existing prior to building. Vansittart made a number of offers of land without restrictions. The BUDC were offered for example $54\frac{1}{4}$ acres for £11,100. (BUDC minutes, 3 May 1933).

126 Interview at Ideal Homestead Ltd's Carlton House, Epsom, Surrey on 12 January 1963.

127 BUDC Special Meeting, 22 February 1933.

128 Special Town Planning Committee Meeting, 28 June 1933. A rather witty comment by Gurney C. Beagley Esq. concerning Ideal Homestead development is noted in the *Bexley R.*, December 1934. At the 1st Annual Banquet of the Corporation of Dartford held on Mayor's Day, in replying to the toast of the 'Visitors' he stated, 'I am conscious of the honour conferred by the Chief Magistrate of this, the youngest borough of Kent, in inviting to this memorable banquet a humble cottager from An Old World Village fast crumbling into a New Ideal Homestead'.

129 Town Planning Committee Meeting, 28 June 1933. At a meeting on 1 May 1935, the Council was still proposing that on any 3 acres with a zoning limit of eight to the acre, only 24 houses were to be allowed, and also that block terrace building would be permissible only where the density was 12 to the acre. But, for example, the built up area enclosed by Hurst Road, Radnor and Crofton Avenues, covering $33\frac{1}{4}$ acres, has an effective density of 11.8 to the acre and is predominantly of terrace housing.

130 R.E. Pahl, 'Spatial structure and social structure', *Working Paper, No. 10* (Centre for Environmental Studies, London, 1968), 13.

131 Editorial comment, *Bexley R.*, 1934, to the effect that other developers in the suburbs had been refused permission by the Southern Railway for the erection of stations, but the importance of Ideal Homestead in the London Region added weight to their request. At that time the firm was constructing 15 estates round Outer London.

132 It is significant that Alonso has added size of site as an important variable in concepts covering the use of parcels of urban land. W. Alonso, *Location and Land Use* (Cambridge, Mass., 1964).

133 Bowley, *op. cit.*, 337.

134 This seems to parallel the situation described by H. Gans for Levittown. H. Gans, *Levittowners – The Anatomy of Suburbia* (1967), 408–24.

135 H. Blumenfeld, in *The Modern Metropolis*, ed. P.B. Speiregen (Cambridge, Mass., 1967), 50.

136 Wissink, *op. cit.*, 242.

137 *Ibid.*, 115.

138 N. Anderson, *The Urban Community – A World Perspective* (1959), 112. 'Thus urban man tends always to be confronted with space-use difficulties to which he must make one type of adjustment or another.'

INDEX

market gardening, 80, 97, 116, 124, 125, 130, 219, 227, 238
Marshall, Barbara, Headingley estate, 165
Marshall family, flax-spinners, Leeds, 182
Martin and Fenwick, surveyors and land agents, Leeds, 161, 189–202
Mattock Lane, Ealing, 102
Metropolitan Board of Works, 106,116, 121
Metropolitan fringe, 212, 218–19, 227, 228, 236, 239, 240–1, 255
Mexborough, earls, Potternewton estate, 162, 170
migration, 16, 63, 65, 81, 83, 239, 240–1
Mill Hill Park estate, Acton, 114, 140
Mill Hill Road, Acton, 104
Mitchell, Frederick, architect, Leeds, 188
Mooreland Road, Bromley, 71
Morum, William, builder, Bromley 71–2
Mount Park estate, Ealing, 130
Mount Pleasant Garden Suburb, Bexleyheath, 224
Muffet, Charles, builder, Bromley, 38, 71
Murray, George, surveyor, 44
Murray Road, Ealing, 130

National Freehold Land Society, 62, 64, 103
National Land Corporation, 130
National Liberal Land Company, 103, 120
National Permanent Mutual Building Society, 64
National Standard Land Company, 128
Naylor's trustees estate, Potternewton, 177, 180–1
New Leeds, Potternewton, 164, 175, 183, 206
Newton Lodge estate, Potternewton, 177, 180
Nokes, John W., landowner, Bromley, 34, 42–3, 46

Oakfield Terrace, Headingley, 185
Oaklands estate, Bexleyheath, 226
Oates, Joseph, merchant, Leeds, 163
occupational structure, Bexley, 236, 241; Bromley, 80
omnibuses, 6, 10, 11, 39, 97–8, 125, 132, 165–6, 168, 176, 219, 243
Osborne Road, Acton, 107, 108
owner-occupied houses, 174, 216, 225, 238, 254; see also house purchase, finance of
Oxford Road, Ealing, 112
Oxford University Chest estate, Bexley, 226, 250, 254

Packington Road, Acton, 108
Paddington, 4, 11, 110
Park Road, Chiswick, 139
Parkhurst-Knoll Road estate, Bexley, 222, 227
parks, 84, 120, 125, 127, 191, 220, 234
Penge, 78, 122
Penge Perseverance Permanent Building Society, 64
People's Co-operative Permanent Building Society, Greenwich, 64
People's Freehold Land Society, Plaistow, Bromley, 58–9, 66, 72
Perryn Road, Acton, 119, 140
physical relief and terrain, influence of, 216, 218, 227, 248, 254
pig-keeping, 108
Pitzhanger Manor, Ealing, 98
Plaistow estate, Bromley, 58–9
planning and Planning Acts, 232–3, 248, 254
planning controls, 220, 248; see also building regulations
playing fields, 184, 227, 255
Plews, William, linen manufacturer and developer, Leeds, 184
Plumstead, 229, 240
population growth, 5, 215; in Bexley, 229, 238; in Bromley, 33–4, 84; outer west London, 95
Potternewton, 163, 183–4, 186, 189–203
pre-development landowners, 17, 30, 40–1, 53, 97, 162, 176, 220, 250, 254
pre-development physical features, 17, 226–7, 234, 250, 254
privacy, 8–9, 12–13

Quayle Jones estate, Bexleyheath, 248, 254

Raggett, J.J., architect, Birmingham, 188
railway companies, Bromley Direct, 36–40; Dartford Loop (S.E.R.), 219, 221; District, 20, 111, 114, 115–16, 122, 129, 134, 138; East Kent, 34; Great Eastern, 19, 133; Great Western, 19, 98, 100, 114–15, 124, 133, 138; Hampstead Junction, 100; Leeds-Thirsk, 19, 170; London, Chatham and Dover, 35, 37, 122; London and Greenwich, 31; London and South Western, 98, 100, 110, 115, 124, 133, 138; Metropolitan, 100, 110, 115; Mid Kent, 34–6, 43; North Kent (S.E.R.), 219; North London, 100, 102, 104, 110, 115, 134; North and South Western Junction, 100, 110; South Eastern, 31, 34, 37; West End and Crystal Palace, 34

272